D0534035

PROFILE OF THE NATION
AN AMERICAN PORTRAIT

Barbara Klier

- no external circ's since Jan 2002
- 2004 ed cur ed. not clear how updated 4/05

INFORMATION PLUS REFERENCE SERIES
Formerly published by Information Plus, Wylie, Texas

GALE GROUP

Detroit
New York
San Francisco
London
Boston
Woodbridge, CT

PROFILE OF THE NATION: AN AMERICAN PORTRAIT

was produced for the Gale Group by Information Plus, Wylie, Texas

Information Plus Staff:

Barbara Klier, Author
Jacquelyn Quiram, Designer
Editorial: Abbey Begun, Cornelia Blair, Nancy R. Jacobs, Virginia Peterson, Mei Ling Rein, Mark A. Siegel

The Gale Group Staff:

Editorial: Rita Runchock, Managing Editor; John F. McCoy, Editor
Graphic Services: Randy Bassett, Image Database Supervisor; Robert Duncan, Senior Imaging Specialist
Product Design: Michelle DiMercurio, Senior Art Director; Michael Logusz, Graphic Artist
Production: NeKita McKee, Buyer; Dorothy Maki, Manufacturing Manager

PROFILE OF A NATION — AN AMERICAN PORTRAIT

CHAPTER I

POPULATION CHARACTERISTICS

The United States has expanded from a small nation of fewer than 4 million persons scattered along the eastern seaboard into a country of more than 270 million extending halfway across the Pacific Ocean to Hawaii and north of the Arctic Circle in Alaska. America's movement westward is reflected in the gradual shift of the center of the American population.

In 1790, the year of the first national census, the mean population center (defined in Table 1.1) lay just east of Baltimore, Maryland. By the Civil War (1861-1865), the population center had moved well into Ohio, and by the end of World War II (1945), the center had reached Illinois.

Reflecting the movement of population out of the Northeast toward the Southwest, the 1980 census located the center of population in Jefferson County, Missouri, near the city of DeSoto, approximately 40 miles south-southwest of the Gateway Arch in St. Louis, Missouri. The 1990 census moved the population center 39.5 miles farther southwest of DeSoto to a heavily wooded area in Crawford County, Missouri. Steelville (population 1,465), the closest town to the population center, lies 9.7 miles to the northwest. (See Figure 1.1.)

1990 POPULATION*

The official 1990 census, performed by the U.S. Bureau of the Census, counted the population of the United States (including armed forces overseas) at 248,709,873, an increase of 22,167,670 people, or 9.8 percent, since 1980. The Bureau of the Census estimates that it missed approximately 5 million, mostly poor, urban people. A study by the Census Bureau indicated that half of the uncounted were children of racial minorities. These persons were not counted for various reasons, including the inability to locate them, people's concerns about privacy, language barriers in immigrant communities, and reluctance on the part of the census-takers to go into areas where many of these people live. A most important goal for the 2000 census is to reduce the undercounts of the poor and the minorities.

Census counts are particularly important because the apportionment of representatives (local, state, and federal), government grants, and the formation of political districts are based on Bureau of the Census counts. The Bureau of the Census generally estimates that its population counts run about 1 to 2 percent below the real number of people in the United States. While overall 1 or 2 percent, or 5 million people, may not sound like much, most of those not counted live in the larger cities, where the miscount may be as high as 4 to 5 percent. Four or 5 percent more in federal grant monies or in political representation can be significant. For example, according to the Children's Defense Fund, a children's advocacy group, the 1990 undercount of population realigned $182 bil-

---

* The Bureau of the Census counts "persons." The Founding Fathers were quite specific that everyone in the country be counted. (Slaves were not citizens, but they were counted. See a copy of the 1790 Census, Figure 1.2.) Because of this, illegal aliens are included in the 10-year census and the monthly estimates prepared by the Bureau of the Census.

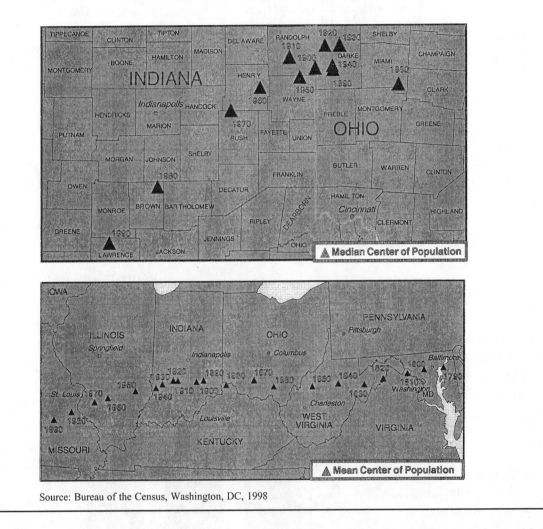

FIGURE 1.1

Centers of Population: 1790 to 1990

[Prior to 1960, excludes Alaska and Hawaii. The median center is located at the intersection of two median lines, a north-south line constructed so that half of the nation's population lives east and half lives west of it, and an east-west line selected so that half of the Nation's population lives north and half lives south of it. The mean center of population is that point at which an imaginary, flat, weightless, and rigid map of the United States would balance if weights of identical value were placed on it so that each weight represented the location of one person on the date of the census]

| YEAR | MEDIAN CENTER | | | | MEAN CENTER | |
	Latitude-N	Longitude-W	Latitude-N	Longitude-W	Approximate location	
1790 (August 2)	(NA)	(NA)	39 16 30	76 11 12	In Kent County, MD, 23 miles E of Baltimore, MD	
1850 (June 1) ..	(NA)	(NA)	38 59 00	81 19 00	In Wirt County, WV, 23 miles SE of Parkersburg, WV[1]	
1900 (June 1) ..	40 03 32	84 49 01	39 09 36	85 48 54	In Bartholomew County, IN, 6 miles SE of Columbus, IN	
1950 (April 1) ..	40 00 12	84 56 51	38 50 21	88 09 33	In Richland County, IL, 8 miles NNW of Olney, IL	
1960 (April 1) ..	39 56 25	85 16 60	38 35 58	89 12 35	In Clinton County, IL, 6.5 miles NW of Centralia, IL	
1970 (April 1) ..	39 47 43	85 31 43	38 27 47	89 42 22	In St. Clair County, IL, 5.3 miles ESE of Mascoutah, IL	
1980 (April 1) ..	39 18 60	86 08 15	38 08 13	90 34 26	In Jefferson County, MO, .25 mile W of DeSoto, MO	
1990 (April 1) ..	38 57 55	86 31 53	37 52 20	91 12 55	In Crawford County, MO, 10 miles SE of Steelville, MO	

NA Not available. [1] West Virginia was set off from Virginia, Dec. 31, 1862, and admitted as a State, June 19, 1863.

Source: Bureau of the Census, Washington, DC, 1998

lion in federal money each year, shifting state allocations for programs such as Medicaid and Head Start.

1998 U.S. AND WORLD POPULATION

In 1998, the Bureau of the Census estimated that the U.S. population had risen to 270.3 million. The United States ranked third in the world in population. Of the 5.9 billion people worldwide in 1998, more than half (3.4 billion) lived in Asia (Figure 1.3). Nearly 1.2 billion lived in China, 984 million in India, 213 million in Indonesia, 170 million in Brazil, and 147 million in Russia. The other 2.5 billion lived in the remaining 220 countries. The United States accounted for less than 5 percent of the world population.

FIGURE 1.2

DISTICTS	Free-white Males of 16 years and upwards, including heads of families	Free-white Males under sixteen years	Free-white Females, including heads of families	All other free persons	Slaves	Total
Vermont	22435	22328	40505	255	16	85539
N. Hampshire	36086	34851	70160	630	158	141885
Maine	24384	24748	46870	538	NONE	96540
Massachusetts	95453	87289	190582	5463	NONE	378787
Rhode Island	16019	15799	32652	3407	948	68825
Connecticut	60523	54403	117448	2808	2764	237946
New York	83700	78122	152320	4654	21324	340120
New Jersey	45251	41416	83287	2762	11423	184139
Pennsylvania	110788	106948	206363	6537	3737	434373
Delaware	11783	12143	22384	3899	8887	59094
Maryland	55915	51339	101395	8043	103036	319728
Virginia	110936	116135	215046	12866	292627	747610
Kentucky	15154	17057	28922	114	12430	73677
N. Carolina	69988	77506	140710	4975	100572	393751
S. Carolina	35576	37722	66880	1801	107094	249073
Georgia	13103	14044	25739	398	29264	82548
	807094	791850	1541263	59150	694280	3893635

Total number of Inhabitants of the United States exclusive of S. Western and N. Territory.	Free white Males of 21 years and upwards.	Free Males under 21 years of age.	Free white Females.	All other Persons.	Slaves.	Total
S.W. territory	6271	10277	15365	361	3417	35691
N. Ditto	—	—	—	—	—	—

Source: Bureau of the Census, Washington, DC

POPULATION GROWTH

The 9.8 percent population growth rate from 1980 to 1990 was the second lowest growth rate in American history. Only the 7.3 percent increase that occurred during the 1930s was less. During that decade of the Great Depression, many people were reluctant to have children because they were not sure they could afford to take care of them.

The highest recent growth rate over a 10-year census period was 18.5 percent during the 1950s. This included the peak years of the post-World War II "baby boom" (1946-1964), during which the average rate of childbirth was more than three births per woman, lead-ing to a large population increase. The drop in population growth has been mainly caused by the drop in the rate of childbearing, which has averaged about two births per woman over the past two decades. (See Figure 1.4 for the annual average percent change in population by decade, 1900 to 2050.)

Population growth rates increased much more slowly in the twentieth century than in the nineteenth century, largely because of a long-term drop in the number of births. At the beginning of the nineteenth century, the average childbearing rate was seven births per woman, more than three times as many as today; however, many children died in infancy. Nonetheless, despite the average number of births dropping, the population growth rate increased in the late nineteenth and early twentieth centuries. During this period, the number of people who died from disease and other causes was declining, while the rate of immigration was increasing from the 1840s to the 1920s.

POPULATION TRENDS

The U.S. population is projected to reach 275 million in 2000 — a growth of 12 million, or 4.5

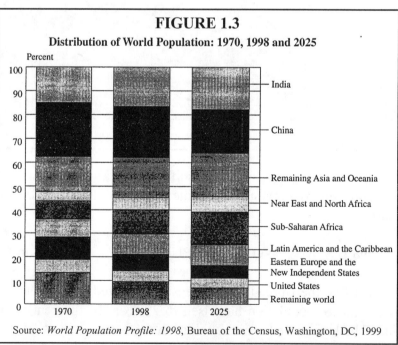

FIGURE 1.3
Distribution of World Population: 1970, 1998 and 2025

Percent — India, China, Remaining Asia and Oceania, Near East and North Africa, Sub-Saharan Africa, Latin America and the Caribbean, Eastern Europe and the New Independent States, United States, Remaining world — 1970, 1998, 2025

Source: *World Population Profile: 1998*, Bureau of the Census, Washington, DC, 1999

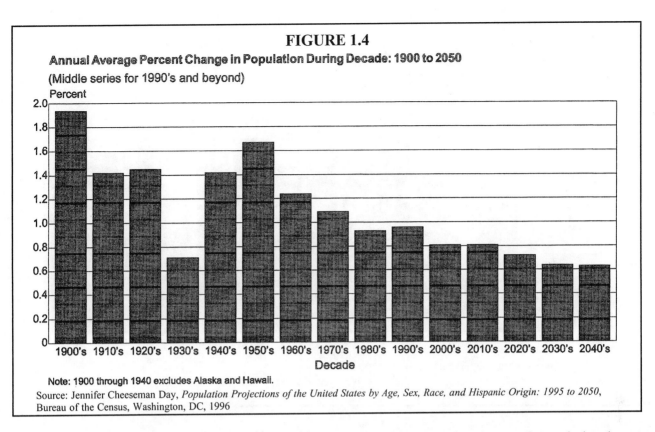

FIGURE 1.4

Annual Average Percent Change in Population During Decade: 1900 to 2050

(Middle series for 1990's and beyond)

Note: 1900 through 1940 excludes Alaska and Hawaii.

Source: Jennifer Cheeseman Day, *Population Projections of the United States by Age, Sex, Race, and Hispanic Origin: 1995 to 2050*, Bureau of the Census, Washington, DC, 1996

percent, since 1995 (middle series projection, Figure 1.5). The U.S. population is projected to top 300 million shortly after 2010, reach 350 million around 2030, and approach 400 million by 2050 (middle series). (See Figure 1.6 for total population growth during this period.)

The average annual rate of population is expected to decrease in the middle series by 30 percent, from 0.88 between 1995 and 2000 to 0.63 between 2040 and 2050. Because the annual rate of immigrants is assumed to remain constant, a slowing natural increase (births minus deaths) is

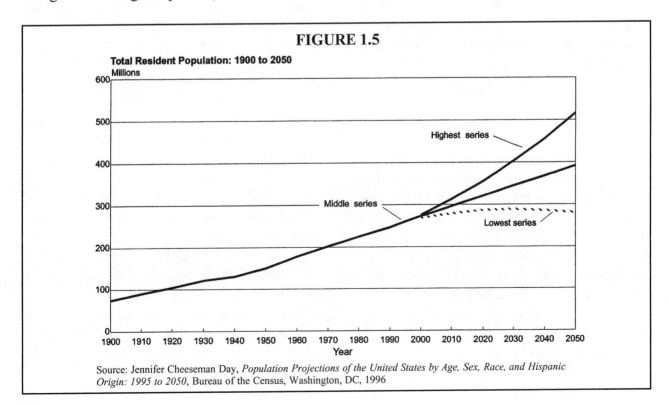

FIGURE 1.5

Total Resident Population: 1900 to 2050

Source: Jennifer Cheeseman Day, *Population Projections of the United States by Age, Sex, Race, and Hispanic Origin: 1995 to 2050*, Bureau of the Census, Washington, DC, 1996

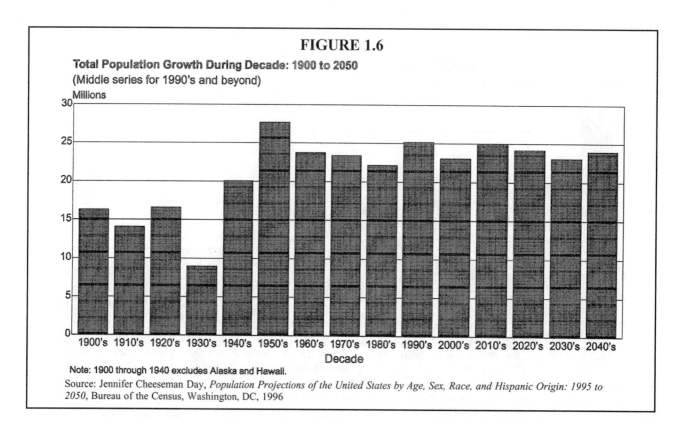

FIGURE 1.6

Total Population Growth During Decade: 1900 to 2050
(Middle series for 1990's and beyond)

Note: 1900 through 1940 excludes Alaska and Hawaii.

Source: Jennifer Cheeseman Day, *Population Projections of the United States by Age, Sex, Race, and Hispanic Origin: 1995 to 2050*, Bureau of the Census, Washington, DC, 1996

likely to be the primary cause of this decrease in the rate of change.

STATE AND COUNTY POPULATIONS

In 1998, California was, by far, the most populous state, with an estimated population of 32.7 million. Texas ranked second (19.8 million), and New York was third (18.2 million). Florida ranked fourth, with almost 15 million. (See Table 1.1 for estimates of state populations.)

The Fastest-Growing States

States with the fastest growth rates continued to be concentrated in the West and South. From 1990 to 1998, five of the six fastest-growing states in the country were in the West. Nevada, where a rapidly growing gambling industry has fueled the population growth, led all states, with a 45.4 percent increase from 1990 to 1998. Arizona's population grew by 27.4 percent during that same period, followed by Idaho (22 percent), Utah (21.9 percent), Colorado (20.5 percent) and Georgia (18 percent). (See Figure 1.7.)

Projections

Between 1995 and 2025, net population change (births minus deaths plus net migration) will be most evident in three states — California, Texas, and Florida. Each will gain more than 6 million persons, 45 percent of the net population change in the United States. (See Figure 1.8.) No other state will gain more than 2.7 million persons. Twelve states that will add between 1.0 million and 2.7 million people during this period will account for about 30 percent of the nation's growth. California, the most populous state, is expected to have 15 percent of the nation's population by 2025.

Top Counties

Not surprisingly, counties with the fastest growth rate in 1998 were also concentrated in the South and West. Of the fastest-growing counties with at least 10,000 people, four were in Georgia, two each in Texas and Colorado, and one each in Virginia and Nevada. All ten counties were in or near metropolitan areas. Forsyth County, part of Atlanta, Georgia, grew the fastest, with a 13 percent increase from 1997 to 1998. (See Table 1.2.) That county's population has increased by 95.4 percent since 1990. Los Angeles County, California, gained the largest number of people, adding 97,027 to its population between 1997 and 1998. Maricopa County, in the Phoenix-Mesa, Arizona, metropolitan area, gained the most people between 1990 and 1998, increasing its population by 661,974 in just eight years.

MOST AMERICANS LIVE IN METROPOLITAN STATISTICAL AREAS

A metropolitan statistical area (MSA) includes a large population center with at least 50,000 residents, together with surrounding communities that are economically and socially tied together. Generally, a metropolitan area is made up of a sizable city with its suburbs and a total population of at least 100,000 people. Most metropolitan areas cross over counties and may also include some rural areas.

Between April 1990 and July 1996, the nation's population grew by 6.7 percent, an increase of 16.6 million people. The country's 273 MSAs and CMSAs (consolidated metropolitan statistical areas) grew at a similar pace of 6.9 percent, an increase of 13.6 million people. Four out of 5 Americans (79.8 percent) lived in metropolitan statistical areas in 1996, the latest year for population estimates of metropolitan areas.

The New York-Northern New Jersey-Long Island, NY-NJ-Conn.-PA., CMSA was the nation's largest metropolitan area in 1996, with nearly 20 million people. Nine other metropolitan areas had populations of more than 4 million in 1996. The 10 largest metropolitan areas were evenly distributed among the nation's four regions, with three each in the Northeast and South and two each in the Midwest and West. (See Table 1.3.)

The Los Angeles-Riverside-Orange County, California, CMSA gained nearly 1 million residents from 1990 to 1996, the largest numeric increase of any metropolitan area. The Atlanta, Georgia, MSA;

TABLE 1.1

STATE	Resident population, 1998 (1,000)
United States	270,299
Alabama	4,352
Alaska	614
Arizona	4,669
Arkansas	2,538
California	32,667
Colorado	3,971
Connecticut	3,274
Delaware	744
District of Columbia	523
Florida	14,916
Georgia	7,642
Hawaii	1,193
Idaho	1,229
Illinois	12,045
Indiana	5,899
Iowa	2,862
Kansas	2,629
Kentucky	3,936
Louisiana	4,369
Maine	1,244
Maryland	5,135
Massachusetts	6,147
Michigan	9,817
Minnesota	4,725
Mississippi	2,752
Missouri	5,439
Montana	880
Nebraska	1,663
Nevada	1,747
New Hampshire	1,185
New Jersey	8,115
New Mexico	1,737
New York	18,175
North Carolina	7,546
North Dakota	638
Ohio	11,209
Oklahoma	3,347
Oregon	3,282
Pennsylvania	12,001
Rhode Island	988
South Carolina	3,836
South Dakota	738
Tennessee	5,431
Texas	19,760
Utah	2,100
Vermont	591
Virginia	6,791
Washington	5,689
West Virginia	1,811
Wisconsin	5,224
Wyoming	481

Source: *State Population Estimates*, Bureau of the Census, Washington, DC, 1998

Dallas-Forth Worth, Texas, CMSA; Houston-Galveston-Brazoria, Texas, CMSA; and Phoenix-Mesa, Arizona, MSA each added more than 500,000 persons. (See Table 1.4.)

The most recent report from the Bureau of the Census noted that these metropolitan areas increased due to high levels of immigration. Although more than 1.2 million people left Los Angeles County from 1990 to 1996, the metropolitan area gained 963,626 people because of immigration and a high number of births. The debate continued about whether immigration pushed people out who were already living in the metropolitan areas or whether those people would have left anyway for better jobs elsewhere and immigrants filled the vacuum.

While some areas lost people from their central cities, the metropolitan areas generally gained population. For example, at the same time that the central area of New York's five boroughs lost more than 900,000 people, the New York CMSA gained 388,843 million people.

The Las Vegas, Nevada-Arizona MSA, fueled by the economic growth of the gaming industry, was the fastest-growing metropolitan area in the country between 1990 and 1996, and Texas had four of the 10 fastest-growing metropolitan areas. (See Table 1.5.) Three of the four Texas cities are border cities with Mexico and have become the home of many immigrants.

The South and the West are home to all 50 of the fastest-growing metropolitan areas and to 8 of 10 of the metropolitan areas with the largest numerical increase. The two regions combined account for 28 of the 47 metropolitan areas with 1 million or more residents.

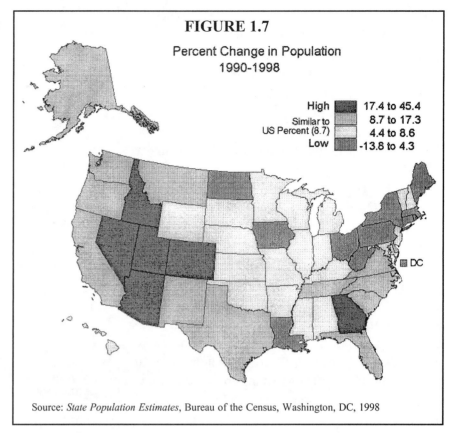

FIGURE 1.7

Percent Change in Population
1990-1998

High	17.4 to 45.4
Similar to US Percent (8.7)	8.7 to 17.3
	4.4 to 8.6
Low	-13.8 to 4.3

Source: *State Population Estimates*, Bureau of the Census, Washington, DC, 1998

CITIES

In 1998, nine cities in the United States had a population of over 1 million people. While New York, Los Angeles, and Chicago, the three largest cities, are also the three largest metropolitan areas, there is little relationship in other MSAs between the population rankings of metropolitan areas and those of their major cities. Houston, for example is the fourth largest city, but the tenth largest metropolitan area. Boston, the seventh largest metropolitan area, is the twentieth largest city.

Both Phoenix, Arizona, and San Antonio, Texas, reached the 1 million mark during the April 1990 to July 1996 period. By the end of that period, Phoenix had become the seventh most populous city, climbing from ninth in 1990. San Antonio rose from tenth to eighth place. Dallas dropped from eighth to ninth. New York City, the nation's largest city, with 7.4 million people, grew by about 97,602 from 1990 to 1998 (1.3 percent). Los Angeles, despite losing population earlier in the decade, grew by nearly 112,000 (3.2 percent) in those eight years, remaining the second largest U.S. city, with a 1998 population of about 3.6 million. (See Table 1.6.)

Fastest-Growing Cities

Smaller cities, with populations between 10,000 and 50,000, grew at a faster rate (8.6 percent) than larger cities (Table 1.7). Between 1990 and 1998, the Mesquite, Nevada, population grew by 441.2 percent, making it the fastest-growing U.S. city among those with populations between 10,000 and 50,000. Frisco, Texas, increased its population by 328.5 percent during the same period. (See Table 1.8.) Phoenix and San Antonio were the country's fastest-growing cities with populations of one million or more, increasing by 21.3 percent and 14.1 percent, respectively (Table 1.6).

FARMS

In 1997, the nation's 1.9 million farms covered 931.8 million acres. The average farm was 487 acres, while the median (half were bigger, half were smaller) farm size was 120 acres. (See Table 1.9.) According to the *1997 Census of Agriculture* (United States Department of Agriculture, National Agricultural Statistics Service, 1999), the number of large farms (those with sales of $100,000 or more) increased six-fold from 1969 to 1997. While total farm count dwindled from 2.7 million in 1969 to 1.9 million in 1997, the number of large farms jumped from 51,995 in 1969 to 345,988 in 1997.

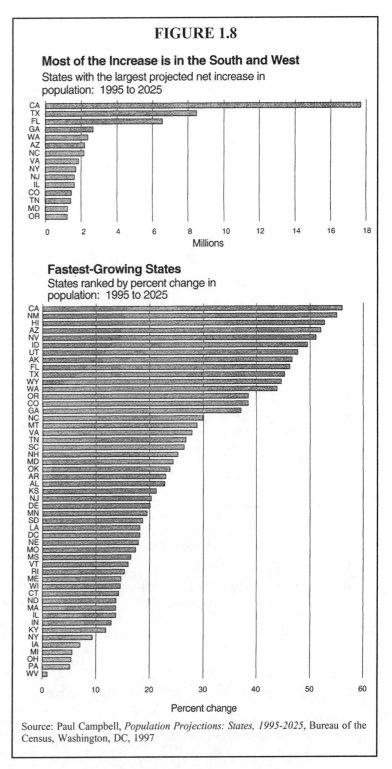

FIGURE 1.8

Most of the Increase is in the South and West
States with the largest projected net increase in population: 1995 to 2025

Fastest-Growing States
States ranked by percent change in population: 1995 to 2025

Source: Paul Campbell, *Population Projections: States, 1995-2025*, Bureau of the Census, Washington, DC, 1997

Half (50.3 percent) of all farms sold less than $10,000 of farm products and accounted for only 1.5 percent of total farm sales. On the other hand, larger farms with sales of $500,000 or more made up only 3.6 percent of all farms, but accounted for more than half (56.6 percent) of all sales. (See Figure 1.9.) Large farms averaged 1,706 acres, compared to 284 acres for smaller farms.

Corporations are more likely to own large farms, while families or individuals were more likely to own small farms. Individual or family ownership is the most common type of organiza-

TABLE 1.2

Ten Fastest-Growing Counties in the United States
with 10,000 or More Persons in 1998

Rank	County	State	Percent Increase: 1997-98
1	Forsyth	Ga.	13.0
2	Douglas	Colo.	11.2
3	Loudoun	Va.	8.2
4	Henry	Ga.	7.2
5	Collin	Texas	6.9
6	Paulding	Ga.	6.9
7	Dawson	Ga.	6.5
8	Elbert	Colo.	6.5
9	Williamson	Texas	6.2
10	Nye	Nev.	6.1

Source: Press Release CB99-50, Bureau of the Census, Washington, DC, 1999

TABLE 1.3

Ten Largest Metropolitan Areas, 1996

Rank	Area	Population
1	New York-Northern New Jersey-Long Island, N.Y.-N.J.-Conn.-Pa., CMSA	19,938,492
2	Los Angeles-Riverside-Orange County, Calif., CMSA	15,495,155
3	Chicago-Gary-Kenosha, Ill.-Ind.-Wis., CMSA	8,599,774
4	Washington-Baltimore, D.C.-Md.-Va.-W. Va., CMSA	7,164,519
5	San Francisco-Oakland-San Jose, Calif., CMSA	6,605,428
6	Philadelphia-Wilmington-Atlantic City, Pa.-N.J.-Del.-Md., CMSA	5,973,463
7	Boston-Worcester-Lawrence, Mass.-N.H.-Maine-Conn., CMSA	5,563,475
8	Detroit-Ann Arbor-Flint, Mich., CMSA	5,284,171
9	Dallas-Fort Worth, Texas, CMSA	4,574,561
10	Houston-Galveston-Brazoria, Texas, CMSA	4,253,428

TABLE 1.4

Ten Biggest Gainers Among Metropolitan Areas, 1990-1996

Rank	Area	Population Gain
1	Los Angeles-Riverside-Orange County, Calif., CMSA	963,626
2	Atlanta, Ga., MSA	581,730
3	Dallas-Fort Worth, Texas, CMSA	537,279
4	Houston-Galveston-Brazoria, Texas, CMSA	522,399
5	Phoenix-Mesa, Ariz., MSA	508,205
6	Washington-Baltimore, D.C.-Md.-Va.-W. Va., CMSA	438,124
7	New York-Northern New Jersey-Long Island, N.Y.-N.J.-Conn.-Pa., CMSA	388,843
8	Chicago-Gary-Kenosha, Ill.-Ind.-Wis., CMSA	359,954
9	San Francisco-Oakland-San Jose, Calif., CMSA	355,547
10	Seattle-Tacoma-Bremerton, Wash., CMSA	350,529

Source of above two tables: Press Release CB97-212, Bureau of the Census, Washington, DC, 1997

TABLE 1.5
Ten Fastest-Growing Metropolitan Areas: 1990-1996

Rank	Area	Percent Increase
1	Las Vegas, Nev.-Ariz., MSA	40.9
2	Laredo, Texas, MSA	32.7
3	McAllen-Edinburg-Mission, Texas, MSA	29.2
4	Boise City, Idaho, MSA	25.9
5	Naples, Fla., MSA	23.7
6	Fayetteville-Springdale-Rogers, Ark., MSA	23.7
7	Austin-San Marcos, Texas, MSA	23.1
8	Phoenix-Mesa, Ariz., MSA	22.7
9	Provo-Orem, Utah, MSA	21.3
10	Brownsville-Harlingen-San Benito, Tx.,MSA	21.1

Source: Press Release CB97-212, Bureau of the Census, Washington, DC, 1997

TABLE 1.6

U.S. Cities with Populations of 500,000 or More in 1998,
Ranked by 1998 Population

Rank	City	1998 Population	Change: 1990 to 1998 Number	Percent
1	New York, N.Y.	7,420,166	97,602	1.3
2	Los Angeles, Calif.	3,597,556	111,999	3.2
3	Chicago, Ill.	2,802,079	18,353	0.7
4	Houston, Texas	1,786,691	132,343	8.0
5	Philadelphia, Pa.	1,436,287	-149,290	-9.4
6	San Diego, Calif.	1,220,666	110,043	9.9
7	Phoenix, Ariz.	1,198,064	210,049	21.3
8	San Antonio, Texas	1,114,130	137,616	14.1
9	Dallas, Texas	1,075,894	68,276	6.8
10	Detroit, Mich.	970,196	-57,778	-5.6
11	San Jose, Calif.	861,284	79,060	10.1
12	San Francisco, Calif.	745,774	21,815	3.0
13	Indianapolis, Ind.	741,304	10,026	1.4
14	Jacksonville, Fla.	693,630	58,400	9.2
15	Columbus, Ohio	670,234	37,289	5.9
16	Baltimore, Md.	645,593	-90,421	-12.3
17	El Paso, Texas	615,032	99,690	19.3
18	Memphis, Tenn.	603,507	-15,145	-2.4
19	Milwaukee, Wis.	578,364	-49,724	-7.9
20	Boston, Mass.	555,447	-18,836	-3.3
21	Austin, Texas	552,435	80,415	17.0
22	Seattle, Wash.	536,978	20,719	4.0
23	Washington, D.C.	523,124	-83,776	-13.8
24	Nashville-Davidson, Tenn.	510,274	21,908	4.5
25	Charlotte, N.C.	504,637	85,079	20.3
26	Portland, Ore.	503,891	17,916	3.7

TABLE 1.7

Population Change in U.S. Cities with 1998 Populations of 10,000 or More,
by Size Category

Population size category (based on 1998 population)	Percent change: 1990-98	Number of cities
1,000,000 or more	3.5	9
500,000 - 999,999	2.0	17
250,000 - 499,999	4.8	41
100,000 - 249,999	7.8	151
50,000 - 99,999	8.2	354
10,000 - 49,999	8.6	2,006
All cities with populations of 10,000 or more	6.6	2,578

Source of above two tables: Press Release CB99-128, Bureau of the Census, Washington, DC, 1999

TABLE 1.8

Five Fastest Growing U.S. Cities with Populations Between
10,000 and 50,000 in 1998, Ranked by Growth Rate

Rank	City	1998 population	1990 Population	Change: 1990 to 1998 Number	Percent
1	Mesquite, Nev.	10,125	1,871	8,254	441.2
2	Frisco, Texas	26,304	6,138	20,166	328.5
3	Fishers, Ind.	25,591	7,189	18,402	256.0
4	Cedar Park, Texas	18,371	5,161	13,210	256.0
5	Lake in the Hills, Ill.	20,417	5,882	14,535	247.1

Source: Press Release CB99-128, Bureau of the Census, Washington, DC, 1999

tion for both groups (Figure 1.10). Of all corporate farms in 1997, 58 percent were large farms. Families or individuals were more likely to own small farms.

Rural Population

Until the early part of this century, the nation's population was mainly rural (open countryside and places with fewer than 2,500 inhabitants that are not suburbs). In 1790, when the first census was taken, 19 out of every 20 persons had a rural residence. The 1920 census was the first time a majority of people lived in urban areas (51.2 percent). In 1997, only 20 percent of families lived in nonmetropolitan areas.

In 1920, farm residents made up 30.2 percent of the total population. This proportion fell to 15.3 percent in 1950, 4.8 percent in 1970, and 2.7 percent in 1980. By 1991, the last year statistics were kept on residents of farms and rural areas, one of every 51 persons (about 1.9 percent) lived on a farm.

RACE AND HISPANIC ORIGIN

The Bureau of the Census bases its population estimates on three components of population change — births, deaths, and immigration. The number of births minus the number of deaths is the "natural increase" in the population. The Bureau researchers then add the number of immigrants minus the number of emigrants (persons who leave one country or region to settle in another) to the

"natural increase" and arrive at a total increase in population.

The Census Bureau estimated the U.S. population, as of August 1, 1999, at 273 million people — 224.9 million were White; 34.9 million, Black; 2.4 million, American Indian, Eskimo, and Aleut; and 10.9 million, Asian and Pacific Islander. The Hispanic population numbered 31.5 million. (See Table 1.10.) Note that Hispanics may be of any race.

While the general population rose 9.8 percent from April 1990 to August 1999, the population among the nation's minorities increased at a much more rapid rate. The White population increased 7.8 percent, from 208.7 million to 224.9 million. The number of Whites not of Hispanic origin rose

TABLE 1.9

State Summary Highlights: 1997

Item	United States
Farms . . . . number..	1 911 859
Land in farms . . . . .acres..	931 795 255
Average size of farm . . . . .acres..	487
Median size of farm . . . . .acres..	120
Estimated market value of land and buildings:	
Average per farm . . . . .dollars..	449 748
Average per acre . . . . .dollars..	933
Estimated market value of all machinery and equipment:	
Average per farm . . . . .dollars..	57 678
Farms by size:	
1 to 9 acres	153 515
10 to 49 acres	410 833
50 to 179 acres	592 972
180 to 499 acres	402 769
500 to 999 acres	175 690
1,000 acres or more	176 080

Source: *1997 Census of Agriculture: United States, Summary and State Data*, vol. I, U.S. Department of Agriculture, Washington, DC, 1999

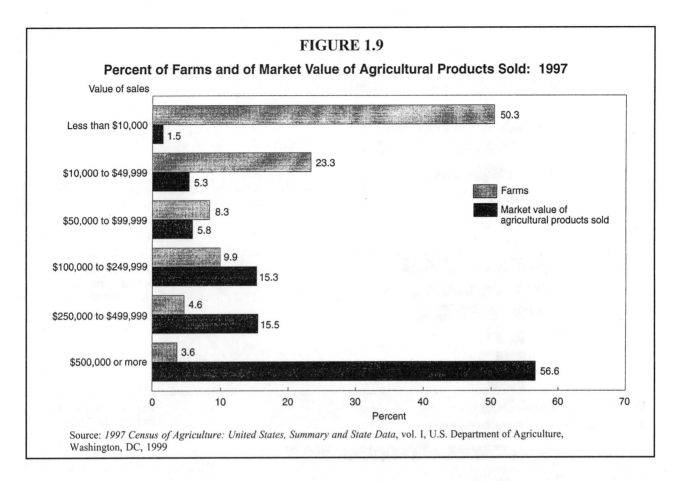

FIGURE 1.9

Percent of Farms and of Market Value of Agricultural Products Sold: 1997

Value of sales

Less than $10,000 — Farms 50.3, Market value 1.5

$10,000 to $49,999 — Farms 23.3, Market value 5.3

$50,000 to $99,999 — Farms 8.3, Market value 5.8

$100,000 to $249,999 — Farms 9.9, Market value 15.3

$250,000 to $499,999 — Farms 4.6, Market value 15.5

$500,000 or more — Farms 3.6, Market value 56.6

Farms

Market value of agricultural products sold

Percent

Source: *1997 Census of Agriculture: United States, Summary and State Data*, vol. I, U.S. Department of Agriculture, Washington, DC, 1999

4 percent, from 188.3 million to 196.2 million. Non-Hispanic Whites made up 72 percent of those living in the United States, down from 83.5 percent in 1970 and 79.6 percent in 1980. (See Table 1.10 for population estimates for April 1990 to August 1999.)

While the majority non-Hispanic White population rose less than half the national average (4 percent) from 1990 to 1999, every minority group grew at a rate faster than the general population increase and, therefore, increased as a proportion of the total population. The Black population rose 14.5 percent; the American Indian, Eskimo, and Aleut population, 16.2 percent; and the Asian and Pacific Islander population, 46 percent. (See Table 1.10.) For more information, see *Minorities — A Changing Role in American Society* (Information Plus, Wylie, Texas, 1998).

Children

In 1998, 65 percent of U.S. children were non-Hispanic White, down from 74 percent in 1980.

About 15 percent were non-Hispanic Black; 15 percent, Hispanic; 4 percent, Asian or Pacific Islander; and 1 percent, American Indian or Alaska Native. The percentages of the child population of Blacks and American Indian or Alaska Natives were fairly stable from 1980 to 1998.

Meanwhile, the percentage of Hispanics increased more rapidly than other racial and ethnic groups, growing from 9 percent of the child population in 1980 to 15 percent in 1998. By 2020, it is projected that more than 1 in 5 children will be Hispanic. The percentage of Asian or Pacific Islander children doubled from 2 to 4 percent between 1980 and 1998. This percentage is expected to continue to grow in the coming decades to 6 percent by 2020. (See Figure 1.11.)

Hispanic-Origin Population

The Hispanic-origin population rose 41 percent, from 22.4 million on April 1, 1990, to 31.5 million by August 1999 (Table 1.10). The Hispanic-origin population accounted for about

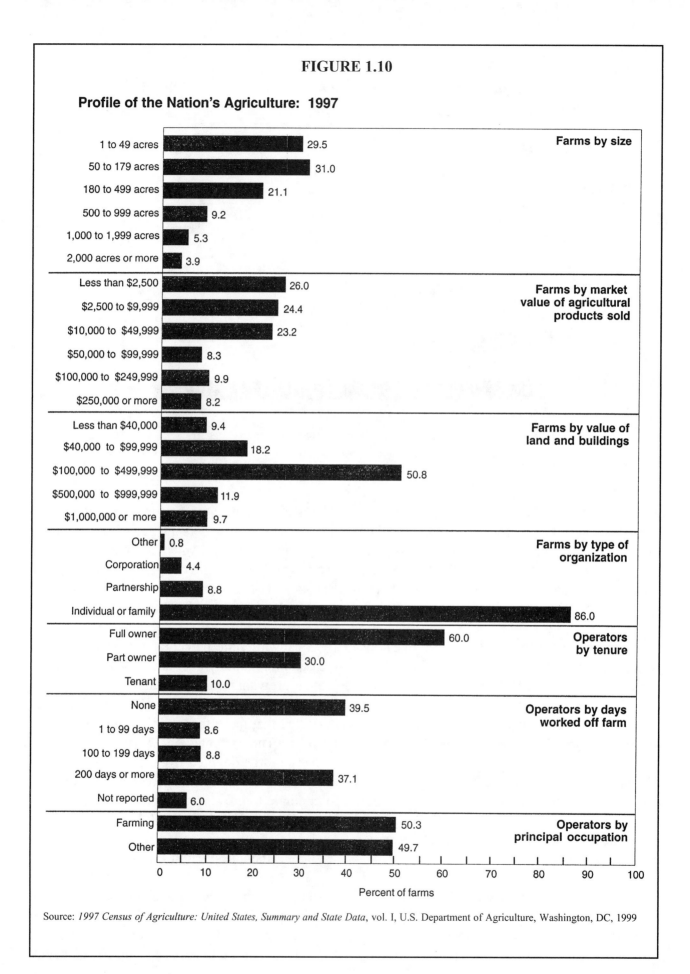

FIGURE 1.10

Profile of the Nation's Agriculture: 1997

Farms by size
- 1 to 49 acres — 29.5
- 50 to 179 acres — 31.0
- 180 to 499 acres — 21.1
- 500 to 999 acres — 9.2
- 1,000 to 1,999 acres — 5.3
- 2,000 acres or more — 3.9

Farms by market value of agricultural products sold
- Less than $2,500 — 26.0
- $2,500 to $9,999 — 24.4
- $10,000 to $49,999 — 23.2
- $50,000 to $99,999 — 8.3
- $100,000 to $249,999 — 9.9
- $250,000 or more — 8.2

Farms by value of land and buildings
- Less than $40,000 — 9.4
- $40,000 to $99,999 — 18.2
- $100,000 to $499,999 — 50.8
- $500,000 to $999,999 — 11.9
- $1,000,000 or more — 9.7

Farms by type of organization
- Other — 0.8
- Corporation — 4.4
- Partnership — 8.8
- Individual or family — 86.0

Operators by tenure
- Full owner — 60.0
- Part owner — 30.0
- Tenant — 10.0

Operators by days worked off farm
- None — 39.5
- 1 to 99 days — 8.6
- 100 to 199 days — 8.8
- 200 days or more — 37.1
- Not reported — 6.0

Operators by principal occupation
- Farming — 50.3
- Other — 49.7

Percent of farms

Source: *1997 Census of Agriculture: United States, Summary and State Data*, vol. I, U.S. Department of Agriculture, Washington, DC, 1999

14

TABLE 1.10

Resident Population Estimates of the United States by Sex, Race, and Hispanic Origin: April 1, 1990 to August 1, 1999 (Numbers in thousands. Consistent with 1990 Decennial Census enumeration.)

	Aug. 1, 1999	July 1, 1999	July 1, 1998	July 1, 1997	July 1, 1996	July 1, 1995	July 1, 1994	July 1, 1993	July 1, 1992	July 1, 1991	July 1, 1990	April 1, 1990
ALL RACES												
Population.........	273,137	272,878	270,299	267,744	265,190	262,765	260,289	257,746	254,995	252,127	249,439	248,765
(Percent of Total)..	100.0	100.0	100.0	100.0	100.0	100.0	100.0	100.0	100.0	100.0	100.0	100.0
Median Age (years)..	35.5	35.5	35.2	34.9	34.7	34.4	34.1	33.7	33.4	33.1	32.8	32.8
Mean Age (years)...	36.4	36.4	36.2	36.1	35.9	35.8	35.7	35.6	35.4	35.3	35.2	35.2
Male Population.....	133,482	133,352	132,046	130,760	129,483	128,272	127,028	125,767	124,404	122,943	121,613	121,271
Female Population...	139,654	139,526	138,252	136,984	135,707	134,493	133,261	131,979	130,590	129,184	127,825	127,494
WHITE												
Population.........	224,865	224,692	223,001	221,317	219,623	218,010	216,365	214,677	212,860	210,961	209,182	208,727
(Percent of Total)..	82.3	82.2	82.5	82.7	82.8	83.0	83.1	83.3	83.5	83.7	83.9	83.9
Median Age (years)..	36.6	36.6	36.3	36.0	35.7	35.4	35.0	34.7	34.4	34.1	33.8	33.7
Mean Age (years)...	37.3	37.3	37.1	37.0	36.9	36.7	36.6	36.5	36.4	36.2	36.1	36.1
Male Population.....	110,462	110,372	109,489	108,615	107,742	106,913	106,060	105,201	104,280	103,290	102,392	102,156
Female Population...	114,403	114,320	113,511	112,702	111,881	111,097	110,305	109,476	108,580	107,671	106,790	106,571
BLACK												
Population.........	34,948	34,903	34,431	33,973	33,518	33,098	32,654	32,179	31,667	31,131	30,623	30,511
(Percent of Total)..	12.8	12.8	12.7	12.7	12.6	12.6	12.5	12.5	12.4	12.3	12.3	12.3
Median Age (years)..	30.1	30.1	29.9	29.7	29.5	29.2	29.0	28.7	28.5	28.2	27.9	27.9
Mean Age (years)...	32.1	32.1	31.9	31.7	31.5	31.3	31.1	31.0	30.9	30.8	30.7	30.7
Male Population.....	16,596	16,573	16,340	16,116	15,895	15,694	15,480	15,252	15,004	14,735	14,492	14,436
Female Population...	18,352	18,329	18,090	17,857	17,623	17,404	17,174	16,927	16,663	16,396	16,132	16,075
AMERICAN INDIAN, ESKIMO, AND ALEUT												
Population.........	2,400	2,396	2,360	2,324	2,289	2,254	2,221	2,185	2,148	2,110	2,074	2,065
(Percent of Total)..	0.9	0.9	0.9	0.9	0.9	0.9	0.9	0.8	0.8	0.8	0.8	0.8
Median Age (years)..	27.7	27.6	27.5	27.2	27.0	26.8	26.7	26.5	26.4	26.2	26.0	26.0
Mean Age (years)...	30.4	30.4	30.2	30.0	29.8	29.5	29.3	29.1	28.9	28.7	28.5	28.5
Male Population.....	1,187	1,186	1,168	1,151	1,133	1,117	1,100	1,083	1,065	1,046	1,028	1,024
Female Population...	1,212	1,211	1,192	1,173	1,155	1,138	1,120	1,102	1,083	1,064	1,046	1,041
ASIAN AND PACIFIC ISLANDER												
Population.........	10,924	10,887	10,507	10,130	9,761	9,403	9,050	8,705	8,319	7,925	7,560	7,462
(Percent of Total)..	4.0	4.0	3.9	3.8	3.7	3.6	3.5	3.4	3.3	3.1	3.0	3.0
Median Age (years)..	31.7	31.7	31.5	31.2	30.9	30.7	30.5	30.2	29.9	29.7	29.5	29.4
Mean Age (years)...	32.6	32.6	32.4	32.2	32.0	31.8	31.6	31.4	31.2	31.0	30.8	30.8
Male Population.....	5,237	5,221	5,049	4,878	4,712	4,549	4,388	4,232	4,055	3,872	3,701	3,655
Female Population...	5,687	5,667	5,459	5,252	5,048	4,854	4,661	4,473	4,264	4,053	3,859	3,807

(continued)

TABLE 1.10 (Continued)

	Aug. 1, 1999	July 1, 1999	July 1, 1998	July 1, 1997	July 1, 1996	July 1, 1995	July 1, 1994	July 1, 1993	July 1, 1992	July 1, 1991	July 1, 1990	April 1, 1990
HISPANIC ORIGIN (of any race)												
Population........	31,469	31,365	30,250	29,160	28,092	27,099	26,152	25,214	24,275	23,384	22,565	22,372
(Percent of Total)..	11.5	11.5	11.2	10.9	10.6	10.3	10.0	9.8	9.5	9.3	9.0	9.0
Median Age (years)..	26.5	26.5	26.4	26.3	26.2	26.1	26.0	25.8	25.7	25.6	25.4	25.3
Mean Age (years)....	28.8	28.8	28.7	28.5	28.4	28.3	28.2	28.1	28.0	27.9	27.8	27.8
Male Population.....	15,824	15,774	15,233	14,706	14,189	13,709	13,244	12,788	12,333	11,898	11,493	11,398
Female Population...	15,645	15,591	15,017	14,454	13,903	13,390	12,908	12,426	11,942	11,486	11,071	10,974
WHITE, NOT HISPANIC												
Population........	196,191	196,113	195,440	194,751	194,029	193,320	192,530	191,689	190,718	189,626	188,588	188,307
(Percent of Total)..	71.8	71.9	72.3	72.7	73.2	73.6	74.0	74.4	74.8	75.2	75.6	75.7
Median Age (years)..	38.1	38.1	37.7	37.4	37.0	36.6	36.3	35.9	35.5	35.2	34.8	34.8
Mean Age (years)....	38.5	38.5	38.3	38.2	38.0	37.8	37.6	37.5	37.3	37.2	37.0	37.0
Male Population.....	96,034	95,990	95,601	95,208	94,806	94,414	93,981	93,535	93,024	92,430	91,897	91,748
Female Population...	100,157	100,123	99,839	99,543	99,223	98,906	98,548	98,154	97,694	97,197	96,690	96,560
BLACK, NOT HISPANIC												
Population........	33,164	33,125	32,718	32,324	31,933	31,573	31,193	30,780	30,332	29,853	29,398	29,299
(Percent of Total)..	12.1	12.1	12.1	12.1	12.0	12.0	12.0	11.9	11.9	11.8	11.8	11.8
Median Age (years)..	30.3	30.3	30.1	29.8	29.6	29.4	29.1	28.9	28.6	28.3	28.1	28.0
Mean Age (years)....	32.3	32.2	32.0	31.8	31.6	31.4	31.3	31.1	31.0	30.9	30.8	30.8
Male Population.....	15,706	15,687	15,485	15,291	15,101	14,929	14,746	14,548	14,330	14,089	13,871	13,822
Female Population...	17,458	17,438	17,233	17,032	16,832	16,644	16,448	16,232	16,001	15,764	15,527	15,477
AMERICAN INDIAN, ESKIMO, AND ALEUT, NOT HISPANIC												
Population........	2,026	2,024	2,001	1,977	1,954	1,931	1,908	1,883	1,857	1,829	1,802	1,796
(Percent of Total)..	0.7	0.7	0.7	0.7	0.7	0.7	0.7	0.7	0.7	0.7	0.7	0.7
Median Age (years)..	28.3	28.3	28.0	27.8	27.6	27.4	27.3	27.1	27.0	26.8	26.6	26.5
Mean Age (years)....	31.1	31.0	30.8	30.6	30.3	30.1	29.9	29.6	29.5	29.3	29.1	29.0
Male Population.....	996	995	983	972	961	950	939	927	914	900	887	884
Female Population...	1,030	1,029	1,017	1,005	993	981	969	956	943	929	915	912
ASIAN AND PACIFIC ISLANDER, NOT HISPANIC												
Population........	10,286	10,251	9,890	9,532	9,181	8,842	8,506	8,180	7,812	7,435	7,086	6,992
(Percent of Total)..	3.8	3.8	3.7	3.6	3.5	3.4	3.3	3.2	3.1	2.9	2.8	2.8
Median Age (years)..	32.0	32.0	31.8	31.5	31.2	31.0	30.8	30.5	30.2	30.0	29.7	29.7
Mean Age (years)....	32.9	32.9	32.7	32.5	32.2	32.0	31.8	31.6	31.4	31.2	31.0	31.0
Male Population.....	4,922	4,906	4,744	4,582	4,425	4,270	4,118	3,970	3,802	3,627	3,464	3,419
Female Population...	5,363	5,345	5,147	4,949	4,756	4,572	4,388	4,210	4,010	3,808	3,622	3,573

Source: Population Estimates Program, Bureau of the Census, Washington, DC, 1999

16

FIGURE 1.11

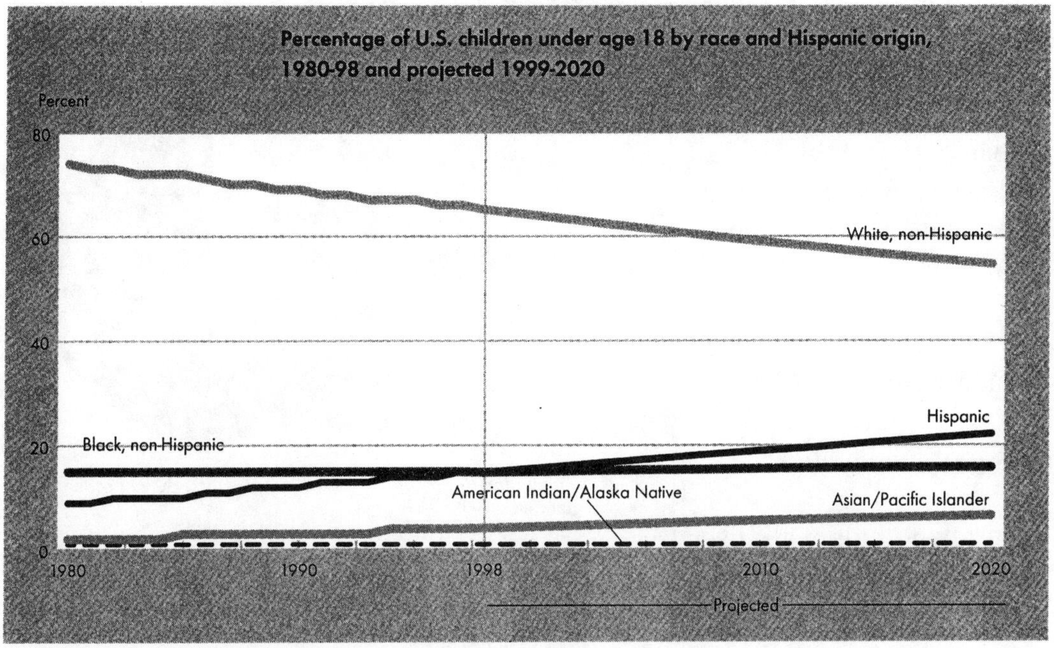

Percentage of U.S. children under age 18 by race and Hispanic origin, 1980-98 and projected 1999-2020

Source: *America's Children: Key National Indicators of Well-Being, 1999*, Federal Interagency Forum on Child and Family Statistics, Washington, DC, 1999

TABLE 1.11

Percent Distribution of the Population by Race and Hispanic Origin: 1990 to 2050

[As of July 1. Resident population]

Year	Total	Race				Hispanic origin[3]	Not of Hispanic origin			
		White	Black	American Indian[1]	Asian[2]		White	Black	American Indian[1]	Asian[2]
ESTIMATE										
1990	100.0	83.9	12.3	0.8	3.0	9.0	75.6	11.8	0.7	2.8
PROJECTIONS										
Middle Series										
1995	100.0	83.0	12.6	0.9	3.6	10.2	73.6	12.0	0.7	3.3
2000	100.0	82.1	12.9	0.9	4.1	11.4	71.8	12.2	0.7	3.9
2005	100.0	81.3	13.2	0.9	4.6	12.6	69.9	12.4	0.8	4.4
2010	100.0	80.5	13.5	0.9	5.1	13.8	68.0	12.6	0.8	4.8
2020	100.0	79.0	14.0	1.0	6.1	16.3	64.3	12.9	0.8	5.7
2030	100.0	77.6	14.4	1.0	7.0	18.9	60.5	13.1	0.8	6.6
2040	100.0	76.1	14.9	1.1	7.9	21.7	56.7	13.3	0.9	7.5
2050	100.0	74.8	15.4	1.1	8.7	24.5	52.8	13.6	0.9	8.2
Lowest Series										
2050	100.0	75.7	15.7	1.2	7.4	22.0	55.8	14.2	1.0	7.0
Highest Series										
2050	100.0	73.5	15.8	1.0	9.7	25.7	50.5	13.8	0.8	9.2

[1]American Indian represents American Indian, Eskimo, and Aleut.
[2]Asian represents Asian and Pacific Islander.
[3]Persons of Hispanic origin may be of any race. The information on the total and Hispanic population shown in this report was collected in the 50 States and the District of Columbia and, therefore, does not include residents of Puerto Rico.

Source: Jennifer Cheeseman Day, *Population Projections of the United States by Age, Sex, Race, and Hispanic Origin: 1995-2025*, Bureau of the Census, Washington, DC, 1996

11.5 percent of the total population of the United States in 1999. Hispanics are expected to number 63 million in 2030 and 88 million in 2050. By then, the Bureau of the Census projects that nearly 1 in 4 Americans will be Hispanic. (See Table 1.11.) Among the reasons for the expected rapid increase in the Hispanic population are

• A higher birth rate for Hispanics than for non-Hispanics.

• High levels of immigration.

In 1996, almost two-thirds of all Hispanics were of Mexican origin. (See Figure 1.12.)

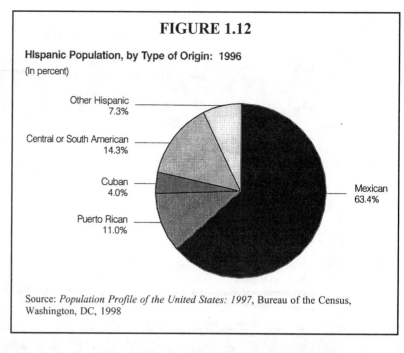

FIGURE 1.12

Hispanic Population, by Type of Origin: 1996
(In percent)

Source: *Population Profile of the United States: 1997*, Bureau of the Census, Washington, DC, 1998

Asians and Pacific Islanders

The number of non-Hispanic Asians and Pacific Islanders in the United States more than doubled from 4 million in 1981 to 10.3 million in August 1999. The Census Bureau estimated the entire Asian and Pacific Islander population (including those of Hispanic origin) at 10.9 million. Immigration to the United States accounted for much of this growth. In 1999, the total Asian and Pacific Islander population accounted for 4 percent of America's population. (See Table 1.10.) By 2050, the proportion of Asians and Pacific Islanders is projected to be 8.7 percent of the total U.S. population (Table 1.11).

In 1996, most of Asians and Pacific Islanders (55 percent) resided in the West, where they made up 9 percent of the total population. Most (94 percent) Asians and Pacific Islanders lived in metropolitan areas. About half of these resided in the suburbs of metropolitan areas, while 45 percent lived in central cities.

Native-American, Eskimo, and Aleut Population

The non-Hispanic Native American (American Indian), Eskimo, and Aleut population rose 11 percent from 1.8 million in 1990 to 2 million in August 1999 and accounted for three-quarters of 1 percent (0.7 percent) of the population (Table 1.10). By 2050, the proportion is expected to rise slightly to just about 1 percent (Table 1.11). Nearly one-half

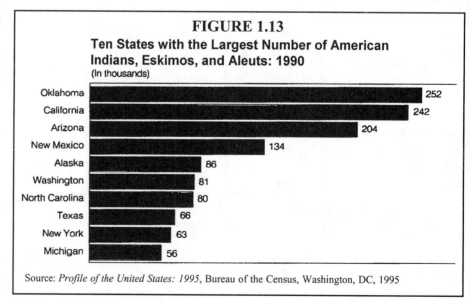

FIGURE 1.13
Ten States with the Largest Number of American Indians, Eskimos, and Aleuts: 1990
(In thousands)

Oklahoma	252
California	242
Arizona	204
New Mexico	134
Alaska	86
Washington	81
North Carolina	80
Texas	66
New York	63
Michigan	56

Source: *Profile of the United States: 1995*, Bureau of the Census, Washington, DC, 1995

TABLE 1.12

Foreign-Born Population Estimates and Historical Decennial Census Data

	Foreign-Born Resident Population		Native Resident Population	
	Number (millions)	Percent of U.S. Population	Number (millions)	Percent of U.S. Population
July 1, 1998	25.2	9.3	245.1	90.7
April 1, 1990	19.8	8.0	228.9	92.0
1980 Census	14.1	6.2	212.5	93.8
1970 Census	9.6	4.7	193.6	95.3
1960 Census	9.7	5.4	169.6	94.6
1950 Census	10.3	6.9	139.9	93.1
1940 Census	11.6	8.8	120.1	91.2
1930 Census	14.2	11.6	108.6	88.4
1920 Census	13.9	13.2	91.8	86.8
1910 Census	13.5	14.7	78.5	85.3
1900 Census	10.3	13.6	65.7	86.4

Source: Press Release CB99-171, Bureau of the Census, Washington, DC, 1999

TABLE 1.13

COUNTRY OF ORIGIN AND YEAR OF ENTRY INTO THE U.S. OF THE FOREIGN BORN, BY CITIZENSHIP STATUS: MARCH 1997

(Numbers in thousands)

	Total Foreign-born		Naturalized Citizen		Not U.S. Citizen	
	Number	Percent	Number	Percent	Number	Percent
Country of Origin						
All countries	25,779	100.0	9,043	100.0	16,736	100.0
Mexico	7,017	27.2	1,044	11.5	5,973	35.7
Cuba	913	3.5	474	5.2	440	2.6
Dominican Republic	632	2.5	195	2.2	437	2.6
El Salvador	607	2.4	110	1.2	497	3.0
Great Britain	606	2.4	237	2.6	369	2.2
China and Hong Kong	1,107	4.3	536	5.9	570	3.4
India	748	2.9	263	2.9	485	2.9
Korea	591	2.3	220	2.4	372	2.2
Philippines	1,132	4.4	657	7.3	475	2.8
Vietnam	770	3.0	385	4.3	385	2.3
Elsewhere	11,655	45.2	4,921	54.4	6,734	40.2
Came to the United States						
All years of entry	25,779	100.0	9,043	100.0	16,736	100.0
Before 1970	4,749	18.4	3,523	39.0	1,226	7.3
1970 to 1979	4,935	19.1	2,580	28.5	2,356	14.1
1980 to 1989	8,555	33.2	2,414	26.7	6,141	36.7
Since 1990	7,539	29.2	526	5.8	7,013	41.9

Source: *March 1997 Current Population Survey*, Bureau of the Census, Washington, DC, 1998

of the American Indian population lived in the West in 1990, 29 percent in the South, 17 percent in the Midwest, and 6 percent in the Northeast. In 1990, four states had an Indian population over 100,000, accounting for 42 percent of the total U.S. American Indian population (Figure 1.13).

Black Population

The non-Hispanic Black population increased from 29.3 million in 1990 to 33.2 million in 1999. (See Table 1.10.) The total Black population increased 14 percent from 30.5 million to 34.9 million. The Black population accounted for approximately 12.8 percent of the total population in 1999, up somewhat from 12.3 percent in 1990 and 11.7 percent in 1980. According to the Census Bureau's projection, the Black population will likely be 15.4 percent of the total population by 2050 (Table 1.11). Most of the growth in the Black population since 1980 (84 percent) has been due to natural increase (births minus deaths). Immigration accounted for the remaining 16 percent.

FOREIGN-BORN POPULATION

In 1998, 9.3 percent of the population of the United States (25.2 million) was foreign-born — nearly double the 4.7 percent foreign-born in 1970. Between 1990 and 1998, the foreign-born population (27.3 percent) increased nearly four times as much as the native* population (7.1 percent). (See Table 1.12.) While the percentage of foreign-born is at its highest level since before World War II, much greater proportions of the U.S. population

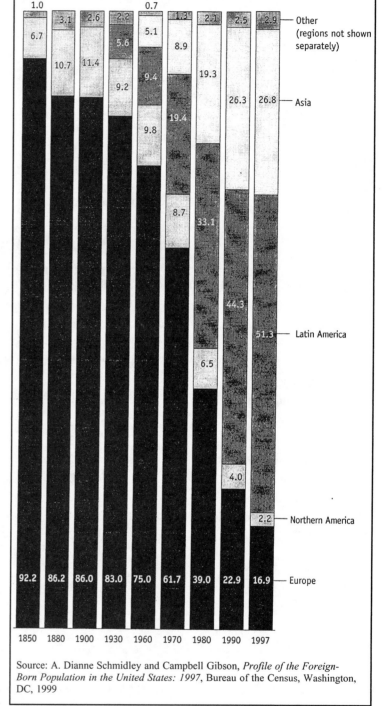

FIGURE 1.14

Foreign-Born Population by Region of Birth: Selected Years, 1850 to 1997

(Percent distribution excluding region not reported. For 1960-90, resident population. For 1997, civilian noninstitutional population plus Armed Forces living off post or with their families on post)

Source: A. Dianne Schmidley and Campbell Gibson, *Profile of the Foreign-Born Population in the United States: 1997*, Bureau of the Census, Washington, DC, 1999

---

* "Natives" are persons born in the United States, Puerto Rico, or an outlying area of the United States, such as Guam or the U.S. Virgin Islands, and persons who were born in a foreign country but who had at least one parent who was a U.S. citizen. All other persons born outside the United States are "foreign-born."

20

TABLE 1.14

Immigrants Admitted by Region and Selected Country of Birth: Fiscal Years 1995-98

Region and country of birth	1998 Number	1998 Percent	1997 Number	1997 Percent	1996 Number	1996 Percent	1995 Number	1995 Percent
1. Mexico	131,575	19.9	146,865	18.4	163,572	17.9	89,932	12.5
2. China, People's Republic	36,884	5.6	41,147	5.2	41,728	4.6	35,463	4.9
3. India	36,482	5.5	38,071	4.8	44,859	4.9	34,748	4.8
4. Philippines	34,466	5.2	49,117	6.2	55,876	6.1	50,984	7.1
5. Dominican Republic	20,387	3.1	27,053	3.4	39,604	4.3	38,512	5.3
6. Vietnam	17,649	2.7	38,519	4.8	42,067	4.6	41,752	5.8
7. Cuba	17,375	2.6	33,587	4.2	26,466	2.9	17,937	2.5
8. Jamaica	15,146	2.3	17,840	2.2	19,089	2.1	16,398	2.3
9. El Salvador	14,590	2.2	17,969	2.3	17,903	2.0	11,744	1.6
10. Korea	14,268	2.2	14,239	1.8	18,185	2.0	16,047	2.2
11. Haiti	13,449	2.0	15,057	1.9	18,386	2.0	14,021	1.9
12. Pakistan	13,094	2.0	12,967	1.6	12,519	1.4	9,774	1.4
13. Colombia	11,836	1.8	13,004	1.6	14,283	1.6	10,838	1.5
14. Russia	11,529	1.7	16,632	2.1	19,668	2.1	14,560	2.0
15. Canada	10,190	1.5	11,609	1.5	15,825	1.7	12,932	1.8
16. Peru	10,154	1.5	10,853	1.4	12,871	1.4	8,066	1.1
17. United Kingdom	9,011	1.4	10,651	1.3	13,624	1.5	12,427	1.7
18. Bangladesh	8,621	1.3	8,681	1.1	8,221	.9	6,072	.8
19. Poland	8,469	1.3	12,038	1.5	15,772	1.7	13,824	1.9
20. Iran	7,883	1.2	9,642	1.2	11,084	1.2	9,201	1.3
Subtotal	443,058	67.1	545,541	68.3	611,602	66.8	465,232	64.6
Other	217,419	32.9	252,837	31.7	304,298	33.2	255,229	35.4

Z Rounds to less than .05 percent.

Source: *Legal Immigration, Fiscal Year 1998*, U.S. Department of Justice, Immigration and Naturalization Service, Washington, DC, 1999

TABLE 1.15

GEOGRAPHICAL MOBILITY OF PEOPLE 1 YEAR OLD AND OLDER, BY SEX, BETWEEN MARCH 1996 AND MARCH 1997

(Numbers in thousands)

	Both Sexes Number	Both Sexes Percent	Male Number	Male Percent	Female Number	Female Percent
Residence in 1996						
Total population 1+	262,976	100.0	128,677	100.0	134,300	100.0
Same house	219,585	83.5	106,973	83.1	112,611	83.9
Different house in the U.S.	42,088	16.0	20,970	16.3	21,118	15.7
- Same county	27,740	10.5	13,776	10.7	13,963	10.4
- Different county	14,348	5.5	7,194	5.6	7,154	5.3
- - Same state	7,960	3.0	4,010	3.1	3,950	2.9
- - Different state	6,389	2.4	3,184	2.5	3,205	2.4
Abroad	1,303	0.5	733	0.6	570	0.4
Total movers	43,391	16.5	21,703	16.9	21,688	16.1

Source: *March 1997 Current Population Survey*, Bureau of the Census, Washington, DC, 1998

were foreign-born during the early part of the twentieth century.

More than one-quarter (29.2 percent) of the foreign-born population of the United States has come into this country since 1990, and another 33.2 percent entered during the 1980s. The remaining 37.5 percent of the foreign-born arrived either during or before the 1970s. In 1997, about 35 percent were naturalized citizens. (See Table 1.13.)

In 1997, over half (51.3 percent) of all foreign-born persons living in the United States were born in Latin America, a percentage which has consis-

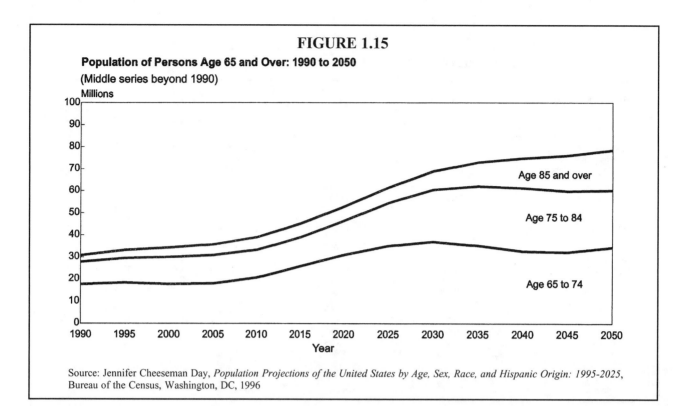

FIGURE 1.15

Population of Persons Age 65 and Over: 1990 to 2050

(Middle series beyond 1990)

Source: Jennifer Cheeseman Day, *Population Projections of the United States by Age, Sex, Race, and Hispanic Origin: 1995-2025*, Bureau of the Census, Washington, DC, 1996

tently increased since 1930 (Figure 1.14). More than one-quarter (27 percent) of the total was born in Mexico. Nearly 27 percent were born in Asia, up from 8.9 percent in 1970. The percentage of Europeans in the foreign-born population has decreased significantly, from 61.7 percent in 1970 to 16.9 percent in 1997. (See Figure 1.14.)

The foreign-born population is not distributed evenly throughout the country. In 1997, five states had a larger percentage of foreign-born residents than the United States as a whole. One-quarter (24.8 percent) of all California residents and one-fifth (19.6 percent) of New York's population were foreign-born. Foreign-born made up 16.4 percent of Florida's population, 15.4 percent of New Jersey residents, and 11.3 percent of Texans.

The foreign-born population included larger proportions of Hispanics and Asians and Pacific Islanders than the native population. In 1997, Hispanics accounted for 44 percent and Asians and Pacific Islanders for 24 percent of the foreign-born population. Together, the two groups accounted for only 9 percent of the native population. On the other hand, the proportions of non-Hispanic Whites and of Blacks were lower in the foreign-born popula-

tion than in the native population. Though non-Hispanic Whites accounted for 77 percent of the native population, they made up 26 percent of the foreign-born population. Blacks represent 13.4 percent of the native population but only 8 percent of the foreign-born population.

IMMIGRATION

In 1998, 660,477 people immigrated to the United States. Mexico was the leading country of origin, with 131,575 persons coming to the United States. Other leading countries were the People's Republic of China (36,884), India (36,482), the Philippines (34,466), and the Dominican Republic (20,387). About two-fifths of the 1998 immigrants came from five countries; two-thirds (67 percent) arrived from only 20 nations. (See Table 1.14.)

In 1998, 40 percent of the immigrants settled in just two states — California (170,126) and New York (96,559). Florida (59,965), Texas (44,428), New Jersey (35,091), and Illinois (33,163) were also popular destinations for immigrants. Since 1971, these six states have been the principal states of intended residence for new immigrants, with

22

TABLE 1.16

Resident Population Estimates of the United States by Age and Sex: August 1, 1999

BOTH SEXES		FEMALES	
Population, all ages	273,137	Population, all ages	139,654
Summary indicators		**Summary indicators**	
Median age..........	35.5	Median age..........	36.6
Mean age............	36.4	Mean age............	37.6
Five-year age groups		**Five-year age groups**	
Under 5 years.......	18,915	Under 5 years.......	9,249
5 to 9 years........	19,951	5 to 9 years........	9,741
10 to 14 years......	19,583	10 to 14 years......	9,554
15 to 19 years......	19,781	15 to 19 years......	9,613
20 to 24 years......	18,099	20 to 24 years......	8,882
25 to 29 years......	18,216	25 to 29 years......	9,162
30 to 34 years......	19,717	30 to 34 years......	9,953
35 to 39 years......	22,553	35 to 39 years......	11,335
40 to 44 years......	22,300	40 to 44 years......	11,243
45 to 49 years......	19,416	45 to 49 years......	9,884
50 to 54 years......	16,515	50 to 54 years......	8,483
55 to 59 years......	12,941	55 to 59 years......	6,727
60 to 64 years......	10,535	60 to 64 years......	5,558
65 to 69 years......	9,455	65 to 69 years......	5,115
70 to 74 years......	8,777	70 to 74 years......	4,910
75 to 79 years......	7,349	75 to 79 years......	4,283
80 to 84 years......	4,832	80 to 84 years......	3,011
85 to 89 years......	2,638	85 to 89 years......	1,786
90 to 94 years......	1,154	90 to 94 years......	845
95 to 99 years......	347	95 to 99 years......	271
100 years and over..	61	100 years and over..	50
Special age categories		**Special age categories**	
5 to 13 years.......	35,631	5 to 13 years.......	17,394
14 to 17 years......	15,674	14 to 17 years......	7,609
18 to 24 years......	26,110	18 to 24 years......	12,788
16 years and over...	210,858	16 years and over...	109,248
18 years and over...	202,916	18 years and over...	105,403
15 to 44 years......	120,666	15 to 44 years......	60,188
65 years and over...	34,613	65 years and over...	20,270
85 years and over...	4,201	85 years and over...	2,952

(continued)

California the leading state since 1976. These figures do not include refugees and asylum seekers. As of October 9, 1999, according to the Bureau of the Census, one international immigrant (net; those entering minus those leaving) entered the United States every 31 seconds. (For further information, see *Immigration and Illegal Aliens — Burden or Blessing?*, Information Plus, Wylie, Texas, 1999.)

GEOGRAPHIC MOBILITY

More than 42 million Americans (16 percent of the population one year old and over) moved in the one-year period between March 1996 and March 1997. Most of these movers (65.9 percent) moved from one residence to another within the same county; 18.9 percent moved between counties within the same state; and 15.2 percent changed states. During that same one-year period, 1.3 million people moved into the United States from abroad. (See Table 1.15.) The overall moving rate is similar to the rates occurring during most of the 1990s and 1980s.

Young adults in their twenties had the highest mobility rates. One-third of persons 20 to 29 years old moved between 1996 and 1997. Moving rates declined as age increased — only 5 percent of those 65 years and older moved. Racial and ethnic minorities moved more. Whites had lower rates of moving (15.3 percent) than Blacks, Asians, or Hispanics (about 20 percent each).

The South was the only region in the nation to experience a significant net change through internal U.S. migration, with a net gain of 391,000 residents from the other three regions. Between 1996 and 1997, the central cities lost 3 million people, while the suburbs gained 2.8 million. About 1.3 million people moved to the United States from abroad, most (92 percent) settling in metropolitan areas.

AN AGING POPULATION

In this century, the rate of growth of the elderly population (persons 65 years old and over) has greatly exceeded the growth rate of the population of the country as a whole. The elderly increased by a factor of 11, from 3 million in 1900 to 34.5 million in 1999. In comparison, the total population increased 3.5 times. Under the Census Bureau's middle series projections, the number of persons 65 years old and over will more than double, to 79 million, by the middle of the next century.

About 1 in 8 Americans was elderly in 1990; by the year 2050, about 1 in 5 will be elderly. (See Figure 1.15 for the growth of the elderly population from 1990 to 2050. The figure is a space graph. The first area represents those 65 to 74 years old, the second area those 75 to 84, and the last space those over 85. The top line is the total elderly population.)

The oldest old (persons 85 years old and over) are a small but rapidly growing group, which now accounts for 1.5 percent of the American population. This population was 4.2 million persons in 1999, about 34 times larger than in 1900. On August 1, 1999, the nation had an estimated 61,000 people aged 100 years or more. Fifty thousand were

TABLE 1.16 (Continued)

Resident Population Estimates of the United States by Age and Sex: August 1, 1999

MALES

Population, all ages 133,482

Summary indicators

Median age..........	34.4
Mean age............	35.1

Five-year age groups

Under 5 years.......	9,666
5 to 9 years........	10,210
10 to 14 years......	10,030
15 to 19 years......	10,168
20 to 24 years......	9,217
25 to 29 years......	9,054
30 to 34 years......	9,764
35 to 39 years......	11,218
40 to 44 years......	11,057
45 to 49 years......	9,532
50 to 54 years......	8,032
55 to 59 years......	6,213
60 to 64 years......	4,978
65 to 69 years......	4,339
70 to 74 years......	3,867
75 to 79 years......	3,066
80 to 84 years......	1,821
85 to 89 years......	852
90 to 94 years......	309
95 to 99 years......	77
100 years and over..	11

Special age categories

5 to 13 years.......	18,238
14 to 17 years......	8,065
18 to 24 years......	13,322
16 years and over...	101,610
18 years and over...	97,513
15 to 44 years......	60,478
65 years and over...	14,343
85 years and over...	1,249

Source: Population Estimates Program, Bureau of the Census, Washington, DC, 1999

women and 11,000 were men. (See Table 1.16 for estimated population by age as of August 1, 1999.) (For more information on the elderly, see *Growing Old in America*, Information Plus, Wylie, Texas 2000.)

In 1998, children comprised 26 percent of the population, down from a peak of 36 percent in

FIGURE 1.16

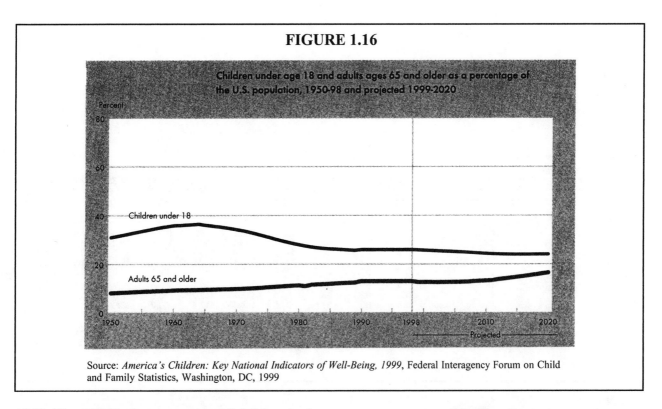

Children under age 18 and adults ages 65 and older as a percentage of the U.S. population, 1950-98 and projected 1999-2020

Percent

Children under 18

Adults 65 and older

Projected

Source: *America's Children: Key National Indicators of Well-Being, 1999*, Federal Interagency Forum on Child and Family Statistics, Washington, DC, 1999

1960. Since 1960, the proportion of children in the U.S. population has been decreasing. They are projected to make up 24 percent of the population in 2020. On the other hand, the elderly have increased as a percentage of the total population. They are expected to comprise 16 percent of the population by 2020. (See Figure 1.16.)

Median Age

Since the proportion of elderly Americans is projected to increase dramatically, it should not be surprising that the median age (half are older; half are younger) of the future U.S. population will be older than it is now. In the middle series, the median age of the population will steadily increase,

FIGURE 1.17

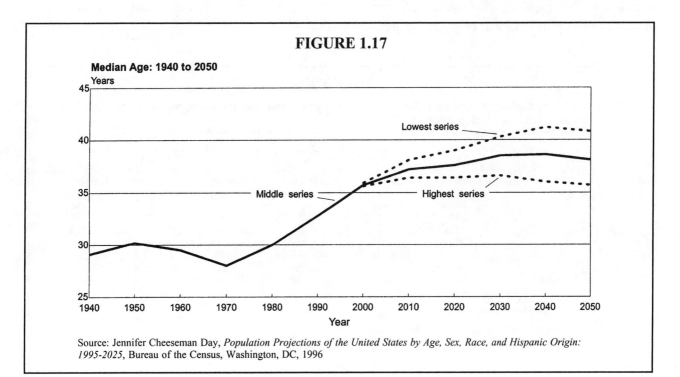

Median Age: 1940 to 2050

Years

Lowest series

Middle series

Highest series

Year

Source: Jennifer Cheeseman Day, *Population Projections of the United States by Age, Sex, Race, and Hispanic Origin: 1995-2025*, Bureau of the Census, Washington, DC, 1996

TABLE 1.17

Crude birth rates, fertility rates, and birth rates by age of mother, according to detailed race and Hispanic origin: United States, selected years 1950–96

[Data are based on the National Vital Statistics System]

Race of mother, Hispanic origin of mother, and year	Crude birth rate[1]	Fertility rate[2]	10–14 years	15–19 years Total	15–17 years	18–19 years	20–24 years	25–29 years	30–34 years	35–39 years	40–44 years	45–49 years
All races				Live births per 1,000 women								
1950	24.1	106.2	1.0	81.6	40.7	132.7	196.6	166.1	103.7	52.9	15.1	1.2
1960	23.7	118.0	0.8	89.1	43.9	166.7	258.1	197.4	112.7	56.2	15.5	0.9
1970	18.4	87.9	1.2	68.3	38.8	114.7	167.8	145.1	73.3	31.7	8.1	0.5
1980	15.9	68.4	1.1	53.0	32.5	82.1	115.1	112.9	61.9	19.8	3.9	0.2
1985	15.8	66.3	1.2	51.0	31.0	79.6	108.3	111.0	69.1	24.0	4.0	0.2
1990	16.7	70.9	1.4	59.9	37.5	88.6	116.5	120.2	80.8	31.7	5.5	0.2
1991	16.3	69.6	1.4	62.1	38.7	94.4	115.7	118.2	79.5	32.0	5.5	0.2
1992	15.9	68.9	1.4	60.7	37.8	94.5	114.6	117.4	80.2	32.5	5.9	0.3
1993	15.5	67.6	1.4	59.6	37.8	92.1	112.6	115.5	80.8	32.9	6.1	0.3
1994	15.2	66.7	1.4	58.9	37.6	91.5	111.1	113.9	81.5	33.7	6.4	0.3
1995	14.8	65.6	1.3	56.8	36.0	89.1	109.8	112.2	82.5	34.3	6.6	0.3
1996	14.7	65.3	1.2	54.4	33.8	86.0	110.4	113.1	83.9	35.3	6.8	0.3

Source: *Health, United States, 1998*, National Center for Health Statistics, Hyattsville, MD, 1998

---

peak at 38.7 in 2035, and then decrease slightly to 38.1 by 2050. (See Figure 1.17.) In 1999, the median age was 35.5 years. (See Table 1.16.)

Baby Boom

The increasing median age is driven by the aging of the population born during the baby boom after World War II (1946-1964). About 29 percent of the population in 1999 was born during the baby boom. As this population ages, the median age will rise. People born during the baby boom will be between the ages of 36 and 54 in 2000. In 2011, the first members of the baby boom will reach 65, and the baby-boom population will have decreased to 25 percent of the total population. The last of the baby-boom population will reach 65 in the year 2029. By that time, the baby-boom population is projected to be only 16 percent of the total population.

TABLE 1.18

Deaths, age-adjusted death rates, and life expectancy at birth, by race and sex; and infant mortality rates, by race: United States, final 1997 and preliminary 1998

Measure and sex	All races[1] 1998	All races[1] 1997	White 1998	White 1997	Black 1998	Black 1997
All deaths	2,338,070	2,314,245	2,020,230	1,996,393	275,469	276,520
Age-adjusted death rate[2]	470.8	479.1	450.4	456.5	683.2	705.3
Male	587.9	602.8	561.9	573.8	874.6	911.9
Female	372.3	375.7	355.7	358.0	535.0	545.5
Life expectancy at birth[3]	76.7	76.5	77.3	77.1	71.5	71.1
Male	73.9	73.6	74.6	74.3	67.8	67.2
Female	79.4	79.4	79.9	79.9	75.0	74.7
All infant deaths	28,486	28,045	18,795	18,539	8,579	8,496
Infant mortality rate[4]	7.2	7.2	6.0	6.0	14.1	14.2

[1]Includes races other than white and black.
[2]Age-adjusted death rates are per 100,000 U.S. standard population.
[3]Life expectancy at birth stated in years.
[4]Infant mortality rates are deaths under 1 year per 1,000 live births in specified group.

Source: Joyce A. Martin et al., "Births and Deaths: Preliminary Data for 1998," *National Vital Statistics Reports*, vol. 47, no. 25, October 5, 1999

TABLE 1.19

Age-adjusted death rates* for 1997, percentage changes in age-adjusted death rates for the 15 leading causes of death, 1996-1997 and 1979-1997, and ratio of age-adjusted death rates, by sex and race of decedent, 1997 -- United States

Rank+	Cause of death (ICD-9& code)	1997 Age-adjusted death rate	Percentage change 1996 to 1997	Percentage change 1979 to 1997	Male:female	Black:white@
1	Diseases of heart (390-398, 402, 404-429)	130.5	-3.0	-34.6	1.8	1.5
2	Malignant neoplasms, including neoplasms of lymphatic and hematopoietic tissues (140-208)	125.6	-1.8	-4.0	1.4	1.3
3	Cerebrovascular diseases (430-438)	25.9	-1.9	-37.7	1.2	1.8
4	Chronic obstructive pulmonary diseases and allied conditions (490-496)	21.1	0.5	44.5	1.5	0.8
5	Accidents** and adverse effects (E800-E949)	30.1	-1.0	-29.8	2.4	1.2
	Motor vehicle accidents (E810-E825)	15.9	-1.9	-31.5	2.1	1.1
	All other accidents and adverse effects (E800-E807, E826-E949)	14.2	0.0	-27.6	2.8	1.4
6	Pneumonia and influenza (480-487)	12.9	0.8	15.2	1.5	1.4
7	Diabetes mellitus (250)	13.5	-0.7	37.8	1.2	2.4
8	Suicide (E950-E959)	10.6	-1.9	-9.4	4.2	0.6
9	Nephritis, nephrotic syndrome, and nephrosis (580-589)	4.4	2.3	2.3	1.5	2.6
10	Chronic liver disease and cirrhosis (571)	7.4	-1.3	-38.3	2.3	1.2
11	Alzheimer's disease (331.0)	2.7	0.0	1250.0	0.9	0.7
12	Septicemia (038)	4.2	2.4	82.6	1.2	2.8
13	Homicide and legal intervention (E960-E978)	8.0	-5.9	-21.6	3.8	6.0
14	Human immunodeficiency virus infection (042-044++)	5.8	-47.7	--&&	3.5	7.5
15	Atherosclerosis (440)	2.1	-4.5	-63.2	1.3	1.0
	All causes	479.1	-2.5	-17.0	1.6	1.5

* Per 100,000 standard population, age-adjusted to the 1940 U.S. population.
+ Based on number of deaths.
& International Classification of Diseases, Ninth Revision.
@ Both groups include Hispanics. Data for other racial groups were not included because of reporting inaccuracies on death certificates and population censuses.
** When a death occurs under "accidental" circumstances, the preferred term within the public health community is "unintentional injury."
++ These codes are not printed in ICD-9 but were introduced as *042-*044 by CDC's National Center for Health Statistics for classifying and coding human immunodeficiency virus infection.
&& Data not available.

Source: "Mortality Patterns — United States, 1997," *Morbidity and Mortality Weekly Report*, vol. 48 , no. 30 , August 6, 1999

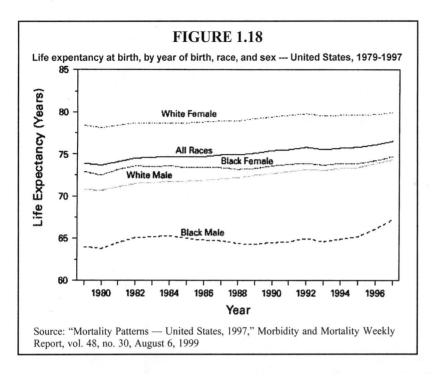

FIGURE 1.18

Life expentancy at birth, by year of birth, race, and sex --- United States, 1979-1997

Source: "Mortality Patterns — United States, 1997," Morbidity and Mortality Weekly Report, vol. 48, no. 30, August 6, 1999

the 1960s and early 1970s. The birth rate was 14.7 births per 1,000 population in 1996. The fertility rate was 65.3 live births per 1,000 women ages 15 to 44. (See Table 1.17 for birth and fertility rates for 1950 through 1996.) The infant mortality rate reached a record low in 1996 (7.2 infant deaths per 1,000 live births), where it remained through 1997 and 1998. (See Table 1.18.) This rate is down sharply from 10.1 infant deaths per 1,000 births in 1987.

DEATH RATES

The death rate dropped from 945 per 100,000 population in 1970 to 860 in 1977 and has remained in the range of 850 to 880 per 100,000 ever since, the lowest levels ever achieved in the United States. The 1998 rate was 865 deaths per 100,000. The age-adjusted death rate, based on the changes in the age distribution of the population, was 470.8 per 100,000 Americans, a record low (Table 1.18). This figure is expected to remain constant because economic and social conditions contributing to a longer life have improved. Table 1.19 shows the leading causes of death. According to the Bureau of the Census, on October 9, 1999, one person died every 14 seconds.

GENDER

In August 1999, the United States had 139.7 million women and 133.5 million men. At the youngest ages (under 15 years), boys outnumbered girls by a ratio of 1.05 to 1.00 or 105.5 boys for every 100 girls. The higher number of males continued until about age 25, when the situation reversed. The female edge then kept getting larger with increasing age. Among the oldest old (85 years and over), there were about 42 men for every 100 women. In August 1999, men had a median age of 34.4 years; women, 36.6 years. (See Table 1.16.)

BIRTHS AND BIRTH RATES

An estimated 3,944,046 babies were born in 1998 (*National Vital Statistics Reports*, Centers for Disease Control and Prevention, vol. 47, no. 25, October 5, 1999). According to the Bureau of the Census, on October 9, 1999, one birth occurred every 8 seconds.

The birth and fertility rates, which increased dramatically in the 1940s and 1950s, declined in

LIFE EXPECTANCY

In 1998, life expectancy at birth reached a record high of 76.7 years. Record high life expectancies were reached for White and Black males (74.6 years and 67.8 years) and for White and Black females (79.9 years and 75.0 years). (See Table 1.18 and Figure 1.18.) Among the world's most populous countries, Japan had the highest life expectancy. Japanese females had a life expectancy of 83 years and Japanese males, 77 years.

CHAPTER II

FAMILIES AND HOUSEHOLDS

TYPES OF HOUSEHOLDS

The Bureau of the Census has two major categories of households: family and nonfamily. A family household consists of the householder (the person who represents the entire household) and at least one additional person related to the householder through marriage, birth, or adoption. A nonfamily household is made up of a householder who either lives alone or exclusively with persons unrelated to the householder.

In 1998, the Bureau of the Census counted 102.5 million households, an increase of 9.2 million households since 1990 and 2.9 million more than the total for 1996. During the 1970s, the number of households rose by a total of 17.4 million, an average of 1.7 million per year. During the 1980s, the number of households increased by about 12.6 million, an average of about 1.3 million households per year. Since 1990, the number of households has increased an average of approximately 1.02 million per year. (See Table 2.1.)

FAMILY HOUSEHOLDS

There were 70.9 million family households in 1998. Their share of households (69.1 percent) fell from about 85 percent in 1960 to 81 percent in 1970, 74 percent in 1980, and 71 percent in 1990. In 1998, family households included 54.3 million married-couple families, 3.9 million families with a male householder (no wife present), and 12.7 million families with a female householder (no husband present). (See Tables 2.1 and 2.2.)

Married-couple families made up 53 percent of all households in 1998, down from 61 percent in 1980, 71 percent in 1970, and 74.5 percent in 1960.

More than half (51 percent) of family households did not have any children under age 18 present in the home. (See Table 2.2.) In 1970, 44 percent of families had no children under 18 at home. These couples had not yet had children, were "empty nesters" whose children had grown up and left home, were couples who chose to remain childless, or were unable to have children. However, families without their own children under 18 at home might not be childless. They might have grandchildren, unrelated foster children, or adult children living in the household.

Racial and Ethnic Differences

In 1998, 84 percent of the 70.9 million family households were maintained by White householders, 12 percent by Black householders, and the remaining by householders of other races. Approximately 10 percent were maintained by Hispanic householders. (Hispanics may be of any race.) (See Table 2.2.)

There were significant racial and ethnic differences among the proportion of married-couple families. While 81 percent of the White family households were married-couple families, 69 percent of Hispanic family households and less than half (47 percent) of Black family households were married-couple families. (See Table 2.2.)

29

TABLE 2.1

Households, by Type: 1970 to Present

(Numbers in thousands)

| Year | Total households | Family households | | Other family | | Nonfamily households | | |
		Total	Married couples	Male househld.	Female househld.	Total	Male househld.	Female househld.
1998	102,528	70,880	54,317	3,911	12,652	31,648	14,133	17,516
1997	101,018	70,241	53,604	3,847	12,790	30,777	13,707	17,070
1996	99,627	69,594	53,567	3,513	12,514	30,033	13,348	16,685
1995	98,990	69,305	53,858	3,226	12,220	29,686	13,190	16,496
1994	97,107	68,490	53,171	2,913	12,406	28,617	12,462	16,155
1993r	96,426	68,216	53,090	3,065	12,061	28,210	12,297	15,914
1993	96,391	68,144	53,171	3,026	11,947	28,247	12,254	15,993
1992	95,669	67,173	52,457	3,025	11,692	28,496	12,428	16,068
1991	94,312	66,322	52,147	2,907	11,268	27,990	12,150	15,840
1990	93,347	66,090	52,317	2,884	10,890	27,257	11,606	15,651
1989	92,830	65,837	52,100	2,847	10,890	26,994	11,874	15,120
1988a	91,124	65,204	51,675	2,834	10,696	25,919	11,282	14,637
1988	91,066	65,133	51,809	2,715	10,608	25,933	11,310	14,624
1987	89,479	64,491	51,537	2,510	10,445	24,988	10,652	14,336
1986	88,458	63,558	50,933	2,414	10,211	24,900	10,648	14,252
1985	86,789	62,706	50,350	2,228	10,129	24,082	10,114	13,968
1984b	85,290	62,015	50,081	2,038	9,896	23,276	9,689	13,587
1984	85,407	61,997	50,090	2,030	9,878	23,410	9,752	13,658
1983	83,918	61,393	49,908	2,016	9,469	22,525	9,514	13,011
1982	83,527	61,019	49,630	1,986	9,403	22,508	9,457	13,051
1981	82,368	60,309	49,294	1,933	9,082	22,059	9,279	12,780
1980c	80,776	59,550	49,112	1,733	8,705	21,226	8,807	12,419
1980	79,108	58,426	48,180	1,706	8,540	20,682	8,594	12,088
1979	77,330	57,498	47,662	1,616	8,220	19,831	8,064	11,767
1978	76,030	56,958	47,357	1,564	8,037	19,071	7,811	11,261
1977	74,142	56,472	47,471	1,461	7,540	17,669	6,971	10,698
1976	72,867	56,056	47,297	1,424	7,335	16,811	6,548	10,263
1975	71,120	55,563	46,951	1,485	7,127	15,557	5,912	9,645
1974	69,859	54,917	46,787	1,421	6,709	14,942	5,654	9,288
1973	68,251	54,264	46,297	1,432	6,535	13,986	5,129	8,858
1972	66,676	53,163	45,724	1,331	6,108	13,513	4,839	8,674
1971	64,778	52,102	44,928	1,254	5,920	12,676	4,403	8,273
1970	63,401	51,456	44,728	1,228	5,500	11,945	4,063	7,882
1969	62,214	50,729	44,086	1,221	5,422	11,485	3,890	7,595
1968	60,813	50,012	43,507	1,195	5,310	10,801	3,658	7,143
1967	59,236	49,086	42,743	1,190	5,153	10,150	3,419	6,731
1966	58,406	48,399	42,263	1,163	4,973	10,007	3,299	6,708

r Revised using population controls based on the 1990 census.
a Data based on 1988 revised processing.
b Incorporates Hispanic-origin population controls.
c Revised using population controls based on the 1980 census.
d Based on 1940 census.

Source: *Household and Family Characteristics: March 1998 (Update)* and earlier updates, Bureau of the Census, Washington, DC, 1998

NONFAMILY HOUSEHOLDS

There were approximately 31.6 million nonfamily households in 1998, about three times as many as the 11.9 million in 1970. Meanwhile, the proportion of all households that were nonfamily households climbed from 19 percent in 1970 to 31 percent in 1998. In recent years, however, the rate of increase in the number of this type of household has slowed significantly. During the 1970s, nonfamily households increased at the av-

erage annual rate of 5.7 percent per year. This rate of increase fell to 2.5 percent per year during the 1980s and declined further to 1.8 percent per year during the 1990s. (See Table 2.1.)

Women maintained most nonfamily households (55.3 percent). About 17.5 million female and 14.1 million male householders lived in nonfamily households in 1998. The proportion of male nonfamily households to all households doubled from 6 percent in 1970 to 14 percent in

TABLE 2.2

Households by Type and Selected Characteristics: 1998

Numbers are in thousands, except averages and percentages.

Characteristics	All households	Family households				Nonfamily households		
		Total	Married couple	Other families Female householder	Male householder	Total	Female householder	Male householder
All households	102,528	70,880	54,317	12,652	3,911	31,648	17,516	14,133
Race and Hispanic origin								
White	86,106	59,511	48,066	8,308	3,137	26,596	14,871	11,725
White not Hispanic	77,936	52,871	43,423	6,826	2,622	25,065	14,164	10,901
Black	12,474	8,408	3,921	3,926	562	4,066	2,190	1,876
Hispanic[1]	8,590	6,961	4,804	1,612	545	1,630	754	875
Size of household								
1 person	26,327	(X)	(X)	(X)	(X)	26,327	15,317	11,010
2 people	32,965	28,722	21,833	5,290	1,598	4,243	1,850	2,393
3 people	17,331	16,640	11,595	3,858	1,187	691	232	459
4 people	15,358	15,090	12,427	2,008	654	268	76	192
5 people	7,048	6,972	5,743	924	306	76	17	59
6 people	2,232	2,195	1,807	293	95	37	21	15
7 or more people	1,267	1,260	911	278	70	7	3	4
Average size	2.62	3.24	3.26	3.18	3.22	1.24	1.17	1.33
Percent with own children under 18	33.9	49.0	46.5	60.8	46.0	(X)	(X)	(X)
Age of householder								
Under 25	5,435	3,019	1,373	1,095	551	2,417	1,080	1,336
25 to 34	19,033	13,639	9,886	2,887	866	5,394	2,070	3,325
35 to 44	23,943	18,872	14,180	3,637	1,055	5,072	1,863	3,208
45 to 54	19,547	14,694	11,734	2,260	701	4,853	2,421	2,431
55 to 64	13,072	9,387	7,936	1,099	352	3,685	2,336	1,348
65 to 74	11,272	6,989	5,841	938	210	4,283	3,080	1,203
75 and over	10,225	4,282	3,368	738	176	5,944	4,664	1,280
Median age	46.3	45.0	46.4	41.4	40.4	50.8	60.8	42.5

Source: Bureau of the Census, Washington, DC

1998, while the proportion of female nonfamily households increased from 12 percent to 17 percent. (See Table 2.1.)

HOUSEHOLD AND FAMILY SIZE

Household size is closely related to the type of household. Over the past generation, changes in household composition and childbearing patterns have resulted in households that, on average, include fewer persons than in the past. The trends toward fewer children per family, more one-parent families, and increased numbers of people living alone are among the major factors contributing to smaller households.

In 1790, the year of the first national census, there were 5.79 persons per household. In 1890, there were 4.76 persons per household. The average had declined by about one member per house-hold over a period of 100 years. It took only another 50 years for household size to drop an additional person (3.76 persons per household in 1940).

Household size fell to 3.14 persons in 1970 and 2.76 persons in 1980. The average number of persons per household in the United States reached a new low of 2.62 persons per household in 1989, where it has remained. Much of this decline resulted from the drop in the average number of younger household members. The average number of persons per family household under age 18 dropped from 1.34 persons in 1970 to 0.96 person in 1990 and 0.99 person in 1998. The average number of children per family with children was 1.87 in 1998.

The proportion of the largest households (those with five persons or more) fell from 21 percent in 1970 to 10 percent in 1998. Medium-sized households with three or four persons accounted for about one-third of households, a proportion that has remained constant over the past two decades. Finally, the smallest households, those comprised of only one or two persons, increased their share of the total from 46 percent in 1970 to 58 percent in 1998. (See Table 2.2.)

AGE OF HOUSEHOLDER

The median age of householders dropped from 48.1 years in 1970 to 46.1 years in 1980, reaching 45.1 years in 1989 and then increasing to 46.3 years in 1998. This leveling off is mainly attributed to the decline in the number of householders in the youngest age categories since 1980. Since 1980, the number of households maintained by persons under 25 years of age has declined from 8 percent of all households to 5 percent in 1998. (See Table 2.2.)

The recent decline in the number of young adult householders is mainly the result of the aging of the 1946-1964 "baby-boom" generation. The leading edge of the baby-boom generation first began forming households during the 1960s. By 1990, baby boomers ranged from 26 to 44 years of age. This group accounted for a large number of households formed during the two decades between 1970 and 1990. As they increased their share of the total, the median age of householders dropped from 48.1 years to 45.3 years during the same period.

The youngest baby boomers turned 35 in 1999. As this large segment of the population continues to grow older and is replaced by the comparatively smaller generation that follows, the median age of householders should be expected to reverse its decline. This turnaround has probably begun, as the median age of householders has increased slightly since 1990 to 46.3 years in 1998. Between 1990 and 1998, the number of households maintained by persons 45 to 54 years of age increased nearly 23 percent. The number of households maintained by those younger than 45 decreased during that period.

Another factor contributing to the decline in the number of younger householders is that today's young adults are not forming their own households at as high a rate as previous generations. Instead, many are returning to or remaining in their parents' homes.

FAMILIES MAINTAINED BY WOMEN

One of the most dramatic changes in the composition of family households during the past quarter century has been the tremendous increase in the number of families maintained by women. In fact, the number of female-headed families doubled between 1970 and 1987. By 1998, about 18 percent of all families were maintained by women, up from 15 percent in 1980 and 11 percent in 1970. (See Table 2.1.)

TABLE 2.3

Provisional Vital Statistics for the United States

[Rates for infant deaths are deaths under 1 year per 1,000 live births; fertility rates are live births per 1,000 women aged 15–44 years; all other rates are per 1,000 total population.]

	Numbers and rates with correction factors[1] for births, marriages, and divorces								
	December				January–December				
	Number		Rate		Number		Rate		
Item	1998	1997	1998	1997	1998	1997	1998	1997	1996
Live births	332,000	324,000	14.4	14.2	3,946,000	3,882,000	14.6	14.5	14.7
Fertility rate.	. . .	. . .	65.0	63.9	. . .	. . .	66.0	65.0	65.4
Deaths	194,000	192,000	8.4	8.4	2,331,000	2,294,000	8.6	8.6	8.7
Infant deaths	2,400	2,200	7.2	6.6	27,600	27,000	7.0	7.0	7.2
Natural increase	138,000	132,000	6.0	5.8	1,615,000	1,588,000	6.0	5.9	6.0
Marriages	170,000	165,000	7.4	7.2	2,244,000	2,384,000	8.3	8.9	8.8
Divorces	98,000	104,000	4.3	4.5	1,135,000	1,163,000	4.2	4.3	4.3

Source: "Births, Marriages, Divorces, and Deaths: Provisional Data for 1998," *National Vital Statistics Reports*, vol. 47, no. 21, July 6, 1999

TABLE 2.4

Percent Married and Living With Their Spouse: 1998

Age	
18 and over	56.0
20-24	18.8
25-29	46.4
30-34	61.2
35-39	64.2
40-44	67.1
45-54	69.2
55-64	70.2
65-74	63.4
75-84	47.7
85 and over	22.8

Source: "More Than Half of All Adults Are Married, But the Proportion Varies with Age," *Census and You*, March/April 1999

There is a significant difference between Blacks and Whites in the proportion of families maintained by women. In 1998, 47 percent of Black family households were maintained by women, compared to 14 percent for Whites. Among Hispanics, women maintained about 1 in 4 families (23 percent) in 1998. (See Table 2.2.)

MARRIED POPULATION

Marriage

In 1998, the National Center for Health Statistics (NCHS) reported approximately 2.2 million marriages. The number of marriages in the United States soared from 1.6 million in 1945 to 2.3 million in 1946 as the World War II soldiers returned to civilian life. In the 1950s, the number of marriages averaged about 1.5 million annually, rising to about 2.3 million in 1972. Since 1980, the number of marriages has averaged about 2.4 million annually.

The marriage rate was 8.3 marriages per 1,000 population in 1998. (See Table 2.3.) This rate has generally declined since the early 1980s and is currently the lowest since 1963. Over the past 25 years, marriage rates have gone through two periods of decline. Marriage rates rose from the early 1960s through 1972, when the rate reached 10.9 per 1,000. Beginning in 1973, the rate dropped,

TABLE 2.5

Estimated Median Age at First Marriage, by Sex: 1890 to the Present

Year	Men	Women
1998	26.7	25.0
1997	26.8	25.0
1996	27.1	24.8
1995	26.9	24.5
1994	26.7	24.5
1993	26.5	24.5
1992	26.5	24.4
1991	26.3	24.1
1990	26.1	23.9
1989	26.2	23.8
1988	25.9	23.6
1987	25.8	23.6
1986	25.7	23.1
1985	25.5	23.3
1984	25.4	23.0
1983	25.4	22.8
1982	25.2	22.5
1981	24.8	22.3
1980	24.7	22.0
1979	24.4	22.1
1978	24.2	21.8
1977	24.0	21.6
1976	23.8	21.3
1975	23.5	21.1
1974	23.1	21.1
1973	23.2	21.0
1972	23.3	20.9
1971	23.1	20.9
1970	23.2	20.8
1969	23.2	20.8
1968	23.1	20.8
1967	23.1	20.6
1966	22.8	20.5
1965	22.8	20.6
1964	23.1	20.5
1963	22.8	20.5
1962	22.7	20.3
1961	22.8	20.3
1960	22.8	20.3
1959	22.5	20.2
1958	22.6	20.2
1957	22.6	20.3
1956	22.5	20.1
1955	22.6	20.2
1954	23.0	20.3
1953	22.8	20.2
1952	23.0	20.2
1951	22.9	20.4
1950	22.8	20.3
1949	22.7	20.3
1948	23.3	20.4
1947	23.7	20.5
1940	24.3	21.5
1930	24.3	21.3
1920	24.6	21.2
1910	25.1	21.6
1900	25.9	21.9
1890	26.1	22.0

Source: Bureau of the Census, Washington, DC

TABLE 2.6

Marital Status and Living Arrangements of Adults 18 Years Old and Over: March 1998

(Numbers in thousands)

Characteristics of adults	Age						
	18 years and over	18 to 24 years	25 to 34 years	35 to 44 years	45 to 64 years	65 to 74 years	75 years over
MARITAL STATUS							
Males	95,009	12,633	19,526	22,055	27,271	7,992	5,533
Married, spouse present	55,303	1,240	9,840	14,230	20,173	6,147	3,674
Married, spouse absent	3,298	183	724	1,001	1,051	184	155
Unmarried	36,407	11,210	8,963	6,823	6,048	1,661	1,704
Never married	25,518	11,066	7,761	4,120	2,053	328	190
Widowed	2,567	-	30	94	425	707	1,311
Divorced	8,322	143	1,171	2,610	3,569	626	202
Females	102,403	12,568	19,828	22,407	29,041	9,882	8,677
Married, spouse present	55,259	2,315	11,428	14,951	19,005	5,181	2,380
Married, spouse absent	3,996	268	914	1,210	1,187	239	178
Unmarried	43,148	9,986	7,486	6,246	8,849	4,462	6,119
Never married	21,043	9,743	5,908	2,721	1,801	425	446
Widowed	11,027	17	90	304	2,223	3,155	5,239
Divorced	11,078	227	1,489	3,222	4,825	882	433
LIVING ARRANGEMENTS							
Males	95,009	12,633	19,526	22,055	27,271	7,992	5,533
Living with relative(s)	75,307	9,988	14,310	17,676	22,560	6,615	4,157
Family householder	45,704	1,286	7,889	11,726	16,663	5,088	3,051
Spouse of householder	12,452	311	2,515	3,405	4,288	1,200	733
Child of householder	12,708	7,399	2,845	1,760	682	22	-
Other, living with relatives	4,443	992	1,061	785	927	305	373
Not living with relatives	19,702	2,645	5,215	4,378	4,712	1,377	1,375
Nonfamily householder	14,122	1,326	3,325	3,208	3,780	1,203	1,280
Living alone	11,000	712	2,222	2,555	3,164	1,111	1,234
Sharing home with nonrelative	3,122	614	1,103	653	616	92	46
Other, not living with relatives	5,580	1,319	1,890	1,170	932	174	95
Females	102,403	12,568	19,828	22,407	29,041	9,882	8,677
Living with relative(s)	80,666	10,020	16,494	19,828	23,649	6,719	3,957
Family householder	25,053	1,609	5,749	7,146	7,418	1,900	1,231
Spouse of householder	41,830	1,564	8,316	11,277	14,672	4,161	1,840
Child of householder	8,917	5,974	1,680	762	477	21	3
Other, living with relatives	4,866	873	749	643	1,082	637	883
Not living with relatives	21,737	2,548	3,334	2,580	5,393	3,163	4,720
Nonfamily householder	17,504	1,068	2,070	1,863	4,758	3,080	4,664
Living alone	15,312	523	1,456	1,499	4,257	2,987	4,590
Sharing home with nonrelative	2,192	545	614	364	501	93	74
Other, not living with relatives	4,233	1,480	1,264	717	635	83	56

- Represents zero or rounds to zero.

Source: *Marital Status and Living Arrangements: March 1998 (Update)*, Bureau of the Census, Washington, DC, 1998

reaching 9.9 per 1,000 in 1977. The rate increased again, reaching 10.6 per 1,000 in 1980-82. Since the early 1980s, the marriage rate generally has been declining. One reason for the recent decline is that the majority of the very large baby-boom generation has aged past their twenties and early thirties, the peak marriage years.

In 1998, according to the Bureau of the Census, about 56 percent of the population 18 years and over were married and living with their spouses. The highest proportion (70.2 percent) was among those from 55 to 64 years old. The percent-

ages among those 65 years and older decreased as the number of widows increased. (See Table 2.4.)

Postponing Marriage

In 1890, the estimated median age at first marriage was 26.1 years for men and 22 years for women. Since that time, the median age at first marriage declined until 1956, when the median age at first marriage reached a low of 22.5 years for men and 20.1 years for women. By 1990, the median age had returned to the 1890 level of 26.1 years for men and an even higher 23.9 years for women. The median age continues to rise. In 1996, the age increased to 27.1 for men and to 24.8 for women. In 1998, the median age for men at first marriage dropped slightly to 26.7, while the median age for women was at a high of 25 years. (See Table 2.5.)

Delayed marriage may lessen the chance of divorce. Studies have shown that marriages at younger ages have a higher probability of divorce than marriages at older ages. However, delayed marriage may also increase the chance of out-of-wedlock childbearing (Arthur J. Norton and Louisa F. Miller, "Marriage, Divorce and Remarriage in the 1990s," *Current Population Reports*, Series P23-180, U.S. Bureau of the Census, Washington, DC, 1992). Researchers have also found that delayed marriage may result in increased cohabitation. (See below for Unmarried-Couple Households.)

Never-Married

In 1998, the never-married over 18 years of age accounted for 58.5 percent of unmarried adults over 18 years of age. The proportion of the never-married among the total adult population over 18 years was 23.6 percent. (See Table 2.6.) Only 4.2 percent of women and men ages 65 to 74 had never been married, while 12 percent of women and 19 percent of men 35 to 44 had never been married.

A much higher proportion of Black women (41 percent) and men (46 percent) age 15 and older were never married than White women (22 percent) and men (29 percent). (See Table 2.7.) The increase in the percentage of adults who have never been married may reflect the increase in adults in nonmarital joint living arrangements rather than an increase in traditional "singles" (Larry L. Bumpass et al., "The Role of Cohabitation in De-

TABLE 2.7

Marital Status of the Population 15 Years Old and Over, by Sex and Race: 1950 to Present

(Numbers in thousands)

| | | | MALES | | | |
| | | | | Unmarried | | |
Years	Total	Married	Unmarried Total	Never Married	Widowed	Divorced
All Races						
1998	101,123	58,633	42,491	31,591	2,569	8,331
1997	100,159	57,923	42,236	31,315	2,690	8,231
1996	98,593	57,656	40,937	30,691	2,478	7,768
1995	97,704	57,570	39,953	30,286	2,284	7,383
1994	96,768	57,068	39,700	30,228	2,222	7,250
1993	94,854	56,833	38,021	28,775	2,468	6,778
1990	91,955	55,833	36,121	27,505	2,333	6,283
1980	81,947	51,813	30,134	24,227	1,977	3,930
1970	70,559	47,109	23,450	19,832	2,051	1,567
1960*	60,273	41,781	18,492	15,274	2,112	1,106
1950*	54,601	36,866	17,735	14,400	2,264	1,071
White						
1998	85,219	51,299	33,920	24,775	2,106	7,038
1997	84,540	50,860	33,680	24,471	2,264	6,945
1996	83,463	50,882	32,581	23,894	2,128	6,559
1995	82,566	50,658	31,909	23,667	1,921	6,321
1994	82,026	50,226	31,800	23,704	1,878	6,218
1993	80,755	50,305	30,451	22,738	1,954	5,759
1990	78,908	49,542	29,367	22,078	1,930	5,359
1980	71,887	46,721	25,167	20,174	1,642	3,351
1970	62,868	42,732	20,135	17,080	1,722	1,333
1960*	54,130	38,042	16,088	13,286	1,816	986
1950*	49,302	33,451	15,850	12,892	1,986	972
Black						
1998	11,283	4,675	6,608	5,191	382	1,035
1997	11,113	4,623	6,491	5,137	340	1,014
1996	10,922	4,515	6,407	5,115	277	1,015
1995	10,825	4,632	6,193	5,031	310	852
1994	10,639	4,486	6,153	5,007	295	851
1993	10,442	4,431	6,012	4,750	426	836
1990	9,948	4,489	5,459	4,319	338	802
1980	8,292	4,053	4,239	3,410	308	521
1970	6,936	3,949	2,987	2,468	307	212
1960*	6,143	3,739	2,404	1,988	296	120
1950*	5,299	3,415	1,885	1,508	278	99

(continued)

TABLE 2.7 (Continued)

Marital Status of the Population 15 Years Old and Over, by Sex and Race:
1950 to Present

(Numbers in thousands)

| | | | FEMALES | | | |
| | | | | Unmarried | | |
Years	Total	Married	Unmarried Total	Never Married	Widowed	Divorced
All Races						
1998	108,168	59,333	48,835	26,713	11,029	11,093
1997	107,076	58,829	48,247	26,073	11,058	11,116
1996	106,031	58,905	47,127	25,528	11,078	10,521
1995	105,028	58,984	46,045	24,693	11,082	10,270
1994	104,032	58,185	45,847	24,645	11,073	10,129
1993	102,400	57,768	44,631	23,534	11,214	9,883
1990	99,838	56,797	43,040	22,718	11,477	8,845
1980	89,914	52,965	36,950	20,226	10,758	5,966
1970	77,766	48,148	29,618	17,167	9,734	2,717
1960*	64,607	42,583	22,024	12,252	8,064	1,708
1950*	57,102	37,577	19,525	11,418	6,734	1,373
White						
1998	89,489	51,410	38,079	19,614	9,351	9,115
1997	88,756	50,987	37,769	19,139	9,404	9,226
1996	88,134	51,388	33,745	18,691	9,392	8,662
1995	87,484	51,390	36,094	18,250	9,399	8,445
1994	86,765	50,766	36,000	18,235	9,424	8,341
1993	86,045	50,668	35,377	17,660	9,512	8,205
1990	84,508	49,986	34,522	17,438	9,800	7,284
1980	77,882	47,277	30,604	16,318	9,296	4,990
1970	68,888	43,286	25,602	14,703	8,559	2,340
1960*	57,860	38,545	19,315	10,796	7,099	1,420
1950*	51,404	34,042	17,362	10,241	5,902	1,219
Black						
1998	13,715	4,983	8,732	5,689	1,370	1,673
1997	13,514	5,058	8,457	5,584	1,307	1,566
1996	13,292	4,947	8,345	5,451	1,330	1,564
1995	13,097	4,942	8,155	5,250	1,380	1,525
1994	12,872	4,863	8,009	5,190	1,322	1,497
1993	12,495	4,820	7,676	4,867	1,401	1,408
1990	11,966	4,813	7,152	4,416	1,392	1,344
1980	10,108	4,508	5,600	3,401	1,319	880
1970	8,108	4,384	3,723	2,248	1,120	355
1960*	6,747	4,038	2,709	1,456	965	288
1950*	5,698	3,534	2,164	1,178	832	154

*1950 and 1960 data are for the population 14 yrs old and over.
 Nonwhite data is shown for Black for these years.

Source: *Marital Status and Living Arrangements: March 1998 (Update)* and earlier updates,
Bureau of the Census, Washington, DC, 1998

White/other races, and 3 percent were Black/other races marriages. Between 1970 and 1998, the number of interracial married couples increased from 310,000 to 1.35 million. (See Table 2.8.)

DIVORCE

In 1998, 9 percent of all those 15 and over were currently divorced, compared to 3 percent in 1970. (See Table 2.7.) This tabulation counts divorced persons who had not remarried at the time the survey was conducted. These statistics do not indicate the number of divorces granted in 1998 or the number of persons who had ever been divorced during their lifetimes.

In 1998, 1,135,000 divorces were granted, a divorce

clining Rates of Marriage," *Journal of Marriage and the Family*, 53: 913-927, 1991). (See below for Unmarried-Couple Households.)

Interracial Married Couples

In 1998, in the vast majority of married couples in the United States, both partners were of the same race. Interracial married couples accounted for only 2.4 percent of all married couples. Of the 1.35 million interracial married couples in 1998, 24 percent were Black/White marriages, 72 percent were

rate of 4.2 per 1,000 population (Table 2.3), the lowest annual divorce rate in over two decades. During the 1950s and early 1960s, the divorce rate was lower, ranging between 2.1 and 2.6 per 1,000 people. Beginning with 1967, the divorce rate increased almost yearly, until it peaked at 5.3 per 1,000 in 1979. The rate was 5.3 per 1,000 again in 1981, but then began to decline, reaching 4.8 per 1,000 by 1987. Since 1987, the rate has varied little.

The National Center for Health Statistics reports that, based on the current figures, statistically

TABLE 2.8

Interracial Married Couples: 1960 to Present

(Numbers in thousands. Includes all interracial married couples with at least one spouse of White or Black race)

| Year | Total married couples | Interracial married couples | | | | | |
| | | Total | Black/White | | | White/ Other race* | Black/ Other race* |
			Total	Black husband White wife	White husband Black wife		
Current Population Survey (CPS)							
1998	55,305	1,348	330	210	120	975	43
1997	54,666	1,264	311	201	110	896	57
1996	54,664	1,260	337	220	117	884	39
1995	54,937	1,392	328	206	122	988	76
1994	54,251	1,283	296	196	100	909	78
1993	54,199	1,195	242	182	60	920	33
1992	53,512	1,161	246	163	83	883	32
1991	53,227	994	231	156	75	720	43
1990	53,256	964	211	150	61	720	33
1989	52,924	953	219	155	64	703	31
1988	52,613	956	218	149	69	703	35
1987	52,286	799	177	121	56	581	41
1986	51,704	827	181	136	45	613	33
1985	51,114	792	164	117	47	599	29
1984	50,864	762	175	111	64	564	23
1983	50,665	719	164	118	46	522	33
1982	50,294	697	155	108	47	515	27
1981	49,896	639	132	104	28	484	23
1980	49,714	651	167	122	45	450	34
Decennial Census							
1990	51,718	1,461	213	159	54	1,173	75
1980	49,514	953	121	94	27	785	47
1970	44,598	310	65	41	24	233	12
1960	40,491	149	51	25	26	90	7

NA Not available.

* "Other race," is any race other than White or Black, such as American Indian, Japanese,Chinese, etc.

Source: *Marital Status and Living Arrangements: March 1998 (Update)* and earlier updates, Bureau of the Census, Washington, DC, 1998

half of all marriages will end in divorce. It should be noted, however, that a certain percentage of people get married and divorced two or more times, adding to the number of divorces. For those not among this group, over half of the marriages will not end in divorce.

UNMARRIED-COUPLE HOUSEHOLDS

In 1998, there were more than 4.2 million unmarried-couple households, compared to 523,000 in 1970. (See Table 2.9.) An unmarried-couple household is composed of two unrelated adults of the opposite sex (one of whom is the householder) living together in a housing unit with or without children under 15 years old. The count of unmarried couple households is intended mainly to esti-mate the number of cohabiting couples, but it may also include households with a roommate, boarder, or paid employee of the opposite sex.

In 1998, there were 8 unmarried couples for every 100 married couples, compared to only 1 for every 100 in 1970 and 6 for every 100 in 1993. About one-third (36 percent) had children under 15 years old present in the home (Table 2.9). These children may be the result of the union of the two people in the relationship, or they may come from earlier marriages or relationships or both.

LIVING ALONE

In 1998, 26.3 million persons — 13 percent of all adults — lived alone. (See Table 2.6.) While women accounted for most persons living alone

(58 percent), the number of men living alone has increased at a faster pace. Between 1970 and 1998, the number of women living alone more than doubled, from 7.3 to 15.3 million. During the same period, the number of men living alone more than tripled, increasing from 3.5 million to 11 million.

Living alone is more common among the elderly, especially among women. Among adults under 35 years old, only 6 percent of women and 9 percent of men lived alone in 1998. For persons 75 years old and over, 53 percent of women, up from 37 percent in 1970, lived by themselves. One-fifth (22 percent) of men over 75 were living alone, slightly more than the 19 percent of the elderly men who lived alone in 1970. Older women are more likely than older men to live alone because they are more likely to outlive their spouses.

TABLE 2.9

Unmarried-Couple Households, by Presence of Children: 1960 to Present

(Numbers in thousands. Data based on Current Population Survey (CPS) unless otherwise specified)

Year	Total	Without children under 15 yrs.	With children under 15 yrs.
1998	4,236	2,716	1,520
1997	4,130	2,660	1,470
1996	3,958	2,516	1,442
1995	3,668	2,349	1,319
1994	3,661	2,391	1,270
1993	3,510	2,274	1,236
1992	3,308	2,187	1,121
1991	3,039	2,077	962
1990	2,856	1,966	891
1989	2,764	1,906	858
1988	2,588	1,786	802
1987	2,334	1,614	720
1986	2,220	1,558	662
1985	1,983	1,380	603
1984	1,988	1,373	614
1983	1,891	1,366	525
1982	1,863	1,387	475
1981	1,808	1,305	502
1980	1,589	1,159	431
1979	1,346	985	360
1978	1,137	865	272
1977	957	754	204
1970 Census	523	327	196
1960 Census	439	242	197

Source: *Marital Status and Living Arrangements: March 1998 (Update)* and earlier updates, Bureau of the Census, Washington, DC, 1998

LIVING ARRANGEMENTS OF YOUNG ADULTS

Significant changes in the living arrangements of young adults have occurred in the past few decades. More young adults are living at home with their parents, more are living alone or sharing their home with a roommate or other nonrelative, more are living in the homes of others, and fewer are maintaining families of their own. Between 1970 and 1998, the proportion of persons 18 to 24 years old maintaining a family (married couples or other persons maintaining families; family householder or spouse of householder) dropped from 38 to 19 percent. The proportion of nonfamily householders (persons living alone or sharing the home they owned/rented with a roommate or other nonrelative) increased from 5 percent to 9 percent. Close to 21 percent of persons 18 to 24 years old

lived in the homes of someone other than their relatives (Table 2.6), up from 10 percent in 1970.

Since 1970, the proportion of adults aged 25 to 34 who maintained their own families has also declined, from 83 percent to 62 percent. While this older group was over three times more likely than the younger group to maintain a family in 1998, they were only about twice as likely in 1970. The proportion of 25- to 34-year-olds living alone or sharing their homes with nonrelatives increased from 5 percent in 1970 to 14 percent in 1998. The total proportion living in the home of someone other than relatives increased from 4 to 22 percent.

Between 1970 and 1980, the proportion of 18- to 24-year-olds living in their parents' homes remained virtually unchanged (47 percent in 1970 and 48 percent in 1980). During the 1980s, the proportion rose 5 percentage points to 53 percent in

38

TABLE 2.10

Young Adults Living at Home: 1960 to Present

(Numbers in thousands. Data based on Current Population Survey (CPS) unless otherwise specified)

Age	Male			Female		
	Total	Child of householder	Percent	Total	Child of householder	Percent
18 to 24 years						
1998	12,633	7,399	59	12,568	5,974	48
1997	12,534	7,501	60	12,452	6,006	48
1996	12,402	7,327	59	12,441	5,955	48
1995	12,545	7,328	58	12,613	5,896	47
1994	12,683	7,547	60	12,792	5,924	46
1993	12,049	7,145	59	12,260	5,746	47
1992	12,083	7,296	60	12,351	5,929	48
1991	12,275	7,385	60	12,627	6,163	49
1990	12,450	7,232	58	12,860	6,135	48
1989	12,574	7,308	58	13,055	6,141	47
1988	12,835	7,792	61	13,226	6,398	48
1987	13,029	7,981	61	13,433	6,375	47
1986	13,324	7,831	59	13,787	6,433	47
1985	13,695	8,172	60	14,149	6,758	48
1984	14,196	8,764	62	14,482	6,779	47
1983	14,344	8,803	61	14,702	7,001	48
1982	14,368	(NA)	(NA)	14,815	(NA)	(NA)
1981	14,367	(NA)	(NA)	14,848	(NA)	(NA)
1980 Census	14,278	7,755	54	14,844	6,336	43
1970 Census	10,398	5,641	54	11,959	4,941	41
1960 Census	6,842	3,583	52	7,876	2,750	35
25 to 34 years						
1998	19,526	2,845	15	19,828	1,680	8
1997	20,039	2,909	15	20,217	1,745	9
1996	20,390	3,213	16	20,528	1,810	9
1995	20,589	3,166	15	20,800	1,759	8
1994	20,873	3,261	16	21,073	1,859	9
1993	20,856	3,300	16	21,007	1,844	9
1992	21,125	3,225	15	21,368	1,874	9
1991	21,319	3,172	15	21,586	1,887	9
1990	21,462	3,213	15	21,779	1,774	8
1989	21,461	3,130	15	21,777	1,728	8
1988	21,320	3,207	15	21,649	1,791	8
1987	21,142	3,071	15	21,494	1,655	8
1986	20,956	2,981	14	21,097	1,686	8
1985	20,184	2,685	13	20,673	1,661	8
1984	19,876	2,626	13	20,297	1,548	8
1983	19,438	2,664	14	19,903	1,520	8
1982	19,090	(NA)	(NA)	19,614	(NA)	(NA)
1981	18,625	(NA)	(NA)	19,203	(NA)	(NA)
1980 Census	18,107	1,894	10	18,689	1,300	7
1970 Census	11,929	1,129	9	12,637	829	7
1960 Census	10,896	1,185	11	11,587	853	7

Note: Unmarried college students living in dormitories are counted as living in their parent(s) home.

Source: *Marital Status and Living Arrangements: March 1998 (Update)* and earlier updates, Bureau of the Census, Washington, DC, 1998

1990. In 1998, the proportion living in their parents' homes remained at 53 percent (59 percent of young men and 48 percent of young women). (See Tables 2.6 and 2.10.)

There is a similar pattern among adults ages 25 to 34. Eight percent of these adults lived with their parents in 1970, 9 percent in 1980, and 12 percent in 1990 and 1998. Increases in the propor-

FIGURE 2.1

Percentage of children under age 18 by presence of parents in household, 1980-98

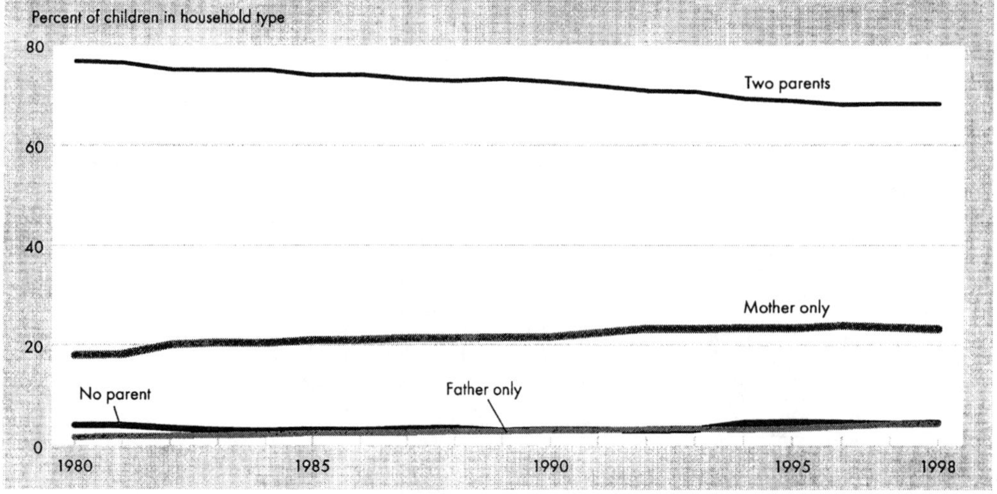

Percent of children in household type

TABLE 2.11

Family structure: Percentage of children under age 18 by presence of parents in household, race, and Hispanic origin, selected years 1980-98

Race and family type	1980	1985	1990	1991	1992	1993	1994[a]	1995[a]	1996[a]	1997[a]	1998[a]
Total											
Two parents[b]	77	74	73	72	71	71	69	69	68	68	68
Mother only[c]	18	21	22	22	23	23	23	23	24	24	23
Father only[c]	2	2	3	3	3	3	3	4	4	4	4
No parent	4	3	3	3	3	3	4	4	4	4	4
White, non-Hispanic											
Two parents[b]	—	—	81	80	79	79	79	78	77	77	76
Mother only[c]	—	—	15	15	16	16	16	16	16	17	16
Father only[c]	—	—	3	3	3	3	3	3	4	4	5
No parent	—	—	2	2	1	1	3	3	3	3	3
Black											
Two parents[b]	42	39	38	36	36	36	33	33	33	35	36
Mother only[c]	44	51	51	54	54	54	53	52	53	52	51
Father only[c]	2	3	4	4	3	3	4	4	4	5	4
No parent	12	7	8	7	7	7	10	11	9	8	9
Hispanic[d]											
Two parents[b]	75	68	67	66	65	65	63	63	62	64	64
Mother only[c]	20	27	27	27	28	28	28	28	29	27	27
Father only[c]	2	2	3	3	4	4	4	4	4	4	4
No parent	3	3	3	4	3	4	5	4	5	5	5

— = not available

[a] Numbers in these years may reflect changes in the Current Population Survey because of newly instituted computer-assisted interviewing techniques and/or because of the change in the population controls to the 1990 Census-based estimates, with adjustments.

[b] Excludes families where parents are not living as a married couple.

[c] Includes some families where both parents are present in the household, but living as unmarried partners.

[d] Persons of Hispanic origin may be of any race.

NOTE: Family structure refers to the presence of biological, adoptive, and stepparents in the child's household. Thus, a child with a biological mother and stepfather living in the household is said to have two parents.

Source of figure and table: *America's Children: Key National Indicators of Well-Being, 1999*, Federal Interagency Forum on Child and Family Statistics, Washington, DC, 1999

TABLE 2.12

Living Arrangements of Children Under 18 Years: March 1998

(Numbers in thousands)

Characteristics of children	Age						
	Under 18 years	Under 1 year	1 and 2 years	3 to 5 years	Under 6 years	6 to 11 years	12 to 17 years
LIVING ARRANGEMENTS OF CHILDREN							
Total children	71,377	3,885	7,770	12,193	23,848	24,226	23,303
Living with:							
Two parents	48,642	2,736	5,489	8,331	16,556	16,638	15,447
One parent	19,777	1,057	2,000	3,412	6,468	6,648	6,660
Mother only	16,634	817	1,646	2,885	5,347	5,732	5,554
Father only	3,143	240	354	527	1,121	916	1,106
Other relative(s)	2,125	54	210	308	573	711	843
Nonrelative(s) only	833	38	71	142	251	229	353
LIVING ARRANGEMENTS OF GRANDCHILDREN[1]							
Total grandchildren	3,989	419	699	740	1,859	1,214	915
Living with:							
Both parents present	503	67	91	113	271	148	84
Mother only present	1,827	299	417	378	1,094	465	268
Father only present	241	27	36	35	98	87	56
Neither parent present	1,417	27	154	214	395	513	508
MARITAL STATUS OF PARENT							
Living with mother only	16,634	817	1,646	2,885	5,347	5,732	5,554
Married, spouse absent	3,558	82	292	609	983	1,337	1,238
Separated	2,783	63	209	490	763	1,058	962
Widowed	671	10	31	45	86	204	382
Divorced	5,704	84	249	657	991	2,071	2,642
Never married	6,700	640	1,073	1,574	3,288	2,120	1,292
Living with father only	3,143	240	354	527	1,121	916	1,106
Married, spouse absent	578	19	32	95	146	200	232
Separated	380	10	10	64	85	149	146
Widowed	123	2	-	18	20	28	75
Divorced	1,397	48	66	136	250	472	675
Never married	1,046	171	255	278	705	217	124

[1]Grandchildren are only those living in the grandparent's home. Excludes grandchildren with grandparents living in the home of the child's parent(s).

- Represents zero or rounds to zero.

Source: *Marital Status and Living Arrangements: March 1998 (Update)*, Bureau of the Census, Washington, DC, 1998

FIGURE 2.2

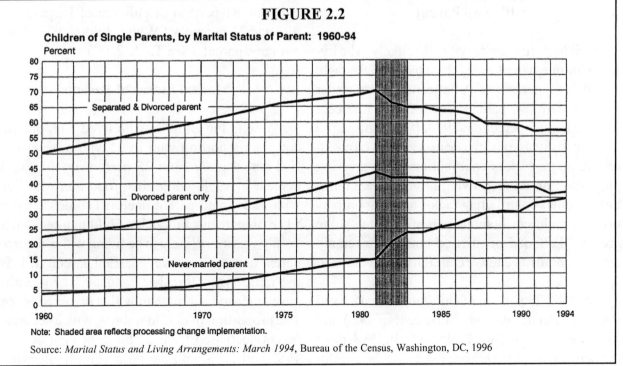

Children of Single Parents, by Marital Status of Parent: 1960-94

Note: Shaded area reflects processing change implementation.

Source: *Marital Status and Living Arrangements: March 1994*, Bureau of the Census, Washington, DC, 1996

TABLE 2.13

Grandchildren Living in the Home of Their Grandparents: 1970 to Present

(Numbers in thousands)

Year	Total children under 18	Grandchildren				
			With parent(s) present			
		Total	Both parents present	Mother only present	Father only present	Without parent(s) present
1998	71,377	3,989	503	1,827	241	1,417
1997	70,983	3,894	554	1,785	247	1,309
1996	70,908	4,060	467	1,943	220	1,431
1995	70,254	3,965	427	1,876	195	1,466
1994	69,508	3,735	436	1,764	175	1,359
1993	66,893	3,368	475	1,647	229	1,017
1992	65,965	3,253	502	1,740	144	867
1991	65,093	3,320	559	1,674	151	937
1990	64,137	3,155	467	1,563	191	935
1980 Census	63,369	2,306	310	922	86	988
1970 Census	69,276	2,214	363	817	78	957

Source: *Marital Status and Living Arrangements: March 1998 (Update)* and earlier updates, Bureau of the Census, Washington, DC, 1998

tion living at home occurred for both men and women, but in all years, men were more likely to live at home than women.

LIVING ARRANGEMENTS OF CHILDREN

Nearly 7 of 10 Children Live with Two Parents

Children are considerably more likely to be living with one parent today than two decades ago. In 1998, 68 percent of American children under 18 lived with two parents, down from 77 percent in 1980 and 85 percent in 1970. (See Figure 2.1.) The rise in divorce and the increase in unwed mothers are major factors contributing to the growing proportion of children living in one-parent families. Another contributing factor to rising proportions of children in single-parent families is the greater likelihood of married couples to remain childless or to have fewer children than in the past.

In 1998, 27 percent of children under 18 lived with one parent, up from 20 percent in 1980 and 12 percent in 1970. (See Table 2.11.) In 1998, most (85 percent) of these children lived with their moth-

ers, although an increasing proportion lived with their fathers. In 1998, 15 percent of the children in a one-parent situation lived with their fathers, up from 10 percent in 1980 and 8 percent in 1970.

Black children and children of Hispanic origin were more likely to be living with one parent than were White children. In 1998, 55 percent of Black children, 31 percent of children of Hispanic origin, and 21 percent of White children were living with one parent. (See Table 2.11.)

Marital Status of Parents

Among the children who lived with one parent, the proportion who lived with a never-married parent grew from 25 percent in 1985 to 39 percent in 1998, while the proportion who lived with a divorced parent declined somewhat from 41 to 36 percent. In 1985, a child in a one-parent family was more likely to be living with a divorced parent than with a never-married parent. In 1998, the child was more likely to be living with a never-married parent than with a divorced parent. The proportion of children living with a separated parent decreased from 23 to 16 percent between 1985 and 1998, and the proportion living with a widowed parent dropped from 8 to 4 percent. (See Table 2.12. Figure 2.2 shows the marital status of single parents from 1960 to 1994.)

The increase in the percentage of children living with one parent reflects the growing number of births to unmarried women. In 1998, there were 1.29 million births to unmarried mothers — 3 out of 10 births (32.8 percent). In 1980, 0.7 million births, fewer than 2 of 10 total births, were to unmarried women.

Grandparents

Grandparents play an important role in raising a small but significant proportion of children. In 1998, almost 4 million grandchildren under 18 lived in the homes of their grandparents. (This figure does not include children whose parents are keeping the household, with the grandparent or grandparents living with them.) (See Table 2.13.)

Since 1970, the proportion of children living with their grandparents has risen from about 3 per-cent to nearly 6 percent. Most of the increase in the number of grandchildren living with grandparents has been among children with only a mother present in the household. Since 1970, the proportion of grandchildren with neither parent present declined from 43 percent to 35.5 percent in 1998, while the proportion with mother only present increased from 37 percent to 46 percent. (See Table 2.13.) Continued high levels of divorce and the rise in out-of-wedlock childbearing were the main reasons for these changes.

In 1997, according to Rachel Pruchno in "Raising Grandchildren: The Experiences of Black and White Grandmothers" (*The Gerontologist*, vol. 39, 209-221, Washington, D.C.), 5.6 percent of American children (4 million) were living with 3.7 million grandparents. About 780,000 households included a grandparent and grandchild, without the grandchild's parents. Black households (9.2 percent) were more likely than White households (2.3 percent) to include children living with grandparents.

CHAPTER III

LABOR FORCE

The number of workers in the American civilian non-institutionalized labor force (not in the army, school, jail, or mental health facilities) grew rapidly over the past generation, almost doubling from 74.5 million in 1965 to 137.7 million in 1998. During this period, the proportion of the working-age population rose from 58.9 to 67.1 percent. (See Table 3.1.) This growth was mainly attributable to the entrance into the work force of the post-World War II baby boom children and the growth in the number and percentage of women entering the work force.

While the proportion of men in the labor force has remained steady over the past 10 years at around 75 percent, participation by women rose from 56 percent in 1987 to 60 percent in 1999 (Table 3.2). In August 1999, married men living with their wives accounted for 32.5 percent of the labor force. Married women living with their husbands made up 25 percent of the work force, and women who maintained families on their own accounted for 6.3 percent.

While 91.6 percent of men and 76.1 percent of women 25 to 54 years of age were in the work force in August 1999, the percentage dropped to 68.1 percent for men and 51.6 percent for women between 55 and 64 years of age. (See Table 3.3.) The proportion of men in this age group in the labor force generally has declined over the past few years, while the percentage of women has increased. A growing percentage of jobs held by this age group are part-time instead of full-time. The low unemployment rate (just under 3 percent) among this older group reflects the fact that many

of these older workers have given up looking for a job or have retired and are, therefore, not in the labor force.

Older workers leave the work force for many reasons, ranging from disability to a genuine desire to retire. For many older people, however, leaving the work force is not a voluntary act. Companies trying to cut expenses sometimes find it in their financial interest to force older, more highly paid workers into retirement and replace them with younger, lower paid workers. Older workers are also more expensive to insure. The increasing desire of many companies to cut down the size of their staffs, frequently by eliminating many middle-management positions, has been particularly detrimental to this age group. They are frequently offered early retirement with some fringe benefits, but they may be laid off with no benefits if they refuse the early retirement.

SERVICE ECONOMY

The American economy has moved away from a goods-producing, or manufacturing, economy toward a service economy. Over the past generation, the service sector has accounted for an increasing proportion of workers. Since 1969, the number of workers in goods-producing industries has remained virtually unchanged while the number working in the service-producing sector has doubled. In 1960, for every goods-producing worker, there were about 1.7 service-producing workers. By 1970, the ratio was 1 to 2; by 1980, it was 1 to 3.4; and by 1998, it was nearly 1 to 4. (See Table 3.4.)

TABLE 3.1

Employment status of the civilian noninstitutional population 16 years and over, 1965 to date

(Numbers in thousands)

Year and month	Civilian noninsti-tutional population	Civilian labor force								Not in labor force
		Number	Percent of population	Employed				Unemployed		
				Number	Percent of population	Agriculture	Nonagricultural industries	Number	Percent of labor force	
				Annual averages						
1965	126,513	74,455	58.9	71,088	56.2	4,361	66,726	3,366	4.5	52,058
1966	128,058	75,770	59.2	72,895	56.9	3,979	68,915	2,875	3.8	52,288
1967	129,874	77,347	59.6	74,372	57.3	3,844	70,527	2,975	3.8	52,527
1968	132,028	78,737	59.6	75,920	57.5	3,817	72,103	2,817	3.6	53,291
1969	134,335	80,734	60.1	77,902	58.0	3,606	74,296	2,832	3.5	53,602
1970	137,085	82,771	60.4	78,678	57.4	3,463	75,215	4,093	4.9	54,315
1971	140,216	84,382	60.2	79,367	56.6	3,394	75,972	5,016	5.9	55,834
1972[1]	144,126	87,034	60.4	82,153	57.0	3,484	78,669	4,882	5.6	57,091
1973[1]	147,096	89,429	60.8	85,064	57.8	3,470	81,594	4,365	4.9	57,667
1974	150,120	91,949	61.3	86,794	57.8	3,515	83,279	5,156	5.6	58,171
1975	153,153	93,775	61.2	85,846	56.1	3,408	82,438	7,929	8.5	59,377
1976	156,150	96,158	61.6	88,752	56.8	3,331	85,421	7,406	7.7	59,991
1977	159,033	99,009	62.3	92,017	57.9	3,283	88,734	6,991	7.1	60,025
1978[1]	161,910	102,251	63.2	96,048	59.3	3,387	92,661	6,202	6.1	59,659
1979	164,863	104,962	63.7	98,824	59.9	3,347	95,477	6,137	5.8	59,900
1980	167,745	106,940	63.8	99,303	59.2	3,364	95,938	7,637	7.1	60,806
1981	170,130	108,670	63.9	100,397	59.0	3,368	97,030	8,273	7.6	61,460
1982	172,271	110,204	64.0	99,526	57.8	3,401	96,125	10,678	9.7	62,067
1983	174,215	111,550	64.0	100,834	57.9	3,383	97,450	10,717	9.6	62,665
1984	176,383	113,544	64.4	105,005	59.5	3,321	101,685	8,539	7.5	62,839
1985	178,206	115,461	64.8	107,150	60.1	3,179	103,971	8,312	7.2	62,744
1986[1]	180,587	117,834	65.3	109,597	60.7	3,163	106,434	8,237	7.0	62,752
1987	182,753	119,865	65.6	112,440	61.5	3,208	109,232	7,425	6.2	62,888
1988	184,613	121,669	65.9	114,968	62.3	3,169	111,800	6,701	5.5	62,944
1989	186,393	123,869	66.5	117,342	63.0	3,199	114,142	6,528	5.3	62,523
1990[1]	189,164	125,840	66.5	118,793	62.8	3,223	115,570	7,047	5.6	63,324
1991	190,925	126,346	66.2	117,718	61.7	3,269	114,449	8,628	6.8	64,578
1992	192,805	128,105	66.4	118,492	61.5	3,247	115,245	9,613	7.5	64,700
1993	194,838	129,200	66.3	120,259	61.7	3,115	117,144	8,940	6.9	65,638
1994[1]	196,814	131,056	66.6	123,060	62.5	3,409	119,651	7,996	6.1	65,758
1995	198,584	132,304	66.6	124,900	62.9	3,440	121,460	7,404	5.6	66,280
1996	200,591	133,943	66.8	126,708	63.2	3,443	123,264	7,236	5.4	66,647
1997[1]	203,133	136,297	67.1	129,558	63.8	3,399	126,159	6,739	4.9	66,837
1998[1]	205,220	137,673	67.1	131,463	64.1	3,378	128,085	6,210	4.5	67,547
				Monthly data, seasonally adjusted[2]						
1998:										
August	205,479	137,481	66.9	131,264	63.9	3,492	127,772	6,217	4.5	67,998
September	205,699	138,081	67.1	131,818	64.1	3,470	128,348	6,263	4.5	67,618
October	205,919	138,116	67.1	131,858	64.0	3,558	128,300	6,258	4.5	67,803
November	206,104	138,193	67.1	132,113	64.1	3,348	128,765	6,080	4.4	67,911
December	206,270	138,547	67.2	132,526	64.2	3,222	129,304	6,021	4.3	67,723
1999:										
January[3]	206,719	139,347	67.4	133,396	64.5	3,299	130,097	5,950	4.3	67,372
February	206,873	139,271	67.3	133,144	64.4	3,328	129,817	6,127	4.4	67,602
March	207,036	138,816	67.0	133,033	64.3	3,281	129,752	5,783	4.2	68,220
April	207,236	139,091	67.1	133,069	64.2	3,384	129,685	6,022	4.3	68,145
May	207,427	139,019	67.0	133,224	64.2	3,295	129,929	5,795	4.2	68,408
June	207,632	139,408	67.1	133,432	64.3	3,354	130,078	5,975	4.3	68,225
July	207,828	139,254	67.0	133,307	64.1	3,292	130,015	5,947	4.3	68,574
August	208,038	139,264	66.9	133,411	64.1	3,219	130,192	5,853	4.2	68,774

[1] Not strictly comparable with prior years.
[2] The population figures are not adjusted for seasonal variation.
[3] Beginning in January 1999, data are not strictly comparable with data for 1998 and earlier years because of revisions in the population controls used in the household survey.

Source: *Employment and Earnings*, vol. 46, no. 9, September 1999

TABLE 3.2

Employment status of the civilian noninstitutional population 16 years and over by sex, 1987 to date

(Numbers in thousands)

Sex, year, and month	Civilian noninsti-tutional population	Civilian labor force								Not in labor force
				Employed				Unemployed		
		Number	Percent of population	Number	Percent of population	Agriculture	Nonagricultural industries	Number	Percent of labor force	
MEN				Annual averages						
1987	86,899	66,207	76.2	62,107	71.5	2,543	59,564	4,101	6.2	20,692
1988	87,857	66,927	76.2	63,273	72.0	2,493	60,780	3,655	5.5	20,930
1989	88,762	67,840	76.4	64,315	72.5	2,513	61,802	3,525	5.2	20,923
1990[1]	90,377	69,011	76.4	65,104	72.0	2,546	62,559	3,906	5.7	21,367
1991	91,278	69,168	75.8	64,223	70.4	2,589	61,634	4,946	7.2	22,110
1992	92,270	69,964	75.8	64,440	69.8	2,575	61,866	5,523	7.9	22,306
1993	93,332	70,404	75.4	65,349	70.0	2,478	62,871	5,055	7.2	22,927
1994[1]	94,355	70,817	75.1	66,450	70.4	2,554	63,896	4,367	6.2	23,538
1995	95,178	71,360	75.0	67,377	70.8	2,559	64,818	3,983	5.6	23,818
1996	96,206	72,087	74.9	68,207	70.9	2,573	65,634	3,880	5.4	24,119
1997[1]	97,715	73,261	75.0	69,685	71.3	2,552	67,133	3,577	4.9	24,454
1998[1]	98,758	73,959	74.9	70,693	71.6	2,553	68,140	3,266	4.4	24,799
				Monthly data, seasonally adjusted[2]						
1998:										
August	98,892	73,754	74.6	70,503	71.3	2,631	67,872	3,251	4.4	25,138
September	99,006	74,202	74.9	70,841	71.6	2,644	68,197	3,361	4.5	24,804
October	99,121	74,189	74.8	70,925	71.6	2,734	68,191	3,264	4.4	24,932
November	99,217	74,345	74.9	71,182	71.7	2,578	68,604	3,163	4.3	24,872
December	99,309	74,437	75.0	71,204	71.7	2,414	68,790	3,233	4.3	24,872
1999:										
January[3]	99,198	74,599	75.2	71,459	72.0	2,456	69,003	3,140	4.2	24,599
February	99,279	74,504	75.0	71,276	71.8	2,424	68,851	3,228	4.3	24,776
March	99,362	74,234	74.7	71,352	71.8	2,406	68,946	2,881	3.9	25,128
April	99,465	74,234	74.6	71,225	71.6	2,534	68,691	3,010	4.1	25,230
May	99,563	74,316	74.6	71,198	71.5	2,413	68,786	3,118	4.2	25,247
June	99,668	74,420	74.7	71,321	71.6	2,434	68,887	3,099	4.2	25,248
July	99,761	74,500	74.7	71,444	71.6	2,450	68,995	3,056	4.1	25,261
August	99,863	74,400	74.5	71,332	71.4	2,409	68,923	3,067	4.1	25,464
				Annual averages						
WOMEN										
1987	95,853	53,658	56.0	50,334	52.5	666	49,668	3,324	6.2	42,195
1988	96,756	54,742	56.6	51,696	53.4	676	51,020	3,046	5.6	42,014
1989	97,630	56,030	57.4	53,027	54.3	687	52,341	3,003	5.4	41,601
1990[1]	98,787	56,829	57.5	53,689	54.3	678	53,011	3,140	5.5	41,957
1991	99,646	57,178	57.4	53,496	53.7	680	52,815	3,683	6.4	42,468
1992	100,535	58,141	57.8	54,052	53.8	672	53,380	4,090	7.0	42,394
1993	101,506	58,795	57.9	54,910	54.1	637	54,273	3,885	6.6	42,711
1994[1]	102,460	60,239	58.8	56,610	55.3	855	55,755	3,629	6.0	42,221
1995	103,406	60,944	58.9	57,523	55.6	881	56,642	3,421	5.6	42,462
1996	104,385	61,857	59.3	58,501	56.0	871	57,630	3,356	5.4	42,528
1997[1]	105,418	63,036	59.8	59,873	56.8	847	59,026	3,162	5.0	42,382
1998[1]	106,462	63,714	59.8	60,771	57.1	825	59,945	2,944	4.6	42,748
				Monthly data, seasonally adjusted[2]						
1998:										
August	106,587	63,727	59.8	60,761	57.0	861	59,900	2,966	4.7	42,860
September	106,693	63,879	59.9	60,977	57.2	826	60,151	2,902	4.5	42,814
October	106,798	63,927	59.9	60,933	57.1	824	60,109	2,994	4.7	42,871
November	106,887	63,848	59.7	60,931	57.0	770	60,161	2,917	4.6	43,039
December	106,960	64,110	59.9	61,322	57.3	808	60,514	2,788	4.3	42,850
1999:										
January[3]	107,521	64,748	60.2	61,937	57.6	843	61,095	2,810	4.3	42,773
February	107,593	64,767	60.2	61,869	57.5	903	60,965	2,899	4.5	42,826
March	107,674	64,582	60.0	61,680	57.3	874	60,806	2,902	4.5	43,092
April	107,771	64,857	60.2	61,845	57.4	850	60,994	3,012	4.6	42,914
May	107,864	64,704	60.0	62,026	57.5	883	61,143	2,677	4.1	43,160
June	107,964	64,988	60.2	62,112	57.5	920	61,191	2,876	4.4	42,977
July	108,067	64,754	59.9	61,863	57.2	843	61,020	2,891	4.5	43,313
August	108,175	64,864	60.0	62,079	57.4	810	61,269	2,786	4.3	43,311

[1] Not strictly comparable with prior years.

[2] The population figures are not adjusted for seasonal variation.

[3] Beginning in January 1999, data are not strictly comparable with data for 1998 and earlier years because of revisions in the population controls used in the household survey.

Source: *Employment and Earnings*, vol. 46, no. 9, September 1999

TABLE 3.3

Employment status of the civilian noninstitutional population by age, sex, and race

(Numbers in thousands)

Age, sex, and race	Civilian noninstitutional population	August 1999								
		Civilian labor force								Not in labor force
		Total	Percent of population	Employed				Unemployed		
				Total	Percent of population	Agriculture	Nonagricultural industries	Number	Percent of labor force	
TOTAL										
16 years and over	208,038	140,090	67.3	134,264	64.5	3,525	130,739	5,826	4.2	67,948
16 to 19 years	16,061	9,014	56.1	7,962	49.6	309	7,653	1,051	11.7	7,048
16 to 17 years	8,070	3,716	46.0	3,237	40.1	146	3,091	479	12.9	4,354
18 to 19 years	7,991	5,298	66.3	4,725	59.1	163	4,562	572	10.8	2,694
20 to 24 years	17,999	14,315	79.5	13,258	73.7	382	12,876	1,057	7.4	3,684
25 to 54 years	118,369	99,082	83.7	95,855	81.0	2,123	93,732	3,227	3.3	19,287
25 to 34 years	37,810	31,879	84.3	30,625	81.0	679	29,947	1,253	3.9	5,931
25 to 29 years	18,263	15,377	84.2	14,704	80.5	346	14,358	673	4.4	2,886
30 to 34 years	19,547	16,502	84.4	15,921	81.4	333	15,588	581	3.5	3,046
35 to 44 years	44,794	37,842	84.5	36,611	81.7	838	35,773	1,231	3.3	6,952
35 to 39 years	22,464	18,867	84.0	18,223	81.1	423	17,800	644	3.4	3,597
40 to 44 years	22,329	18,975	85.0	18,388	82.3	416	17,972	587	3.1	3,354
45 to 54 years	35,765	29,361	82.1	28,619	80.0	606	28,013	742	2.5	6,404
45 to 49 years	19,383	16,308	84.1	15,867	81.9	361	15,506	441	2.7	3,075
50 to 54 years	16,382	13,053	79.7	12,752	77.8	245	12,507	301	2.3	3,329
55 to 64 years	23,065	13,708	59.4	13,338	57.8	432	12,906	370	2.7	9,357
55 to 59 years	12,739	8,875	69.7	8,639	67.8	234	8,405	236	2.7	3,864
60 to 64 years	10,326	4,833	46.8	4,699	45.5	198	4,501	134	2.8	5,493
65 years and over	32,545	3,972	12.2	3,851	11.8	280	3,571	121	3.1	28,573
65 to 69 years	9,274	2,079	22.4	2,016	21.7	98	1,917	64	3.1	7,195
70 to 74 years	8,633	1,111	12.9	1,080	12.5	78	1,001	31	2.8	7,522
75 years and over	14,637	782	5.3	755	5.2	103	652	26	3.3	13,856
Men										
16 years and over	99,863	75,190	75.3	72,348	72.4	2,617	69,731	2,842	3.8	24,674
16 to 19 years	8,171	4,681	57.3	4,138	50.6	240	3,898	543	11.6	3,490
16 to 17 years	4,142	1,954	47.2	1,708	41.3	114	1,594	246	12.6	2,188
18 to 19 years	4,030	2,727	67.7	2,430	60.3	126	2,304	297	10.9	1,303
20 to 24 years	8,919	7,572	84.9	7,035	78.9	309	6,726	537	7.1	1,348
25 to 54 years	57,977	53,119	91.6	51,622	89.0	1,542	50,080	1,497	2.8	4,858
25 to 34 years	18,470	17,255	93.4	16,647	90.1	487	16,160	608	3.5	1,215
25 to 29 years	8,861	8,216	92.7	7,898	89.1	257	7,641	318	3.9	645
30 to 34 years	9,609	9,039	94.1	8,749	91.0	231	8,519	290	3.2	570
35 to 44 years	22,058	20,444	92.7	19,910	90.3	627	19,283	535	2.6	1,613
35 to 39 years	11,084	10,303	93.0	10,040	90.6	330	9,710	263	2.6	781
40 to 44 years	10,974	10,141	92.4	9,870	89.9	296	9,573	271	2.7	833
45 to 54 years	17,449	15,419	88.4	15,065	86.3	427	14,637	354	2.3	2,030
45 to 49 years	9,487	8,557	90.2	8,352	88.0	268	8,084	206	2.4	929
50 to 54 years	7,962	6,862	86.2	6,713	84.3	160	6,553	148	2.2	1,101
55 to 64 years	10,985	7,478	68.1	7,292	66.4	314	6,978	187	2.5	3,507
55 to 59 years	6,110	4,790	78.4	4,672	76.5	168	4,504	117	2.4	1,320
60 to 64 years	4,875	2,689	55.2	2,619	53.7	145	2,474	70	2.6	2,187
65 years and over	13,811	2,340	16.9	2,261	16.4	213	2,049	79	3.4	11,471
65 to 69 years	4,251	1,199	28.2	1,160	27.3	77	1,083	39	3.2	3,052
70 to 74 years	3,854	666	17.3	650	16.9	56	594	17	2.5	3,188
75 years and over	5,706	475	8.3	451	7.9	80	372	23	4.9	5,231
Women										
16 years and over	108,175	64,900	60.0	61,917	57.2	908	61,008	2,984	4.6	43,275
16 to 19 years	7,890	4,333	54.9	3,824	48.5	69	3,755	508	11.7	3,557
16 to 17 years	3,928	1,762	44.9	1,528	38.9	32	1,497	234	13.3	2,166
18 to 19 years	3,962	2,571	64.9	2,296	58.0	37	2,259	275	10.7	1,391
20 to 24 years	9,080	6,743	74.3	6,223	68.5	73	6,150	520	7.7	2,337
25 to 54 years	60,392	45,963	76.1	44,233	73.2	581	43,652	1,730	3.8	14,429
25 to 34 years	19,340	14,624	75.6	13,978	72.3	191	13,787	646	4.4	4,716
25 to 29 years	9,402	7,161	76.2	6,806	72.4	89	6,717	355	5.0	2,241
30 to 34 years	9,938	7,462	75.1	7,172	72.2	102	7,070	291	3.9	2,476
35 to 44 years	22,736	17,398	76.5	16,701	73.5	211	16,490	697	4.0	5,338
35 to 39 years	11,380	8,563	75.2	8,183	71.9	92	8,090	381	4.4	2,817
40 to 44 years	11,356	8,834	77.8	8,518	75.0	119	8,399	316	3.6	2,521
45 to 54 years	18,316	13,942	76.1	13,554	74.0	179	13,376	388	2.8	4,374
45 to 49 years	9,896	7,750	78.3	7,515	75.9	93	7,422	235	3.0	2,146
50 to 54 years	8,420	6,191	73.5	6,039	71.7	86	5,953	153	2.5	2,228
55 to 64 years	12,080	6,230	51.6	6,047	50.1	118	5,929	183	2.9	5,850
55 to 59 years	6,629	4,086	61.6	3,967	59.8	66	3,901	119	2.9	2,544
60 to 64 years	5,451	2,144	39.3	2,080	38.2	53	2,028	64	3.0	3,306
65 years and over	18,734	1,632	8.7	1,589	8.5	67	1,522	43	2.6	17,102
65 to 69 years	5,024	881	17.5	855	17.0	21	834	25	2.9	4,143
70 to 74 years	4,779	445	9.3	430	9.0	23	408	14	3.3	4,334
75 years and over	8,931	307	3.4	304	3.4	23	281	3	.9	8,624

Source: *Employment and Earnings*, vol. 46, no. 9, September 1999

TABLE 3.4

Employees on nonfarm payrolls by major industry, 1947 to date

(In thousands)

Year and month	Total	Total private	Goods-producing				Service-producing						Government		
			Total	Mining	Construction	Manufacturing	Total	Transportation and public utilities	Wholesale trade	Retail trade	Finance, insurance, and real estate	Services	Federal	State	Local
Annual averages															
1947	43,857	38,382	18,509	955	2,009	15,545	25,348	4,166	2,478	6,477	1,728	5,025	1,892	(1)	(1)
1948	44,866	39,216	18,774	994	2,198	15,582	26,092	4,189	2,612	6,659	1,800	5,181	1,863	(1)	(1)
1949	43,754	37,897	17,565	930	2,194	14,441	26,189	4,001	2,610	6,654	1,828	5,239	1,908	(1)	(1)
1950	45,197	39,170	18,506	901	2,364	15,241	26,691	4,034	2,643	6,743	1,888	5,356	1,928	(1)	(1)
1951	47,819	41,430	19,959	929	2,637	16,393	27,860	4,226	2,735	7,007	1,956	5,547	2,302	(1)	(1)
1952	48,793	42,185	20,198	898	2,668	16,632	28,595	4,248	2,821	7,184	2,035	5,699	2,420	(1)	(1)
1953	50,202	43,556	21,074	866	2,659	17,549	29,128	4,290	2,862	7,385	2,111	5,835	2,305	(1)	(1)
1954	48,990	42,238	19,751	791	2,646	16,314	29,239	4,084	2,875	7,360	2,200	5,969	2,188	(1)	(1)
1955	50,641	43,727	20,513	792	2,839	16,882	30,128	4,141	2,934	7,601	2,298	6,240	2,187	1,168	3,558
1956	52,369	45,091	21,104	822	3,039	17,243	31,264	4,244	3,027	7,831	2,389	6,497	2,209	1,250	3,819
1957	52,855	45,239	20,967	828	2,962	17,176	31,889	4,241	3,037	7,848	2,438	6,708	2,217	1,328	4,071
1958	51,322	43,483	19,513	751	2,817	15,945	31,811	3,976	2,989	7,761	2,481	6,765	2,191	1,415	4,230
1959[2]	53,270	45,186	20,411	732	3,004	16,675	32,857	4,011	3,092	8,035	2,549	7,087	2,233	1,484	4,366
1960	54,189	45,836	20,434	712	2,926	16,796	33,755	4,004	3,153	8,238	2,628	7,378	2,270	1,536	4,547
1961	53,999	45,404	19,857	672	2,859	16,326	34,142	3,903	3,142	8,195	2,688	7,619	2,279	1,607	4,708
1962	55,549	46,660	20,451	650	2,948	16,853	35,098	3,906	3,207	8,359	2,754	7,982	2,340	1,668	4,881
1963	56,653	47,429	20,640	635	3,010	16,995	36,013	3,903	3,258	8,520	2,830	8,277	2,358	1,747	5,121
1964	58,283	48,686	21,005	634	3,097	17,274	37,278	3,951	3,347	8,812	2,911	8,660	2,348	1,856	5,392
1965	60,763	50,689	21,926	632	3,232	18,062	38,839	4,036	3,477	9,239	2,977	9,036	2,378	1,996	5,700
1966	63,901	53,116	23,158	627	3,317	19,214	40,743	4,158	3,608	9,637	3,058	9,498	2,564	2,141	6,080
1967	65,803	54,413	23,308	613	3,248	19,447	42,495	4,268	3,700	9,906	3,185	10,045	2,719	2,302	6,371
1968	67,897	56,058	23,737	606	3,350	19,781	44,158	4,318	3,791	10,308	3,337	10,567	2,737	2,442	6,660
1969	70,384	58,189	24,361	619	3,575	20,167	46,023	4,442	3,919	10,785	3,512	11,169	2,758	2,533	6,904
1970	70,880	58,325	23,578	623	3,588	19,367	47,302	4,515	4,006	11,034	3,645	11,548	2,731	2,664	7,158
1971	71,211	58,331	22,935	609	3,704	18,623	48,276	4,476	4,014	11,338	3,772	11,797	2,696	2,747	7,437
1972	73,675	60,341	23,668	628	3,889	19,151	50,007	4,541	4,127	11,822	3,908	12,276	2,684	2,859	7,790
1973	76,790	63,058	24,893	642	4,097	20,154	51,897	4,656	4,291	12,315	4,046	12,857	2,663	2,923	8,146
1974	78,265	64,095	24,794	697	4,020	20,077	53,471	4,725	4,447	12,539	4,148	13,441	2,724	3,039	8,407
1975	76,945	62,259	22,600	752	3,525	18,323	54,345	4,542	4,430	12,630	4,165	13,892	2,748	3,179	8,758
1976	79,382	64,511	23,352	779	3,576	18,997	56,030	4,582	4,562	13,193	4,271	14,551	2,733	3,273	8,865
1977	82,471	67,344	24,346	813	3,851	19,682	58,125	4,713	4,723	13,792	4,467	15,302	2,727	3,377	9,023
1978	86,697	71,026	25,585	851	4,229	20,505	61,113	4,923	4,985	14,556	4,724	16,252	2,753	3,474	9,446
1979	89,823	73,876	26,461	958	4,463	21,040	63,363	5,136	5,221	14,972	4,975	17,112	2,773	3,541	9,633
1980	90,406	74,166	25,658	1,027	4,346	20,285	64,748	5,146	5,292	15,018	5,160	17,890	2,866	3,610	9,765
1981	91,152	75,121	25,497	1,139	4,188	20,170	65,655	5,165	5,375	15,171	5,298	18,615	2,772	3,640	9,619
1982	89,544	73,707	23,812	1,128	3,904	18,780	65,732	5,081	5,295	15,158	5,340	19,021	2,739	3,640	9,458
1983	90,152	74,282	23,330	952	3,946	18,432	66,821	4,952	5,283	15,587	5,466	19,664	2,774	3,662	9,434
1984	94,408	78,384	24,718	966	4,380	19,372	69,690	5,156	5,568	16,512	5,684	20,746	2,807	3,734	9,482
1985	97,387	80,992	24,842	927	4,668	19,248	72,544	5,233	5,727	17,315	5,948	21,927	2,875	3,832	9,687
1986	99,344	82,651	24,533	777	4,810	18,947	74,811	5,247	5,761	17,880	6,273	22,957	2,899	3,893	9,901
1987	101,958	84,948	24,674	717	4,958	18,999	77,284	5,362	5,848	18,422	6,533	24,110	2,943	3,967	10,100
1988	105,209	87,823	25,125	713	5,098	19,314	80,084	5,512	6,030	19,023	6,630	25,504	2,971	4,076	10,339
1989	107,884	90,105	25,254	692	5,171	19,391	82,630	5,614	6,187	19,475	6,668	26,907	2,988	4,182	10,609
1990	109,403	91,098	24,905	709	5,120	19,076	84,497	5,777	6,173	19,601	6,709	27,934	3,085	4,305	10,914
1991	108,249	89,847	23,745	689	4,650	18,406	84,504	5,755	6,081	19,284	6,646	28,336	2,966	4,355	11,081
1992	108,601	89,956	23,231	635	4,492	18,104	85,370	5,718	5,997	19,356	6,602	29,052	2,969	4,408	11,267
1993	110,713	91,872	23,352	610	4,668	18,075	87,361	5,811	5,981	19,773	6,757	30,197	2,915	4,488	11,438
1994	114,163	95,036	23,908	601	4,986	18,321	90,256	5,984	6,162	20,507	6,896	31,579	2,870	4,576	11,682
1995	117,191	97,885	24,265	581	5,160	18,524	92,925	6,132	6,378	21,187	6,806	33,117	2,822	4,635	11,849
1996	119,608	100,189	24,493	580	5,418	18,495	95,115	6,253	6,482	21,597	6,911	34,454	2,757	4,606	12,056
1997	122,690	103,133	24,962	596	5,691	18,675	97,727	6,408	6,648	21,966	7,109	36,040	2,699	4,582	12,276
1998	125,826	106,007	25,347	590	5,985	18,772	100,480	6,600	6,831	22,296	7,407	37,526	2,686	4,612	12,521
Monthly data, seasonally adjusted															
1998:															
August	126,170	106,301	25,344	585	6,005	18,754	100,826	6,625	6,846	22,353	7,445	37,688	2,688	4,633	12,548
September	126,361	106,470	25,333	583	6,009	18,741	101,028	6,637	6,871	22,382	7,467	37,780	2,689	4,647	12,555
October	126,567	106,654	25,306	578	6,042	18,686	101,261	6,657	6,876	22,392	7,494	37,929	2,711	4,633	12,569
November	126,841	106,893	25,298	574	6,085	18,639	101,543	6,671	6,891	22,443	7,520	38,070	2,723	4,637	12,588
December	127,186	107,213	25,354	570	6,173	18,611	101,832	6,684	6,901	22,525	7,542	38,207	2,701	4,652	12,620
1999:															
January	127,378	107,386	25,315	560	6,170	18,585	102,063	6,708	6,924	22,556	7,570	38,313	2,702	4,644	12,646
February	127,730	107,676	25,329	553	6,238	18,538	102,401	6,723	6,937	22,648	7,581	38,458	2,713	4,670	12,671
March	127,813	107,726	25,285	550	6,232	18,503	102,528	6,732	6,947	22,611	7,595	38,556	2,710	4,680	12,697
April	128,134	108,035	25,288	538	6,277	18,473	102,846	6,750	6,965	22,724	7,611	38,697	2,688	4,688	12,723
May	128,162	108,085	25,199	531	6,239	18,429	102,963	6,758	6,977	22,748	7,621	38,782	2,666	4,677	12,734
June	128,443	108,338	25,180	526	6,258	18,396	103,263	6,781	6,993	22,796	7,636	38,952	2,664	4,675	12,766
July[p]	128,781	108,625	25,248	529	6,272	18,447	103,533	6,797	7,011	22,895	7,644	39,030	2,657	4,683	12,816
August[p]	128,905	108,702	25,153	526	6,243	18,384	103,752	6,809	7,031	22,892	7,655	39,162	2,659	4,701	12,843

[1] Not available.

[2] Data include Alaska and Hawaii beginning in 1959. This inclusion resulted in an increase of 212,000 (0.4 percent) in the nonfarm total for the March 1959 benchmark month.

[p] = preliminary.

NOTE: Establishment survey estimates are currently projected from March 1998 benchmark levels. When more recent benchmark data are introduced, all unadjusted data (beginning April 1998) and all seasonally adjusted data (beginning January 1995) are subject to revision.

Source: *Employment and Earnings*, vol. 46, no. 9, September 1999

TABLE 3.5

The 10 industries with the fastest wage and salary employment growth, 1998-2008
(Numbers in thousands of jobs)

Industry	Employment		Change	
	1998	2008	Number	Percent
Computer and data processing services	1,599	3,472	1,872	117
Health services, not elsewhere classified	1,209	2,018	809	67
Residential care	747	1,171	424	57
Management and public relations	1,034	1,500	466	45
Personnel supply services	3,230	4,623	1,393	43
Miscellaneous equipment rental and leasing	258	369	111	43
Museums, botanical and zoological gardens	93	131	39	42
Research and testing services	614	861	247	40
Miscellaneous transportation services	236	329	94	40
Security and commodity brokers	645	900	255	40

Source: *BLS Releases New 1998-2008 Employment Projections*, Bureau of Labor Statistics, Washington, DC, November 30, 1999

Over the 1998-2008 period, the Bureau of Labor Statistics (BLS) expects the service-producing industries to account for virtually all of the job growth. Table 3.5 shows the 10 industries projected to grow the fastest. Half of these fastest-growing industries belong to four industry groups: health services, business services, social services, and engineering, management, and related services. These four industries are expected to account for nearly half of all nonfarm wage and salary jobs added to the economy over the next decade.

Over the past decade (1988-1998), in the goods-producing area, only the construction industry has employed a growing number of workers, while the numbers working in mining have fallen significantly, and manufacturing has managed to stay somewhat level. Nonetheless, from 1947 to 1998, the proportion of manufacturing jobs has fallen from 35 percent of all jobs to 15 percent. Manufacturing jobs are expected to decline even further by 2008, while construction will be the only goods-producing industry to add jobs in the next decade.

About 19.8 million persons (about 16 percent of the nonfarm working population) worked for the government in 1998. Between 1990 and 1998, the federal government lost 13 percent of its workers, while state and local government workforces increased by 7 and 15 percent, respectively.

OCCUPATIONS

In August 1999, an almost equal proportion of workers was employed in managerial or professional areas and in technical, sales, or administrative support fields (30.2 percent and 29 percent, respectively). Other leading occupational categories were service occupations* (13.7); operators, fabricators, and laborers (13.6 percent); and precision production, craft, and repair (10.7 percent). (See Table 3.6.) Professional specialty occupations and service workers — on opposite ends of educational and earnings categories — are projected to account for 45 percent of job growth over the 1998-2008 period.

Of the 10 occupations projected to grow the fastest over the next decade, the top five are computer-related (often referred to as information technology occupations). (See Table 3.7.) Table 3.8 shows the 10 occupations expected to add the most jobs between 1998 and 2008. These 10 occupa-

---

* It is important to understand the difference between a service industry and a service occupation. A service industry provides a service to the economy but employs more than service workers. For example, a restaurant is a service industry. It may employ workers involved in service, but it also employs secretaries, managers, and accountants, whose occupations are not considered service occupations.

TABLE 3.6

Employed persons by occupation, race, and sex

(Percent distribution)

Occupation and race	Total		Men		Women	
	Aug. 1998	Aug. 1999	Aug. 1998	Aug. 1999	Aug. 1998	Aug. 1999
TOTAL						
Total, 16 years and over (thousands)	132,206	134,264	71,537	72,348	60,669	61,917
Percent	100.0	100.0	100.0	100.0	100.0	100.0
Managerial and professional specialty	29.2	30.2	27.9	28.6	30.6	32.0
Executive, administrative, and managerial	14.5	14.5	15.1	15.0	13.9	13.9
Professional specialty	14.6	15.6	12.8	13.6	16.7	18.1
Technical, sales, and administrative support	29.5	29.0	19.8	19.4	41.1	40.3
Technicians and related support	3.3	3.3	2.9	2.9	3.7	3.7
Sales occupations	12.2	12.1	11.2	11.1	13.3	13.3
Administrative support, including clerical	14.1	13.7	5.7	5.4	24.0	23.3
Service occupations	13.7	13.7	10.2	10.4	17.8	17.5
Private household	.6	.6	.1	.1	1.3	1.3
Protective service	1.9	2.0	2.9	3.0	.8	.8
Service, except private household and protective	11.1	11.1	7.3	7.3	15.7	15.4
Precision production, craft, and repair	10.9	10.7	18.4	18.1	2.0	2.0
Operators, fabricators, and laborers	13.7	13.6	19.2	19.2	7.3	7.0
Machine operators, assemblers, and inspectors	5.9	5.4	6.8	6.2	4.7	4.4
Transportation and material moving occupations	3.9	4.1	6.6	6.9	.8	.8
Handlers, equipment cleaners, helpers, and laborers	3.9	4.1	5.8	6.1	1.8	1.7
Farming, forestry, and fishing	3.0	2.9	4.5	4.2	1.3	1.2
White						
Total, 16 years and over (thousands)	111,511	112,846	61,328	61,901	50,183	50,945
Percent	100.0	100.0	100.0	100.0	100.0	100.0
Managerial and professional specialty	30.3	31.1	29.0	29.5	32.0	33.1
Executive, administrative, and managerial	15.3	15.3	16.0	15.9	14.5	14.5
Professional specialty	15.0	15.9	13.0	13.6	17.4	18.6
Technical, sales, and administrative support	29.6	29.1	19.8	19.6	41.5	40.6
Technicians and related support	3.2	3.3	2.8	2.9	3.7	3.7
Sales occupations	12.5	12.5	11.7	11.6	13.4	13.5
Administrative support, including clerical	13.9	13.3	5.3	5.0	24.4	23.4
Service occupations	12.4	12.5	9.0	9.2	16.5	16.6
Private household	.6	.6	.1	.1	1.3	1.3
Protective service	1.8	1.8	2.7	2.7	.7	.7
Service, except private household and protective	10.0	10.1	6.3	6.4	14.5	14.6
Precision production, craft, and repair	11.3	11.3	19.1	18.9	1.9	2.0
Operators, fabricators, and laborers	13.1	12.9	18.3	18.3	6.7	6.3
Machine operators, assemblers, and inspectors	5.5	5.0	6.6	6.0	4.2	3.9
Transportation and material moving occupations	3.8	3.9	6.3	6.6	.7	.8
Handlers, equipment cleaners, helpers, and laborers	3.8	3.9	5.5	5.7	1.7	1.6
Farming, forestry, and fishing	3.3	3.1	4.8	4.6	1.5	1.4
Black						
Total, 16 years and over (thousands)	14,663	15,156	6,950	7,124	7,713	8,033
Percent	100.0	100.0	100.0	100.0	100.0	100.0
Managerial and professional specialty	19.2	21.3	15.8	17.8	22.3	24.4
Executive, administrative, and managerial	9.6	9.4	8.5	8.0	10.6	10.5
Professional specialty	9.6	11.9	7.3	9.7	11.7	13.9
Technical, sales, and administrative support	29.3	29.6	18.3	18.4	39.3	39.5
Technicians and related support	3.3	3.1	3.1	2.4	3.5	3.7
Sales occupations	9.8	9.2	7.1	7.2	12.3	10.9
Administrative support, including clerical	16.1	17.2	8.0	8.7	23.4	24.8
Service occupations	22.9	21.4	19.7	18.6	25.9	23.9
Private household	.5	.7	.1	.1	.9	1.2
Protective service	3.6	3.6	5.8	5.6	1.6	1.8
Service, except private household and protective	18.8	17.2	13.8	12.9	23.3	20.9
Precision production, craft, and repair	7.9	7.3	14.7	13.3	1.8	1.9
Operators, fabricators, and laborers	19.1	19.2	28.7	29.5	10.5	10.0
Machine operators, assemblers, and inspectors	7.9	7.8	9.0	8.8	6.8	6.8
Transportation and material moving occupations	5.9	6.0	10.7	11.3	1.5	1.2
Handlers, equipment cleaners, helpers, and laborers	5.4	5.4	8.9	9.4	2.1	1.9
Farming, forestry, and fishing	1.5	1.3	2.9	2.4	.3	.3

NOTE: Beginning in January 1999, data reflect revised population controls used in the household survey.

Source: *Employment and Earnings*, vol. 46, no. 9, September 1999

tions will account for nearly one-fifth of total employment growth.

Women are far more likely than men to work in administrative support, including clerical, and in service occupations. Men dominate such categories as precision production, craft, and repair; operators, fabricators, and laborers; and farming, forestry, and fishing. (See Table 3.6.)

Blacks are less likely than Whites to work in managerial and professional specialties, sales, and precision production positions. Blacks are more likely than Whites to work as operators, fabricators, and laborers and in service occupations. Black women are more likely to be in managerial and professional specialties and sales and administrative support than Black men. (See Table 3.6.)

THE UNEMPLOYED

The U.S. unemployment rate reached a post-World War II high of 9.7 percent in 1982. It remained high at 9.6 percent in 1983 as the result of the most severe economic recession since the Great Depression of the 1930s. The unemployment rate then dropped, approaching 5 percent in 1989, but again began increasing, staying just under 7 percent for most of 1991 and rising to 7.5 percent in 1992. As the economy improved, the rate fell to 6.9 percent in 1993. By 1998, the U.S. unemployment rate dropped to 4.5 percent. (See Table 3.9.) By August 1999, the rate had fallen to 4.2 percent, due to a booming economy. However, some previously laid-off workers, especially those over 55 years old, had stopped looking for work and were not counted in the unemployment rate (see below).

TABLE 3.7

The 10 fastest growing occupations, 1998-2008
(Numbers in thousands of jobs)

Occupation	Employment		Change	
	1998	2008	Number	Percent
Computer engineers	299	622	323	108
Computer support specialists	429	869	439	102
Systems analysts	617	1,194	577	94
Database administrators	87	155	67	77
Desktop publishing specialists	26	44	19	73
Paralegals and legal assistants	136	220	84	62
Personal care and home health aides	746	1,179	433	58
Medical assistants	252	398	146	58
Social and human service assistants	268	410	141	53
Physician assistants	66	98	32	48

TABLE 3.8

The 10 occupations with the largest job growth, 1998-2008
(Numbers in thousands of jobs)

Occupation	Employment		Change	
	1998	2008	Number	Percent
Systems analysts	617	1,194	577	94
Retail salespersons	4,056	4,620	563	14
Cashiers	3,198	3,754	556	17
General managers and top executives	3,362	3,913	551	16
Truck drivers, light and heavy	2,970	3,463	493	17
Office clerks, general	3,021	3,484	463	15
Registered nurses	2,079	2,530	451	22
Computer support specialists	429	869	439	102
Personal care and home health aides	746	1,179	433	58
Teacher assistants	1,192	1,567	375	31

Source of both tables: *BLS Releases New 1998-2008 Employment Projections*, Bureau of Labor Statistics, Washington, DC, November 30, 1999

TABLE 3.9

Unemployment rates, approximating U.S. concepts, in nine countries, quarterly data seasonally adjusted

Country	Annual average		1997				1998		
	1997	1998	I	II	III	IV	I	II	III
United States..........................	4.9	4.5	5.2	5.0	4.9	4.7	4.6	4.4	4.5
Canada..................................	9.2	8.3	9.6	9.4	9.0	8.9	8.6	8.4	8.3
Australia................................	8.6	8.0	8.7	8.7	8.6	8.3	8.1	8.1	8.2
Japan....................................	3.4	4.1	3.3	3.4	3.4	3.5	3.7	4.2	4.3
France...................................	12.4	11.8	12.4	12.5	12.5	12.3	12.0	11.8	11.7
Germany................................	7.8	7.5	7.7	7.8	7.8	7.8	7.7	7.6	7.4
Italy[1]..................................	12.3	12.3	12.3	12.3	12.2	12.3	12.2	12.3	12.4
Sweden..................................	10.1	8.4	10.9	10.6	9.7	9.1	8.7	8.6	8.4
United Kingdom.......................	7.0	6.3	7.4	7.2	6.9	6.6	6.4	6.2	6.3

[1] Quarterly rates are for the first month of the quarter.
− Data not available.

NOTE: Quarterly figures for France, Germany, and the United Kingdom are calculated by applying annual adjustment factors to current published data, and therefore should be viewed as less precise indica... unemployment under U.S. concepts than the annual figures. See on the data" for information on breaks in series. For further qualif... and historical data, see *Comparative Labor Force Statistics, 10 Co*... (Bureau of Labor Statistics, August 1996).

Source: *Monthly Labor Review*, vol. 122, no. 7, July 1999

In 1998, the United States had one of the lowest unemployment rates of the industrialized countries. Japan (4.1 percent) had the lowest rate, although it was much higher than Japan's 1991 rate of 2.1 percent. Italy (12.3 percent) and France (11.8 percent) had particularly high rates. (See Table 3.9.)

Unemployment rates in the United States vary from state to state. In April 1999, Washington, DC (6.8 percent), West Virginia (6.7 percent), New Mexico (6.4 percent), and Alaska (5.9 percent) had the highest unemployment rates. Minnesota (2.1 percent), New Hampshire and South Dakota (2.4

TABLE 3.10

Unemployment rates by State, seasonally adjusted

State	Apr. 1998	Mar. 1999	Apr. 1999[P]	State	Apr. 1998	Mar. 1999	Apr. 1999[P]
Alabama..................................	4.3	4.4	4.6	Missouri..................................	4.5	2.9	3.2
Alaska....................................	5.6	6.3	5.9	Montana.................................	5.7	5.4	5.4
Arizona..................................	4.3	4.2	4.3	Nebraska................................	2.7	2.3	2.5
Arkansas................................	5.6	4.4	4.3	Nevada..................................	4.8	3.8	4.1
California................................	5.9	5.8	5.6	New Hampshire.......................	3.0	3.0	2.4
Colorado................................	4.0	2.7	3.0	New Jersey.............................	4.7	4.5	4.5
Connecticut............................	3.4	3.2	3.4	New Mexico............................	6.0	6.2	6.4
Delaware................................	4.1	3.2	3.3	New York................................	5.7	5.0	5.0
District of Columbia..................	9.2	7.2	6.8	North Carolina.........................	3.6	3.2	2.8
Florida...................................	4.4	4.2	4.2	North Dakota...........................	3.2	2.9	2.6
Georgia..................................	4.3	4.2	3.9	Ohio......................................	4.1	3.9	4.2
Hawaii....................................	6.1	5.9	5.5	Oklahoma...............................	4.5	4.3	4.1
Idaho.....................................	5.0	4.7	4.7	Oregon...................................	5.5	5.6	5.3
Illinois...................................	4.3	3.8	3.9	Pennsylvania...........................	4.6	4.4	4.2
Indiana...................................	3.0	2.6	2.5	Rhode Island...........................	5.2	3.0	3.1
Iowa......................................	2.8	2.7	2.7	South Carolina.........................	3.6	3.7	4.2
Kansas...................................	3.9	3.5	3.3	South Dakota...........................	2.9	2.5	2.4
Kentucky................................	4.8	4.3	4.2	Tennessee..............................	4.3	4.3	4.1
Louisiana...............................	6.0	5.1	5.1	Texas....................................	4.7	4.5	4.6
Maine....................................	4.2	3.4	3.6	Utah......................................	4.0	3.4	3.0
Maryland................................	4.8	3.7	3.8	Vermont.................................	3.2	3.1	2.6
Massachusetts........................	3.2	2.8	2.9	Virginia..................................	2.8	2.8	2.7
Michigan................................	3.7	4.0	3.9	Washington.............................	4.6	4.6	4.5
Minnesota..............................	2.4	2.2	2.1	West Virginia...........................	6.9	6.7	6.7
Mississippi.............................	5.5	5.1	4.6	Wisconsin...............................	2.9	3.2	3.1
				Wyoming................................	4.8	4.4	4.4

[P] = preliminary

Source: *Monthly Labor Review*, vol. 122, no. 7, July 1999

TABLE 3.11

Unemployment rates by sex and age, monthly data seasonally adjusted

[Civilian workers]

Sex and age	Annual average		1998								1999				
	1997	1998	May	June	July	Aug.	Sept.	Oct.	Nov.	Dec.	Jan.	Feb.	Mar.	Apr.	May
Total, 16 years and over	4.9	4.5	4.4	4.5	4.5	4.5	4.5	4.5	4.4	4.3	4.3	4.4	4.2	4.3	4.2
16 to 24 years	11.3	10.4	10.2	10.6	10.4	10.8	10.9	10.5	9.9	9.8	10.1	10.2	10.0	10.0	9.4
16 to 19 years	16.0	14.6	14.3	14.8	14.2	14.9	15.2	15.7	15.0	14.0	15.5	14.1	14.3	14.1	12.6
16 to 17 years	18.2	17.2	16.3	18.0	15.7	17.1	17.6	18.2	18.0	16.9	18.4	15.5	16.6	16.9	15.9
18 to 19 years	14.5	12.8	13.1	12.6	13.1	13.5	13.5	14.0	13.0	12.1	13.1	13.1	12.8	12.3	10.6
20 to 24 years	8.5	7.9	7.7	8.1	8.2	8.4	8.2	7.3	6.9	7.2	6.9	7.7	7.4	7.6	7.5
25 years and over	3.8	3.4	3.3	3.4	3.4	3.3	3.4	3.4	3.3	3.3	3.2	3.3	3.1	3.2	3.2
25 to 54 years	3.9	3.5	3.4	3.5	3.5	3.5	3.5	3.5	3.4	3.4	3.3	3.4	3.1	3.3	3.2
55 years and over	3.0	2.7	2.5	2.6	2.8	2.6	2.7	2.7	3.0	3.0	2.9	2.9	2.9	2.9	2.6
Men, 16 years and over	4.9	4.4	4.3	4.4	4.5	4.4	4.5	4.4	4.3	4.3	4.2	4.3	3.9	4.1	4.2
16 to 24 years	11.8	11.1	11.1	11.1	11.3	11.3	11.9	10.9	10.3	10.8	10.7	10.1	9.9	10.5	10.2
16 to 19 years	16.9	16.2	15.9	15.9	15.9	15.9	17.4	16.7	16.5	16.4	16.9	14.6	15.0	14.8	13.3
16 to 17 years	19.1	19.1	18.3	20.5	18.0	18.9	20.2	20.9	20.0	19.9	19.7	15.3	16.9	19.2	17.7
18 to 19 years	15.4	14.1	14.5	12.9	14.3	14.2	15.1	13.7	14.4	14.0	14.7	14.1	13.6	12.2	10.6
20 to 24 years	8.9	8.1	8.3	8.3	8.5	8.5	8.6	7.5	6.6	7.3	7.1	7.5	7.0	8.0	8.3
25 years and over	3.6	3.2	3.1	3.2	3.3	3.2	3.2	3.2	3.1	3.2	3.1	3.2	2.7	2.9	3.1
25 to 54 years	3.7	3.3	3.2	3.3	3.4	3.3	3.2	3.3	3.1	3.1	3.1	3.3	2.8	2.9	3.1
55 years and over	3.1	2.8	2.5	2.5	3.0	2.6	3.0	2.9	3.1	3.1	2.8	3.0	2.6	2.6	2.7
Women, 16 years and over	5.0	4.6	4.5	4.7	4.5	4.7	4.5	4.7	4.6	4.3	4.3	4.5	4.5	4.6	4.1
16 to 24 years	10.7	9.8	9.2	10.1	9.5	10.4	9.8	10.1	9.5	8.7	9.5	10.2	10.0	9.5	8.6
16 to 19 years	15.0	12.9	12.6	13.6	12.2	13.8	12.9	14.8	13.3	11.3	13.9	13.7	13.6	13.4	11.8
16 to 17 years	17.2	15.1	14.2	15.1	13.2	15.5	14.9	15.4	15.9	13.8	16.9	15.7	16.2	14.5	13.8
18 to 19 years	13.6	11.5	11.6	12.3	11.7	12.8	11.9	14.3	11.4	10.2	11.5	12.1	11.9	12.5	10.6
20 to 24 years	8.1	7.8	7.0	7.9	7.7	8.2	7.8	7.1	7.1	7.1	6.7	8.0	7.8	7.1	6.7
25 years and over	3.9	3.6	3.6	3.6	3.5	3.5	3.6	3.6	3.6	3.5	3.4	3.3	3.4	3.6	3.2
25 to 54 years	4.1	3.8	3.7	3.7	3.6	3.7	3.7	3.8	3.8	3.6	3.5	3.5	3.5	3.7	3.4
55 years and over	2.9	2.6	2.5	2.6	2.6	2.7	2.3	2.5	2.9	2.8	3.1	2.7	3.2	3.3	2.6

TABLE 3.12

Selected unemployment indicators, monthly data seasonally adjusted

[Unemployment rates]

Selected categories	Annual average		1998								1999				
	1997	1998	May	June	July	Aug.	Sept.	Oct.	Nov.	Dec.	Jan.	Feb.	Mar.	Apr.	May
Characteristic															
Total, all workers	4.9	4.5	4.4	4.5	4.5	4.5	4.5	4.5	4.4	4.3	4.3	4.4	4.2	4.3	4.2
Both sexes, 16 to 19 years	16.0	14.6	14.3	14.8	14.2	14.9	15.2	15.7	15.0	14.0	15.5	14.1	14.3	14.1	12.6
Men, 20 years and over	4.2	3.7	3.6	3.7	3.8	3.7	3.7	3.6	3.5	3.6	3.4	3.7	3.2	3.4	3.6
Women, 20 years and over	4.4	4.1	3.9	4.1	4.0	4.0	4.0	4.0	4.0	3.9	3.7	3.8	3.9	4.1	3.6
White, total	4.2	3.9	3.8	4.0	3.8	3.9	3.9	3.9	3.8	3.8	3.8	3.8	3.6	3.8	3.7
Both sexes, 16 to 19 years	13.6	12.6	12.2	13.4	11.5	12.9	12.8	13.5	13.0	12.6	13.0	11.8	11.9	12.1	11.0
Men, 16 to 19 years	14.3	14.1	14.0	14.4	13.2	14.2	14.7	14.1	14.1	14.5	14.1	12.2	12.6	11.9	10.9
Women, 16 to 19 years	12.8	10.9	10.1	12.3	9.7	11.5	10.8	13.0	11.6	10.6	11.9	11.4	11.1	11.6	10.1
Men, 20 years and over	3.6	3.2	3.2	3.3	3.3	3.3	3.3	3.2	3.1	3.2	3.1	3.3	2.8	3.0	3.2
Women, 20 years and over	3.7	3.4	3.3	3.4	3.4	3.5	3.4	3.4	3.4	3.3	3.3	3.2	3.3	3.6	3.2
Black, total	10.0	8.9	8.9	8.5	9.6	8.9	9.0	8.6	8.6	7.9	7.8	8.3	8.1	7.7	7.5
Both sexes, 16 to 19 years	32.4	27.6	29.9	22.5	28.1	29.2	28.1	29.2	28.7	27.5	29.8	29.2	31.0	28.1	24.1
Men, 16 to 19 years	36.5	30.1	31.2	22.4	30.2	29.7	32.7	34.7	33.0	27.3	34.2	31.6	32.9	33.0	26.2
Women, 16 to 19 years	28.7	25.3	27.4	22.6	27.0	26.8	25.7	23.5	22.1	17.6	25.0	27.0	29.1	23.5	22.0
Men, 20 years and over	8.5	7.4	6.9	7.1	8.7	7.6	7.1	6.9	7.0	6.7	5.9	6.7	5.8	6.1	6.6
Women, 20 years and over	8.8	7.9	8.3	7.8	7.9	7.6	7.9	7.5	7.6	7.0	6.6	7.1	7.2	6.8	6.4
Hispanic origin, total	7.7	7.2	6.9	7.5	7.2	7.4	7.4	7.3	7.3	7.6	6.6	6.7	5.8	6.9	6.7
Married men, spouse present	2.7	2.4	2.4	2.2	2.3	2.3	2.3	2.3	2.2	2.3	2.3	2.4	2.1	2.3	2.4
Married women, spouse present	3.1	2.9	2.8	2.9	2.8	3.1	2.7	2.8	2.9	2.8	2.8	2.8	2.7	2.9	2.5
Women who maintain families	8.1	7.2	7.5	7.1	6.9	6.8	7.6	6.9	6.9	6.3	6.1	6.5	6.7	7.2	6.0
Full-time workers	4.8	4.3	4.3	4.4	4.4	4.4	4.3	4.3	4.2	4.2	4.1	4.3	4.0	4.2	4.0
Part-time workers	5.5	5.3	4.9	5.2	5.2	5.3	5.3	5.5	5.4	5.2	5.2	4.9	4.9	4.9	5.1
Industry															
Nonagricultural wage and salary workers	5.0	4.6	4.5	4.6	4.6	4.7	4.8	4.6	4.5	4.4	4.3	4.3	4.2	4.4	4.2
Mining	3.8	3.2	1.6	4.0	3.9	3.6	3.0	2.4	2.2	4.3	7.4	7.7	5.3	9.3	5.9
Construction	9.0	7.5	8.0	7.9	6.8	7.4	8.6	6.7	7.0	6.4	7.3	7.5	6.7	7.4	7.2
Manufacturing	4.2	3.9	3.6	3.6	4.3	3.9	4.0	3.9	3.8	4.0	3.5	3.7	3.4	3.3	3.4
Durable goods	3.5	3.4	3.0	3.0	4.1	3.5	3.7	3.2	3.2	3.4	3.4	3.3	2.9	3.1	3.3
Nondurable goods	5.1	4.7	4.6	4.6	4.6	4.5	4.6	5.1	4.8	4.9	3.8	4.3	4.1	3.7	3.6
Transportation and public utilities	3.5	3.4	3.1	3.5	3.4	3.5	3.5	3.5	3.2	3.2	2.5	3.2	2.9	2.8	3.3
Wholesale and retail trade	6.2	5.5	5.3	5.6	5.6	5.6	5.7	5.6	5.2	5.5	5.2	5.2	5.4	5.4	5.3
Finance, insurance, and real estate	3.0	2.5	2.1	2.2	2.1	2.7	2.4	2.5	2.8	2.8	2.4	2.4	1.9	3.2	2.1
Services	4.6	4.5	4.7	4.6	4.6	4.7	4.5	4.7	4.6	4.1	4.1	4.0	4.2	4.1	3.9
Government workers	2.6	2.3	2.4	2.2	2.4	2.2	2.2	2.2	2.1	2.0	2.2	2.3	2.1	2.5	2.6
Agricultural wage and salary workers	9.1	8.3	8.0	8.4	8.2	7.4	7.9	6.7	7.6	8.3	9.6	11.3	9.5	9.7	10.7

Source of both tables: *Monthly Labor Review*, vol. 122, no. 7, July 1999 percent each), and Indiana and Nebraska (2.5 percent each) had the lowest rates. (See Table 3.10.)

Age

Unemployment does not occur evenly in all occupations or sectors of society. Workers under 25 years of age are far more likely to be unemployed than older workers. (See Table 3.11.) Their jobs are frequently more marginal, and younger workers leave their jobs more often than older ones do. They also have less seniority to protect themselves against layoffs.

Race

In May 1999, Blacks (7.5 percent) and Hispanics (6.7 percent) were considerably more likely to be out of work than Whites (3.7 percent). Many Blacks work in occupations that have suffered as the American economy has changed from an industrial to a service economy. In May 1999, Black teenagers experienced an unemployment rate of about 24.1 percent, compared to 11.0 percent for White teenagers. Black male teenagers were more likely to be unemployed than Black female teenagers. (See Table 3.12.)

Occupations and Industries

Some occupations are more susceptible to unemployment than others. People working in managerial and professional specialties were much less likely to find themselves unemployed than those laboring as operators, fabricators, and laborers. (See Table 3.13.) In 1999, those working in the

TABLE 3.13

Unemployed persons by occupation and sex

Occupation	Thousands of persons		Unemployment rates					
	Total		Total		Men		Women	
	Aug. 1998	Aug. 1999	Aug. 1998	Aug. 1999	Aug. 1998	Aug. 1999	Aug. 1998	Aug. 1999
Total, 16 years and over[1]	6,173	5,826	4.5	4.2	4.0	3.8	5.0	4.6
Managerial and professional specialty	858	860	2.2	2.1	1.6	1.9	2.8	2.2
Executive, administrative, and managerial	356	396	1.8	2.0	1.5	1.8	2.3	2.2
Professional specialty	503	464	2.5	2.2	1.7	2.1	3.3	2.2
Technical, sales, and administrative support	1,509	1,443	3.7	3.6	2.9	2.7	4.2	4.0
Technicians and related support	76	97	1.7	2.2	1.2	2.7	2.2	1.7
Sales occupations	748	663	4.4	3.9	3.1	2.4	5.8	5.3
Administrative support, including clerical	684	682	3.5	3.6	3.5	3.4	3.5	3.6
Service occupations	1,306	1,094	6.7	5.6	5.8	5.0	7.4	6.1
Private household	89	83	10.0	9.1	([2])	([2])	10.5	8.9
Protective service	60	90	2.3	3.3	1.4	2.8	5.8	5.4
Service, except private household and protective	1,157	921	7.3	5.8	7.5	5.8	7.2	5.9
Precision production, craft, and repair	606	628	4.1	4.2	3.9	3.8	5.6	7.7
Mechanics and repairers	159	155	3.3	3.2	3.2	2.6	5.3	13.1
Construction trades	268	327	4.5	5.3	4.4	5.2	10.1	10.3
Other precision production, craft, and repair	178	146	4.3	3.7	4.1	3.1	5.1	5.8
Operators, fabricators, and laborers	1,215	1,134	6.3	5.9	6.0	5.3	7.1	7.7
Machine operators, assemblers, and inspectors	415	421	5.1	5.5	4.5	4.3	6.0	7.4
Transportation and material moving occupations	269	231	4.9	4.0	4.4	3.9	9.8	4.7
Handlers, equipment cleaners, helpers, and laborers	531	481	9.3	8.1	9.5	7.7	8.5	9.9
Construction laborers	139	88	13.5	8.2	13.6	7.7	([2])	([2])
Other handlers, equipment cleaners, helpers, and laborers	392	393	8.4	8.1	8.3	7.7	8.4	9.6
Farming, forestry, and fishing	162	163	3.9	4.1	4.0	3.7	3.4	5.5
No previous work experience	506	477	–	–	–	–	–	–
16 to 19 years	340	331	–	–	–	–	–	–
20 to 24 years	81	76	–	–	–	–	–	–
25 years and over	85	70	–	–	–	–	–	–

[1] Includes a small number of persons whose last job was in the Armed Forces.
[2] Data not shown where base is less than 75,000.

NOTE: Beginning in January 1999, data reflect revised population controls used in the household survey.

Source: *Employment and Earnings*, vol. 46, no. 9, September 1999

TABLE 3.14

Unemployed persons by industry and sex

Industry	Thousands of persons		Unemployment rates					
	Total		Total		Men		Women	
	Aug. 1998	Aug. 1999	Aug. 1998	Aug. 1999	Aug. 1998	Aug. 1999	Aug. 1998	Aug. 1999
Total, 16 years and over	6,173	5,826	4.5	4.2	4.0	3.8	5.0	4.6
Nonagricultural private wage and salary workers	4,851	4,448	4.6	4.1	4.2	3.8	5.0	4.6
Mining	23	26	3.7	4.2	3.9	3.8	2.7	7.3
Construction	407	453	5.6	6.0	5.8	5.8	4.3	7.7
Manufacturing	797	756	3.7	3.8	3.4	3.3	4.4	4.9
Durable goods	453	455	3.5	3.7	3.5	3.3	3.5	5.0
Lumber and wood products	46	50	5.7	6.2	6.2	6.4	3.0	5.5
Furniture and fixtures	36	32	4.8	4.9	4.5	4.2	5.6	6.5
Stone, clay, and glass products	17	23	2.7	3.7	2.7	3.5	2.5	4.1
Primary metal industries	46	19	5.7	2.5	6.4	2.6	2.5	2.0
Fabricated metal products	52	44	3.4	3.3	3.9	3.0	2.2	4.2
Machinery and computing equipment	78	86	3.1	3.6	3.3	3.6	2.4	3.4
Electrical machinery, equipment, and supplies	63	58	3.3	3.2	2.8	1.5	4.2	6.1
Transportation equipment	62	93	2.6	4.0	2.3	2.8	3.5	7.9
Automobiles	32	51	2.5	3.8	2.5	2.3	2.3	8.4
Other transportation equipment	30	42	2.7	4.3	2.1	3.4	4.9	7.1
Professional and photographic equipment	15	19	1.9	2.6	.8	3.0	3.5	2.0
Other durable goods industries	38	30	5.1	4.2	5.0	4.1	5.2	4.3
Nondurable goods	344	301	4.1	3.8	3.2	3.2	5.4	4.7
Food and kindred products	87	75	5.0	4.3	4.7	3.3	5.8	6.0
Textile mill products	18	27	2.6	5.2	1.6	5.3	4.0	5.1
Apparel and other textile products	70	69	9.0	9.4	6.1	10.1	10.4	9.1
Paper and allied products	16	17	2.3	2.9	1.5	3.4	4.4	1.4
Printing and publishing	60	52	3.5	3.1	3.4	3.5	3.5	2.7
Chemicals and allied products	17	14	1.2	1.0	1.8	.8	.1	1.3
Rubber and miscellaneous plastics products	54	29	5.2	3.0	2.5	2.1	10.6	5.0
Other nondurable goods industries	21	19	5.7	5.7	5.4	4.5	6.3	8.5
Transportation and public utilities	274	261	3.7	3.3	3.5	3.2	4.3	3.5
Transportation	196	190	4.3	3.9	3.9	3.9	5.4	4.2
Communications and other public utilities	77	71	2.8	2.3	2.6	2.0	3.1	2.8
Wholesale and retail trade	1,483	1,271	5.5	4.7	4.7	4.0	6.3	5.4
Wholesale trade	188	168	3.6	3.3	3.0	2.6	4.9	4.5
Retail trade	1,296	1,104	5.9	5.0	5.3	4.4	6.5	5.6
Finance, insurance, and real estate	210	198	2.6	2.4	2.2	2.0	3.0	2.7
Service industries	1,658	1,482	4.8	4.1	4.3	3.8	5.0	4.3
Professional services	667	588	3.3	2.8	2.5	2.5	3.6	3.0
Other service industries	991	894	6.9	5.9	5.8	4.8	8.0	7.1
Agricultural wage and salary workers	120	148	4.9	6.6	4.4	6.0	6.3	8.4
Government, self-employed, and unpaid family workers	696	753	2.4	2.5	1.9	2.2	3.0	2.8
No previous work experience	506	477	–	–	–	–	–	–

NOTE: Beginning in January 1999, data reflect revised population controls used in the household survey.

Source: *Employment and Earnings*, vol. 46, no. 9, September 1999

construction, lumber and wood products, apparel, and agricultural industries were more likely to find themselves without jobs than those in the primary metal, professional and photographic equipment, paper, chemicals, communications, finance, insurance and real estate, and professional services industries. (See Table 3.14.)

How Long Does Unemployment Last?

In 1998, the average length of unemployment was 14.5 weeks, down from 18.8 weeks in 1994. On average, 42 percent of the unemployed had been unemployed for less than five weeks, and somewhat less than one-third (31 percent) had been out of work for five to 14 weeks. About 12 percent were out of work 15 to 26 weeks and 14 percent for more than 27 weeks. (See Table 3.15.) Men (14.6 weeks in August 1999) tended to stay unemployed somewhat longer than women (11.8 weeks). Generally, the older the job seeker, the longer it took to find work. (See Table 3.16.)

Because better-paying jobs usually take longer to find, men 45 years and older, who were more likely to be seeking higher paying employment than

TABLE 3.15

Duration of unemployment, monthly data seasonally adjusted

[Numbers in thousands]

Weeks of unemployment	Annual average		1998								1999				
	1997	1998	May	June	July	Aug.	Sept.	Oct.	Nov.	Dec.	Jan.	Feb.	Mar.	Apr.	May
Less than 5 weeks..........................	2,538	2,622	2,608	2,553	2,626	2,652	2,638	2,754	2,546	2,614	2,353	2,601	2,478	2,788	2,467
5 to 14 weeks..........................	2,138	1,950	1,967	2,022	1,975	1,956	1,968	1,896	1,983	1,839	2,071	1,944	1,891	1,867	1,816
15 weeks and over..........................	2,062	1,637	1,509	1,641	1,606	1,644	1,636	1,598	1,611	1,578	1,469	1,550	1,434	1,446	1,523
15 to 26 weeks..........................	995	763	671	833	783	810	732	732	752	754	753	766	736	773	794
27 weeks and over..........................	1,067	875	838	808	823	834	904	866	859	824	716	784	697	673	729
Mean duration, in weeks...............	15.8	14.5	14.7	14.1	14.3	13.7	14.3	14.1	14.4	14.1	13.4	13.8	13.5	13.1	13.4
Median duration, in weeks..............	8.0	6.7	6.1	6.7	6.7	6.8	6.6	5.9	6.7	6.7	6.9	7.0	6.9	6.1	6.7

Source: *Monthly Labor Review*, vol. 122, no. 7, July 1999

TABLE 3.16

Unemployed persons by age, sex, race, marital status, and duration of unemployment

Sex, age, race, and marital status	August 1999							
	Thousands of persons						Weeks	
	Total	Less than 5 weeks	5 to 14 weeks	15 weeks and over			Average (mean) duration	Median duration
				Total	15 to 26 weeks	27 weeks and over		
TOTAL								
Total, 16 years and over	5,826	2,498	1,976	1,352	633	719	13.1	6.7
16 to 19 years	1,051	499	429	123	81	43	8.1	5.1
20 to 24 years	1,057	526	350	180	91	89	10.6	4.6
25 to 34 years	1,253	532	403	318	163	155	13.3	7.2
35 to 44 years	1,231	507	396	327	144	183	14.8	7.3
45 to 54 years	742	276	225	242	93	149	17.4	7.9
55 to 64 years	370	117	130	123	51	71	18.2	8.9
65 years and over	121	40	43	39	10	29	19.4	8.6
Men, 16 years and over	2,842	1,223	899	720	301	419	14.6	6.9
16 to 19 years	543	249	226	68	50	17	8.1	5.6
20 to 24 years	537	282	162	92	38	54	11.3	4.3
25 to 34 years	608	271	168	169	81	88	13.9	6.6
35 to 44 years	535	209	170	156	54	102	18.4	7.9
45 to 54 years	354	124	95	135	41	94	20.6	9.0
55 to 64 years	187	63	53	70	28	42	20.2	9.3
65 years and over	79	24	25	30	9	22	20.0	10.5
Women, 16 years and over	2,984	1,275	1,077	632	332	300	11.8	6.6
16 to 19 years	508	250	202	56	30	26	8.1	4.7
20 to 24 years	520	244	188	88	52	35	9.8	5.3
25 to 34 years	646	261	235	149	83	67	12.7	7.7
35 to 44 years	697	298	227	172	91	81	12.0	6.8
45 to 54 years	388	151	130	107	52	55	14.5	7.2
55 to 64 years	183	54	76	53	23	29	16.1	8.5
65 years and over	43	16	18	8	1	7	([1])	([1])
Race								
White, 16 years and over	4,246	1,930	1,397	920	408	512	12.4	5.9
Men	2,148	955	674	520	198	321	13.9	6.5
Women	2,099	975	723	400	210	191	10.8	5.4
Black, 16 years and over	1,318	467	475	376	188	188	16.1	8.6
Men	564	214	187	162	79	83	17.6	8.0
Women	754	253	287	214	109	105	15.0	9.0
Marital status								
Men, 16 years and over:								
Married, spouse present	911	391	261	260	105	154	15.6	7.0
Widowed, divorced, or separated	383	150	97	136	49	88	18.6	8.6
Single (never married)	1,548	683	541	324	147	177	12.9	6.5
Women, 16 years and over:								
Married, spouse present	1,017	415	399	203	125	77	10.7	6.7
Widowed, divorced, or separated	633	279	196	158	66	91	14.1	6.2
Single (never married)	1,333	580	481	272	140	131	11.5	6.6

[1] Data not shown where base is less than 75,000.

NOTE: Beginning in January 1999, data reflect revised population controls used in the household survey.

Source: *Employment and Earnings*, vol. 46, no. 9, September 1999

TABLE 3.17

Unemployed persons by occupation, industry, and duration of unemployment

Occupation and industry	August 1999							
	Thousands of persons						Weeks	
	Total	Less than 5 weeks	5 to 14 weeks	15 weeks and over			Average (mean) duration	Median duration
				Total	15 to 26 weeks	27 weeks and over		
OCCUPATION								
Managerial and professional specialty	860	329	330	201	80	122	13.7	7.4
Technical, sales, and administrative support	1,443	624	494	324	178	146	11.7	6.7
Service occupations	1,094	466	385	243	109	134	12.5	6.8
Precision production, craft, and repair	628	310	174	144	77	66	12.6	4.8
Operators, fabricators, and laborers	1,134	553	304	277	124	153	14.2	5.0
Farming, forestry, and fishing	163	77	46	39	10	29	14.4	5.1
INDUSTRY[1]								
Agriculture	148	70	49	29	9	19	11.6	5.5
Construction	458	220	136	101	47	54	12.2	5.5
Manufacturing	758	347	204	207	99	108	15.0	6.6
Durable goods	455	216	109	130	69	61	14.9	6.1
Nondurable goods	303	132	95	76	30	47	15.2	6.9
Transportation and public utilities	282	130	82	70	33	36	12.1	5.9
Wholesale and retail trade	1,285	559	464	262	132	130	11.7	6.1
Finance, insurance, and real estate	199	104	54	40	26	14	8.9	4.3
Services	1,783	765	633	385	191	194	12.4	6.7
Public administration	129	41	45	43	16	27	19.4	9.0
No previous work experience	477	120	238	119	53	66	16.2	8.4

[1] Includes wage and salary workers only.
NOTE: Beginning in January 1999, data reflect revised population controls used in the household survey.

TABLE 3.18

Unemployed persons by reason for unemployment, sex, age, and race

(Numbers in thousands)

Reason	Total, 16 years and over		Men, 20 years and over		Women, 20 years and over		Both sexes, 16 to 19 years		White		Black	
	Aug. 1998	Aug. 1999	Aug. 1998	Aug. 1999	Aug. 1998	Aug. 1999	Aug. 1998	Aug. 1999	Aug. 1998	Aug. 1999	Aug. 1998	Aug. 1999
NUMBER OF UNEMPLOYED												
Total unemployed	6,173	5,826	2,359	2,299	2,639	2,475	1,175	1,051	4,448	4,246	1,466	1,318
Job losers and persons who completed temporary jobs	2,715	2,559	1,399	1,314	1,135	1,112	181	133	2,026	1,922	586	523
On temporary layoff	782	784	320	346	421	404	42	34	622	633	135	118
Not on temporary layoff	1,932	1,775	1,079	968	714	707	140	100	1,404	1,289	452	405
Permanent job losers	1,342	1,250	776	691	514	507	51	52	988	935	293	258
Persons who completed temporary jobs	590	525	303	277	199	200	88	48	417	354	159	147
Job leavers	795	866	292	361	383	339	120	167	617	701	144	141
Reentrants	2,157	1,925	588	584	1,036	919	534	421	1,487	1,310	585	513
New entrants	506	477	80	41	86	105	340	331	318	314	151	141
PERCENT DISTRIBUTION												
Job losers and persons who completed temporary jobs	44.0	43.9	59.3	57.1	43.0	44.9	15.4	12.7	45.6	45.3	40.0	39.7
On temporary layoff	12.7	13.5	13.6	15.0	16.0	16.3	3.5	3.2	14.0	14.9	9.2	8.9
Not on temporary layoff	31.3	30.5	45.8	42.1	27.0	28.6	11.9	9.5	31.6	30.3	30.8	30.8
Job leavers	12.9	14.9	12.4	15.7	14.5	13.7	10.2	15.9	13.9	16.5	9.8	10.7
Reentrants	34.9	33.0	24.9	25.4	39.3	37.1	45.4	40.0	33.4	30.8	39.9	38.9
New entrants	8.2	8.2	3.4	1.8	3.3	4.3	29.0	31.4	7.1	7.4	10.3	10.7
UNEMPLOYED AS A PERCENT OF THE CIVILIAN LABOR FORCE												
Job losers and persons who completed temporary jobs	2.0	1.8	2.0	1.9	1.9	1.8	2.0	1.5	1.7	1.6	3.6	3.2
Job leavers	.6	.6	.4	.5	.6	.6	1.3	1.8	.5	.6	.9	.9
Reentrants	1.6	1.4	.8	.8	1.7	1.5	5.8	4.7	1.3	1.1	3.6	3.1
New entrants	.4	.3	.1	.1	.1	.2	3.7	3.7	.3	.3	.9	.9

NOTE: Beginning in January 1999, data reflect revised population controls used in the household survey.

Source of both tables: *Employment and Earnings*, vol. 46, no. 9, September 1999

TABLE 3.19

Persons not in the labor force by desire and availability for work, age, and sex

(In thousands)

Category	Total		Age						Sex			
			16 to 24 years		25 to 54 years		55 years and over		Men		Women	
	Aug. 1998	Aug. 1999	Aug. 1998	Aug. 1999	Aug. 1998	Aug. 1999	Aug. 1998	Aug. 1999	Aug. 1998	Aug. 1999	Aug. 1998	Aug. 1999
Total not in the labor force	67,100	67,948	10,211	10,732	19,033	19,287	37,856	37,929	24,352	24,674	42,748	43,275
Do not want a job now[1]	61,920	63,206	8,447	9,047	16,512	17,115	36,961	37,045	22,360	22,810	39,560	40,396
Want a job[1]	5,180	4,742	1,765	1,685	2,521	2,172	895	884	1,992	1,863	3,188	2,879
Did not search for work in previous year	3,274	3,040	1,039	977	1,547	1,350	687	713	1,216	1,146	2,058	1,894
Searched for work in previous year[2]	1,907	1,702	725	708	974	822	207	172	777	717	1,130	985
Not available to work now	655	568	259	240	355	291	42	37	197	192	459	377
Available to work now	1,251	1,134	466	468	619	532	166	134	580	525	671	609
Reason not currently looking:												
Discouragement over job prospects[3]	280	265	99	122	130	117	51	26	168	153	112	112
Reasons other than discouragement	971	869	368	346	489	415	115	108	412	372	559	497
Family responsibilities	166	140	42	27	114	107	11	5	22	25	145	114
In school or training	147	143	115	101	32	37	–	–	59	66	88	77
Ill health or disability	95	77	20	6	54	44	21	28	52	44	43	32
Other[4]	563	510	191	213	289	226	82	70	280	236	283	273

[1] Includes some persons who are not asked if they want a job.
[2] Persons who had a job in the prior 12 months must have searched since the end of that job.
[3] Includes believes no work available, could not find work, lacks necessary schooling or training, employer thinks too young or old, and other types of discrimination.

[4] Includes those who did not actively look for work in the prior 4 weeks for such reasons as child-care and transportation problems, as well as a small number for which reason for nonparticipation was not ascertained.

NOTE: Beginning in January 1999, data reflect revised population controls used in the household survey.

TABLE 3.20

Persons at work in nonfarm occupations by sex and usual full- or part-time status

(Numbers in thousands)

Occupation and sex	August 1999							
		Worked 1 to 34 hours					Average hours	
				For noneconomic reasons				
	Total at work	Total	For economic reasons	Usually work full time	Usually work part time	Worked 35 hours or more	Total at work	Persons who usually work full time
Total, 16 years and over[1]	120,572	26,861	3,080	7,925	15,856	93,711	39.9	43.2
Managerial and professional specialty	35,993	6,569	441	2,845	3,283	29,424	41.9	44.3
Executive, administrative, and managerial	18,394	2,643	114	1,372	1,157	15,751	43.7	45.3
Professional specialty	17,599	3,926	327	1,472	2,126	13,673	40.1	43.1
Technical, sales, and administrative support	36,600	9,541	860	2,368	6,312	27,059	38.1	42.1
Technicians and related support	4,172	830	67	323	440	3,342	39.5	41.8
Sales occupations	15,357	4,342	481	803	3,058	11,015	39.2	44.3
Administrative support, including clerical	17,071	4,369	312	1,242	2,814	12,703	36.8	40.3
Service occupations	17,097	5,940	857	894	4,189	11,157	36.1	42.1
Private household	780	410	49	32	329	371	30.2	41.5
Protective service	2,460	358	45	129	184	2,102	42.9	45.1
Service, except private household and protective	13,857	5,172	763	733	3,676	8,685	35.2	41.5
Precision production, craft, and repair	13,592	1,665	306	800	560	11,927	42.7	43.8
Operators, fabricators, and laborers	17,290	3,147	616	1,018	1,512	14,144	40.9	43.2
Machine operators, assemblers, and inspectors	6,922	1,000	208	471	320	5,922	40.9	42.1
Transportation and material moving occupations	5,148	714	134	225	355	4,435	44.3	46.4
Handlers, equipment cleaners, helpers, and laborers	5,220	1,433	274	322	837	3,787	37.6	41.5

[1] Excludes farming, forestry, and fishing occupations.

NOTE: Beginning in January 1999, data reflect revised population controls used in the household survey.

Source of both tables: *Employment and Earnings*, vol. 46, no. 9, September 1999

either women or younger people, remained unemployed longer. Blacks were out of work longer than Whites. Widowed, divorced, or separated men and women were unemployed longer than those who had never been married or those who were still living with their spouses. Married men living with their wives were out of work longer than never-married men. (See Table 3.16.)

Duration of unemployment can depend on the type of job held and the time of the year. At the end of summer 1999, finance, insurance, and real estate employees had the least amount of time unemployed (an average of 8.9 weeks). Those involved in public administration were unemployed for an average of 19.4 weeks. (See Table 3.17.)

Forty-three percent of those unemployed in service occupations were out of work less than five weeks, and 22 percent were still looking for work after 15 weeks. Almost 4 of 10 (38 percent) of those seeking managerial and professional positions were unemployed less than five weeks, and 23 percent still lacked jobs after 15 weeks. (See Table 3.17.)

Construction workers were more in demand. Nearly half (48 percent) found work within five weeks, although 22 percent still needed jobs after 15 weeks. Manufacturing jobs, too, were in demand. Forty-six percent of manufacturing workers were out of work less than five weeks, although 27 percent were still looking for work after 15 weeks. (See Table 3.17.)

In August 1999, most of those classified as unemployed had lost their jobs or had completed temporary jobs (43.9 percent). Another 14.9 percent had left their jobs. About 42 percent of the men and nearly 29 percent of the women had been laid off permanently. (See Table 3.18.)

Displaced Workers

Between 1995 and 1996, 2.2 million workers were displaced, losing jobs they had held for three or more years because their plants or companies closed or moved, they had insufficient work, or their positions were abolished. Eighty-three percent were reemployed when surveyed in February 1998. About half of those were employed in a different major industry, often experiencing more severe earnings losses than those who were reemployed in the same industry from which they had been displaced.

In general, the risk of job loss decreases as the number of years of educational attainment increases. The risk also declines with increasing number of years on the job.

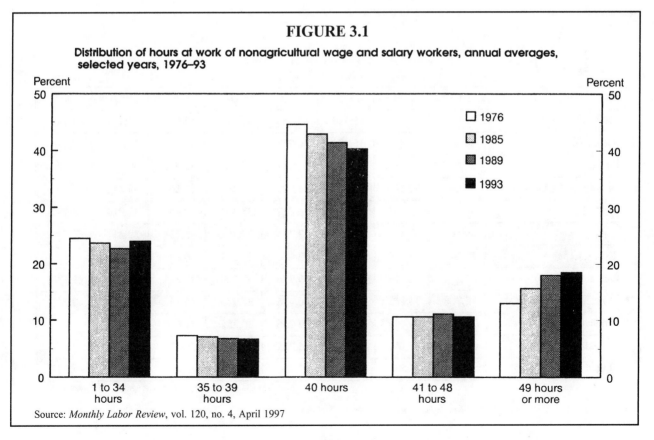

FIGURE 3.1

Distribution of hours at work of nonagricultural wage and salary workers, annual averages, selected years, 1976–93

Source: *Monthly Labor Review*, vol. 120, no. 4, April 1997

The labor force includes those working and those unemployed still looking for work. In August 1999, more than half (56 percent) of persons not in the labor force were ages 55 or older. Only 7 percent of those who were no longer part of the labor force still wanted a job, and 36 percent of those who wanted a job had looked for work during the previous year. Some of the reasons those who were available for work gave for not currently

TABLE 3.21

Annual Number of Hours Worked Per Person

	1990	1991	1992	1993	1994	1995	1996	1997
Australia	1869	1858	1850	1874	1879	1876	1867	1866
Canada	1737.6	1717.2	1714.1	1718.4	1734.7	1737.2	1732.4	
Japan	2031	1998	1965	1905	1898	1889		
United States	1942.6	1936	1918.9	1945.9	1945.3	1952.3	1950.6	1966
New Zealand	1820.1	1801.4	1811.8	1843.5	1850.6	1843.1	1838	
France						1638.4	1666	1656
Germany, Fed.Rep. of	1610	1590	1604.7	1583.7	1579.5	1562.7	1559.5	
Ireland	1728	1708	1688	1672	1660	1648	1656	
Norway	1432	1427.3	1436.9	1434	1431	1414	1407	1399
Sweden						1544.4	1553.8	1552
Switzerland		1640	1637	1633	1639	1643		
United Kingdom							1732	1731
Denmark (Male)	1644.5	1620.15	1669	1660.55	1688.85			
Netherlands (Male)	1619.3	1623.55	1689.25	1684.2	1679.35			

TABLE 3.22

Value Added Per Person Employed

	1990	1991	1992	1993	1994	1995	1996	1997
Belgium	43,911	44,554	45,510	45,384	46,947	47,676	48,193	49,187
Denmark	34,543	35,351	35,404	36,778	38,804	39,119	39,780	40,214
Finland	33,287	32,518	33,760	35,512	37,481	38,518	39,199	39,722
Hong Kong, China	36,009	37,280	39,759	41,293	42,462	43,864	44,412	
Ireland	34,603	35,534	36,049	36,827	38,469	40,792	42,916	44,253
Japan	36,669	37,406	37,407	37,374	37,597	38,134	39,434	
Korea, Republic of	21,243	22,374	23,016	23,971	25,261	26,787	28,166	
Spain	36,782	37,538	38,618	39,924	41,203	41,245	40,997	41,138
Sweden	33,768	34,168	35,192	36,416	37,975	38,796	39,619	40,741
Taiwan, China	25,258	26,496	27,649	29,006	30,252	31,679	33,438	
United Kingdom	35,001	35,164	35,744	36,775	38,047	38,419	38,890	
United States	45,377	45,606	46,434	47,350	48,043	48,493	49,150	49,905

Updated by CL. Approved by KMK. Last update: 30 September 1999.

Souce of both tables: Data drawn on *Key Indicators of the Labour Market 1999*. Copyright © International Labour Organization 1999

TABLE 3.23

Persons at work 1 to 34 hours in all and nonagricultural industries by reason for working less than 35 hours and usual full- or part-time status

(Numbers in thousands)

Reason for working less than 35 hours	August 1999					
	All industries			Nonagricultural industries		
	Total	Usually work full time	Usually work part time	Total	Usually work full time	Usually work part time
Total, 16 years and over	27,837	9,483	18,354	26,932	9,231	17,701
Economic reasons	3,238	1,340	1,898	3,102	1,271	1,831
Slack work or business conditions	1,759	984	775	1,677	940	736
Could only find part-time work	1,068	–	1,068	1,046	–	1,046
Seasonal work	145	90	55	120	72	48
Job started or ended during week	267	267	–	259	259	–
Noneconomic reasons	24,598	8,143	16,455	23,830	7,960	15,870
Child-care problems	745	73	671	729	73	656
Other family or personal obligations	5,011	684	4,327	4,874	671	4,202
Health or medical limitations	652	–	652	615	–	615
In school or training	4,827	133	4,694	4,690	122	4,568
Retired or Social Security limit on earnings	1,911	–	1,911	1,766	–	1,766
Vacation or personal day	4,701	4,701	–	4,619	4,619	–
Holiday, legal or religious	63	63	–	63	63	–
Weather-related curtailment	146	146	–	117	117	–
All other reasons	6,543	2,343	4,199	6,358	2,295	4,063
Average hours:						
Economic reasons	22.9	23.4	22.5	22.8	23.3	22.5
Other reasons	21.6	24.0	20.4	21.7	24.1	20.5

NOTE: Beginning in January 1999, data reflect revised population controls used in the household survey.

TABLE 3.24

Multiple jobholders by selected demographic and economic characteristics

(Numbers in thousands)

Characteristic	Both sexes				Men				Women			
	Number		Rate[1]		Number		Rate[1]		Number		Rate[1]	
	Aug. 1998	Aug. 1999	Aug. 1998	Aug. 1999	Aug. 1998	Aug. 1999	Aug. 1998	Aug. 1999	Aug. 1998	Aug. 1999	Aug. 1998	Aug. 1999
AGE												
Total, 16 years and over[2]	7,462	7,298	5.6	5.4	4,015	3,909	5.6	5.4	3,447	3,389	5.7	5.5
16 to 19 years	431	488	5.4	6.1	173	239	4.2	5.8	258	250	6.6	6.5
20 years and over	7,031	6,810	5.7	5.4	3,842	3,671	5.7	5.4	3,189	3,139	5.6	5.4
20 to 24 years	756	718	5.9	5.4	378	316	5.5	4.5	378	402	6.4	6.5
25 years and over	6,275	6,092	5.6	5.4	3,464	3,355	5.7	5.5	2,812	2,737	5.5	5.3
25 to 54 years	5,537	5,352	5.8	5.6	3,043	2,915	5.9	5.6	2,494	2,437	5.7	5.5
55 years and over	738	740	4.5	4.3	421	439	4.6	4.6	317	301	4.4	3.9
55 to 64 years	648	604	5.1	4.5	359	361	5.1	5.0	290	243	5.0	4.0
65 years and over	90	136	2.5	3.5	63	78	3.0	3.5	27	58	1.8	3.6
RACE AND HISPANIC ORIGIN												
White	6,386	6,184	5.7	5.5	3,484	3,339	5.7	5.4	2,903	2,845	5.8	5.6
Black	783	802	5.3	5.3	380	390	5.5	5.5	403	413	5.2	5.1
Hispanic origin	451	456	3.4	3.3	269	264	3.3	3.2	181	191	3.4	3.4
MARITAL STATUS												
Married, spouse present	3,945	3,879	5.3	5.1	2,444	2,382	5.7	5.5	1,501	1,497	4.7	4.5
Widowed, divorced, or separated	1,332	1,252	6.5	6.1	495	472	5.9	5.6	837	780	6.9	6.4
Single (never married)	2,184	2,167	6.0	5.8	1,076	1,056	5.3	5.1	1,109	1,112	6.8	6.7
FULL- OR PART-TIME STATUS												
Primary job full time, secondary job part time	4,344	3,992	–	–	2,541	2,350	–	–	1,803	1,641	–	–
Primary and secondary jobs both part time	1,408	1,514	–	–	469	499	–	–	939	1,014	–	–
Primary and secondary jobs both full time	271	332	–	–	184	260	–	–	87	72	–	–
Hours vary on primary or secondary job	1,384	1,418	–	–	796	777	–	–	588	641	–	–

[1] Multiple jobholders as a percent of all employed persons in specified group.

[2] Includes a small number of persons who work part time on their primary job and full time on their secondary jobs(s), not shown separately.

NOTE: Detail for the above race and Hispanic-origin groups will not sum to totals because data for the "other races" group are not presented and Hispanics are included in both the white and black population groups. Beginning in January 1999, data reflect revised population controls used in the household survey.

Source of both tables: *Employment and Earnings*, vol. 46, no. 9, September 1999

TABLE 3.25

Employment Status of High School and College Students 15 Years Old and Over,
By Level of School, Attendance Status, Age, Gender, Race, and Hispanic Origin: October 1998

Numbers in thousands.

All Races	Total	Full-time students				Part-time students			
		Total	Employed Full-time	Employed Part-time	Not Employed	Total	Employed Full-time	Employed Part-time	Not Employed
Total									
Total	28,190	22,832	1,810	6,984	14,038	5,358	3,786	856	716
Enrolled in High School									
15 years old	3,739	3,739	15	414	3,310	-	-	-	-
16 and 17 years old	7,297	7,297	104	2,350	4,844	-	-	-	-
18 and 19 years old	1,235	1,235	103	378	755	-	-	-	-
20 years old and over	372	372	143	27	202	-	-	-	-
Enrolled in College									
15 to 17 year olds	123	107	7	39	62	17	5	6	5
18 to 19 years old	3,670	3,265	204	1,267	1,795	405	153	162	90
20 to 21 years old	3,092	2,677	296	1,126	1,254	415	224	109	82
22 to 24 years old	2,561	1,890	316	729	846	671	461	147	63
25 to 29 years old	2,148	1,092	276	390	427	1,056	791	130	134
30 to 34 years old	1,266	443	144	93	205	823	654	90	79
35 years and over	2,686	714	203	173	338	1,972	1,497	212	263

Source: Bureau of the Census, Washington, DC, 1999

looking were discouragement over job prospects (23 percent), in school or training (13 percent), family responsibilities (12 percent), and ill health or disability (7 percent). (See Table 3.19.)

HOW MANY HOURS DO AMERICANS WORK?

In August 1999, about 78 percent of nonfarm American workers were working full-time (35 hours or more), while the remaining 22 percent were working part-time (fewer than 35 hours). The average worker labored 39.9 hours per week, while the average full-time employee worked 43.2 hours. (See Table 3.20.)

Who Is Working the Longer Workweeks?

Economists working for the Bureau of Labor Statistics found that the average number of hours worked each week has changed little since the mid-1970s, but the proportion of persons working very long work weeks has risen. Figure 3.1 shows that the proportion of nonagricultural wage and salary workers who worked exactly 40 hours per week

declined, while the share working 49 hours or more rose. The proportions working fewer than 40 hours and 41 to 48 hours remained fairly stable. In 1997, about 30 percent of men and 15 percent of women usually worked more than 44 hours a week. One man in 10 and 1 woman in 30 often worked more than 54 hours a week.

Some occupations required more time than others. Transportation and material-moving workers worked 44.3 hours (46.4 hours for workers on full-time schedules). Executive, administrative, and managerial people averaged about 44 hours (45.3 hours a week for full-time). On the other hand, private household workers averaged only 30.2 hours a week (41.5 hours for full-time) (Table 3.20).

Professionals and managers were among those most likely to work very long workweeks. This may reflect the considerable responsibilities associated with many of these types of jobs. In addition, employers are often not required by law to pay overtime premiums to workers in these occupations, as they must do for most hourly paid workers. These salaried workers tend to be better paid.

TABLE 3.26

Contingency rates by occupation and industry, February 1995 and February 1997

[Percent]

Occupation and industry	Contingency rates[1]					
	Estimate 1		Estimate 2		Estimate 3	
	1995	1997	1995	1997	1995	1997
Occupation						
Total, 16 years and older	2.2	1.9	2.8	2.4	4.9	4.4
Managerial and professional specialty	1.7	1.4	2.1	1.7	4.8	4.2
Executive, administrative, and managerial	8	.7	1.1	1.0	2.7	2.2
Professional specialty	2.6	2.0	3.1	2.4	6.8	6.0
Technical, sales, and administrative support	2.1	2.1	2.5	2.6	4.4	4.3
Technicians and related support	1.3	1.8	1.9	2.7	4.2	4.7
Sales occupations	1.2	1.1	1.6	1.5	2.6	2.1
Administrative support, including clerical	3.1	3.0	3.4	3.5	5.8	6.0
Service occupations	3.0	2.3	4.1	3.2	5.8	5.0
Precision, production, craft, and repair	2.3	1.8	2.9	2.3	4.6	4.1
Operators, fabricators, and laborers	2.7	2.2	3.1	3.0	5.4	4.4
Farming, forestry, and fishing	2.2	2.0	3.2	3.0	5.6	5.9
Industry						
Total, 16 years and older	2.2	1.9	2.8	2.4	4.9	4.4
Agriculture	2.4	1.6	3.3	2.6	5.0	5.2
Mining	1.0	1.1	1.0	1.8	2.6	4.0
Construction	4.5	3.7	5.7	4.7	8.4	7.2
Manufacturing	1.3	.9	1.6	1.1	3.1	2.1
Transportation and public utilities	1.2	.7	1.3	1.2	2.9	2.6
Wholesale trade	.7	.8	1.0	1.3	2.3	2.1
Retail trade	1.6	1.5	2.0	1.7	3.0	2.6
Finance, insurance, and real estate	.7	1.1	.8	1.3	2.0	2.1
Services	3.4	2.8	4.3	3.7	7.5	6.7
Public administration	1.2	1.2	1.2	1.2	3.6	4.2

[1] Contingency rates are calculated by dividing the number of contingent workers in a specified worker group by the total number of employed persons in the same worker group. Estimate 1 above is calculated using the narrowest definition of contingent work; estimate 3 uses the broadest definition.

Source: *Monthly Labor Review*, vol. 121, no. 11, November 1998

In contrast, sales and transportation workers, who also work long workweeks, are not, on average, highly paid. In these cases, a large proportion of workers may work more hours per week due to the direct relationship of hours and earnings (the more they work, the more they earn). For example, commissioned sales workers clearly have an incentive to work long workweeks. Indeed, full-time sales workers employed by motor vehicle and boat dealerships averaged 49 hours per week, on average, in 1997. In contrast, full-time retail sales workers, occupations in which significant commissions are a less common form of pay, averaged right at 40 hours. Fewer than 8 percent of janitors and cleaners, bookkeepers, nursing aides, and secretaries worked extended hours.

Americans Working Longer Than Workers in Japan, Korea, and Europe

A recent study by the U.N. International Labor Organization (ILO) found that Americans spend more time on the job than any other workers in the developed world. Their time at work has increased from an average of 1,883 hours in 1980 to 1,966 in 1997. In comparison, Japanese workers averaged 2,121 hours on the job in 1980 and 1,889 in 1995, the most recent data available. (See Table 3.21.) According to ILO director general Juan Somavia, "The number of hours worked is one important indicator of a country's overall quality of life. While the benefits of hard work are clear, working more is not the same as working better...."

Lower working hours may also reflect higher productivity."

Overall, American workers continue to be the world's most productive. In 1997, they contributed an average of $49,905 to the economy with their work (Table 3.22). However, measured by how much value they create for each hour they worked, they have fallen behind France. French workers spent 300 fewer hours on the job than American workers in 1997, yet added more value per hour of work — $32 per hour compared to $30.66. In Ireland, which, like America, has had strong economic growth in the 1990s, workers spent 310 hours less than their American counterparts in 1997.

PART-TIME WORK

People work part time for various reasons. In August 1999, 34 percent of part-time employees were usually full-time workers who, for some reason, now had to work part time. Twelve percent of part-time workers took part-time work due to economic conditions. These economic reasons, usually caused by employers' circumstances, included slack work, material shortages, or the availability of only part-time work. Most (88 percent) workers who usually worked part time did so for noneconomic reasons: they did not want to work full time or were unavailable, perhaps because they were going to school, were taking care of children, or had other family or personal obligations. (See Table 3.23.)

MULTIPLE JOBS

In August 1999, 5.4 percent of workers held multiple jobs. The multiple-job rate among men actually declined from 7 percent in 1970 to 5.4 percent in 1999. The proportion of women holding more than one job increased from 2 percent in 1970 to 6 percent in 1997, dropping somewhat to 5.5 in 1999. Single women (6.7 percent) and widowed, divorced, and separated women (6.4 percent) were the most likely to have more than one job. Married women (4.5 percent) and single men (5.1 percent) were the least likely. (See Table 3.24.)

STUDENTS WITH JOBS

In 1998, more than 1 in 4 American high schoolers (28 percent) worked while going to school. Most worked part time. In college, even

TABLE 3.27

Employed contingent workers by reason for contingency and preference for noncontingent work, February 1997

[Percent distribution]

Reason	Contingent workers[1]		
	Estimate 1	Estimate 2	Estimate 3
Total			
Total, 16 years and older (thousands)	2,385	2,663	5,140
Percent	100.0	100.0	100.0
Economic reasons	38.2	39.6	30.5
Only type of work could find	23.2	24.8	18.2
Hope job leads to permanent employment	8.1	8.0	6.7
Other economic reason	7.0	6.8	5.6
Personal reasons	48.7	47.3	48.5
Flexibility of schedule and only wanted to work a short period of time	11.2	12.6	11.7
Family or personal obligations and child-care problems	2.9	2.8	3.2
In school or training	21.6	19.7	19.2
Money is better	1.7	1.5	1.4
Other personal reason	11.2	10.7	13.0
Reason not available	13.1	13.1	20.9
Prefer noncontingent employment			
Total, 16 years and older (thousands)	1,436	1,755	3,096
Percent	100.0	100.0	100.0
Economic reasons	57.9	55.2	45.8
Only type of work could find	36.1	35.6	28.3
Hope job leads to permanent employment	12.3	11.1	10.1
Other economic reason	9.5	8.5	7.5
Personal reasons	28.3	26.6	29.6
Flexibility of schedule and only wanted to work a short period of time	6.3	6.5	6.1
Family or personal obligations and child-care problems	2.5	2.5	2.2
In school or training	10.0	8.8	10.6
Money is better	1.8	1.5	1.3
Other personal reason	7.9	7.3	9.3
Reason not available	13.6	18.2	24.6

[1] Contingent workers are defined as individuals who do not perceive themselves as having an explicit or implicit contract with their employers for ongoing employment. Estimate 1 above is calculated using the narrowest definition of contingent work; estimate 3 uses the broadest definition.

Source: *Monthly Labor Review*, vol. 121, no. 11, November 1998

TABLE 3.28

Workers in alternative arrangements as a percent of total employment, February 1995 and 1997

Type of alternative arrangement	Percent of total employed, February 1995	Percent of total employed, February 1997
Independent contractors Workers identified as independent contractors, independent consultants, or freelance workers, whether they were self-employed or wage and salary workers	6.7	6.7
On-call workers Workers called to work only as needed, although they can be scheduled to work for several days or weeks in a row	1.6	1.6
Temporary help agency workers Workers paid by a temporary help agency, whether or not their job actually was temporary	1.0	1.0
Workers provided by contract firms Workers employed by a company that provides them or their services to others under contract and who are usually assigned to only one customer and usually work at the customer's worksite	.5	.6

Source: *Monthly Labor Review*, vol. 121, no. 11, November 1998

more students worked (64 percent). Approximately 34 percent of college students worked full time, and 30 percent worked part time. (See Table 3.25.) In both high school and college, equal percentages of male and female students had jobs. White high school students (31 percent) were more likely to work than Black (18 percent) or Hispanic (17 percent) students.

CONTINGENT WORKERS

The Bureau of Labor Statistics (BLS) defined contingent work as any job in which an individual does not have an explicit or implicit contract for long-term employment. This includes independent contractors, on-call workers, and those working for temporary help services. The February 1997 *Current Population Survey* estimated that between 2.4 and 5.6 million workers (1.9 to 4.4 percent of total employment) were in contingent jobs.

The differences arise due to alternative definitions. The narrowest estimate (1) included wage and salary workers who held their jobs for one year or less and expected to be employed for an additional year or less. The middle estimates (2) added the self-employed and independent contractors. The third estimate (3) dropped the time limit on wage and salary workers and included any worker

who believed his or her job was temporary. (See Table 3.26.)

Contingent workers were more likely to be in professional specialties, administrative support, and farming occupations and were less likely to be in managerial or sales occupations. It might seem surprising that contingent workers were over-represented in professional specialty occupations. However, this category includes teachers, who had an above-average rate of contingency. In fact, postsecondary teachers accounted for 28.4 percent of all contingent workers in the professional specialty category, according to Estimate 3. Apparently, colleges and universities use many adjunct or temporary teachers with short-term contracts. It could also be, however, that the uncertainties of the tenure process play an important role in how college and university teachers look at their jobs.

Others in the professional category include biological and life scientists (19.8 percent), musicians (12.6 percent), physicians (9.9 percent), and actors and directors (9.9 percent). These figures indicate that many contingent workers are highly skilled. The higher proportion of contingent workers in the administrative support occupation, which includes occupations such as clerks, data entry

TABLE 3.29

Employed persons with alternative and traditional work arrangements, by selected characteristics, February 1997

[Percent distribution]

Characteristic	Workers with alternative arrangements				Workers with traditional arrangements
	Independent contractors	On-call workers	Temporary help agency workers	Workers provided by contract firms	
Age and sex					
Total, 16 years and older (thousands)	8,456	1,996	1,300	809	114,199
Percent	100.0	100.0	100.0	100.0	100.0
16 to 19 years	.8	9.7	6.1	2.0	5.0
20 to 24 years	2.4	11.9	16.5	8.2	9.8
25 to 34 years	18.3	22.4	30.3	34.2	25.4
35 to 44 years	31.1	25.4	21.5	31.1	27.7
45 to 54 years	26.5	14.4	16.2	14.2	20.4
55 to 64 years	13.9	9.7	6.7	7.7	9.2
65 years and older	7.0	6.5	2.8	2.7	2.5
Men, 16 years and older	66.6	49.0	44.7	69.8	52.7
16 to 19 years	.3	5.3	2.8	1.1	2.5
20 to 24 years	1.5	6.4	9.6	7.7	5.1
25 to 34 years	11.4	11.8	15.2	24.0	13.7
35 to 44 years	20.7	12.1	6.9	22.0	14.6
45 to 54 years.	17.7	6.9	6.2	9.1	10.5
55 to 64 years	9.9	3.9	2.2	5.1	4.9
65 years and older	5.1	2.6	1.8	.9	1.4
Women, 16 years and older .	33.4	51.0	55.3	30.2	47.3
16 to 19 years	.5	4.3	3.2	.7	2.4
20 to 24 years	.9	5.5	6.9	.5	4.7
25 to 34 years	7.0	10.6	15.2	10.3	11.7
35 to 44 years	10.4	13.4	14.5	9.1	13.1
45 to 54 years	8.8	7.5	10.0	5.1	9.9
55 to 64 years	4.0	5.8	4.5	2.6	4.3
65 years and older	1.9	3.9	1.1	1.9	1.1
Race and Hispanic origin					
White	90.7	89.3	75.1	81.6	84.8
Black	5.3	7.8	21.3	12.9	10.9
Hispanic origin	7.3	13.3	12.3	6.3	9.6

NOTE: Workers with traditional arrangements are those who do not fall into any of the "alternative arrangements" categories. Details for the above race and Hispanic-origin groups will not sum to totals because data for the "other races" group are not presented and Hispanics are included in both the white and black population groups. Details for other characteristics may not sum to totals because of rounding.

Source: *Monthly Labor Review*, vol. 121, no. 11, November 1998

keyers, teachers' aides, and receptionists, comes closer to the stereotypical notion that contingent workers hold jobs that require relatively little formal training.

Although contingent workers were found in every industry, contingent workers were much more likely to be concentrated in construction and services industries. (See Table 3.26.) Specific industries within the services category that had high contingency rates were personnel supply services (44.4 percent), private household services (15.7 percent), educational services (11.4 percent), entertainment and recreation services (6.8 percent), and social services (6.2 percent). It is important to recognize that, although those in the services industry make up a large proportion of contingent workers, most workers in this industry were not contingent.

Part-time workers were more likely than full-time workers to hold contingent jobs. About 10 percent of employees in part-time jobs were contingent workers, compared with about 3 percent of those with full-time jobs. Contingent workers were also more likely to hold more than one job.

Nearly three-fifths of contingent workers would rather hold a noncontingent job. About half reported a personal reason for holding a contingent job, such as flexibility of schedule or in school or training. Far more of those who preferred a noncontingent job cited economic reasons. (See Table 3.27.)

TABLE 3.30

Employed persons with alternative and traditional work arrangements, by educational attainment and sex, February 1997

[Percent distribution]

Educational attainment and sex	Workers with alternative arrangements				Workers with traditional arrangements
	Independent contractors	On-call workers	Temporary help agency workers	Workers provided by contract firms	
Total, 25 to 64 years (thousands)	7,590	1,437	970	705	94,424
Percent	100.0	100.0	100.0	100.0	100.0
Less than a high school diploma	8.7	13.4	11.1	7.1	9.7
High school graduate, no college	30.3	28.7	30.7	36.9	32.8
Less than a bachelor's degree	26.8	32.0	36.3	23.3	28.0
College graduate	34.1	25.9	21.9	32.7	29.5
Men, 25 to 64 years old (thousands)	5,047	692	397	486	49,873
Percent	100.0	100.0	100.0	100.0	100.0
Less than a high school diploma	9.9	18.6	13.9	6.4	11.3
High school graduate, no college	31.3	33.4	27.5	35.6	31.9
Less than a bachelor's degree	25.2	30.3	35.1	24.9	26.4
College graduate	33.5	17.6	23.5	33.1	30.4
Women, 25 to 64 years old (thousands)	2,543	745	573	219	44,551
Percent	100.0	100.0	100.0	100.0	100.0
Less than a high school diploma	6.2	8.6	9.2	9.1	7.9
High school graduate, no college	28.4	24.3	33.0	39.5	33.8
Less than a bachelor's degree	30.0	33.6	37.2	20.0	29.8
College graduate	35.3	33.6	20.6	31.4	28.5

NOTE: Workers with traditional arrangements are those who do not fall into any of the "alternative arrangements" categories. Details may not sum to totals due to rounding.

Source: *Monthly Labor Review*, vol. 121, no. 11, November 1998

ALTERNATIVE WORK ARRANGEMENTS

Employees in alternative work arrangements are defined either as individuals whose employment is arranged through an employment intermediary or individuals whose place, time, and quantity of work are potentially unpredictable. These include workers such as independent contractors, on-call workers, workers paid by temporary help firms, and workers whose services are provided through contract firms. (See Table 3.28.) Since many observers have claimed that the number of temporary workers has been increasing, the Bureau of Labor Statistics decided to include questions on these types of workers in its February 1995 *Current Population Survey*. This survey was repeated in February 1997. In general, the percentage of total employment within each arrangement, as well as the characteristics of the workers, was very similar to the previous survey.

The BLS found that approximately 12.6 million persons, or 10 percent of the work force, fell into at least one of the four categories. The largest category was independent contractors, with 8.5 million, followed by on-call workers (2 million),

temporary help agency workers (1.3 million), and contract company employees (809,000). (See Tables 3.29 and 3.30 for selected characteristics of workers in alternative work arrangements).

OCCUPATIONAL INJURIES, ILLNESSES, AND FATALITIES

The rate of occupational injury and illness in full-time workers increased during the 1980s and the early 1990s. There were 7.9 cases per 100 workers in 1986, increasing to a high of 8.9 in 1992 and then dropping to 7.1 in 1997. In 1986, there were 65.8 lost workdays per 100 workers, and in 1992, there were 93.8 lost workdays. Beginning with the 1993 survey, estimates on lost workdays were no longer generated. The number of workdays lost varied by the type of industry and occupation. In 1992, the food and related products industry lost 211.9 days per 100 full-time workers, while finance, insurance, and real estate occupations lost only 32.9 days.

In 1997, 6,218 workers were killed on the job. Forty-two percent involved transportation incidents, over half of which were highway accidents;

18 percent were assaults and violent acts; 17 percent involved contact with objects and equipment, and 11 percent were falls. Nine percent involved exposure to harmful substances or environments, and 3 percent were fires and explosions.

UNION AFFILIATION

Union membership has decreased dramatically over the past two decades. In 1975, 28.9 percent of the nation's workers were union members. This proportion dropped to 21.9 percent in 1982, 15.8

TABLE 3.31

Union affiliation of employed wage and salary workers by selected characteristics

(Numbers in thousands)

| Characteristic | 1997 | | | | | 1998 | | | | |
| | Total employed | Members of unions[1] | | Represented by unions[2] | | Total employed | Members of unions[1] | | Represented by unions[2] | |
		Total	Percent of employed	Total	Percent of employed		Total	Percent of employed	Total	Percent of employed
SEX AND AGE										
Total, 16 years and over	114,533	16,110	14.1	17,923	15.6	116,730	16,211	13.9	17,918	15.4
16 to 24 years	18,571	968	5.2	1,140	6.1	19,164	1,014	5.3	1,151	6.0
25 years and over	95,962	15,142	15.8	16,783	17.5	97,566	15,198	15.6	16,767	17.2
25 to 34 years	29,408	3,434	11.7	3,870	13.2	29,121	3,332	11.4	3,711	12.7
35 to 44 years	31,461	4,987	15.9	5,571	17.7	31,865	5,013	15.7	5,511	17.3
45 to 54 years	22,714	4,645	20.5	5,092	22.4	23,579	4,737	20.1	5,220	22.1
55 to 64 years	9,871	1,894	19.2	2,045	20.7	10,427	1,923	18.4	2,110	20.2
65 years and over	2,509	182	7.3	205	8.2	2,574	193	7.5	214	8.3
Men, 16 years and over	59,825	9,763	16.3	10,619	17.7	60,973	9,850	16.2	10,638	17.4
16 to 24 years	9,666	612	6.3	691	7.1	9,927	637	6.4	719	7.2
25 years and over	50,159	9,150	18.2	9,928	19.8	51,046	9,213	18.0	9,919	19.4
25 to 34 years	15,832	2,132	13.5	2,359	14.9	15,656	2,112	13.5	2,301	14.7
35 to 44 years	16,430	3,068	18.7	3,346	20.4	16,768	3,055	18.2	3,264	19.5
45 to 54 years	11,471	2,718	23.7	2,908	25.4	11,874	2,771	23.3	2,982	25.1
55 to 64 years	5,101	1,130	22.1	1,198	23.5	5,404	1,177	21.8	1,265	23.4
65 years and over	1,324	103	7.8	118	8.9	1,343	98	7.3	108	8.0
Women, 16 years and over	54,708	6,347	11.6	7,304	13.4	55,757	6,362	11.4	7,280	13.1
16 to 24 years	8,906	355	4.0	449	5.0	9,237	377	4.1	432	4.7
25 years and over	45,802	5,992	13.1	6,855	15.0	46,520	5,985	12.9	6,848	14.7
25 to 34 years	13,575	1,302	9.6	1,512	11.1	13,464	1,219	9.1	1,410	10.5
35 to 44 years	15,030	1,919	12.8	2,225	14.8	15,097	1,958	13.0	2,248	14.9
45 to 54 years	11,242	1,927	17.1	2,184	19.4	11,705	1,967	16.8	2,238	19.1
55 to 64 years	4,770	764	16.0	847	17.8	5,023	746	14.9	845	16.8
65 years and over	1,184	80	6.7	87	7.3	1,231	95	7.7	106	8.6
RACE, HISPANIC ORIGIN, AND SEX										
White, 16 years and over	96,104	13,088	13.6	14,538	15.1	97,531	13,118	13.5	14,460	14.8
Men	50,941	8,171	16.0	8,859	17.4	51,700	8,166	15.8	8,788	17.0
Women	45,163	4,917	10.9	5,679	12.6	45,831	4,952	10.8	5,673	12.4
Black, 16 years and over	13,346	2,394	17.9	2,688	20.1	13,894	2,460	17.7	2,739	19.7
Men	6,201	1,251	20.2	1,378	22.2	6,452	1,337	20.7	1,458	22.6
Women	7,145	1,143	16.0	1,309	18.3	7,443	1,123	15.1	1,282	17.2
Hispanic origin, 16 years and over	11,881	1,407	11.8	1,602	13.5	12,374	1,471	11.9	1,634	13.2
Men	7,153	904	12.6	1,023	14.3	7,360	937	12.7	1,017	13.8
Women	4,728	503	10.6	579	12.2	5,015	534	10.6	617	12.3
FULL- OR PART-TIME STATUS[3]										
Full-time workers	93,578	14,619	15.6	16,227	17.3	95,595	14,825	15.5	16,323	17.1
Part-time workers	20,710	1,449	7.0	1,653	8.0	20,862	1,354	6.5	1,559	7.5

[1] Data refer to members of a labor union or an employee association similar to a union.

[2] Data refer to members of a labor union or an employee association similar to a union as well as workers who report no union affiliation but whose jobs are covered by a union or an employee association contract.

[3] The distinction between full- and part-time workers is based on hours usually worked. Beginning in 1994, these data will not sum to totals because full- or part-time status on the principal job is not identifiable for a small number of multiple jobholders.

NOTE: Data refer to the sole or principal job of full- and part-time workers. Excluded are all self-employed workers regardless of whether or not their businesses are incorporated. Detail for the above race and Hispanic-origin groups will not sum to totals because data for the "other races" group are not presented and Hispanics are included in both the white and black population groups. Beginning in January 1998, data reflect new composite estimation procedures and revised population controls used in the household survey.

Source: *Employment and Earnings*, vol. 46, no. 1, January 1999

percent in 1992, and just 13.9 percent in 1998. A total of 15.4 percent of the workforce was represented by unions in 1998. (This latter figure includes workers who were not union members but whose jobs were covered by a union contract.) The recession of the early 1980s, the movement of jobs overseas, the decline in traditionally unionized heavy industry, management's desire to eliminate union power, the threat of job loss, and unimaginative union leadership all contributed to the decline in union membership.

TABLE 3.32

Union affiliation of employed wage and salary workers by occupation and industry

(Numbers in thousands)

Occupation and industry	1997					1998				
	Total employed	Members of unions[1]		Represented by unions[2]		Total employed	Members of unions[1]		Represented by unions[2]	
		Total	Percent of employed	Total	Percent of employed		Total	Percent of employed	Total	Percent of employed
OCCUPATION										
Managerial and professional specialty	31,946	4,208	13.2	4,951	15.5	33,102	4,252	12.8	5,015	15.2
Executive, administrative, and managerial	14,908	763	5.1	959	6.4	15,473	812	5.2	1,017	6.6
Professional specialty	17,037	3,445	20.2	3,992	23.4	17,629	3,440	19.5	3,998	22.7
Technical, sales, and administrative support	34,796	3,158	9.1	3,648	10.5	35,379	3,239	9.2	3,677	10.4
Technicians and related support	4,111	427	10.4	501	12.2	4,150	433	10.4	498	12.0
Sales occupations	13,055	559	4.3	659	5.0	13,378	544	4.1	620	4.6
Administrative support, including clerical	17,631	2,172	12.3	2,488	14.1	17,851	2,262	12.7	2,558	14.3
Service occupations	16,204	2,141	13.2	2,356	14.5	16,594	2,209	13.3	2,398	14.5
Protective service	2,248	897	39.9	965	42.9	2,399	991	41.3	1,048	43.7
Service, except protective service	13,956	1,244	8.9	1,391	10.0	14,195	1,218	8.6	1,350	9.5
Precision production, craft, and repair	12,069	2,723	22.6	2,864	23.7	12,274	2,708	22.1	2,834	23.1
Operators, fabricators, and laborers	17,629	3,791	21.5	4,008	22.7	17,443	3,713	21.3	3,894	22.3
Machine operators, assemblers, and inspectors	7,717	1,690	21.9	1,764	22.9	7,498	1,603	21.4	1,672	22.3
Transportation and material moving occupations	4,931	1,199	24.3	1,279	25.9	4,935	1,204	24.4	1,267	25.7
Handlers, equipment cleaners, helpers, and laborers	4,981	901	18.1	964	19.4	5,010	906	18.1	956	19.1
Farming, forestry, and fishing	1,890	88	4.6	97	5.1	1,938	90	4.6	100	5.2
INDUSTRY										
Private wage and salary workers	96,386	9,363	9.7	10,255	10.6	98,329	9,306	9.5	10,104	10.3
Agriculture[3]	1,681	36	2.2	40	2.4	1,739	26	1.5	31	1.8
Nonagricultural industries	94,705	9,327	9.8	10,215	10.8	96,590	9,280	9.6	10,073	10.4
Mining	607	84	13.9	87	14.3	589	72	12.2	79	13.4
Construction	5,739	1,067	18.6	1,118	19.5	5,946	1,056	17.8	1,093	18.4
Manufacturing	19,961	3,253	16.3	3,441	17.2	19,763	3,127	15.8	3,315	16.8
Durable goods	11,908	2,090	17.5	2,198	18.5	11,999	1,990	16.6	2,097	17.5
Nondurable goods	8,053	1,164	14.5	1,243	15.4	7,763	1,138	14.7	1,218	15.7
Transportation and public utilities	6,949	1,804	26.0	1,909	27.5	7,147	1,843	25.8	1,931	27.0
Transportation	4,212	1,118	26.5	1,177	27.9	4,316	1,108	25.7	1,156	26.8
Communications and public utilities	2,737	686	25.1	731	26.7	2,831	735	26.0	775	27.4
Wholesale and retail trade	23,676	1,315	5.6	1,469	6.2	24,230	1,283	5.3	1,387	5.7
Wholesale trade	4,296	251	5.8	284	6.6	4,425	259	5.9	275	6.2
Retail trade	19,379	1,065	5.5	1,186	6.1	19,805	1,024	5.2	1,113	5.6
Finance, insurance, and real estate	7,070	155	2.2	199	2.8	7,420	150	2.0	195	2.6
Services	30,704	1,647	5.4	1,993	6.5	31,493	1,750	5.6	2,073	6.6
Government workers	18,147	6,747	37.2	7,668	42.3	18,401	6,905	37.5	7,815	42.5
Federal	3,217	1,030	32.0	1,266	39.4	3,269	1,105	33.8	1,299	39.7
State	5,031	1,485	29.5	1,679	33.4	5,150	1,431	27.8	1,667	32.4
Local	9,899	4,232	42.7	4,723	47.7	9,982	4,370	43.8	4,849	48.6

[1] Data refer to members of a labor union or an employee association similar to a union.

[2] Data refer to members of a labor union or an employee association similar to a union as well as workers who report no union affiliation but whose jobs are covered by a union or an employee association contract.

[3] Data for 1997 have been corrected.

NOTE: Data refer to the sole or principal job of full- and part-time workers. Excluded are all self-employed workers regardless of whether or not their businesses are incorporated. Beginning in January 1998, data reflect new composite estimation procedures and revised population controls used in the household survey.

Source: *Employment and Earnings*, vol. 46, no. 1, January 1999

Instead of demanding better hours, more pay, and improved working conditions — the traditional union demands — most unions agreed to "give backs" (surrendering existing benefits) and lower salaries in exchange for job guarantees during the 1980s. However, many companies continued to develop factories overseas or purchase heavily from foreign producers, which resulted in fewer jobs for American workers and more plant shutdowns.

In the mid-1990s, concerned about their declining membership, unions became more aggressive in recruiting members. Although concerned about eroding benefits, wages, and jobs, many workers were still wary of unions. The reputation of some union leaders, both past and present, disturbed them, and many workers feared losing their jobs if they became involved in union activities. The 1997 UPS strike promoted a more positive public view of unions.

TABLE 3.33

Median weekly earnings of full-time wage and salary workers by union affiliation and selected characteristics

Characteristic	1997				1998			
	Total	Members of unions[1]	Represented by unions[2]	Non-union	Total	Members of unions[1]	Represented by unions[2]	Non-union
SEX AND AGE								
Total, 16 years and over	$503	$640	$632	$478	$523	$659	$653	$499
16 to 24 years	306	385	384	302	319	415	410	315
25 years and over	540	655	648	511	572	673	667	537
25 to 34 years	481	579	572	466	502	595	591	489
35 to 44 years	579	675	666	548	597	683	678	576
45 to 54 years	607	704	697	578	620	716	712	592
55 to 64 years	558	661	657	512	592	697	692	560
65 years and over	393	614	609	374	405	610	597	383
Men, 16 years and over	579	683	679	539	598	699	696	573
16 to 24 years	317	402	404	313	334	430	424	326
25 years and over	615	697	693	595	639	712	709	617
25 to 34 years	515	607	603	503	544	618	615	524
35 to 44 years	651	712	708	630	677	722	719	660
45 to 54 years	713	744	741	698	732	755	755	719
55 to 64 years	669	702	701	649	699	738	737	674
65 years and over	452	677	672	415	482	657	659	445
Women, 16 years and over	431	577	568	411	456	596	593	430
16 to 24 years	292	353	351	289	305	389	382	301
25 years and over	462	587	581	437	485	605	602	463
25 to 34 years	427	521	514	416	451	542	542	439
35 to 44 years	482	592	585	461	498	605	605	479
45 to 54 years	495	627	620	465	516	651	645	488
55 to 64 years	433	582	575	408	476	602	596	448
65 years and over	348	(3)	586	324	350	548	522	329
RACE, HISPANIC ORIGIN, AND SEX								
White, 16 years and over	519	$663	654	494	545	683	678	513
Men	595	699	695	569	615	719	716	591
Women	444	595	587	421	468	610	607	443
Black, 16 years and over	400	533	523	371	426	578	572	398
Men	432	577	573	396	468	597	592	424
Women	375	504	496	349	400	537	533	376
Hispanic origin, 16 years and over	351	506	501	331	370	540	541	350
Men	371	538	526	348	390	585	584	367
Women	318	440	430	309	337	478	481	322

[1] Data refer to members of a labor union or an employee association similar to a union.
[2] Data refer to members of a labor union or an employee association similar to a union as well as workers who report no union affiliation but whose jobs are covered by a union or an employee association contract.
[3] Data not shown where base is less than 50,000.
NOTE: Data refer to the sole or principal job of full-time workers. Excluded are all self-employed workers regardless of whether or not their businesses are incorporated. Detail for the above race and Hispanic-origin groups will not sum to totals because data for the "other races" group are not presented and Hispanics are included in both the white and black population groups. Beginning in January 1998, data reflect new composite estimation procedures and revised population population controls used in the household survey.

Source: *Employment and Earnings*, vol. 46, no. 1, January 1999

TABLE 3.34

Percent of full-time employees participating in employer-provided benefit plans, and in selected features within plans, medium and large private establishments, selected years, 1980–97

Item	1980	1982	1984	1986	1988	1989	1991	1993	1995	1997
Scope of survey (in 000's).................................	21,352	21,043	21,013	21,303	31,059	32,428	31,163	28,728	33,374	38,409
Number of employees (in 000's):										
With medical care...	20,711	20,412	20,383	20,238	27,953	29,834	25,865	23,519	25,546	29,340
With life insurance...	20,498	20,201	20,172	20,451	28,574	30,482	29,293	26,175	29,078	33,495
With defined benefit plan..............................	17,936	17,676	17,231	16,190	19,567	20,430	18,386	16,015	17,417	19,202
Time-off plans										
Participants with:										
Paid lunch time..	10	9	9	10	11	10	8	9	–	–
Average minutes per day.............................	–	25	26	27	29	26	30	29	–	–
Paid rest time...	75	76	73	72	72	71	67	68	–	–
Average minutes per day.............................	–	25	26	26	26	26	28	26	–	–
Paid funeral leave...	–	–	–	88	85	84	80	83	80	81
Average days per occurrence......................	–	–	–	3.2	3.2	3.3	3.3	3.0	3.3	3.7
Paid holidays...	99	99	99	99	96	97	92	91	89	89
Average days per year.................................	10.1	10.0	9.8	10.0	9.4	9.2	10.2	9.4	9.1	9.3
Paid personal leave......................................	20	24	23	25	24	22	21	21	22	20
Average days per year.................................	–	3.8	3.6	3.7	3.3	3.1	3.3	3.1	3.3	3.5
Paid vacations...	100	99	99	100	98	97	96	97	96	95
Paid sick leave [1]...	62	67	67	70	69	68	67	65	58	56
Unpaid maternity leave..................................	–	–	–	–	33	37	37	60	–	–
Unpaid paternity leave..................................	–	–	–	–	16	18	26	53	–	–
Unpaid family leave	–	–	–	–	–	–	–	–	84	93
Insurance plans										
Participants in medical care plans.................	97	97	97	95	90	92	83	82	77	76
Percent of participants with coverage for:										
Home health care...	–	–	46	66	76	75	81	86	78	85
Extended care facilities.................................	58	62	62	70	79	80	80	82	73	78
Physical exam..	–	–	8	18	28	28	30	42	56	63
Percent of participants with employee contribution required for:										
Self coverage..	26	27	36	43	44	47	51	61	67	69
Average monthly contribution.......................	–	–	$11.93	$12.80	$19.29	$25.31	$26.60	$31.55	$33.92	$39.14
Family coverage..	46	51	58	63	64	66	69	76	78	80
Average monthly contribution.......................	–	–	$35.93	$41.40	$60.07	$72.10	$96.97	$107.42	$118.33	$130.07
Participants in life insurance plans................	96	96	96	96	92	94	94	91	87	87
Percent of participants with:										
Accidental death and dismemberment insurance...	69	72	74	72	78	71	71	76	77	74
Survivor income benefits...............................	–	–	–	10	8	7	6	5	7	6
Retiree protection available...........................	–	64	64	59	49	42	44	41	37	33
Participants in long-term disability insurance plans...	40	43	47	48	42	45	40	41	42	43
Participants in sickness and accident insurance plans...	54	51	51	49	46	43	45	44	–	–
Participants in short-term disability plans [1].............	–	–	–	–	–	–	–	–	53	55
Retirement plans										
Participants in defined benefit pension plans..........	84	84	82	76	63	63	59	56	52	50
Percent of participants with:										
Normal retirement prior to age 65.........................	55	58	63	64	59	62	55	52	52	52
Early retirement available...............................	98	97	97	98	98	97	98	95	96	95
Ad hoc pension increase in last 5 years..............	–	–	47	35	26	22	7	6	4	10
Terminal earnings formula.............................	53	52	54	57	55	64	56	61	58	56
Benefit coordinated with Social Security.............	45	45	56	62	62	63	54	48	51	49
Participants in defined contribution plans...............	–	–	–	60	45	48	48	49	55	57
Participants in plans with tax-deferred savings arrangements...	–	–	–	33	36	41	44	43	54	55
Other benefits										
Employees eligible for:										
Flexible benefits plans...................................	–	–	–	2	5	9	10	12	12	13
Reimbursement accounts [2]............................	–	–	–	5	12	23	36	52	38	32
Premium conversion plans.............................	–	–	–	–	–	–	–	–	5	7

[1] The definitions for paid sick leave and short-term disability (previously sickness and accident insurance) were changed for the 1995 survey. Paid sick leave now includes only plans that specify either a maximum number of days per year or unlimited days. Short-terms disability now includes all insured, self-insured, and State-mandated plans available on a per-disability basis, as well as the unfunded per-disability plans previously reported as sick leave. Sickness and accident insurance, reported in years prior to this survey, included only insured, self-insured, and State-mandated plans providing per-disability bene- fits at less than full pay.

[2] Prior to 1995, reimbursement accounts included premium conversion plans, which specifically allow medical plan participants to pay required plan premiums with pretax dollars. Also, reimbursement accounts that were part of flexible benefit plans were tabulated separately.

NOTE: Dash indicates data not available.

Source: *Monthly Labor Review*, vol. 122, no. 7, July 1999

In 1998, men (16.2 percent) were more likely to be union members than women (11.4 percent), and Blacks (17.7 percent) were more likely to be unionized than Whites (13.5 percent) or Hispanics (11.9 percent). (See Table 3.31.) Blacks were more likely to be union members because they were more likely to work in blue-collar or government jobs, while Whites were more likely to work in managerial jobs.

TABLE 3.35

Percent of full-time employees participating in employer-provided benefit plans, and in selected features within plans, small private establishments and State and local governments, 1987, 1990, 1992, 1994, and 1996

Item	Small private establishments				State and local governments			
	1990	1992	1994	1996	1987	1990	1992	1994
Scope of survey (in 000's)...............................	32,466	34,360	35,910	39,816	10,321	12,972	12,466	12,907
Number of employees (in 000's):								
With medical care..................	22,402	24,396	23,536	25,599	9,599	12,064	11,219	11,192
With life insurance..................	20,778	21,990	21,955	24,635	8,773	11,415	11,095	11,194
With defined benefit plan..................	6,493	7,559	5,480	5,883	9,599	11,675	10,845	11,708
Time-off plans								
Participants with:								
Paid lunch time..................	8	9	–	–	17	11	10	–
Average minutes per day..................	37	37	–	–	34	36	34	–
Paid rest time..................	48	49	–	–	58	56	53	–
Average minutes per day..................	27	26	–	–	29	29	29	–
Paid funeral leave..................	47	50	50	51	56	63	65	62
Average days per occurrence..................	2.9	3.0	3.1	3.0	3.7	3.7	3.7	3.7
Paid holidays..................	84	82	82	80	81	74	75	73
Average days per year[1]..................	9.5	9.2	7.5	7.6	10.9	13.6	14.2	11.5
Paid personal leave..................	11	12	13	14	38	39	38	38
Average days per year..................	2.8	2.6	2.6	3.0	2.7	2.9	2.9	3.0
Paid vacations..................	88	88	88	86	72	67	67	66
Paid sick leave [2]..................	47	53	50	50	97	95	95	94
Unpaid leave..................	17	18	–	–	57	51	59	–
Unpaid paternity leave..................	8	7	–	–	30	33	44	–
Unpaid family leave..................	–	–	47	48	–	–	–	93
Insurance plans								
Participants in medical care plans..................	69	71	66	64	93	93	90	87
Percent of participants with coverage for:								
Home health care..................	79	80	–	–	76	82	87	84
Extended care facilities..................	83	84	–	–	78	79	84	81
Physical exam..................	26	28	–	–	36	36	47	55
Percent of participants with employee contribution required for:								
Self coverage..................	42	47	52	52	35	38	43	47
Average monthly contribution..................	$25.13	$36.51	$40.97	$42.63	$15.74	$25.53	$28.97	$30.20
Family coverage..................	67	73	76	75	71	65	72	71
Average monthly contribution..................	$109.34	$150.54	$159.63	$181.53	$71.89	$117.59	$139.23	$149.70
Participants in life insurance plans..................	64	64	61	62	85	88	89	87
Percent of participants with:								
Accidental death and dismemberment insurance..................	78	76	79	77	67	67	74	64
Survivor income benefits..................	1	1	2	1	1	1	1	2
Retiree protection available..................	19	25	20	13	55	45	46	46
Participants in long-term disability insurance plans..................	19	23	20	22	31	27	28	30
Participants in sickness and accident insurance plans..................	6	26	26	–	14	21	22	21
Participants in short-term disability plans [2]..................	–	–	–	29	–	–	–	–
Retirement plans								
Participants in defined benefit pension plans..................	20	22	15	15	93	90	87	91
Percent of participants with:								
Normal retirement prior to age 65..................	54	50	–	47	92	89	92	92
Early retirement available..................	95	95	–	92	90	88	89	87
Ad hoc pension increase in last 5 years..................	7	4	–	–	33	16	10	13
Terminal earnings formula..................	58	54	–	53	100	100	100	99
Benefit coordinated with Social Security..................	49	46	–	44	18	8	10	49
Participants in defined contribution plans..................	31	33	34	38	9	9	9	9
Participants in plans with tax-deferred savings arrangements..................	17	24	23	28	28	45	45	24
Other benefits								
Employees eligible for:								
Flexible benefits plans..................	1	2	3	4	5	5	5	5
Reimbursement accounts [3]..................	8	14	19	12	5	31	50	64
Premium conversion plans..................	–	–	–	7	–	–	–	–

[1] Methods used to calculate the average number of paid holidays were revised in 1994 to count partial days more precisely. Average holidays for 1994 are not comparable with those reported in 1990 and 1992.

[2] The definitions for paid sick leave and short-term disability (previously sickness and accident insurance) were changed for the 1996 survey. Paid sick leave now includes only plans that specify either a maximum number of days per year or unlimited days. Short-term disability now includes all insured, self-insured, and State-mandated plans available on a per-disability basis, as well as the unfunded per-disability plans previously reported as sick leave.

Sickness and accident insurance, reported in years prior to this survey, included only insured, self-insured, and State-mandated plans providing per-disability benefits at less than full pay.

[3] Prior to 1996, reimbursement accounts included premium conversion plans, which specifically allow medical plan participants to pay required plan premiums with pretax dollars. Also, reimbursement accounts that were part of flexible benefit plans were tabulated separately.

NOTE: Dash indicates data not available.

Source: *Monthly Labor Review*, vol. 122, no. 7, July 1999

Not surprisingly, more blue-collar workers were unionized than managers. Protective service workers (police and firefighters) were most likely to be members of (41.3 percent) or represented by (43.7 percent) unions. A significant proportion of persons in professional specialties, many of whom were teachers, were either members of unions (19.5 percent) or covered by union agreements (22.7 percent). By industry, transportation and public utility workers (25.8 percent) and government workers (37.5 percent), including teachers, were, by far, the most unionized groups. (See Table 3.32.)

Union workers were generally better paid than nonunion workers. In 1998, the median earnings for a union member was $659 per week, compared to a nonunion worker who earned $499 (Table 3.33).

WORK STOPPAGES (STRIKES)

The number of work stoppages (strikes) has decreased dramatically over the past several decades. In 1974, there were 424 work stoppages, resulting in 31.8 million days idle. (This figure is calculated by multiplying the number of workers by the number of days they were on strike.) For most of the remainder of the 1970s, there were 200 to 300 work stoppages a year.

This changed dramatically during the 1980s. The number fell from 187 in 1980 to only 40 in 1988, rising slightly to 44 in 1990, with just 5.9 million days idle. In 1992, the number of work stoppages decreased to 35, involving nearly 4 million days. In 1994, the number of stoppages rose to 45, involving 5.0 million days. This dropped again to 37 stoppages in 1996, with 4.9 million days. In 1998, 34 work stoppages resulted in 5.1 million workdays of idleness. The decrease in the number of strikes is tied to the decline in union membership and the strong economy of the mid-1990s.

EMPLOYEE BENEFIT PLANS

In 1997, most workers (95 percent) in medium and large private establishments got paid vacations. Over half (56 percent) received paid sick leave, but only 20 percent got paid personal leave. Seventy-six percent participated in health insurance plans, down sharply from 97 percent in 1984. (See Table 3.34.)

In 1996, 86 percent of employees in small private firms received paid vacations while only two-thirds of state and local government workers (66 percent — 1994 figures) did. Workers for state and local governments (87 percent) were more likely to have medical care plans than those who worked for small firms (66 percent) in 1994. (See Table 3.35.)

CHAPTER IV

INCOME AND POVERTY

The federal government measures family and household income in a number of different ways. While the Bureau of the Census conducts most of the surveys, small differences can result from surveys being taken at different times of the year or with a slightly different focus. In many cases, the person being interviewed may not answer all the questions, and therefore, the figures may vary from category to category. Furthermore, none of these statistics are absolutely accurate — they are all estimates based on the best current survey methods.

All demographic surveys suffer from under-coverage of the population resulting from missed housing units and missed persons within sample households. Weighting procedures that account for missing persons try to correct the under-coverage, but its final impact on estimates is unknown. In addition, most of the statistics try to consider inflation. To do this, the researchers usually select a base year and then present their findings in the dollars of that year.

DEFINITIONS — HOUSEHOLDS AND FAMILIES

This section presents the results of surveys on both households and families and is based on several *Current Population Reports* prepared by the Bureau of the Census in Washington, D.C., including *Money Income in the United States: 1998* (1999), *Poverty in the United States: 1998* (1999); and *Asset Ownership of Households: 1993* (1995). Households include family and nonfamily households. A nonfamily household is one in which a person maintaining the household either lives alone or with nonrelatives only, such as a roommate or a boarder. A family is a group of two or more persons related by birth, marriage, or adoption and living together.

MEDIAN INCOMES

Households and Family

The Bureau of the Census measures both the median income (one-half earn more than this figure, and one-half earn less) and the mean (average) income, although it more frequently focuses on the median income. In 1998, for the fourth consecutive year, median incomes rose, after experiencing several years of decline. In 1998, the median household income was about $38,885, up significantly from the previous year's $37,581. (See Table 4.1.) This was the highest median income level ever recorded.

In 1998, overall household income exceeded the 1989 pre-recessionary peak of $37,884 (in 1998 dollars) by 2.6 percent (Table 4.1). In 1994, real median household income was 6.3 percent below the 1989 level; in 1995, it was 3.8 percent below the 1989 level; and in 1996, it was 2.7 percent below the 1989 level.

The working wife has become an essential feature of the American economy and an important influence on the economic level of the family. In 1998, 68.8 million women at least 15 years old worked in the labor force, 56.3 percent of them working full-time, year-round. The number of

TABLE 4.1

Comparison of Summary Measures of Income by Selected Characteristics: 1989, 1997, and 1998

[Households and people as of March of the following year.]

Characteristics	1998 Median income — Number (1,000)	1998 Median income — Value (dollars)	1998 Median income — 90-percent confidence interval (+/−) (dollars)	Median income in 1997 (in 1998 dollars) — Value (dollars)	Median income in 1997 (in 1998 dollars) — 90-percent confidence interval (+/−) (dollars)	Median income in 1989[r] (in 1998 dollars) — Value (dollars)	Median income in 1989[r] (in 1998 dollars) — 90-percent confidence interval (+/−) (dollars)	Percent change in real income 1997 to 1998 — Percent change	Percent change in real income 1997 to 1998 — 90-percent confidence interval (+/−)	Percent change in real income 1989[r] to 1998 — Percent change	Percent change in real income 1989[r] to 1998 — 90-percent confidence interval (+/−)
HOUSEHOLDS											
All households	103,874	38,885	378	37,581	286	37,884	344	*3.5	0.6	*2.6	0.8
Type of Household											
Family households.	71,535	47,469	410	46,053	394	45,343	413	*3.1	0.6	*4.7	0.8
Married-couple families	54,770	54,276	530	52,486	388	50,702	458	*3.4	0.6	*7.0	0.9
Female householder, no husband present	12,789	24,393	655	23,399	657	22,662	603	*4.2	2.0	*7.6	2.5
Male householder, no wife present. .	3,976	39,414	1,633	37,205	1,201	39,717	1,607	*5.9	2.8	−0.8	3.5
Nonfamily households.	32,339	23,441	467	22,043	347	22,568	363	*6.3	1.3	*3.9	1.6
Female householder	17,971	18,615	462	17,887	428	18,143	474	*4.1	1.8	2.6	2.2
Male householder	14,368	30,414	559	28,022	770	29,489	660	*8.5	1.8	*3.1	1.8
Race and Hispanic Origin of Householder											
All races[1]	103,874	38,885	378	37,581	286	37,884	344	*3.5	0.6	*2.6	0.8
White.	87,212	40,912	336	39,579	413	39,852	320	*3.4	0.7	*2.7	0.7
Non-Hispanic White.	78,577	42,439	401	41,209	354	40,792	331	*3.0	0.6	*4.0	0.8
Black.	12,579	25,351	653	25,440	720	23,950	789	−0.3	1.9	*5.8	2.7
Asian and Pacific Islander	3,308	46,637	2,135	45,954	2,102	47,337	2,007	1.5	3.2	−1.5	3.7
Hispanic origin[2]	9,060	28,330	898	27,043	792	28,631	882	*4.8	1.8	−1.1	2.7
Age of Householder											
15 to 24 years.	5,770	23,564	730	22,935	822	24,401	755	2.7	2.4	−3.4	2.6
25 to 34 years.	18,819	40,069	696	38,769	755	39,041	603	*3.4	1.3	*2.6	1.5
35 to 44 years.	23,968	48,451	730	47,081	637	49,310	675	*2.9	1.0	−1.7	1.2
45 to 54 years.	20,158	54,148	877	52,683	727	54,575	893	*2.8	1.1	−0.8	1.4
55 to 64 years.	13,571	43,167	989	42,000	763	40,569	878	*2.8	1.5	*6.4	2.0
65 years and over	21,589	21,729	395	21,084	406	20,719	381	*3.1	1.3	*4.9	1.6
Nativity of the Householder											
Native born.	92,853	39,677	390	38,229	381	(NA)	(NA)	*3.8	0.7	(X)	(X)
Foreign born.	11,021	32,963	1,230	31,806	802	(NA)	(NA)	3.6	2.3	(X)	(X)
Naturalized citizen.	4,877	41,028	1,808	(NA)	(NA)	(NA)	(NA)	(X)	(X)	(X)	(X)
Not a citizen	6,143	28,278	1,199	27,379	971	(NA)	(NA)	3.3	2.8	(X)	(X)
Region											
Northeast.	19,877	40,634	772	39,535	877	42,780	709	*2.8	1.5	*−5.0	1.5
Midwest	24,489	40,609	600	38,913	747	37,685	642	*4.4	1.3	*7.8	1.5
South	36,959	35,797	500	34,880	580	33,933	471	*2.6	1.1	*5.5	1.3
West	22,549	40,983	661	39,772	910	40,705	696	*3.0	1.4	0.7	1.4
Residence											
Inside metropolitan areas	83,441	40,983	352	39,994	448	40,776	346	*2.5	0.7	0.5	0.7
Inside central cities	32,144	33,151	638	32,039	456	(NA)	(NA)	*3.5	1.5	(X)	(X)
Outside central cities	51,297	46,402	512	45,364	568	(NA)	(NA)	*2.3	0.8	(X)	(X)
Outside metropolitan areas	20,433	32,022	630	30,525	690	29,393	636	*4.9	1.5	*8.9	1.9
EARNINGS OF FULL-TIME, YEAR-ROUND WORKERS											
Male	56,951	35,345	219	34,199	535	35,727	242	*3.4	0.9	*−1.1	0.6
Female	38,785	25,862	194	25,362	259	24,614	270	*2.0	0.7	*5.1	0.9
PER CAPITA INCOME											
All races[1]	271,743	20,120	199	19,541	202	18,280	132	*3.0	0.7	*10.1	0.8
White	223,294	21,394	237	20,743	239	19,385	147	*3.1	0.8	*10.4	0.8
Non-Hispanic White	193,074	22,952	268	22,246	271	(NA)	(NA)	*3.2	0.9	(X)	(X)
Black.	35,070	12,957	322	12,543	346	11,406	253	*3.3	1.9	*13.6	2.1
Asian and Pacific Islander	10,897	18,709	1,094	18,510	1,128	(NA)	(NA)	1.1	4.4	(X)	(X)
Hispanic origin[2]	31,689	11,434	410	10,941	393	10,770	294	*4.5	2.3	*6.2	2.7

*Statistically significant change at the 90-percent confidence level.   [r]Revised to reflect the population distribution reported in the 1990 census.

[1]Data for American Indians, Eskimos, and Aleuts are not shown separately. Data for this population group are not tabulated from the CPS because of its small size.

[2]Hispanics may be of any race.

Source: *Money Income in the United States: 1998*, Bureau of the Census, Washington, DC, 1999

wives in the paid labor force doubled from 15.8 million (36.6 percent of all married-couple families) in 1968 to 33.7 million (about 61 percent) in 1998.

Regions and States

For the first time since data were first tabulated (in 1975), median household income levels

TABLE 4.2

Median Income of Households by State

[Income in 1998 dollars.]

States	Three-year average 1996-1998		Two-year moving averages				Differences in 2-year moving averages 1997-1998 less 1996-1997	
			1997-1998		1996-1997			
	Median income	Standard error	Median income	Standard error	Median income	Standard error	Difference	Percent change
United States	37,779	137	38,233	167	37,227	148	* 1,007	* 2.7
Alabama	33,394	1,003	34,351	1,210	31,958	1,211	* 2,393	* 7.5
Alaska	51,421	1,236	49,717	1,418	51,786	1,354	−2,069	* −4.0
Arizona	34,402	909	35,170	1,057	33,058	1,085	* 2,112	* 6.4
Arkansas	27,471	784	27,117	958	27,373	900	−256	−0.9
California	40,522	548	40,623	604	40,317	710	307	0.8
Colorado	44,349	1,075	45,253	1,282	43,224	1,389	* 2,028	* 4.7
Connecticut	44,978	1,832	45,589	1,961	44,213	2,174	1,376	3.1
Delaware	42,000	1,260	42,581	1,583	42,270	1,470	310	0.7
District of Columbia	32,999	911	32,895	953	32,783	1,099	112	0.3
Florida	33,234	442	33,935	561	32,396	462	* 1,538	* 4.7
Georgia	36,553	891	37,950	869	35,497	1,117	* 2,453	* 6.9
Hawaii	41,932	1,325	41,199	1,580	42,484	1,400	−1,285	−3.0
Idaho	35,554	903	35,302	1,009	34,991	1,131	311	0.9
Illinois	42,065	730	42,552	843	41,509	805	1,043	2.5
Indiana	38,580	958	39,613	1,152	38,004	1,048	1,609	* 4.2
Iowa	35,276	954	35,664	1,029	34,405	1,189	1,259	3.7
Kansas	35,867	1,115	36,875	1,338	35,445	1,297	1,430	4.0
Kentucky	34,633	1,101	35,113	1,314	33,823	1,308	1,289	3.8
Louisiana	32,317	1,072	32,757	1,329	32,608	1,199	148	0.5
Maine	34,989	854	34,461	977	34,664	1,060	−202	−0.6
Maryland	47,711	1,456	48,714	1,515	46,558	1,742	2,156	4.6
Massachusetts	42,017	1,236	42,511	1,392	41,853	1,412	658	1.6
Michigan	40,639	758	40,583	841	40,048	950	536	1.3
Minnesota	44,579	1,159	45,576	1,508	42,906	1,155	* 2,671	* 6.2
Mississippi	28,592	924	29,031	1,056	28,329	1,140	703	2.5
Missouri	37,640	1,307	38,662	1,628	36,360	1,512	* 2,302	* 6.3
Montana	30,348	914	30,622	943	29,733	1,153	889	3.0
Nebraska	35,661	1,086	35,823	1,274	35,284	1,278	538	1.5
Nevada	39,751	1,061	39,608	1,166	39,749	1,347	−141	−0.4
New Hampshire	42,511	1,228	43,297	1,438	41,288	1,410	2,009	4.9
New Jersey	49,303	971	49,297	1,184	49,041	1,115	256	0.5
New Mexico	29,386	863	31,049	1,058	28,308	948	* 2,741	* 9.7
New York	36,845	508	36,875	585	36,571	584	304	0.8
North Carolina	36,407	696	36,118	803	36,692	813	−574	−1.6
North Dakota	31,717	891	31,229	1,055	32,424	1,074	−1,195	−3.7
Ohio	37,005	832	37,811	1,038	36,046	829	* 1,765	* 4.9
Oklahoma	31,357	789	32,783	935	30,172	893	* 2,612	* 8.7
Oregon	37,922	1,197	38,447	1,538	37,350	1,297	1,098	2.9
Pennsylvania	37,791	713	38,558	846	37,179	818	* 1,380	· * 3.7
Rhode Island	38,150	1,464	38,012	2,026	36,881	1,416	1,131	3.1
South Carolina	34,692	1,037	34,031	1,213	35,404	1,272	−1,373	−3.9
South Dakota	31,205	755	31,471	895	30,415	906	1,056	3.5
Tennessee	32,397	897	32,602	1,104	31,550	1,033	1,052	3.3
Texas	35,254	555	35,702	642	34,990	693	713	2.0
Utah	42,073	1,084	43,870	1,315	40,960	1,318	* 2,911	* 7.1
Vermont	36,196	1,097	37,485	1,374	34,607	1,260	2,878	* 8.3
Virginia	42,572	1,326	43,490	1,695	42,181	1,419	1,309	3.1
Washington	43,593	1,128	46,339	1,286	41,679	1,402	* 4,660	* 11.2
West Virginia	26,950	831	27,310	883	27,072	1,104	238	0.9
Wisconsin	41,032	997	40,769	1,002	40,884	1,255	−115	−0.3
Wyoming	33,783	878	34,597	1,143	33,050	981	* 1,547	* 4.7
New York, NY CMSA	41,908	529	41,777	608	41,968	636	−191	−0.5
Los Angeles, CA CMSA	39,111	637	39,520	819	38,682	739	838	2.2

* Statistically significant at the 90-percent confidence level.

Source: *Money Income in the United States: 1998*, Bureau of the Census, Washington, DC, 1999

in all four regions increased. In 1998, the West had the highest median household income ($40,983), followed by the Northeast ($40,634) and the Midwest ($40,609). The South had the lowest median household income ($35,797). (See Table 4.1.)

When comparing the relative ranking of states, the U.S. Census Bureau considers three-year averages a more accurate indicator. For 1996 through 1998, incomes were highest in Alaska, New Jersey, Maryland, Connecticut, Minnesota, and Colorado. Incomes were lowest in West Virginia, Arkansas, Mississippi, and New Mexico. (See Table 4.2.)

Residence

Households located in central cities of large metropolitan areas (one million or more population) had a median income of $33,151, compared to a median income of $46,402 of households located in the suburbs of large metropolitan areas. The median income in households outside metropolitan areas was $32,022 in 1998. (See Table 4.1.)

Race and Hispanic Origin

In 1998, Asians and Pacific Islanders continued to have the highest median household income ($46,637) among the racial and Hispanic-origin groups. Non-Hispanic White households ($42,439) had the second highest, followed by Hispanic-origin households ($28,330) and Black households

($25,351). (See Table 4.1 and Figure 4.1.) (Persons of Hispanic origin may be of any race.)

Although Asians and Pacific Islanders as a group had the highest median household income in 1998, their income per household member was lower than the income per household member of non-Hispanic White households. (The income per household member measure represents the average amount of income available to each household member.) The larger average size of Asian and Pacific Islander households (3.15 persons compared to 2.47 for non-Hispanic White households) produced an income per household member of $19,107 in 1998, less than the $22,633 for non-Hispanic White households. The income per household member for Black households was $12,402, and for Hispanics, $11,071, based on average household sizes of 2.75 and 3.46, respectively.

The typical White family earned considerably more ($49,023) than the typical Black ($29,404) or Hispanic ($29,608) family. One reason for this large disparity was the larger proportion of minority families headed by female householders. When the incomes of White ($54,736), Black ($47,383),

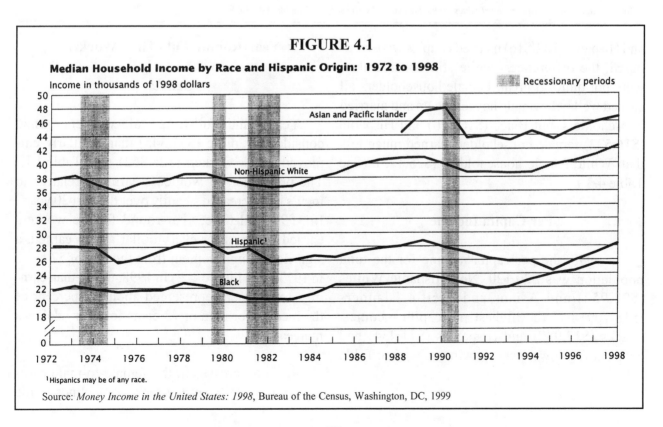

FIGURE 4.1

Median Household Income by Race and Hispanic Origin: 1972 to 1998

Income in thousands of 1998 dollars

Recessionary periods

Asian and Pacific Islander

Non-Hispanic White

Hispanic¹

Black

¹Hispanics may be of any race.

Source: *Money Income in the United States: 1998*, Bureau of the Census, Washington, DC, 1999

TABLE 4.3

Median Income of Families by Selected Characteristics, Race, and Hispanic Origin of Householder: 1998, 1997, and 1996

[Families as of March of the following year. An asterisk (*) preceding percent change indicates statistically significant change at the 90-percent confidence level.]

Characteristic	1998			1997			1996			Percent change in real median income (1997-1998)
		Median income			Median income			Median income		
	Number (1,000)	Value (dollars)	Standard error (dollars)	Number (1,000)	Value (dollars)	Standard error (dollars)	Number (1,000)	Value (dollars)	Standard error (dollars)	
ALL RACES										
All families	71 551	46 737	241	70 884	44 568	267	70 241	42 300	209	* 3.3
Type of Family										
Married-couple families	54 778	54 180	321	54 321	51 591	231	53 604	49 707	305	* 3.4
Wife in paid labor force	33 680	63 751	379	33 535	60 669	291	33 242	58 381	322	* 3.5
Wife not in paid labor force	21 098	37 161	369	20 786	36 027	305	20 362	33 748	393	1.6
Male householder, no wife present	3 977	35 681	850	3 911	32 960	839	3 847	31 600	549	* 6.6
Female householder, no husband present..	12 796	22 163	325	12 652	21 023	308	12 790	19 911	306	* 3.8
WHITE										
All families	60 077	49 023	283	59 515	46 754	259	58 934	44 756	266	* 3.2
Type of Family										
Married-couple families	48 461	54 736	335	48 070	52 098	247	47 650	50 190	257	* 3.5
Wife in paid labor force	29 378	64 480	402	29 344	61 441	309	29 308	58 995	333	* 3.3
Wife not in paid labor force	19 083	37 755	416	18 726	36 343	319	18 342	34 214	406	* 2.3
Male householder, no wife present	3 087	37 798	1 099	3 137	34 802	950	2 944	32 439	962	* 6.9
Female householder, no husband present..	8 529	25 175	414	8 308	22 999	465	8 339	22 373	408	* 7.8
BLACK										
All families	8 452	29 404	713	8 408	28 602	629	8 455	26 522	470	1.2
Type of Family										
Married-couple families	3 979	47 383	1 165	3 921	45 372	755	3 851	41 963	965	2.8
Wife in paid labor force	2 852	55 579	984	2 716	51 702	748	2 636	50 805	1 002	* 5.9
Wife not in paid labor force	1 127	27 927	1 056	1 205	28 757	1 499	1 216	27 594	1 173	-4.4
Male householder, no wife present	660	27 087	1 178	562	25 654	1 212	657	26 338	2 006	4.0
Female householder, no husband present..	3 813	16 770	418	3 926	16 879	438	3 947	15 530	503	-2.2
HISPANIC ORIGIN[1]										
All families	7 273	29 608	568	6 961	28 142	655	6 631	26 179	495	* 3.6
Type of Family										
Married-couple families	4 945	34 816	745	4 804	33 914	902	4 520	31 930	611	1.1
Wife in paid labor force	2 726	45 188	980	2 650	42 280	893	2 536	40 956	778	* 5.2
Wife not in paid labor force	2 219	24 939	716	2 153	23 749	724	1 984	22 769	675	3.4
Male householder, no wife present	600	29 227	1 357	545	25 543	1 780	494	25 875	1 249	* 12.7
Female householder, no husband present..	1 728	16 532	710	1 612	14 994	703	1 617	12 952	677	* 8.6

Source: *Money Income in the United States: 1998*, Bureau of the Census, Washington, DC, 1999

and Hispanic ($34,816) married couples were compared, the differences, while still considerable, were not quite so great. Female householders all earned well below male householders and married householders, but Black ($16,770) and Hispanic ($16,532) female householders earned much less than White female householders ($25,175). (See Table 4.3.)

Per Capita Income

In 1998, the per capita income for the total population was $20,120. Non-Hispanic Whites ($22,952) and Asians and Pacific Islanders ($18,709) had the highest per capita incomes. Blacks ($12,957) and Hispanics ($11,434) had considerably lower per capita incomes. (See Table 4.1.)

Year-Round, Full-Time Workers

Gender

Year-round, full-time male workers earned considerably more ($35,345) than similarly employed female workers ($25,862). (See Table 4.1.) The proportion of women's earnings relative to men's has increased steadily over the past 20 years. In 1997, full-time, year-round female workers earned 74 cents for every dollar a man earned, a significant improvement from the low of 57 cents in 1973. (See Figure 4.2.) In 1998, the median earnings for women represented about 73 percent of the median for men or 73 cents for every dollar a man earned.

Recent increases in the female-to-male earnings ratio have been due more to declines in the earnings of men than to increases in the earnings of women. Since 1989, the earnings of men have declined by 1.1 percent, while the earnings of women have increased by 5.1 percent. (See Table 4.1.) According to many observers, factors that contribute to the gender wage gap include differences in education, years and continuity of work experience, types of occupations or industries traditionally chosen by women workers, and union status.

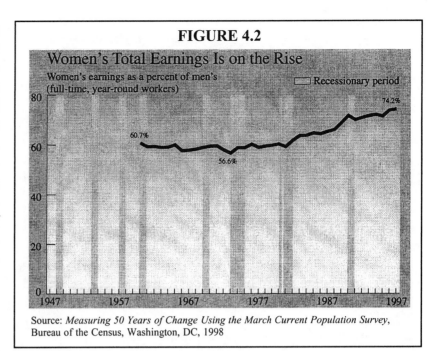

FIGURE 4.2

Women's Total Earnings Is on the Rise

Women's earnings as a percent of men's (full-time, year-round workers)   ☐ Recessionary period

Source: *Measuring 50 Years of Change Using the March Current Population Survey,* Bureau of the Census, Washington, DC, 1998

Education

Education is a very important factor influencing income. Median earnings increase sharply as educational attainment increases. The 1998 median earnings of those households whose householders had a ninth to twelfth grade education (no diploma) were $20,724; for high school graduates, $34,373; for those with an associate's degree, $48,604; and for those with a bachelor's degree or postgraduate degree, such as a master's, $66,474. (See Table 4.4.)

Compared to men with the same educational attainment, women with less than a ninth grade education earned 76 percent of what men earned. Women who attended high school but did not graduate earned about 68 percent of men's median income. Women with a high school diploma or a bachelor's degree earned 71 percent; with a professional degree, 61 percent; and with a doctorate, 75 percent of the median income of men with similar degrees. (See Figure 4.3.)

MONEY INCOME DISTRIBUTION

In 1998, just over two-fifths of American households (43.3 percent) earned between $15,000 and $49,999, while about one-fifth (18 percent) made less than $15,000. Close to two-fifths (38.6 percent) earned $50,000 or more. (See Table 4.4.) The proportions have changed somewhat over the past thirty years. In 1967, after adjusting for infla-

tion, 55 percent of American households made $15,000 to $49,999; 22.3 percent earned less than $15,000; and 22.6 percent made more than $50,000. The proportion making $100,000 or more rose from 2.9 percent in 1967 to 8.1 percent in 1993 and 10.5 percent in 1998. While 11.3 percent of White households in 1998 made $100,000 or more, only 4.6 percent of Hispanic and 4 percent of Black households earned that much.

Income Inequality

Another, more significant, way to show how income is divided in the United States is to determine how much of the nation's total income is earned by each economic quintile (one-fifth) of the population. Since 1967, the proportion of income made by the highest-earning 20 percent of the population has increased from 43.8 percent to 49.2 percent, while the share of the middle 60 percent dropped from 52.3 percent in 1967 to 47.2 percent in 1998. Meanwhile, the lowest-earning 20 percent accounted for 4.0 percent in 1967 and just 3.6 percent of total income in 1998. The share of income controlled by the top 5 percent of households increased from 17.5 percent in 1967 to 21.4 percent in 1998. (See Figure 4.4.)

Another way to look at the growth in inequality over time is to compare incomes at selected

79

TABLE 4.4

Selected Characteristics—Households by Total Money Income in 1998

[Numbers in thousands. Households as of March of the following year.]

Characteristic	Total	Less than $5,000	$5,000 to $9,999	$10,000 to $14,999	$15,000 to $24,999	$25,000 to $34,999	$35,000 to $49,999	$50,000 to $74,999	$75,000 to $99,999	$100,000 and over	Median income Value (dollars)	Median income Standard error (dollars)	Mean income Value (dollars)	Mean income Standard error (dollars)
All households	103 874	3 373	7 332	8 093	14 587	13 698	16 660	19 272	9 934	10 926	38 885	230	51 855	280
TYPE OF RESIDENCE														
Inside metropolitan areas	83 441	2 687	5 408	6 193	11 103	10 669	13 091	15 643	8 636	10 012	40 983	215	54 725	330
Inside central cities	32 144	1 562	2 909	3 042	4 878	4 320	4 931	5 134	2 581	2 788	33 151	388	46 467	460
1 million or more	20 513	997	1 954	1 987	2 999	2 628	3 065	3 269	1 686	1 928	33 559	500	47 529	595
Under 1 million	11 631	566	955	1 054	1 879	1 692	1 867	1 865	895	859	32 488	535	44 593	716
Outside central cities.........	51 297	1 125	2 499	3 151	6 225	6 349	8 159	10 509	6 055	7 224	46 402	311	59 901	449
1 million or more	35 028	671	1 523	1 974	3 830	4 083	5 452	7 312	4 421	5 762	49 940	395	63 998	571
Under 1 million	16 269	454	976	1 177	2 395	2 266	2 707	3 198	1 634	1 462	39 428	564	51 079	693
Outside metropolitan areas	20 433	686	1 924	1 900	3 484	3 029	3 569	3 629	1 298	914	32 022	383	40 131	547
REGION														
Northeast	19 877	687	1 468	1 580	2 614	2 358	3 007	3 582	2 048	2 532	40 634	469	55 041	624
Midwest	24 489	646	1 541	1 834	3 304	3 353	3 940	5 032	2 418	2 422	40 609	365	52 430	592
South	36 959	1 391	2 989	2 925	5 683	5 100	5 907	6 473	3 168	3 323	35 797	304	48 284	467
West.......................	22 549	648	1 334	1 755	2 985	2 887	3 806	4 185	2 300	2 648	40 983	403	54 274	632
RACE AND HISPANIC ORIGIN OF HOUSEHOLDER														
White	87 212	2 263	5 352	6 468	11 937	11 480	14 230	16 862	8 730	9 889	40 912	205	54 207	319
Black	12 579	918	1 773	1 338	2 183	1 700	1 795	1 659	708	507	25 351	397	34 139	456
Hispanic origin[1]	9 060	441	912	989	1 620	1 477	1 432	1 271	503	416	28 330	546	38 280	814
TYPE OF HOUSEHOLD														
Family households.............	71 535	1 650	2 537	3 653	8 639	8 996	12 192	15 676	8 489	9 702	47 469	249	60 406	371
Married-couple families.......	54 770	627	914	1 841	5 488	6 329	9 454	13 301	7 739	9 077	54 276	322	68 010	452
Male householder, no wife present	3 976	97	138	209	641	675	759	845	319	293	39 414	993	48 306	1 053
Female householder, no husband present	12 789	925	1 486	1 603	2 510	1 992	1 979	1 530	431	333	24 393	398	31 608	496
Nonfamily households..........	32 339	1 723	4 795	4 440	5 948	4 701	4 468	3 596	1 444	1 224	23 441	285	32 938	319
Male householder	14 368	726	1 358	1 364	2 475	2 237	2 415	2 128	849	816	30 414	340	40 127	565
Living alone...............	10 966	642	1 283	1 201	2 119	1 783	1 768	1 338	425	408	26 021	334	34 572	626
Female householder	17 971	998	3 437	3 076	3 473	2 464	2 053	1 467	595	408	18 615	281	27 190	342
Living alone...............	15 640	947	3 366	2 951	3 155	2 144	1 638	959	295	186	16 406	236	23 362	321
AGE OF HOUSEHOLDER														
Under 65 years	82 286	2 741	4 128	4 645	9 694	10 627	14 029	17 386	9 104	9 930	44 697	274	56 688	327
15 to 24 years	5 770	493	582	668	1 325	944	932	551	151	123	23 564	445	30 947	995
25 to 34 years	18 819	673	833	1 193	2 521	2 932	3 502	4 192	1 713	1 260	40 069	423	47 960	540
35 to 44 years	23 968	606	888	1 132	2 426	2 950	4 387	5 529	3 002	3 049	48 451	444	60 103	616
45 to 54 years	20 158	475	813	790	1 831	2 119	3 123	4 621	2 724	3 663	54 148	534	67 293	729
55 to 64 years	13 571	494	1 013	863	1 590	1 681	2 086	2 494	1 515	1 835	43 167	601	57 952	865
65 years and over	21 589	632	3 204	3 448	4 893	3 071	2 631	1 886	829	995	21 729	240	33 432	468
65 to 74 years	11 373	306	1 406	1 353	2 400	1 742	1 645	1 257	587	678	26 112	399	38 580	691
75 years and over	10 216	327	1 798	2 095	2 493	1 329	986	629	243	317	17 885	283	27 700	609
Mean age of householder	48.6	45.8	57.0	55.6	51.7	47.9	46.1	45.0	46.0	47.8	(X)	(X)	(X)	(X)
SIZE OF HOUSEHOLD														
One person	26 606	1 588	4 649	4 151	5 273	3 926	3 406	2 297	720	594	20 154	221	27 982	324
Two people	34 262	872	1 310	2 051	5 115	4 991	5 936	6 871	3 327	3 788	41 512	301	54 930	515
Three people	17 386	411	661	844	1 941	2 014	2 999	3 971	2 247	2 297	49 069	518	60 356	708
Four people	15 030	255	381	544	1 241	1 567	2 536	3 723	2 206	2 578	55 886	607	67 691	770
Five people	6 962	167	204	310	622	729	1 161	1 680	976	1 113	53 706	911	66 523	1 336
Six people	2 367	46	95	126	256	299	383	473	330	360	49 080	1 500	63 626	2 125
Seven people or more	1 261	33	33	66	138	171	239	256	128	196	46 646	1 676	62 922	3 063
Mean size of household	2.61	2.06	1.74	1.98	2.23	2.45	2.72	2.97	3.18	3.25	(X)	(X)	(X)	(X)
NUMBER OF EARNERS														
No earners	21 263	2 056	5 005	3 984	4 702	2 400	1 594	893	299	330	14 442	147	20 946	242
One earner	36 216	1 150	2 007	3 350	7 134	6 787	6 670	5 121	1 947	2 050	31 162	183	42 498	461
Two earners or more	46 396	167	321	759	2 752	4 511	8 396	13 257	7 687	8 545	60 787	258	73 323	453
Two earners	36 501	146	308	712	2 527	3 935	7 117	10 427	5 481	5 848	57 388	319	69 238	486
Three earners...............	7 409	21	12	47	213	506	1 066	2 223	1 558	1 763	70 012	816	84 455	1 326
Four earners or more	2 485	0	1	0	12	71	213	608	648	933	86 676	1 640	100 147	1 953
Mean number of earners	1.41	0.45	0.37	0.62	0.90	1.23	1.55	1.88	2.11	2.18	(X)	(X)	(X)	(X)
WORK EXPERIENCE OF HOUSEHOLDER														
Total	103 874	3 373	7 332	8 093	14 587	13 698	16 660	19 272	9 934	10 926	38 885	230	51 855	280
Worked	74 296	1 177	2 038	3 571	8 487	9 867	13 421	16 937	8 929	9 869	48 179	263	60 766	353
Worked at full-time jobs	64 566	690	1 179	2 485	6 882	8 626	11 941	15 419	8 298	9 046	50 562	223	63 102	383
50 weeks or more	54 963	283	448	1 676	5 302	7 240	10 323	13 853	7 542	8 296	53 033	301	66 088	420
27 to 49 weeks	6 194	60	301	447	998	968	1 136	1 103	599	582	39 041	808	52 071	1 211
26 weeks or less	3 409	346	430	363	581	418	482	463	158	167	24 525	1 140	34 993	1 078
Worked at part-time jobs	9 730	487	859	1 086	1 605	1 241	1 480	1 518	631	823	31 470	618	45 266	857
50 weeks or more	4 867	118	363	561	872	667	721	763	337	465	32 276	852	47 585	1 244
27 to 49 weeks	2 325	89	217	234	384	268	407	371	147	209	33 945	1 312	47 049	1 791
26 weeks or less	2 538	280	280	290	349	306	352	384	147	149	27 249	1 194	39 184	1 540
Did not work	29 578	2 196	5 294	4 522	6 100	3 831	3 239	2 335	1 005	1 056	19 093	193	29 471	362

See footnotes at end of table.

(continued)

Selected Characteristics—Households by Total Money Income in 1998—Con.

[Numbers in thousands. Households as of March of the following year.]

Characteristic	Total	Less than $5,000	$5,000 to $9,999	$10,000 to $14,999	$15,000 to $24,999	$25,000 to $34,999	$35,000 to $49,999	$50,000 to $74,999	$75,000 to $99,999	$100,000 and over	Median income Value (dollars)	Median income Standard error (dollars)	Mean income Value (dollars)	Mean income Standard error (dollars)
EDUCATIONAL ATTAINMENT[2]														
Total	98 104	2 880	6 750	7 425	13 262	12 754	15 727	18 721	9 783	10 802	40 296	194	53 084	290
Less than 9th grade	7 047	414	1 573	1 327	1 537	918	668	402	104	104	16 154	347	23 501	610
9th to 12th grade (no diploma) ..	9 407	586	1 473	1 346	2 056	1 304	1 289	890	286	177	20 724	336	28 234	479
High school graduate (includes equivalency)	30 613	1 010	2 258	2 613	4 840	4 831	5 534	5 729	2 347	1 450	34 373	334	42 352	370
Some college, no degree	17 833	437	771	1 126	2 357	2 579	3 330	3 852	1 842	1 539	41 658	374	51 220	597
Associate degree	7 468	146	246	387	772	918	1 376	1 875	924	824	48 604	818	57 317	1 066
Bachelor's degree or more......	25 738	287	430	626	1 700	2 204	3 531	5 973	4 280	6 707	66 474	499	83 096	755
Bachelor's degree	16 781	191	323	422	1 251	1 616	2 465	4 070	2 758	3 684	62 188	549	75 213	796
Master's degree	5 961	60	71	134	340	429	805	1 337	1 061	1 723	71 086	955	87 497	1 692
Professional degree	1 623	23	19	51	64	81	132	282	200	771	95 309	3 560	127 499	4 787
Doctorate degree	1 373	13	17	18	45	77	129	284	261	528	84 100	3 491	107 847	3 700

[1]Hispanics may be of any race.
[2]Restricted to people 25 years and over.

Source: *Money Income in the United States: 1998*, Bureau of the Census, Washington, DC, 1999

positions in the income distribution. A household at the 95th percentile in 1998 (top 5 percent) had $132,199 or more in income, at least 8.2 times that of a household at the twentieth percentile ($16,116 or less). Three decades before, in 1967, a household at the 95th percentile had at least 6.3 times the income of a household at the twentieth percentile. (See Table 4.5.)

Examining the change in average real household income for each quintile is still another way to consider growth in inequality. The average income of households in the top quintile grew 58.3 percent, from $80,584 (in 1998 dollars) in 1967 to $127,529 in 1998, and the fourth quintile increased 35.5 percent, from $44,468 to $60,266. During the same period, the average income in the lowest quintile grew by only 26.3 percent, from $7,301 to

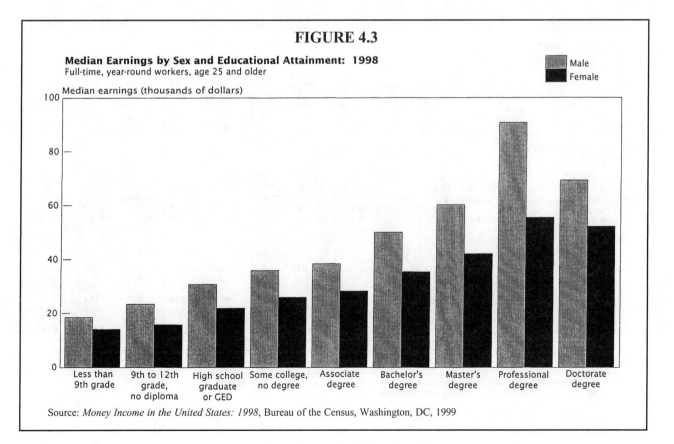

FIGURE 4.3

Median Earnings by Sex and Educational Attainment: 1998
Full-time, year-round workers, age 25 and older

Male
Female

Median earnings (thousands of dollars)

Less than 9th grade | 9th to 12th grade, no diploma | High school graduate or GED | Some college, no degree | Associate degree | Bachelor's degree | Master's degree | Professional degree | Doctorate degree

Source: *Money Income in the United States: 1998*, Bureau of the Census, Washington, DC, 1999

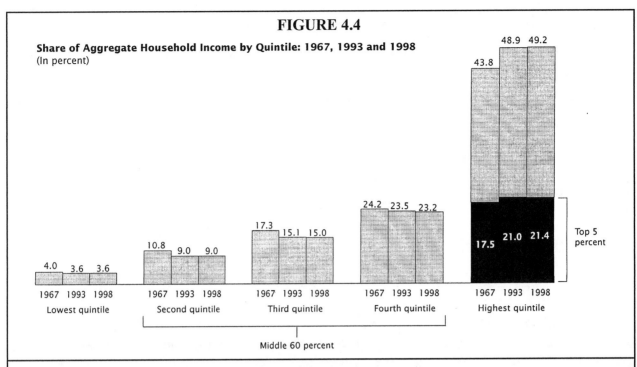

FIGURE 4.4

Share of Aggregate Household Income by Quintile: 1967, 1993 and 1998
(In percent)

TABLE 4.5

Selected Measures of Household Income Dispersion: 1967 to 1998

[Income in 1998 dollars]

Measures of income dispersion	1998	1997	1996	1995[1]	1990	1985	1980[2]	1975[3]	1970	1968	1967
HOUSEHOLD INCOME AT SELECTED PERCENTILES											
20th percentile upper limit	16,116	15,640	15,342	15,402	15,589	15,149	14,965	14,574	14,552	14,367	13,471
50th (median)	38,885	37,581	36,872	36,446	37,343	35,778	35,076	34,224	34,471	33,478	32,075
80th percentile upper limit	75,000	72,614	70,659	69,654	68,848	66,365	62,784	59,446	57,863	54,858	53,170
95th percentile lower limit	132,199	128,521	124,187	120,860	118,163	110,984	101,999	94,787	91,477	85,824	85,317
HOUSEHOLD INCOME RATIOS OF SELECTED PERCENTILES											
95th/20th..................	8.20	8.22	8.09	7.85	7.58	7.33	6.82	6.50	6.29	5.97	6.33
95th/50th..................	3.40	3.42	3.37	3.32	3.16	3.10	2.91	2.77	2.65	2.56	2.66
80th/50th..................	1.93	1.93	1.92	1.91	1.84	1.85	1.79	1.74	1.68	1.64	1.66
80th/20th..................	4.65	4.64	4.61	4.52	4.42	4.38	4.20	4.08	3.98	3.82	3.95
20th/50th..................	0.41	0.42	0.42	0.42	0.42	0.42	0.43	0.43	0.42	0.43	0.42
MEAN HOUSEHOLD INCOME OF QUINTILES											
Lowest quintile..............	9,223	9,010	8,930	8,931	8,973	8,782	8,879	8,800	8,008	7,921	7,301
Second quintile	23,288	22,442	21,917	21,816	22,486	21,708	21,428	20,894	21,293	20,935	19,906
Third quintile	38,967	37,756	36,866	36,478	37,141	35,955	35,268	34,186	34,289	33,201	31,783
Fourth quintile	60,266	58,479	57,057	56,076	55,997	54,072	51,928	49,645	48,336	46,319	44,468
Highest quintile	127,529	124,676	120,005	117,021	108,671	99,741	91,211	86,457	85,581	81,120	80,584
SHARES OF HOUSEHOLD INCOME OF QUINTILES											
Lowest quintile..............	3.6	3.6	3.7	3.7	3.9	4.0	4.3	4.4	4.1	4.2	4.0
Second quintile	9.0	8.9	9.0	9.1	9.6	9.7	10.3	10.5	10.8	11.1	10.8
Third quintile................	15.0	15.0	15.1	15.2	15.9	16.3	16.9	17.1	17.4	17.5	17.3
Fourth quintile	23.2	23.2	23.3	23.3	24.0	24.6	24.9	24.8	24.5	24.4	24.2
Highest quintile	49.2	49.4	49.0	48.7	46.6	45.3	43.7	43.2	43.3	42.8	43.8
Gini coefficient of income inequality..................	0.456	0.459	0.455	0.450	0.428	0.419	0.403	0.397	0.394	0.388	0.399

[1]Reflects the implementation of 1990 census adjusted population controls, 1990 census sample redesign, a change in data collection method from paper-pencil to computer-assisted interviewing (CAI), and changes in income reporting limits. For detailed information concerning the impact of these changes, see Current Population Reports, Series P60-191, *A Brief Look at Postwar U.S. Income Inequality.*
[2]Reflects implementation of 1980 census population controls.
[3]Reflects implementation of 1970 census population controls.

Source of figure and table: *Money Income in the United States: 1998*, Bureau of the Census, Washington, DC, 1999

$9,223 (in 1998 dollars). The next lowest quintiles grew at an even slower pace: the second quintile —17 percent; the third quintile — 22.6 percent. (See Table 4.5.)

Ratio to Poverty Threshold

Studying the changes in the ratio of family income to poverty thresholds is also a way to look at the changes in income distribution. Poverty thresholds (levels) represent the amounts of annual income, depending on family size and composition, below which a family or individual is considered poor. For example, in 1998, the poverty threshold for one person was $8,316, while the threshold for four persons was $16,660. (See below for a discussion of poverty.)

A ratio of 1.00 indicates that the family has an income equal to the poverty threshold for its size and composition. The average ratio in the bottom quintile in 1967 was .97, while the average in the top quintile was 6.06. By 1997, the ratio in the bottom fifth was .99, while the average ratio in the top fifth was 10.02 (10 times the poverty threshold). Though the income-to-poverty ratio for the highest quintile grew 65 percent from 1967 to 1997, the lowest quintile's ratio was virtually unchanged, indicating a widening income gap. The ratio for the middle quintile rose from 2.67 in 1967 to 3.45 in 1996. (See Figure 4.5.) (See below for more information on the income-to-poverty ratio.)

Reasons for Income Inequality

Several factors have contributed to this growing inequality of income. The elderly population, which generally earns less than the average, is growing. An increasing number of people are living in nonfamily situations (mainly those who live alone or with nonrelatives), a category that usually makes less money than the traditional family. The proportion of families

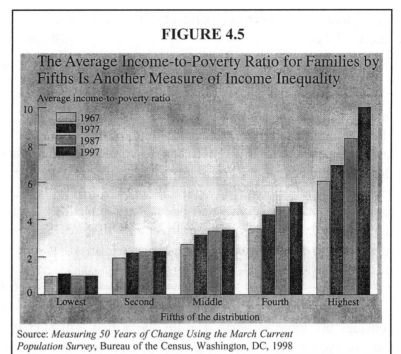

FIGURE 4.5

The Average Income-to-Poverty Ratio for Families by Fifths Is Another Measure of Income Inequality

Source: *Measuring 50 Years of Change Using the March Current Population Survey*, Bureau of the Census, Washington, DC, 1998

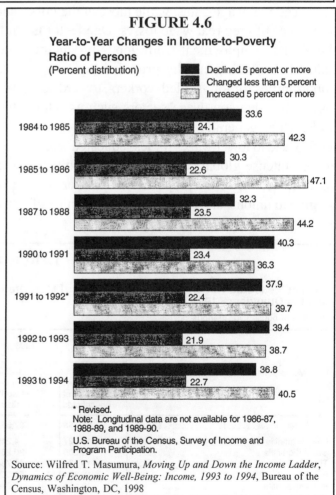

FIGURE 4.6

Year-to-Year Changes in Income-to-Poverty Ratio of Persons
(Percent distribution)

* Revised.
Note: Longitudinal data are not available for 1986-87, 1988-89, and 1989-90.

U.S. Bureau of the Census, Survey of Income and Program Participation.

Source: Wilfred T. Masumura, *Moving Up and Down the Income Ladder, Dynamics of Economic Well-Being: Income, 1993 to 1994*, Bureau of the Census, Washington, DC, 1998

headed by a female householder, no husband present, has also increased. Between 1970 and 1998, families with a female householder, no husband present, rose from 10.7 percent of all families to 17.8 percent.

Other factors that the Bureau of the Census believes may contribute to the growing inequality of income distribution include the aging of the "baby boom" generation, which is earning more, and a greater number of women working outside the home and contributing to family income. The increasing tendency over this period for men with higher-than-average earnings to marry women with higher-than-average earnings has also contributed to widening the gap between high-income and low-income households.

In addition, the wage distribution has become considerably more unequal. The highly skilled, trained, and educated workers at the top have experienced real wage gains, while those at the bottom have suffered real wage losses. One factor is the shift in employment from goods-producing industries, which generally provided high-wage opportunities for low-skilled workers, toward services and other low-wage sectors such as retail trade, which generally pay less. Other factors that tend to lead to lower wages for less educated workers are intense global competition and immigration, the decline of the proportion of workers belonging to unions, and the drop in the real value of the minimum wage. Still others are the increasing need for computer skills and the growing use of temporary workers. (See Chapter III.)

Fluctuations in Income

Most Americans experience significant fluctuations in their economic well-being from year to year. About three-fourths of the population see their economic well-being go either up or down by at least 5 percent from one year to the next as a result of changes in living arrangements, program participation, work status, or other circumstances.

One measure of economic well-being is the income-to-poverty ratio, or income ratio, the ratio of a person's annual family income to the family's poverty threshold or level (see above). Figure 4.6 shows the proportion of Americans whose income ratios rose or dropped significantly (5 percent or more) or remained the same (less than 5 percent change) from year to year. The proportion of persons whose income ratios rose from one year to the next was smaller in the 1990s than in the 1980s, reaching its minimum during the 1990-1991 recession (downturn in the economy). Conversely, the percentage of people who experienced declines in their income ratios yearly grew larger from the last decade to the present one.

TABLE 4.6

Median Measured Net Worth and Distribution of Measured Net Worth by Monthly Household Income Quintiles: 1993 and 1991

[Number of households in thousands]

Monthly household income quintiles[1]	1993			1991 (in 1993 dollars)		
	Number of households	Median measured net worth (dollars)	Distribution of measured net worth	Number of households	Median measured net worth (dollars)	Distribution of measured net worth
Total	96,468	37,587	100.0	94,692	38,500	100.0
Lowest quintile............................	19,327	4,249	7.2	18,977	5,406	7.0
Second quintile	19,306	20,230	12.2	18,912	20,315	12.2
Third quintile..............................	19,279	30,788	15.9	18,969	30,263	15.8
Fourth quintile	19,304	50,000	20.6	18,928	51,779	20.4
Highest quintile	19,251	118,996	44.1	18,905	121,423	44.6

[1]Quintile upper limits for 1993 were: lowest quintile – $1,071; second quintile – $1,963; third quintile – $2,995; fourth quintile – $4,635. Upper limits for 1991 were: lowest quintile – $1,135; second quintile – $2,027; third quintile – $3,089; fourth quintile – $4,721.

Source: T. J. Eller and Wallace Fraser, *Asset Ownership of Households: 1993*, Bureau of the Census, Washington, DC, 1995

TABLE 4.7

Percent of Households Owning Assets and Median Value of Holdings by Monthly Household Income Quintile for Selected Asset Types: 1993 and 1991

[Excludes group quarters]

Monthly household income quintiles[1]	Interest-earning assets at financial institutions[2]	Other interest-earning assets[3]	Stocks and mutual fund shares	Equity in own home	Equity in motor vehicles	Equity in own business or profession	IRA or Keogh accounts
PERCENT OF HOUSEHOLDS OWNING ASSETS							
1993							
Total	71.1	8.6	20.9	64.3	85.7	10.8	23.1
Lowest quintile.........................	42.2	2.6	4.4	41.5	58.2	6.1	5.4
Second quintile	62.9	5.1	11.6	55.9	85.1	7.5	14.0
Third quintile	73.7	7.3	18.1	63.4	93.1	9.6	20.5
Fourth quintile	84.6	9.1	26.0	74.8	95.8	11.6	28.3
Highest quintile	92.2	19.1	44.3	86.0	96.4	19.4	47.1
1991							
Total	73.2	9.0	20.7	64.7	86.4	11.7	22.9
Lowest quintile.........................	43.2	2.3	5.8	43.8	58.4	6.6	5.1
Second quintile	65.8	5.1	11.5	55.7	87.0	8.7	12.2
Third quintile	77.4	7.5	16.2	64.3	93.0	10.0	19.9
Fourth quintile	86.2	8.8	25.4	74.0	96.3	12.8	29.4
Highest quintile	93.4	21.3	44.8	86.0	97.4	20.5	48.1
MEDIAN VALUE OF HOLDINGS FOR ASSET OWNERS							
1993 (dollars)							
Total	2,999	12,998	6,960	46,669	5,140	7,000	12,985
Lowest quintile	1,594	9,999	3,300	38,940	1,657	946	10,000
Second quintile	1,999	12,999	4,916	40,973	3,348	1,980	11,000
Third quintile	1,998	12,499	4,650	42,984	4,625	4,800	9,500
Fourth quintile	2,747	9,999	5,900	41,850	6,491	9,500	11,800
Highest quintile	5,999	14,999	9,992	66,068	9,898	17,075	16,100
1991 (in 1993 dollars)							
Total	3,709	16,058	5,490	43,070	5,555	10,203	11,886
Lowest quintile	2,468	6,571	4,081	36,040	1,555	6,360	8,372
Second quintile	2,624	15,900	3,988	41,340	3,533	5,088	8,904
Third quintile	2,384	14,205	5,062	37,100	4,872	4,770	10,562
Fourth quintile	3,179	15,899	3,816	41,870	6,935	10,176	10,388
Highest quintile	7,738	20,140	9,010	63,494	10,017	15,928	15,370

[1]Quintile upper limits for 1993 were: lowest quintile – $1,071; second quintile – $1,963; third quintile – $2,995; fourth quintile – $4,635. Upper limits for 1991 were: lowest quintile – $1,135; second quintile – $2,027; third quintile – $3,089; fourth quintile – $4,721.
[2]Includes passbook savings accounts, money market deposit accounts, certificates of deposits, and interest-earning checking accounts.
[3]Includes money market funds, U.S. Government securities, municipal and corporate bonds, and other interest-earning assets.

Source: T. J. Eller and Wallace Fraser, *Asset Ownership of Households: 1993*, Bureau of the Census, Washington, DC, 1995

Although statistics, such as median income, do not change much in real terms from one year to the next, income ratios do shift for most Americans. Figure 4.6 shows that, from one year to the next, about one-fourth of all Americans had stable income ratios. Therefore, the large majority (about three-fourths) were subject to considerable changes from year to year, regardless of the status of the business cycle (ups and downs in the economy from times of prosperity to times of recession). Over the course of a lifetime, the average American will likely experience a number of these shifts.

While the state of the economy is an important factor in determining which way these fluctuations go, it is not the only factor. People had an even (50-50) chance or better to have an income-ratio rise of 5 percent or more from one year to the next if, over the course of two years,

• They began to work year-round, full-time.

• The number of workers in the household increased.

85

TABLE 4.8

Median Measured Net Worth by Race and Hispanic Origin of Householder and Monthly Household Income Quintile: 1993 and 1991

[Excludes group quarters]

Monthly household income quintile	Total		White		Black		Hispanic origin[1]	
	1993	1991 (in 1993 dollars)	1993	1991 (in 1993 dollars)	1993	1991 (in 1993 dollars)	1993	1991 (in 1993 dollars)
All households (thousands)	96,468	94,692	82,190	81,409	11,248	10,768	7,403	6,407
Median measured net worth (dollars). . . .	37,587	38,500	45,740	47,075	4,418	4,844	4,656	5,557
Measured Net Worth by Income Quintile[2]								
Lowest quintile:								
Households (thousands)	19,327	18,977	14,662	14,480	4,066	4,041	2,272	1,835
Median measured net worth (dollars). .	4,249	5,406	7,605	10,743	250	0	499	529
Second quintile:								
Households (thousands)	19,306	18,912	16,162	16,006	2,663	2,436	1,760	1,557
Median measured net worth (dollars). .	20,230	20,315	27,057	26,665	3,406	3,446	2,900	3,214
Third quintile:								
Households (thousands)	19,279	18,969	16,591	16,388	2,126	2,124	1,437	1,312
Median measured net worth (dollars). .	30,788	30,263	36,341	35,510	8,480	8,302	6,313	7,501
Fourth quintile:								
Households (thousands)	19,304	18,928	17,218	17,043	1,454	1,353	1,115	1,009
Median measured net worth (dollars). .	50,000	51,779	54,040	55,950	20,745	21,852	20,100	20,564
Highest quintile:								
Households (thousands)	19,252	18,905	17,558	17,492	937	814	819	694
Median measured net worth (dollars). .	118,996	121,423	123,350	128,298	45,023	56,922	55,923	72,168

[1]Persons of Hispanic origin may be of any race.
[2]Quintile upper limits for 1993 were: lowest quintile – $1,071; second quintile – $1,963; third quintile – $2,995; fourth quintile – $4,635. Upper limits for 1991 were: lowest quintile – $1,135; second quintile – $2,027; third quintile – $3,089; fourth quintile – $4,721.

Source: T. J. Eller and Wallace Fraser, *Asset Ownership of Households: 1993*, Bureau of the Census, Washington, DC, 1995

- They married or otherwise became part of a married-couple family.

- The number of adults in their household increased or the number of dependent children decreased.

Conversely, most people saw their income ratios decline significantly when they ceased to

- Be married.

- Work year-round, full-time.

The lower one's current annual income is, the more likely it will rise the following year, and the less likely it will fall. For instance, among those whose 1993 family income was below the poverty level, 53 percent saw their income ratios rise 5 percent or more the following year, while 26 percent experienced drops. On the other hand, among those at the top of the ladder (families with incomes four or more times the 1993 poverty level), 45 per-

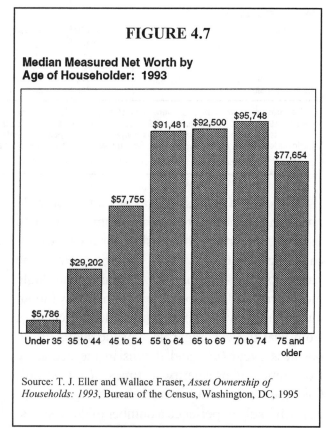

FIGURE 4.7

Median Measured Net Worth by Age of Householder: 1993

Under 35: $5,786
35 to 44: $29,202
45 to 54: $57,755
55 to 64: $91,481
65 to 69: $92,500
70 to 74: $95,748
75 and older: $77,654

Source: T. J. Eller and Wallace Fraser, *Asset Ownership of Households: 1993*, Bureau of the Census, Washington, DC, 1995

TABLE 4.9

Median Measured Net Worth by Type of Household and Age of Householder: 1993 and 1991

[Excludes group quarters]

Type of household by age of householder	1993			1991		
		Median measured net worth (dollars)			Median measured net worth (in 1993 dollars)	
	Number of households (thousands)	Total	Excluding equity in own home	Number of households (thousands)	Total	Excluding equity in own home
Married-couple households	52,891	61,905	17,051	52,616	63,599	19,557
Less than 35 years	12,141	12,941	5,677	12,247	12,702	5,548
35 to 54 years	23,983	61,874	17,436	23,080	64,047	19,801
55 to 64 years	7,568	127,752	43,543	7,849	123,138	47,158
65 years and over........................	9,199	129,790	44,410	9,040	142,517	59,200
Male householders	15,397	13,500	5,157	15,297	12,698	5,963
Less than 35 years	5,285	4,300	2,890	5,746	5,027	3,668
35 to 54 years	6,157	18,426	6,156	5,409	18,391	7,420
55 to 64 years	1,437	44,670	10,905	1,514	32,330	5,988
65 years and over........................	2,518	60,741	12,927	2,627	69,157	17,489
Female householders......................	28,180	13,294	3,363	27,179	15,518	3,762
Less than 35 years	6,935	1,342	790	7,038	1,383	953
35 to 54 years	8,908	8,405	2,652	7,959	11,294	3,308
55 to 64 years	3,286	44,762	6,475	3,211	41,635	6,229
65 years and over........................	9,050	57,679	9,560	8,972	62,746	13,015

Source: T. J. Eller and Wallace Fraser, *Asset Ownership of Households: 1993*, Bureau of the Census, Washington, DC, 1995

cent experienced declines, while 31 percent posted gains.

HOW MUCH IS A PERSON WORTH?

"How much is a person worth?" is normally asked as an economic question, not a moral or social one. In its latest study on net worth, the Bureau of the Census, in *Asset Ownership of House-* *holds: 1993* (Washington, DC, 1995), found that the average household net worth — the value of assets (what you own) less any debts (what you owe) — was $37,587 for 1993, compared to $43,617 in 1988, a drop of 14 percent, or $6,030, after adjusting for inflation. This was not statistically different from the 1991 median net worth of $38,500. (The Bureau of the Census cautions that financial holdings of certain types of wealth tend

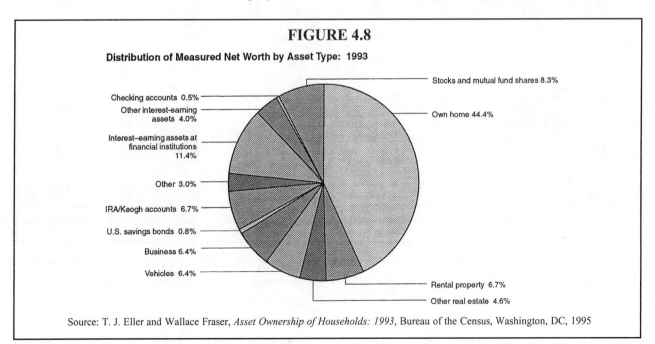

FIGURE 4.8

Distribution of Measured Net Worth by Asset Type: 1993

Checking accounts 0.5%
Other interest-earning assets 4.0%
Interest–earning assets at financial institutions 11.4%
Other 3.0%
IRA/Keogh accounts 6.7%
U.S. savings bonds 0.8%
Business 6.4%
Vehicles 6.4%
Stocks and mutual fund shares 8.3%
Own home 44.4%
Rental property 6.7%
Other real estate 4.6%

Source: T. J. Eller and Wallace Fraser, *Asset Ownership of Households: 1993*, Bureau of the Census, Washington, DC, 1995

TABLE 4.10

1995 Survey of Consumer Finances

Family characteristic	Mortgage and home equity	Installment	Other lines of credit	Credit card	Investment real estate	Other debt	Any debt
	Percentage of families holding debt						
All families	**41.1** (.6)	**46.5** (.8)	**1.9** (.2)	**47.8** (.8)	**6.3** (.4)	**9.0** (.6)	**75.2** (.7)
Income (1995 dollars)							
Less than 10,000	8.9	25.9	*	25.4	1.6	6.6	48.5
10,000–24,999	24.8	41.3	1.4	41.9	2.5	8.7	67.3
25,000–49,999	47.3	54.3	2.0	56.7	5.8	8.5	83.9
50,000–99,999	68.7	60.7	3.2	62.8	9.5	10.0	89.9
100,000 and more	73.6	37.0	4.0	37.0	27.9	15.8	86.4
Age of head (years)							
Less than 35	32.9	62.2	2.6	55.4	2.6	7.8	83.8
35–44	54.1	60.7	2.2	55.8	6.5	11.1	87.2
45–54	61.9	54.0	2.3	57.3	10.4	14.1	86.5
55–64	45.8	36.0	1.4	43.4	12.5	7.5	75.2
65–74	24.8	16.7	1.3	31.3	5.0	5.5	54.5
75 and more	7.1	9.6	††	18.3	1.5	3.6	30.1
Race or ethnicity of head							
White non-Hispanic	43.5	46.4	2.1	47.5	6.9	9.1	75.8
Nonwhite or Hispanic	32.7	46.9	1.3	48.8	4.4	8.5	73.1
Current work status of head							
Professional, managerial	63.4	56.2	3.7	56.8	10.5	10.9	90.3
Technical, sales, clerical	51.4	61.1	2.0	60.1	4.1	12.3	88.6
Precision production	53.3	64.5	2.3	64.8	5.4	9.1	88.3
Machine operators and laborers	44.1	61.3	.9	56.9	6.8	9.5	86.0
Service occupations	34.6	50.3	*	53.1	2.2	9.0	82.6
Self-employed	51.3	45.6	3.6	44.9	15.4	10.0	81.9
Retired	19.0	18.4	.3	26.6	3.6	4.8	45.9
Other not working	17.9	42.8	*	38.7	2.7	9.8	65.0
Housing status							
Owner	63.6	46.0	1.5	51.4	7.9	8.7	80.2
Renter or other	0	47.5	2.6	41.2	3.5	9.5	66.2
	Median value of holdings for families holding debt (thousands of 1995 dollars)						
All families	**51.0** (2.1)	**6.1** (.3)	**3.5** (.7)	**1.5** (.1)	**28.0** (2.9)	**2.0** (.2)	**22.5** (1.2)
Income (1995 dollars)							
Less than 10,000	14.0	2.9	*	.6	15.0	2.0	2.6
10,000–24,999	26.0	3.9	3.0	1.2	18.3	1.2	9.2
25,000–49,999	46.0	6.6	3.0	1.4	25.0	1.5	23.4
50,000–99,999	68.0	9.0	2.2	2.2	34.0	2.5	65.0
100,000 and more	103.4	8.5	19.5	3.0	36.8	7.0	112.2
Age of head (years)							
Less than 35	63.0	7.0	1.4	1.4	22.8	1.5	15.2
35–44	60.0	5.6	2.0	1.8	30.0	1.7	37.6
45–54	48.0	7.0	5.7	2.0	28.1	2.5	41.0
55–64	36.0	5.9	3.5	1.3	26.0	4.0	25.8
65–74	19.0	4.9	3.8	.8	36.0	2.0	7.7
75 and more	15.9	3.9	††	.4	8.0	3.0	2.0
Race or ethnicity of head							
White non-Hispanic	54.0	6.4	3.5	1.5	29.0	2.0	27.2
Nonwhite or Hispanic	36.5	5.0	.8	1.2	25.0	1.5	12.2
Current work status of head							
Professional, managerial	79.0	8.2	2.5	2.2	26.3	2.7	65.1
Technical, sales, clerical	52.6	8.0	.6	1.7	25.0	1.6	30.1
Precision production	50.0	6.3	1.5	1.4	35.0	2.0	29.5
Machine operators and laborers ...	36.8	5.2	1.6	1.3	17.0	1.0	15.2
Service occupations	38.5	5.1	*	1.3	13.0	1.0	12.0
Self-employed	62.0	5.8	8.0	2.6	50.0	4.8	42.2
Retired	23.3	4.4	3.8	1.0	23.0	2.5	6.5
Other not working	45.0	5.0	*	.8	20.0	1.7	7.5
Housing status							
Owner	51.0	6.9	5.0	1.5	27.0	2.5	46.0
Renter or other	*	5.0	1.5	1.3	28.0	1.5	4.9

Source: "Family Finances in the U.S.: Recent Evidence from the Survey of Consumer Finances," *Federal Reserve Bulletin*, January 1997, Federal Reserve System, Washington, DC

to be underreported, so these figures might be somewhat low.)

Households with considerable net worth generally have the chance to offer their members greater opportunities. They are better able to buy the things they want, to feel more secure, to travel, to send their children to college, and to help their grown children get started. Greater net worth can buy political influence and power or at least present the opportunity to meet those who have that power. Net worth is a major factor in determining a household's position and power in American society.

Net Worth

The Census Bureau found huge disparities in net worth among the various sectors of society. As was the case with income (see above), the highest quintile (the upper one-fifth in net worth) controlled most (44 percent) of the wealth, and the lowest quintile owned only 7.2 percent. While the median net worth of the lowest quintile was only $4,249, the median net worth of the highest quintile was $118,996. (See Table 4.6.)

In 1993, the ownership rate of home equity varied significantly with income, from 42 percent for the lowest income group to 86 percent for the wealthiest group. Ownership rates in stocks and mutual fund shares (4 to 44 percent), retirement accounts such as IRAs or Keogh accounts (5 to 47 percent), and business equity (6 to 19 percent) also varied widely between the lowest and highest income groups. (See Table 4.7.)

Race, Age, and Households

In 1993, the median net worth of White households ($45,740) was 10 times that of Black households ($4,418) and Hispanic households ($4,656).

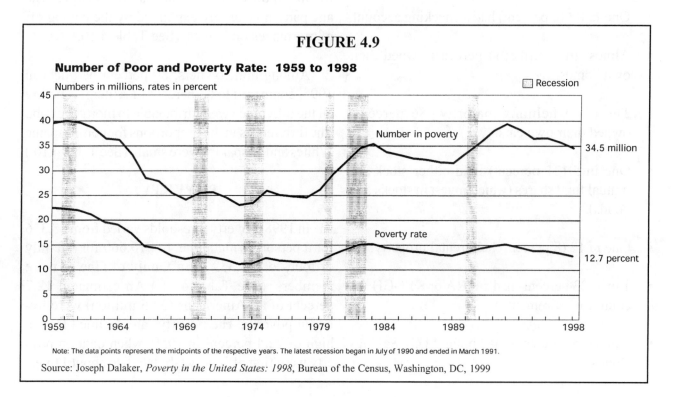

FIGURE 4.9

Number of Poor and Poverty Rate: 1959 to 1998

Note: The data points represent the midpoints of the respective years. The latest recession began in July of 1990 and ended in March 1991.

Source: Joseph Dalaker, *Poverty in the United States: 1998*, Bureau of the Census, Washington, DC, 1999

(See Table 4.8.) Net worth tended to rise with age through 74 years of age and then drop. (See Figure 4.7.)

Married-couple households were worth considerably more than households headed by a single man or woman. Both male- and female-maintained households had median net worth approximately one-fifth that of married-couple households in 1993. When net worth levels were compared within age groups, households maintained by women younger than 55 years of age had a much lower median net worth than their male counterparts. (See Table 4.9.) Not surprisingly, those who had been working for the full year, those owning their own homes, and those who earned higher incomes tended to have a greater net financial worth.

Assets

In the 1993 study on net worth, the Bureau of the Census asked the respondents what type of financial assets they owned.

- 7 of 10 Americans (71 percent) had some type of interest-bearing account at financial institutions.

- One-half (46 percent) had a checking account.

- Almost two-thirds (64 percent) owned their own homes.

- The overwhelming majority (86 percent) owned their own cars.

- One in 5 (21 percent) held either stocks or mutual fund shares (which invest in stocks and bonds).

- One in 12 (8 percent) held rental property.

- 1 in 4 (23 percent) had an IRA or KEOGH account for retirement.

- 1 in 6 (18.5 percent) had bought U.S. Savings Bonds.

Home ownership accounted for 44 percent of total net worth. Interest-earning accounts made up the next largest share of net worth (11.4 percent), while stocks and bonds accounted for 8 percent. (See Figure 4.8.)

DEBT

The Federal Reserve Board's Survey of Consumer Finances (SCF), conducted in 1983, 1989, 1992, and 1995, provides information on family debt. Most families (75 percent) had some type of debt (including mortgage debt) in 1995 (Table 4.10).

The median of debt tends to increase with family income, likely because of borrowing associated with the acquisition of nonfinancial assets (homes, cars, etc.). In 1995, indebted households with incomes below $25,000 typically owed less than $10,000, but those with incomes over $100,000 typically owed $112,000 (Table 4.10).

By age group, the proportion of families borrowing varies only a little for the groups with heads younger than 65, but it falls off quickly for those 65 years and over. The drop-off in median borrowing in these older groups is even sharper. The age pattern is largely explained by the paying off of mortgages on homes. (See Table 4.10.)

Among homeowners, 80 percent had debt in 1995, compared to 66 percent of renters — nearly all the difference was attributable to mortgage debt. The differences in the proportions for non-Hispanic Whites and Hispanics were small. (See Table 4.10.)

POVERTY

In 1998, poverty thresholds varied from $8,316 for a person living alone, to $16,660 for a family of four, to $33,339 for a family of nine or more members. (See Table 4.11.) An estimated 12.7 percent of all Americans (34.5 million) were living in poverty. The poverty rate declined from a high of 22.4 percent in 1959, when data on poverty were first officially tabulated, to about 11 per-

TABLE 4.12

People and Families in Poverty by Selected Characteristics: 1989, 1997, and 1998

Numbers in thousands

Characteristic	Below poverty, 1998				Below poverty, 1997				Below poverty, 1989			
	Number	90-pct. C.I. (±)	Percent	90-pct. C.I. (±)	Number	90-pct. C.I. (±)	Percent	90-pct. C.I. (±)	Number	90-pct. C.I. (±)	Percent	90-pct. C.I. (±)
PEOPLE												
Total	34,476	920	12.7	0.3	35,574	931	13.3	0.3	32,415	859	13.1	0.3
Family Status												
In families..................	25,370	804	11.2	0.4	26,217	814	11.6	0.4	24,882	765	11.8	0.4
Householder...............	7,186	248	10.0	0.4	7,324	252	10.3	0.4	6,895	232	10.4	0.4
Related children under 18......	12,845	479	18.3	0.7	13,422	485	19.2	0.7	12,541	454	19.4	0.7
Related children under 6	4,775	309	20.6	1.4	5,049	316	21.6	1.4	5,116	306	22.5	1.4
In unrelated subfamilies	628	66	48.8	6.0	670	67	46.5	5.5	727	67	54.6	6.1
Reference person	247	41	47.4	9.2	259	41	45.0	8.5	284	41	51.8	9.1
Children under 18	361	89	50.5	14.2	403	94	48.9	13.0	430	92	60.5	15.3
Unrelated individual	8,478	275	19.9	0.7	8,687	280	20.8	0.7	6,807	230	19.3	0.7
Male	3,465	161	17.0	0.8	3,447	161	17.4	0.9	2,577	132	15.8	0.8
Female	5,013	201	22.6	1.0	5,240	206	24.0	1.0	4,230	174	22.3	1.0
Race and Hispanic Origin												
White, total..................	23,454	776	10.5	0.3	24,396	790	11.0	0.4	21,294	712	10.2	0.3
White, not Hispanic..........	15,799	646	8.2	0.3	16,491	660	8.6	0.3	15,499	615	8.3	0.3
Black, total	9,091	434	26.1	1.2	9,116	434	26.5	1.3	9,525	423	30.8	1.4
Asian and Pacific Islander, total ...	1,360	181	12.5	1.7	1,468	186	14.0	1.8	1,032	155	14.2	2.1
Hispanic origin, all races.......	8,070	411	25.6	1.3	8,308	413	27.1	1.3	6,086	357	26.3	1.5
Age												
Under 18 years...............	13,467	487	18.9	0.7	14,113	495	19.9	0.7	13,154	462	20.1	0.7
18 to 64 years	17,623	674	10.5	0.4	18,085	681	10.9	0.4	15,950	617	10.4	0.4
18 to 24 years...............	4,312	201	16.6	0.8	4,416	204	17.5	0.8	4,132	189	15.4	0.7
25 to 34 years...............	4,582	214	11.9	0.6	4,759	219	12.1	0.6	4,873	212	11.2	0.5
35 to 44 years...............	4,082	202	9.1	0.5	4,251	207	9.6	0.5	3,115	171	8.3	0.5
45 to 54 years...............	2,444	158	6.9	0.4	2,439	158	7.2	0.5	1,873	133	7.5	0.5
55 to 59 years...............	1,165	110	9.2	0.9	1,092	107	9.0	0.9	971	97	9.5	0.9
60 to 64 years...............	1,039	104	10.1	1.0	1,127	109	11.2	1.1	986	97	9.4	0.9
65 years and over	3,386	179	10.5	0.6	3,376	179	10.5	0.6	3,312	171	11.4	0.6
Nativity												
Native.......................	29,707	860	12.1	0.4	30,336	869	12.5	0.4	NA	NA	NA	NA
Foreign-born.................	4,769	413	18.0	1.6	5,238	433	19.9	1.6	NA	NA	NA	NA
Naturalized citizen...........	1,087	199	11.0	2.0	1,111	201	11.4	2.1	NA	NA	NA	NA
Not a citizen	3,682	364	22.2	2.2	4,127	385	25.0	2.3	NA	NA	NA	NA
Region												
Northeast	6,357	385	12.3	0.8	6,474	388	12.6	0.8	5,213	336	10.2	0.7
Midwest	6,501	428	10.3	0.7	6,493	428	10.4	0.7	7,088	429	12.0	0.7
South	12,992	612	13.7	0.7	13,748	628	14.6	0.7	13,277	594	15.6	0.7
West........................	8,625	505	14.0	0.8	8,858	512	14.6	0.9	6,838	433	12.8	0.8
Residence												
Inside metropolitan areas	26,997	827	12.3	0.4	27,273	829	12.6	0.4	23,726	748	12.3	0.4
Inside central cities	14,921	630	18.5	0.8	15,018	632	18.8	0.8	14,151	589	18.5	0.8
Outside central cities..........	12,076	569	8.7	0.4	12,255	572	9.0	0.4	9,574	489	8.2	0.4
Outside metropolitan areas.......	7,479	554	14.4	1.1	8,301	582	15.9	1.1	8,690	571	15.9	1.1
FAMILIES												
Total	7,186	248	10.0	0.4	7,324	252	10.3	0.4	6,895	232	10.4	0.4
White, total.................	4,829	196	8.0	0.3	4,990	199	8.4	0.3	4,457	179	7.9	0.3
White, not Hispanic..........	3,264	156	6.1	0.3	3,357	160	6.3	0.3	3,287	151	6.4	0.3
Black, total	1,981	118	23.4	1.5	1,985	118	23.6	1.5	2,108	118	27.9	1.7
Asian and Pacific Islander, total ...	270	43	11.0	1.8	244	41	10.2	1.8	201	35	12.2	2.2
Hispanic origin, all races.......	1,648	109	22.7	1.5	1,721	110	24.7	1.6	1,227	89	23.7	1.8
Type of Family												
Married-couple	2,879	146	5.3	0.3	2,821	145	5.2	0.3	2,965	143	5.7	0.3
White......................	2,400	132	5.0	0.3	2,312	130	4.8	0.3	2,347	125	5.0	0.3
White, not Hispanic	1,639	107	3.8	0.2	1,501	102	3.5	0.2	1,776	107	4.1	0.3
Black......................	290	44	7.3	1.1	312	46	8.0	1.2	444	53	11.7	1.4
Hispanic origin, all races	775	72	15.7	1.5	836	76	17.4	1.6	592	61	16.4	1.8
Female householder, no husband present.....................	3,831	171	29.9	1.5	3,995	176	31.6	1.5	3,575	158	32.6	1.6
White......................	2,123	123	24.9	1.6	2,305	130	27.7	1.7	1,886	112	25.8	1.7
White, not Hispanic	1,428	100	20.7	1.6	1,598	107	23.4	1.7	1,341	92	21.7	1.6
Black......................	1,557	105	40.8	3.1	1,563	105	39.8	3.0	1,553	100	46.7	3.4
Hispanic origin, all races	756	72	43.7	4.7	767	72	47.6	5.1	576	59	48.0	5.7

Source: Joseph Dalaker, *Poverty in the United States: 1998*, Bureau of the Census, Washington, DC, 1999

cent for most of the 1970s. It began rising in 1980, reaching 15.2 percent in 1983. Since then, it declined to 13.1 percent in 1989, increased to 15.1 percent in 1993, and then declined to 12.7 in 1998. (See Figure 4.9.)

Characteristics of the Poor

Age

In 1998, half the nation's poor were either children under 18 years old (39 percent) or the elderly (9.8 percent). Children accounted for 26 percent and the elderly for 13 percent of the total population, making the children overrepresented in the poverty population and the elderly under-represented. However, a higher proportion of elderly (6.4 percent) than nonelderly (4.0 percent) were concentrated just over their respective poverty thresholds (between 100 percent and 125 percent of their thresholds); 17.8 percent of the nation's 11.6 million "near poor" persons were elderly.

In 1998, the poverty rate for all children under 18 years of age was 18.9 percent (Table 4.12 and Figure 4.10). This was the first time since 1980 that the poverty rate for children has been lower than 20 percent. Among children under age six living in families with a female householder, no spouse present, 54.8 percent were poor, compared to 10.1 percent of such children in married-couple families. Figure 4.11 shows how much better children in married-couple families fare economically than those headed by females.

In 1998, the poverty rate for people 18 to 64 years of age was 10.5 percent. (See Figure 4.10.) About 16.6 percent of persons 18 to 24 years of age, 6.9 percent of persons 45 to 54 years of age, and 10.5 percent of those 65 years old and over lived in poverty. (See Table 4.12.) Prior to 1974, the poverty rate for children was less than that of the elderly. Since 1974, it has been higher than the rates of other age groups.

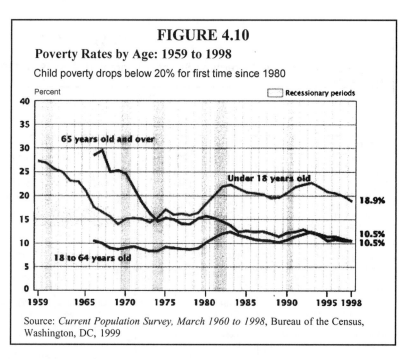

FIGURE 4.10

Poverty Rates by Age: 1959 to 1998

Child poverty drops below 20% for first time since 1980

Source: *Current Population Survey, March 1960 to 1998*, Bureau of the Census, Washington, DC, 1999

Race and Nativity

In 1998, the poverty rate for Whites was 10.5 percent; for non-Hispanic Whites, 8.2 percent; for Blacks, 26.1 percent; and for Asians or Pacific Islanders, 12.5 percent. The poverty rate for persons of Hispanic origin was 25.6 percent. (See Table 4.12.)

Although the poverty rate for Whites was much lower than the rates for other groups, the majority

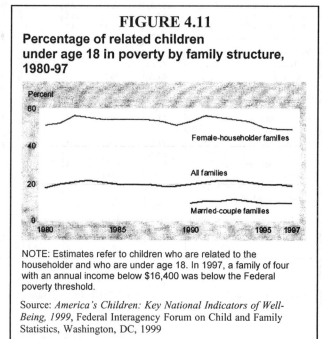

FIGURE 4.11

Percentage of related children under age 18 in poverty by family structure, 1980-97

NOTE: Estimates refer to children who are related to the householder and who are under age 18. In 1997, a family of four with an annual income below $16,400 was below the Federal poverty threshold.

Source: *America's Children: Key National Indicators of Well-Being, 1999*, Federal Interagency Forum on Child and Family Statistics, Washington, DC, 1999

TABLE 4.13

Poverty Status of Families by Type of Family, Presence of Related Children, Race, and Hispanic Origin: 1959 to 1998

[Numbers in thousands. Families as of March of the following year]

Year and characteristic	All families			Married-couple families			Male householder, no wife present			Female householder, no husband present		
		Below poverty level			Below poverty level			Below poverty level			Below poverty level	
	Total	Number	Percent	Total	Number	Percent	Total	Number	Percent	Total	Number	Percent
ALL RACES												
With and Without Children Under 18 Years												
1998	71,551	7,186	10.0	54,778	2,879	5.3	3,977	476	12.0	12,796	3,831	29.9
1997	70,884	7,324	10.3	54,321	2,821	5.2	3,911	508	13.0	12,652	3,995	31.6
1996	70,241	7,708	11.0	53,604	3,010	5.6	3,847	531	13.8	12,790	4,167	32.6
1995	69,597	7,532	10.8	53,570	2,982	5.6	3,513	493	14.0	12,514	4,057	32.4
1994	69,313	8,053	11.6	53,865	3,272	6.1	3,228	549	17.0	12,220	4,232	34.6
With Children Under 18 Years												
1998	37,268	5,628	15.1	26,226	1,822	6.9	2,108	350	16.6	8,934	3,456	38.7
1997	37,427	5,884	15.7	26,430	1,863	7.1	2,175	407	18.7	8,822	3,614	41.0
1996	37,204	6,131	16.5	26,184	1,964	7.5	2,063	412	20.0	8,957	3,755	41.9
1995	36,719	5,976	16.3	26,034	1,961	7.5	1,934	381	19.7	8,751	3,634	41.5
1994	36,782	6,408	17.4	26,367	2,197	8.3	1,750	395	22.6	8,665	3,816	44.0
WHITE												
With and Without Children Under 18 Years												
1998	60,077	4,829	8.0	48,461	2,400	5.0	3,087	306	9.9	8,529	2,123	24.9
1997	59,515	4,990	8.4	48,070	2,312	4.8	3,137	373	11.9	8,308	2,305	27.7
1996	58,934	5,059	8.6	47,650	2,416	5.1	2,945	367	12.5	8,339	2,276	27.3
1995	58,872	4,994	8.5	47,877	2,443	5.1	2,711	351	12.9	8,284	2,200	26.6
1994	58,444	5,312	9.1	47,905	2,629	5.5	2,508	354	14.1	8,031	2,329	29.0
With Children Under 18 Years												
1998	29,984	3,665	12.2	22,634	1,503	6.6	1,659	236	14.2	5,691	1,926	33.8
1997	30,060	3,895	13.0	22,783	1,516	6.7	1,775	310	17.5	5,502	2,069	37.6
1996	29,826	3,863	13.0	22,757	1,548	6.8	1,568	283	18.0	5,501	2,032	36.9
1995	29,713	3,839	12.9	22,663	1,583	7.0	1,496	276	18.4	5,554	1,980	35.6
1994	29,548	4,025	13.6	22,839	1,708	7.5	1,319	253	19.2	5,390	2.064	38.3
BLACK												
With and Without Childen Under 18 Years												
1998	8,452	1,981	23.4	3,979	290	7.3	660	134	20.3	3,813	1,557	40.8
1997	8,408	1,985	23.6	3,921	312	8.0	561	110	19.6	3,926	1,563	39.8
1996	8,455	2,206	26.1	3,851	352	9.1	657	130	19.8	3,947	1,724	43.7
1995	8,055	2,127	26.4	3,713	314	8.5	573	112	19.5	3,769	1,701	45.1
1994	8,093	2,212	27.3	3,842	336	8.7	535	161	30.1	3,716	1,715	46.2
With Children Under 18 Years												
1998	5,491	1,673	30.5	2,198	189	8.6	353	87	24.6	2,940	1,397	47.5
1997	5,647	1,721	30.5	2,275	205	9.0	312	80	25.6	3,060	1,436	46.9
1996	5,695	1,941	34.1	2,174	239	11.0	401	109	27.2	3,120	1,593	51.0
1995	5,340	1,821	34.1	2,119	209	9.9	337	79	23.4	2,884	1,533	53.2
1994	5,439	1,954	35.9	2,147	245	11.4	341	118	34.6	2,951	1,591	53.9

(continued)

of poor people in 1998 were White (68 percent). About 46 percent were non-Hispanic Whites; Blacks, 26 percent; and Asians or Pacific Islanders, 4 percent of the nation's poor. About one-fourth (23 percent) of the poor were persons of Hispanic origin. (Those of Hispanic origin may be of any race, but over 90 percent were included in the White racial category.) (See Table 4.12.)

TABLE 4.13 (Continued)

Poverty Status of Families by Type of Family, Presence of Related Children, Race, and Hispanic Origin: 1959 to 1998—Con.

[Numbers in thousands. Families as of March of the following year]

Year and characteristic	All families			Married-couple families			Male householder, no wife present			Female householder, no husband present		
		Below poverty level			Below poverty level			Below poverty level			Below poverty level	
	Total	Number	Percent	Total	Number	Percent	Total	Number	Percent	Total	Number	Percent
HISPANIC ORIGIN¹												
With and Without Children Under 18 Years												
1998	7,273	1,648	22.7	4,945	775	15.7	600	117	19.6	1,728	756	43.7
1997	6,961	1,721	24.7	4,804	836	17.4	545	118	21.7	1,612	767	47.6
1996	6,631	1,748	26.4	4,520	815	18.0	494	110	22.3	1,617	823	50.9
1995	6,287	1,695	27.0	4,247	803	18.9	436	100	22.9	1,604	792	49.4
1994	6,202	1,724	27.8	4,236	827	19.5	481	124	25.8	1,485	773	52.1
With Children Under 18 Years												
1998	5,078	1,454	28.6	3,398	656	19.3	325	91	28.0	1,355	707	52.2
1997	4,910	1,492	30.4	3,293	692	21.0	325	99	30.5	1,292	701	54.2
1996	4,689	1,549	33.0	3,124	687	22.0	291	102	35.1	1,274	760	59.7
1995	4,422	1,470	33.2	2,902	657	22.6	237	78	32.9	1,283	735	57.3
1994	4,377	1,497	34.2	2,923	698	23.9	272	99	36.4	1,182	700	59.2

ʳFor 1992, figures are based on 1990 census population controls. For 1991, figures are revised to correct for nine omitted weights from the original March 1992 CPS file. For 1988 and 1987, figures are based on new processing procedures and are also revised to reflect corrections to the files after publication of the 1988 advance report, *Money Income and Poverty Status in the United States: 1988*, P-60, No. 166.

(NA) Not available.

¹People of Hispanic origin may be of any race.

Note: Prior to 1979, unrelated subfamilies were included in all families. Beginning in 1979, unrelated subfamilies are excluded from all families.

Source: Joseph Dalaker, *Poverty in the United States: 1998*, Bureau of the Census, Washington, DC, 1999

In 1998, the foreign-born population was disproportionately poor, compared to natives of the United States. Immigrants had a 1998 poverty rate of 18 percent, compared to 12.1 percent for the native-born. While the 25.2 million foreign-born individuals made up only 9.3 percent of the total population, they were 13.8 percent of the poor. Of the foreign-born population, 16.7 million people were not naturalized citizens; 22 percent of these noncitizens were poor in 1998, compared to 11 percent for naturalized citizens (which was lower than the poverty rate for natives at 12.1 percent).

Working and Nonworking

In 1998, 6.3 percent of workers were poor, compared to 21.1 percent of those who did not work during the year. Forty-one percent of poor people 16 years old and over worked. Only 13 percent of the poor worked year-round, full-time. For all people 16 years old and over, 70 percent worked, and 46 percent worked year-round, full-time.

Families in Poverty

In 1998, 10 percent of all families were living in poverty. Married-couple families had a poverty rate of 5.3 percent. For families with a female householder, no spouse present, the poverty rate was 29.9 percent. Not surprisingly, families headed by female householders were overrepresented among the poor. While only 18 percent of all families in the United States had a female householder with no spouse present, 53 percent of all poor families had a female householder. Among those persons not in families (the 31.6 million unrelated individuals — persons living alone or with nonrelatives only), 19.9 percent were poor. Unrelated individuals made up 25 percent of the poverty population, compared to only 15 percent of the entire U.S. population. (See Table 4.12.)

In 1998, White families had a far lower poverty rate (8 percent) than Black families (23.4 percent) or families with a householder of Hispanic origin (22.7 percent). (See Table 4.13.) The poverty rate for Hispanic-origin married couples was 15.7 percent, compared to 7.3 percent for Blacks and 5 percent for Whites. Two of 5 Black families (40.8 percent), more than 2 of 5 Hispanic families (43.7 percent) and 1 of 4 (24.9 percent) White families with a female householder and no husband present were below the poverty level.

Black families headed by males with no spouse present had a poverty rate of 20.3 percent. Hispanic families headed by males with no spouse present had a poverty rate of 19.6 percent, while similar White families had a poverty rate of 9.9 percent. (See Table 4.13.) Female-householder families made up 79 percent of all poor Black families, compared to 46 percent of poor Hispanic-origin families and 44 percent of poor White families.

Families with Children

Families with children were more likely to be in poverty than families without children because family income had to be stretched further to support additional persons. Among the general population, 10 percent of the families with and without children under age 18 lived in poverty, compared to 15.1 percent with children under age 18. Married couples with children (6.9 percent) were far less likely to live below the poverty level than families with children with male householders, no wife present (16.6 percent), or families with children with female householders, no husband present (38.7 percent).

There were significant differences based on race and Hispanic origin. Among White families with children under 18, 12.2 percent lived below the poverty line. About 3 of every 10 Black families (30.5 percent) and Hispanic families (28.6 percent) with children lived below the poverty level. (See Table 4.13.)

Female-Headed Families

In all instances, a far greater percentage of female-headed families lived below the poverty

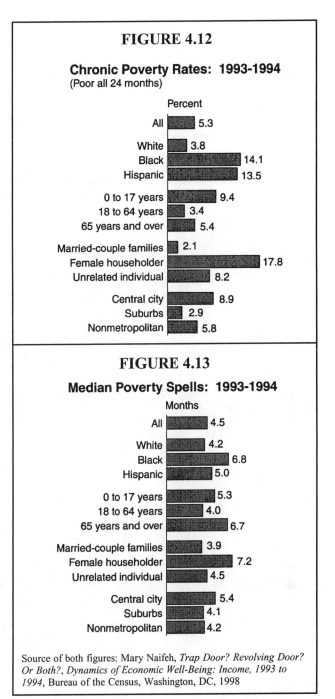

FIGURE 4.12

Chronic Poverty Rates: 1993-1994
(Poor all 24 months)

Percent

All	5.3
White	3.8
Black	14.1
Hispanic	13.5
0 to 17 years	9.4
18 to 64 years	3.4
65 years and over	5.4
Married-couple families	2.1
Female householder	17.8
Unrelated individual	8.2
Central city	8.9
Suburbs	2.9
Nonmetropolitan	5.8

FIGURE 4.13

Median Poverty Spells: 1993-1994

Months

All	4.5
White	4.2
Black	6.8
Hispanic	5.0
0 to 17 years	5.3
18 to 64 years	4.0
65 years and over	6.7
Married-couple families	3.9
Female householder	7.2
Unrelated individual	4.5
Central city	5.4
Suburbs	4.1
Nonmetropolitan	4.2

Source of both figures: Mary Naifeh, *Trap Door? Revolving Door? Or Both?*, *Dynamics of Economic Well-Being: Income, 1993 to 1994*, Bureau of the Census, Washington, DC, 1998

line than male-headed families, and a greater percentage of both lived in poverty than did married couples. Families headed by females have been a growing proportion of all poor families. In 1959, such families accounted for about one-fourth (23 percent) of all the families living in poverty. By 1986, female-headed families accounted for half (51 percent) of all families living in poverty, increasing to 53 percent in 1998.

On the other hand, the proportion of female-headed families living in poverty has actu-

TABLE 4.14

Average Monthly Participation Rates and Median Family Benefits by Selected Characteristics: 1993 and 1994

Characteristic	Any means-tested program[1]		AFDC/GA		SSI		Food stamps		Medicaid		Housing assistance		1993		1994	
	1993	1994	1993	1994	1993	1994	1993	1994	1993	1994	1993	1994	Median	Standard error	Median	Standard error
Total number of recipients[3]	39,162	39,514	14,675	14,438	4,841	5,106	25,713	25,383	27,984	29,332	13,044	12,206	(X)	(X)	(X)	(X)
As percent of the population.	15.2	15.2	5.7	5.5	1.9	2.0	10.0	9.7	10.9	11.3	5.1	4.7	485	4.0	476	3.0
Race and Hispanic Origin[4]																
White	11.7	11.8	3.8	3.7	1.4	1.5	7.4	7.2	8.1	8.5	3.5	3.3	444	4.5	435	3.5
Not of Hispanic origin.	9.4	9.4	2.8	2.6	1.3	1.3	5.7	5.4	6.4	6.8	2.8	2.6	400	6.0	399	5.0
Black	36.6	36.0	16.4	16.4	4.5	4.7	26.0	25.6	26.8	27.5	14.9	13.2	560	4.0	542	9.0
Hispanic origin	32.3	31.7	13.7	12.9	3.0	2.9	22.9	21.9	23.4	23.0	10.9	10.0	557	18.0	556	12.5
Not of Hispanic origin. . . .	13.3	13.2	4.8	4.7	1.8	1.8	8.5	8.3	9.4	9.9	4.4	4.1	466	4.5	460	3.0
Age																
Under 18 years	26.2	26.5	13.2	12.9	0.0	0.0	19.6	19.3	21.2	22.1	8.0	7.4	604	4.5	587	6.0
18 to 64 years	11.0	10.8	3.4	3.3	2.0	2.1	6.9	6.6	6.8	7.1	3.8	3.4	444	2.0	443	3.0
65 years and over	12.0	11.7	0.2	0.2	5.5	5.4	4.2	4.1	8.1	8.0	5.2	5.2	204	3.5	200	5.0
Sex																
Male.	13.0	13.0	4.5	4.3	1.4	1.4	8.4	8.2	8.8	9.2	4.4	3.9	490	7.5	479	5
Female.	17.2	17.3	6.8	6.7	2.4	2.5	11.5	11.2	12.8	13.2	5.7	5.4	483	5	473	5.5
Educational Attainment (people 18 years old and over)																
Less than 4 years of high school.	25.8	25.6	6.5	5.9	7.5	7.7	15.3	14.8	17.5	17.8	9.0	8.4	432	7	433	5.5
High school graduate, no college.	10.5	10.5	2.9	3.0	1.9	2.0	6.2	6.1	6.4	6.7	3.6	3.5	396	10	386	10.5
1 or more years of college	4.6	4.5	1.2	1.2	0.8	0.9	2.4	2.3	2.7	2.8	1.9	1.7	420	13	433	11
Disability Status (people 15 to 64 years old)																
With a work disability	25.0	25.5	6.4	6.3	9.3	10.0	15.1	14.6	18.9	20.0	6.6	6.5	459	5	454	7
With no work disability . . .	8.7	8.5	3.2	3.1	0.3	0.4	5.7	5.6	4.8	5.0	3.4	3.0	466	9.5	448	7
Residence																
Metropolitan	14.7	14.7	5.9	5.9	1.7	1.9	9.5	9.4	10.6	11.1	5.3	4.9	517	5.5	521	6
Central city	23.0	22.4	10.4	9.9	2.7	2.7	15.8	15.2	17.0	17.0	9.1	8.3	574	7.5	564	5.5
Noncentral city	9.3	9.5	3.1	3.2	1.1	1.3	5.5	5.5	6.5	7.0	2.9	2.6	444	5	447	8
Nonmetropolitan.	17.0	16.6	4.8	4.4	2.4	2.3	11.5	10.7	11.6	11.9	4.2	3.9	401	9.5	354	7
Region																
Northeast	14.8	14.6	6.4	6.0	1.9	1.9	8.9	8.6	10.9	10.9	5.9	5.6	599	11	610	13
Midwest	12.5	12.6	5.4	5.3	1.2	1.3	8.7	8.5	9.1	9.5	4.6	4.4	538	9.5	486	5
South	16.5	16.4	4.5	4.3	2.4	2.5	11.5	11.4	10.5	11.1	5.0	4.2	377	2	368	5.5
West.	16.7	16.8	7.3	7.4	2.0	2.0	10.0	9.6	13.4	13.9	4.9	4.9	630	7	624	7.5
Family Status																
In families.	15.6	15.6	6.5	6.4	1.4	1.5	10.8	10.6	11.4	11.8	4.8	4.4	531	6	512	6.5
In married-couple families.	9.1	8.9	2.2	2.2	0.9	0.9	5.5	5.2	5.8	6.1	2.5	2.0	377	2	380	4.5
In families with a female householder, no spouse present . . .	44.3	44.3	26.3	24.9	3.4	3.4	34.9	33.8	36.1	36.3	15.4	15.0	614	4	599	3
Unrelated individuals	12.8	12.4	0.7	0.6	4.5	4.7	5.2	4.9	7.7	7.9	6.3	6.1	169	13.5	188	12.5
Employment and Labor Force Status (people 18 years old and over)																
Employed full time	4.0	3.8	0.4	0.5	0.2	0.3	1.8	1.7	1.2	1.4	1.8	1.6	235	6.5	239	10
Employed part time	8.6	9.2	1.8	2.0	0.9	1.1	4.9	5.4	4.6	5.4	3.1	3.0	297	6.5	299	6
Unemployed.	26.6	26.9	10.4	11.3	1.9	1.5	19.9	20.2	16.0	17.0	9.1	9.0	455	6.5	446	10.5
Not in labor force	21.3	21.3	6.3	6.0	6.9	7.1	12.6	12.3	15.9	16.1	7.1	6.7	460	3.5	458	3.5

(continued)

96

TABLE 4.14 (Continued)

Average Monthly Participation Rates and Median Family Benefits by Selected Characteristics: 1993 and 1994—Con.

Characteristic	Any means-tested program[1]		AFDC/GA		SSI		Food stamps		Medicaid		Housing assistance		1993		1994	
													Median	Standard error	Median	Standard error
	1993	1994	1993	1994	1993	1994	1993	1994	1993	1994	1993	1994				
Marital Status (people 18 years old and over)																
Married	6.6	6.2	1.4	1.3	1.0	1.1	3.9	3.7	3.5	3.5	2.1	1.7	604	7.5	587	9
Separated, divorced, or widowed	19.6	19.6	5.0	4.8	5.9	6.1	11.2	11.1	13.6	13.9	7.4	7.3	358	10.5	359	8.5
Never married	15.6	15.6	5.1	4.9	3.6	3.8	8.9	8.6	10.5	11.0	6.0	5.6	363	11.5	371	9.5
Family Income-to-Poverty Ratio																
Under 1.00	60.5	60.3	29.7	28.3	6.2	6.7	49.6	48.3	47.0	47.7	20.8	20.0	558	6.5	541	6.5
1.00 and over	6.7	7.0	1.2	1.4	1.1	1.1	2.6	2.8	4.1	4.6	2.1	1.9	349	11.5	364	8

X Not applicable.

[1] Means-tested programs include AFDC, general assistance, SSI, food stamps, medicaid, and housing assistance.
[2] Median monthly family benefits include AFDC, general assistance, SSI, and food stamps only.
[3] In thousands.
[4] Hispanics may be of any race.

Source: Wilfred T. Masumura, *Moving Up and Down the Income Ladder, Dynamics of Economic Well-Being: Income, 1993 to 1994*, Bureau of the Census, Washington, DC, 1998

TABLE 4.15

People Living in Households With Difficulties Meeting Basic Needs, by Income Quintile, Age, Race and Hispanic Origin, and Gender: 1995

(In percent)

Characteristic	Type of difficulty with basic needs							
	Didn't meet essential expenses[1]	Didn't pay full gas, electric, or oil bill	Didn't pay full rent or mortgage	Needed to see dentist but didn't go	Needed to see doctor but didn't go	Had telephone disconnected	Had gas, electric oil, disconnected	Evicted from house or apartment
Total	**12.8**	**9.9**	**6.8**	**7.0**	**5.7**	**3.7**	**1.9**	**0.4**
Income Quintile Measures[2]								
Lowest quintile	25.0	19.9	14.0	12.1	10.7	8.8	4.0	1.1
Second quintile	15.8	12.2	8.2	9.2	7.9	5.2	2.1	0.4
Third quintile	10.9	8.5	6.0	6.7	4.8	2.1	1.5	0.5
Fourth quintile	6.5	4.4	3.0	3.8	2.8	1.3	1.0	0.1
Fifth quintile	4.2	2.8	1.5	2.1	1.7	0.6	0.4	0.0
Age								
0 to 17 years	18.7	15.4	10.1	8.8	7.0	6.2	3.0	0.6
18 to 29 years	13.6	10.5	7.6	8.3	6.3	5.0	2.4	0.5
30 to 59 years	11.6	8.6	6.3	6.8	5.8	2.9	1.5	0.4
60 years and over	5.1	3.1	1.4	2.9	2.7	0.5	0.4	0.1
Race and Hispanic Origin[3]								
White, not Hispanic	10.9	7.8	5.5	6.5	5.3	2.5	1.3	0.3
Black, not Hispanic	21.3	18.2	11.0	7.0	6.6	9.5	4.2	1.0
Hispanic origin	18.2	16.2	11.6	10.6	8.2	6.8	3.4	0.4
Gender								
Male	12.3	9.6	6.7	6.8	5.5	3.6	1.9	0.4
Female	13.3	10.1	6.8	7.2	5.9	3.9	1.8	0.4
Gender of Householder								
Male	10.1	7.5	5.3	6.0	4.9	2.4	1.2	0.3
Female	18.4	14.8	9.7	9.0	7.6	6.5	3.2	0.7
Health Insurance Coverage								
Not insured	22.8	18.0	13.1	15.5	14.9	6.6	3.9	0.8
Insured	9.9	7.5	4.9	4.5	3.1	2.9	1.3	0.3

[1] Indicates response to the opening question in this section of the survey "During the past 12 months has there been a time when your household did not meet its essential expenses?" This was asked independently of answers to questions about specific problems also listed on this table.

[2] Income quintiles group people according to household income, ranging from the lowest fifth of the population to the highest.

[3] Data for White and Black exclude Hispanics. Hispanics may be of any race.

U.S. Census Bureau, Survey of Income and Program Participation, 1993 panel, administered 1995.

Source: Kurt J. Bauman, *Extended Measures of Well-Being: Meeting Basic Needs*, Bureau of the Census, Washington, DC, 1999

ally dropped over the past several decades. In 1959, almost 43 percent of all female-headed families were living in poverty. By 1979, the proportion had dropped to 30 percent. By 1993, it had risen to about 36 percent. In 1998, 30 percent of female-headed families were poor. (See Tables 4.12 and 4.13.)

Poverty in Geographic Regions

In 1998, the poverty rate was highest in the West (14 percent) and the South (13.7 percent, a record low), followed by the Northeast (12.3 percent) and the Midwest (10.3 percent). (See Table 4.12.) The South continues to have the largest proportion of the nation's poor population — 38 percent. Nationwide, poverty rates varied from 8.4 percent in New Hampshire to 22.7 percent in the District of Columbia and 22.4 percent in New Mexico.

TABLE 4.16

Food Sufficiency, Days Without Food and Food Budget Shortfall, by Income Quintile, Age, Race, Hispanic Origin, and Gender: 1995

Characteristic	Not enough or not the kind of food wanted (Percent)	Not enough food		
		Percent	Avg. number of days without food in last 30 days	Avg. budget shortfall in last 30 days (Dollars)
Total	**18.8**	**4.8**	**9**	**95**
Income Quintile Measures[1]				
Lowest quintile	35.1	11.2	9	86
Second quintile	24.8	6.6	9	110
Third quintile	15.1	3.2	9	98
Fourth quintile	9.8	1.5	6	115
Fifth quintile	6.4	0.8	6	42
Age				
0 to 17 years	25.1	7.3	8	100
18 to 29 years	20.6	5.6	9	91
30 to 59 years	16.7	4.1	9	96
60 years and over	11.5	1.9	11	67
Race and Hispanic Origin[2]				
White, not Hispanic	14.6	3.2	10	107
Black, not Hispanic	30.4	9.3	7	59
Hispanic origin	35.0	11.7	7	104
Gender				
Male	18.3	4.7	8	96
Female	19.2	5.0	9	94
Gender of Householder				
Male	15.9	3.3	8	93
Female	24.8	8.0	9	96
Health Insurance Coverage				
Not insured	32.8	9.7	9	106
Insured	14.7	3.4	9	93

[1] Income quintiles group people according to household income, ranging from the lowest fifth of the population to the highest.

[2] Data for White and Black exclude Hispanics. Hispanics may be of any race.

U.S. Census Bureau, Survey of Income and Program Participation, 1993 panel, administered 1995.

Source: Kurt J. Bauman, *Extended Measures of Well-Being: Meeting Basic Needs*, Bureau of the Census, Washington, DC, 1999

The poverty rate was higher in nonmetropolitan areas (14.4 percent) than in metropolitan areas (12.3 percent). The poverty rate in central cities (18.5 percent) was twice that of suburban areas (8.7 percent). (See Table 4.12.) In 1998, 43 percent of the poor lived in the central cities.

Who Stays Poor?

The Bureau of the Census studied poor Americans over a two-year period in 1993 and 1994. The Census Bureau found that only about one-third of those who were poor in an average month in 1994 were poor in all of 1993 and 1994. Blacks and Hispanics were less likely to get out of poverty, as were children, people in female-headed households, and those not working. A noticeable proportion

of the population was chronically poor — 5.3 percent were poor all 24 months of 1993 and 1994 (Figure 4.12). One-half of all poverty spells lasted 4.5 months or longer, and Blacks had significantly longer poverty spells than Whites. One half of all poverty spells experienced by Blacks lasted longer

TABLE 4.17

Thinking just about your own financial situation, do you consider yourself to be rich, upper income, middle income, lower income, or poor?

Own Financial Situation – Trend

	May 17-20 1990	Apr 25-28 1996
Rich	•	1
Upper income	7	8
Middle income	59	58
Lower income	23	24
Poor	10	9
No opinion	1	•
	100%	100%

• Less than 0.5%

Source: *The Gallup Poll Monthly*, May 1996, Princeton, NJ

TABLE 4.18*

Looking ahead, how likely is it that you will ever be rich? Would you say it is very likely, somewhat likely, somewhat unlikely or very unlikely?

Chances of Becoming Rich – Trend

	May 17-20 1990	Apr 25-28 1996
Very likely	9%	10%
Somewhat likely	23	24
Not very likely	32	37
Not at all likely	35	27
No opinion	1	2
	100%	100%

*This question was asked of all who reported that they were not "rich" (Table 4.17).

TABLE 4.19

All in all, if you had your choice, would you want to be rich, or not?

Like to Be Rich? – Trend

	May 17-20 1990	Apr 25-28 1996
Yes	59%	60%
No	38	37
No opinion	3	3
	100%	100%

Source of both tables: *The Gallup Poll Monthly*, May 1996, Princeton, NJ

sons ages 18 to 64 years and 11.7 percent of persons 65 and over. (See Table 4.14.)

Over half of the poor (60.3 percent) received means-tested assistance, compared to 7.0 percent of the nonpoor. Persons in married-couple families (8.9 percent) were less likely than those in families with female households, no spouse present (44.3 percent), to participate in the programs (Table 4.14). During the 1993-1994 period, the median length of time participants received benefits from these programs was 7.4 months.

Individuals were more likely to participate in Medicaid than in any other program. In 1994, the average monthly partici-

than 6.8 months, compared with 4.2 months for Whites and 5 months for Hispanics. (See Figure 4.13.)

Who Gets Assistance?

In 1994, approximately 1 in 7 Americans participated in major means-tested assistance programs. (Means-tested programs are those that require the income and/or assets of the individual or family to be below a specified level in order to qualify for benefits.) On average, 40 million persons, or 15.2 percent of the population, were assisted in 1994, 12.6 million more program participants than the 27.4 million in 1987.

In 1994, over one-third of Blacks (36 percent) participated in one or more major means-tested assistance programs, compared to 11.8 percent of Whites. About 31.7 percent of Hispanics received assistance. More than a quarter of the nation's children (26.5 percent) participated in at least one of these programs, compared to 10.8 percent of per-

TABLE 4.20

Just thinking about your own situation, how much money per year would you need to make in order to consider yourself rich?

Income Needed to Be Rich

Less than $40,000	8%
$40,000-$59,999	10
$60,000-$79,999	8
$80,000-$99,999	3
$100,000	21
$101,001-$149,999	1
$150,000-$199,999	5
$200,000-$249,999	9
$250,000-$299,999	4
$300,000-$499,999	5
$500,000-$999,999	8
$1,000,000	4
$1,000,001-$4,999,999	2
$5,000,000 or more	2
No opinion	10
	100%

Mean:	$885,000
Median:	$100,000

Source: *The Gallup Poll Monthly*, May 1996, Princeton, NJ

pation rate for Medicaid, 11.3 percent, was higher than that of food stamps, AFDC/General Assistance, housing assistance, or Supplementary Security Income (SSI). (See Table 4.14.) While a higher proportion participated in Medicaid, the length of stay on each of these programs was similar. The median stay on Medicaid was 8 months; for food stamps, 8.2 months; and for AFDC, 8.3 months.

Basic Needs

In 1995, about 1 of every 5 Americans lived in a household that had at least one problem meeting basic needs. Eleven percent lived in households where more than one of these difficulties occurred. One-fourth of the poor, those in the lowest income quintile, could not meet essential expenses at some time during 1995. About 1 in 10 households did not pay the full gas, electric, or oil bill, and nearly 7 percent did not pay their full rent or mortgage. Nearly every type of difficulty was more common among children and female-headed households. Blacks and Hispanics were more likely than Whites to have difficulty meeting basic needs. (See Table 4.15.)

Health and Nutrition

In 1995, the poor (the lowest income quintile) were more than twice as likely as the nonpoor (the third quintile and above) to live in households that reported a member did not see a doctor or dentist when needed. People without insurance were about 4 times more likely to report not seeing a doctor or dentist than those who had insurance coverage. (See Table 4.15.) The poor were far more likely to report not having enough food to eat, as were children, Blacks and Hispanics, and female householders. (See Table 4.16.)

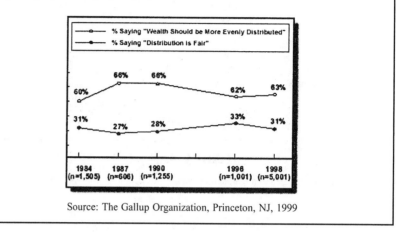

FIGURE 4.14

Is Distribution of Money and Wealth in America Today Considered Fair or Not?--Trend

Do you feel that the distribution of money and wealth in this country today is fair, or do you feel that the money and wealth in this country should be more evenly distributed among a larger percentage of the people?

Source: The Gallup Organization, Princeton, NJ, 1999

OPINIONS ON INCOME AND WEALTH

In 1996, most people polled by the Gallup Organization classified themselves as middle income (Table 4.17). More than one-quarter of those who thought they were not rich felt that it was not at all likely they would be rich, and another one-third felt that becoming rich was not very likely (Table 4.18). Not surprisingly, most (60 percent) would have liked to be rich (Table 4.19). Seven of 10 thought that they needed to earn at least $100,000 to be considered rich (Table 4.20).

The Gallup Organization also asked if the respondents thought the distribution of money and wealth in this country was fair. In 1998, almost one-third of the respondents thought it was, while almost two-thirds (63 percent) thought it was not. Since Gallup's first measurement of this opinion in 1984, the percentage of respondents feeling that the distribution was unfair has remained within a narrow range, between 60 and 66 percent. (See Figure 4.14.)

CHAPTER V

HEALTH*

Health-care expenditures by Americans have soared from $73.2 billion in 1970 to $247.3 billion in 1980, $699.4 billion in 1990, and an estimated $1 trillion in 1997. Per capita spending for health care increased to $3,925 in 1997, more than double the $1,735 just a dozen years before in 1985. (See Table 5.1.)

In 1970, 7.1 percent of the gross domestic product (GDP — total value of goods and services produced within the United States) went for health care; by 1997, the percentage had nearly doubled to 13.5 percent. (See Table 5.1 and Figure 5.1.) Over the past four years, the percentage of the GDP spent on health care has remained stable. The leveling-off was, in part, because of a slowdown in health spending and, in part, because of a strong economy. America's health expenditure rate is significantly higher than most other Western industrialized countries. (See Table 5.2.)

In 1997, national health expenditures grew 4.8 percent, about half the growth rate of 1990 (10.2 percent), partly because of lower inflation and partly because of slower growth in health-care use. (See Table 5.1.) Slower growth in the use of health care and health-care costs are also due to the rise of health maintenance organizations (see below) and managed care, an attempt to control costs and profitably deliver health care by health insurance companies.

WHERE DOES THE SPENDING GO?

In 1997, about 88.7 percent of total health-care spending went for personal health care ($969 billion). The remaining 11.3 percent was mainly spent on program administration, government public health activities, research, and buildings. (See Table 5.3.)

The $371.1 billion for hospital care was the largest proportion (34 percent) expended on personal health care. About $217.6 billion (19.9 percent) was spent on physicians' services. Physicians may also influence other spending since they usually determine who will be hospitalized, what type and quantity of services the hospital patient will receive, and what type of drugs will be administered. Insurance programs, however, are having an ever greater role in making these decisions. Nursing home care (7.6 percent), drugs and medical sundries (10 percent), and dentists' services (4.6 percent) accounted for most of the remaining personal health-care expenditures. (See Table 5.3.)

While general inflation has played a role in the increase in the cost of health care, health-care costs have generally run well ahead of inflation. During the 1990s, the annual rate of increase in the medical-care component of the Consumer Price Index (the CPI measures the rate of inflation) declined every year from 7.5 percent in 1990 to 3.2 percent in 1998. Nonetheless, from 1990 to 1998, the av-

---

* For a complete discussion of health issues, see *Health — A Concern for Every American*, Information Plus, Wylie, Texas, 1999

TABLE 5.1

Gross domestic product, national health expenditures, Federal and State and local government expenditures, and average annual percent change: United States, selected years 1960–97

[Data are compiled by the Health Care Financing Administration]

Gross domestic product, national health expenditures, and government health expenditures	1960	1965	1970	1975	1980	1985	1990	1994	1995	1996	1997
					Amount in billions						
Gross domestic product (GDP)	$ 527	$ 719	$1,036	$1,631	$2,784	$4,181	$ 5,744	$ 6,947	$ 7,270	$ 7,662	$ 8,111
					Percent						
National health expenditures as percent of GDP	5.1	5.7	7.1	8.0	8.9	10.3	12.2	13.6	13.7	13.6	13.5
Source of funds for national health expenditures					Amount in billions						
National health expenditures	$ 26.9	$ 41.1	$ 73.2	$130.7	$247.3	$428.7	$ 699.4	$ 947.7	$ 993.7	$1,042.5	$1,092.4
Private funds	20.2	30.9	45.5	75.7	142.5	254.5	416.2	524.9	538.5	561.1	585.3
Public funds	6.6	10.3	27.7	55.0	104.8	174.2	283.2	422.8	455.2	481.4	507.1
					Percent distribution						
National health expenditures	100.0	100.0	100.0	100.0	100.0	100.0	100.0	100.0	100.0	100.0	100.0
Private funds	75.2	75.0	62.2	57.9	57.6	59.4	59.5	55.4	54.2	53.8	53.6
Public funds	24.8	25.0	37.8	42.1	42.4	40.6	40.5	44.6	45.8	46.2	46.4
Per capita health expenditures					Amount						
National health expenditures	$ 141	$ 202	$ 341	$ 582	$1,052	$1,735	$ 2,690	$ 3,500	$ 3,637	$ 3,781	$ 3,925
Private health expenditures	106	151	212	337	606	1,030	1,601	1,939	1,971	2,035	2,103
Public health expenditures	35	50	129	245	446	705	1,089	1,561	1,666	1,746	1,822
Federal government expenditures					Amount in billions						
Total	$ 89.6	$122.4	$209.1	$371.3	$622.5	$974.2	$1,284.5	$1,561.4	$1,634.7	$1,695.0	$1,741.0
Health	2.9	4.8	17.8	36.4	72.0	123.2	195.2	301.2	326.0	348.0	367.0
State and local government expenditures											
Total	$ 38.4	$ 57.2	$108.2	$198.0	$307.0	$437.8	$ 648.8	$ 852.3	$ 886.0	$ 922.6	$ 960.1
Health	3.7	5.5	9.9	18.6	32.8	51.0	88.0	121.6	129.2	133.4	140.0
Health as a percent of total					Percent						
Federal government expenditures	3.3	3.9	8.5	9.8	11.6	12.6	15.2	19.3	19.9	20.5	21.1
State and local government expenditures	9.7	9.5	9.1	9.4	10.7	11.7	13.6	14.3	14.6	14.5	14.6
Growth				Average annual percent change from previous year shown							
Gross domestic product	...	6.4	7.6	9.5	11.3	8.5	6.6	4.9	4.6	5.4	5.9
National health expenditures											
Total	...	8.9	12.2	12.3	13.6	11.6	10.2	7.9	4.9	4.9	4.8
Per capita	...	7.4	11.1	11.3	12.6	10.5	9.2	6.8	3.9	4.0	3.8
Private health expenditures											
Total	...	8.8	12.2	12.3	13.6	12.3	10.3	6.0	2.6	4.2	4.3
Per capita	...	7.3	12.2	12.3	13.6	11.2	9.2	4.9	1.7	3.3	3.4
Public health expenditures											
Total	...	9.1	12.2	12.3	13.6	10.7	10.2	10.5	7.7	5.7	5.3
Per capita	...	7.6	12.2	12.3	13.6	9.6	9.1	9.4	6.7	4.8	4.4
Federal government expenditures											
Total	...	6.4	11.3	12.2	10.9	9.4	5.7	5.0	4.7	3.7	2.7
Health	...	10.6	29.9	15.4	14.6	11.3	9.6	11.5	8.2	6.8	5.5
State and local government expenditures											
Total	...	8.3	13.6	12.8	9.2	7.4	8.2	7.1	4.0	4.1	4.1
Health	...	7.9	12.6	13.5	12.0	9.2	11.5	8.4	6.2	3.2	5.0

... Category not applicable.

NOTES: These data include revisions in health expenditures and differ from previous editions of *Health, United States*. They reflect Social Security Administration population revisions as of July 1998.

National Health Statistics Group, Office of the Actuary. National health expenditures, 1997. Health Care Financing Review vol 20 no 1. HCFA pub no 03412. Health Care Financing Administration. Washington: U.S. Government Printing Office, March 1999.

Source: *Health, United States, 1999*, National Center for Health Statistics, Hyattsville, MD, 1999

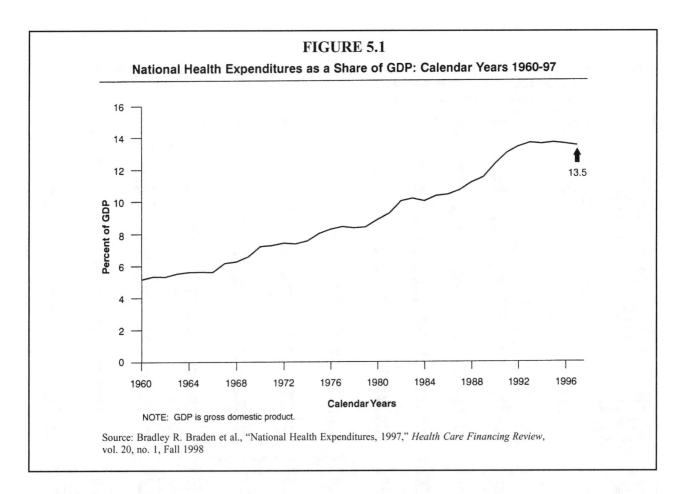

FIGURE 5.1

National Health Expenditures as a Share of GDP: Calendar Years 1960-97

NOTE: GDP is gross domestic product.

Source: Bradley R. Braden et al., "National Health Expenditures, 1997," *Health Care Financing Review*, vol. 20, no. 1, Fall 1998

erage annual growth rate for the medical-care component of the CPI (4.7 percent) was significantly higher than the average overall inflation rate of 2.8 percent. In 1998, the annual medical-care inflation rate was double the annual overall rate of inflation. In 1998, the annual inflation increase for hospital services (3.3 percent) was similar to that of professional medical services (3.2 percent) and medical-care commodities (3.0 percent). (See Table 5.4.)

WHO PAYS FOR IT?

All Americans pay for the nation's health-care system — whether directly out-of-pocket, through health insurance premiums, or indirectly through taxes that help support government payments. In 1997, direct out-of-pocket payments (for example, the money paid directly to the doctor, dentist, or pharmacy and not later reimbursed by an insurance company) accounted for 19.4 percent of all personal health-care expenditures (Table 5.5).

Private health insurance companies and the government are the major third-party payers of health expenditures. (The patient is the first party and the doctor, pharmacist, or hospital is the second party.) The government (44.6 percent), private health insurance (32.3 percent), and other private sources (3.7 percent), such as charities and philanthropy, paid for 81 percent of the nation's personal health-care bill. (See Table 5.5.)

Some observers believe one of the major reasons medical costs have increased so rapidly is the high proportion paid by third parties. In 1997, third-party sources paid for almost all (96.6 percent) of the cost of hospital bills, over four-fifths (84.4 percent) of doctors' bills, more than two-thirds (68.8 percent) of nursing home costs, and half (53 percent) of dental bills. Third parties also paid half (51 percent) of the cost of vision products (eyeglasses) and other medical durables (wheelchairs, crutches, and hearing aids) and 51.3 percent of drug expenditures. (See Table 5.6.)

TABLE 5.2

Total health expenditures as a percent of gross domestic product and per capita health expenditures in dollars: Selected countries and years 1960–97

[Data compiled by the Organization for Economic Cooperation and Development]

Country	1960	1965	1970	1975	1980	1985	1990	1994	1995	1996	1997[1]
	Health expenditures as a percent of gross domestic product										
Australia	4.9	5.1	5.7	7.5	7.3	7.7	8.2	8.4	8.4	8.5	8.4
Austria	4.4	4.7	5.4	7.3	7.9	6.7	7.1	7.8	8.0	8.0	7.9
Belgium	3.4	3.9	4.1	5.9	6.6	7.4	7.6	8.1	7.9	7.8	7.6
Canada	5.5	6.0	7.1	7.2	7.3	8.4	9.2	9.9	9.7	9.6	9.0
Czechoslovakia	---	---	---	---	---	---	5.5	8.3	7.5	7.2	7.0
Denmark	3.6	4.8	6.1	6.5	6.8	6.3	6.5	6.6	8.0	8.0	7.4
Finland	3.9	4.9	5.7	6.4	6.5	7.3	8.0	7.9	7.6	7.4	7.2
France	4.2	5.2	5.8	7.0	7.6	8.5	8.9	9.7	9.9	9.7	9.6
Germany	4.3	4.6	5.7	8.0	8.1	8.5	8.2	10.3	10.4	10.5	10.4
Greece	2.4	2.6	3.3	3.4	3.6	4.0	4.2	5.5	5.8	6.8	7.1
Hungary	---	---	---	---	---	---	6.6	7.3	7.1	6.7	6.5
Iceland	3.3	3.9	5.0	5.8	6.2	7.3	8.0	8.1	8.2	8.2	8.0
Ireland	3.8	4.2	5.3	7.7	8.8	7.8	6.6	7.6	7.0	7.0	7.0
Italy	3.6	4.3	5.2	6.2	7.0	7.1	8.1	8.4	7.7	7.8	7.6
Japan	---	---	4.4	5.5	6.4	6.7	6.0	6.9	7.2	7.2	7.3
Korea	---	---	2.1	2.5	2.9	3.9	3.9	4.6	3.9	4.0	4.0
Luxembourg	---	---	3.7	5.1	6.2	6.1	6.6	6.5	6.7	6.8	7.1
Mexico	---	---	---	---	---	---	---	4.7	4.9	4.6	4.7
Netherlands	3.8	4.3	5.9	7.5	7.9	7.9	8.3	8.8	8.8	8.6	8.6
New Zealand	4.3	---	5.2	6.7	6.0	5.3	7.0	7.1	7.3	7.3	7.7
Norway	3.0	3.6	4.6	6.1	7.0	6.6	7.8	8.0	8.0	7.9	7.5
Poland	---	---	---	---	---	---	4.4	4.4	4.5	5.0	5.2
Portugal	---	---	2.8	5.6	5.8	6.3	6.5	7.8	8.2	8.3	7.8
Spain	1.5	2.6	3.7	4.9	5.7	5.7	6.9	7.3	7.3	7.4	7.4
Sweden	4.7	5.5	7.1	7.9	9.4	9.0	8.8	7.6	8.5	8.6	8.6
Switzerland	3.3	3.8	5.2	7.0	7.3	8.1	8.4	9.5	9.6	10.2	10.1
Turkey	---	---	2.4	2.7	3.3	2.2	2.5	5.2	3.3	3.8	4.0
United Kingdom	3.9	4.1	4.5	5.5	5.6	5.9	6.0	6.9	6.9	6.9	6.7
United States	5.1	5.7	7.1	8.0	8.9	10.3	12.2	13.6	13.7	13.6	13.5
	Per capita health expenditures[2]										
Australia	$98	$125	$212	$443	$669	$989	$1,316	$1,609	$1,699	$1,775	$1,805
Austria	67	92	166	377	697	815	1,180	1,573	1,641	1,748	1,793
Belgium	53	82	131	311	588	890	1,247	1,653	1,664	1,708	1,747
Canada	105	151	255	433	729	1,206	1,691	2,005	2,029	2,065	2,095
Czechoslovakia	---	---	---	---	---	---	538	735	---	904	904
Denmark	67	120	215	348	595	816	1,069	1,344	1,708	1,802	1,848
Finland	55	92	165	312	521	852	1,292	1,289	1,370	1,380	1,447
France	73	121	208	398	716	1,088	1,539	1,868	1,971	1,983	2,051
Germany	91	127	230	498	860	1,274	1,642	2,020	2,128	2,278	2,339
Greece	16	27	60	106	190	288	389	634	703	888	974
Hungary	---	---	---	---	---	---	---	459	---	602	602
Iceland	50	85	139	295	637	929	1,375	1,571	1,789	1,893	2,005
Ireland	37	52	98	240	468	586	748	1,201	1,204	1,276	1,324
Italy	50	81	157	295	591	834	1,322	1,559	1,503	1,584	1,589
Japan	27	64	132	269	535	823	1,082	1,454	1,576	1,677	1,741
Korea	---	---	14	32	71	171	310	525	483	537	587
Luxembourg	---	---	150	315	617	895	1,499	1,962	2,077	2,139	2,340
Mexico	---	---	---	---	---	---	---	379	361	358	391
Netherlands	68	99	205	408	693	932	1,325	1,643	1,743	1,766	1,838
New Zealand	92	---	177	358	463	592	937	1,151	1,238	1,270	1,352
Norway	47	74	135	308	639	910	1,365	1,754	1,809	1,928	1,814
Poland	---	---	---	---	---	---	---	219	---	371	371
Portugal	---	---	45	154	264	387	616	939	1,025	1,071	1,125
Spain	14	37	83	190	332	455	813	992	1,042	1,115	1,168
Sweden	90	146	274	476	867	1,174	1,492	1,339	1,590	1,675	1,728
Switzerland	93	137	270	523	850	1,297	1,782	2,280	2,403	2,499	2,547
Turkey	---	---	23	41	77	73	119	272	190	232	260
United Kingdom	77	98	149	278	453	670	957	1,213	1,234	1,317	1,347
United States	141	202	341	582	1,052	1,735	2,690	3,500	3,637	3,781	3,925

- - - Data not available.

[1]Preliminary figures.

[2]Per capita health expenditures for each country have been adjusted to U.S. dollars using gross domestic product purchasing power parities for each year.

NOTE: Some numbers in this table have been revised and differ from previous editions of *Health, United States*.

Schieber GJ, Poullier JP, and Greenwald LG. U.S. health expenditure performance: An international comparison and data update. Health Care Financing Review vol 13 no 4. Washington: Health Care Financing Administration. September 1992; Anderson GF and Poullier JP. Health spending, access, and outcomes: Trends in industrialized countries. Health Affairs vol 18 no 3. May/June 1999; Office of National Health Statistics, Office of the Actuary. National health expenditures, 1997. Health Care Financing Review vol 20 no 1. HCFA pub no 03412. Washington: Health Care Financing Administration. March 1999; Organization for Economic Cooperation and Development Health Data File: Unpublished data.

Source: *Health, United States, 1999*, National Center for Health Statistics, Hyattsville, MD, 1999

TABLE 5.3

National health expenditures, average annual percent change, and percent distribution, according to type of expenditure: United States, selected years 1960–97

[Data are compiled by the Health Care Financing Administration]

Type of expenditure	1960	1965	1970	1975	1980	1985	1990	1994	1995	1996	1997
						Amount in billions					
All expenditures	$26.9	$41.1	$73.2	$130.7	$247.3	$428.7	$699.4	$947.7	$993.7	$1,042.5	$1,092.4
Health services and supplies	25.2	37.7	67.9	122.3	235.6	412.3	674.8	917.2	963.1	1,010.6	1,057.5
Personal health care	23.6	35.2	63.8	114.5	217.0	376.4	614.7	834.0	879.3	924.0	969.0
Hospital care	9.3	14.0	28.0	52.6	102.7	168.3	256.4	335.7	347.2	360.8	371.1
Physician services	5.3	8.2	13.6	23.9	45.2	83.6	146.3	193.0	201.9	208.5	217.6
Dentist services	2.0	2.8	4.7	8.0	13.3	21.7	31.6	42.4	45.0	47.5	50.6
Nursing home care	0.8	1.5	4.2	8.7	17.6	30.7	50.9	71.1	75.5	79.4	82.8
Other professional services	0.6	0.9	1.4	2.7	6.4	16.6	34.7	49.6	53.6	57.5	61.9
Home health care	0.1	0.1	0.2	0.6	2.4	5.6	13.1	26.2	29.1	31.2	32.3
Drugs and other medical nondurables	4.2	5.9	8.8	13.0	21.6	37.1	59.9	81.6	88.9	98.3	108.9
Vision products and other medical durables	0.6	1.0	1.6	2.5	3.8	6.7	10.5	12.5	13.1	13.4	13.9
Other personal health care	0.7	0.8	1.3	2.5	4.0	6.1	11.2	21.9	25.1	27.4	29.9
Program administration and net cost of health insurance	1.2	1.9	2.7	4.9	11.9	24.3	40.5	55.1	53.3	52.5	50.0
Government public health activities[1]	0.4	0.6	1.3	2.9	6.7	11.6	19.6	28.2	30.4	34.0	38.5
Research and construction	1.7	3.4	5.3	8.4	11.6	16.4	24.5	30.5	30.6	32.0	34.9
Noncommercial research	0.7	1.5	2.0	3.3	5.5	7.8	12.2	15.9	16.7	17.2	18.0
Construction	1.0	1.9	3.4	5.1	6.2	8.5	12.3	14.6	13.9	14.8	16.9
						Percent distribution					
All expenditures	100.0	100.0	100.0	100.0	100.0	100.0	100.0	100.0	100.0	100.0	100.0
Health services and supplies	93.7	91.6	92.7	93.6	95.3	96.2	96.5	96.8	96.9	96.9	96.8
Personal health care	88.0	85.5	87.1	87.6	87.8	87.8	87.9	88.0	88.5	88.6	88.7
Hospital care	34.5	34.1	38.2	40.2	41.5	39.3	36.7	35.4	34.9	34.6	34.0
Physician services	19.7	19.9	18.5	18.3	18.3	19.5	20.9	20.4	20.3	20.0	19.9
Dentist services	7.3	6.8	6.4	6.1	5.4	5.0	4.5	4.5	4.5	4.6	4.6
Nursing home care	3.2	3.6	5.8	6.6	7.1	7.2	7.3	7.5	7.6	7.6	7.6
Other professional services	2.3	2.1	1.9	2.1	2.6	3.9	5.0	5.2	5.4	5.5	5.7
Home health care	0.2	0.2	0.3	0.5	1.0	1.3	1.9	2.8	2.9	3.0	3.0
Drugs and other medical nondurables	15.8	14.3	12.0	10.0	8.7	8.6	8.6	8.6	8.9	9.4	10.0
Vision products and other medical durables	2.4	2.4	2.2	2.0	1.5	1.6	1.5	1.3	1.3	1.3	1.3
Other personal health care	2.6	2.0	1.8	1.9	1.6	1.4	1.6	2.3	2.5	2.6	2.7
Program administration and net cost of health insurance	4.3	4.7	3.7	3.8	4.8	5.7	5.8	5.8	5.4	5.0	4.6
Government public health activities[1]	1.4	1.5	1.8	2.2	2.7	2.7	2.8	3.0	3.1	3.3	3.5
Research and construction	6.3	8.4	7.3	6.4	4.7	3.8	3.5	3.2	3.1	3.1	3.2
Noncommercial research	2.6	3.7	2.7	2.5	2.2	1.8	1.7	1.7	1.7	1.6	1.6
Construction	3.7	4.7	4.6	3.9	2.5	2.0	1.8	1.5	1.4	1.4	1.6

. . . Category not applicable.

[1]Includes personal care services delivered by government public health agencies.

NOTE: These data include revisions in health expenditures and differ from previous editions of *Health, United States*.

National Health Statistics Group, Office of the Actuary. National health expenditures, 1997. Health Care Financing Review vol 20 no 1. HCFA pub no 03412. Health Care Financing Administration. Washington: U.S. Government Printing Office, March 1999.

Source: *Health, United States, 1999*, National Center for Health Statistics, Hyattsville, MD, 1999

Medicare and Medicaid

Medicare, designed to help older Americans with their medical bills, is the largest federal program and paid for 21.6 percent of the nation's personal health-care bill in 1997. Medicare provided $208.9 billion in health-care services to 38.4 million aged and disabled enrollees — not all of whom used the services. From 1990 to 1997, Medicare expenditures almost doubled. (See Table 5.5.) In 1997, most Medicare benefits (59.2 percent) went for hospital care, while most of the remainder (22.2 percent) bought physicians' services (Table 5.6).

In 1997, Medicaid, a health insurance program for certain low-income and needy individuals, spent $152.3 billion, 15.7 percent of all personal health-care expenses. (See Table 5.5.) Federal, state, and local governments jointly fund this program. Medicaid is heavily weighted towards insti-

TABLE 5.4

Consumer Price Index and average annual percent change for all items, selected items, and medical care components: United States, selected years 1960–98

[Data are based on reporting by samples of providers and other retail outlets]

Items and medical care components	1960	1970	1980	1985	1990	1995	1996	1997	1998
					Consumer Price Index (CPI)				
All items	29.6	38.8	82.4	107.6	130.7	152.4	156.9	160.5	163.0
All items excluding medical care	30.2	39.2	82.8	107.2	128.8	148.6	152.8	156.3	158.6
All services	24.1	35.0	77.9	109.9	139.2	168.7	174.1	179.4	184.2
Selected items									
Food	30.0	39.2	86.8	105.6	132.4	148.4	153.3	157.3	160.7
Apparel	45.7	59.2	90.9	105.0	124.1	132.0	131.7	132.9	133.0
Housing	- - -	36.4	81.1	107.7	128.5	148.5	152.8	156.8	160.4
Energy	22.4	25.5	86.0	101.6	102.1	105.2	110.1	111.5	102.9
Medical care	22.3	34.0	74.9	113.5	162.8	220.5	228.2	234.6	242.1
Components of medical care									
Medical care services	19.5	32.3	74.8	113.2	162.7	224.2	232.4	239.1	246.8
Professional medical services	- - -	37.0	77.9	113.5	156.1	201.0	208.3	215.4	222.2
Physicians' services	21.9	34.5	76.5	113.3	160.8	208.8	216.4	222.9	229.5
Dental services	27.0	39.2	78.9	114.2	155.8	206.8	216.5	226.6	236.2
Eye care[1]	- - -	- - -	- - -	- - -	117.3	137.0	139.3	141.5	144.1
Services by other medical professionals[1]	- - -	- - -	- - -	- - -	120.2	143.9	146.6	151.8	155.4
Hospital and related services	- - -	- - -	69.2	116.1	178.0	257.8	269.5	278.4	287.5
Hospital services[2]	- - -	- - -	- - -	- - -	- - -	- - -	- - -	101.7	105.0
Inpatient services[2]	- - -	- - -	- - -	- - -	- - -	- - -	- - -	101.3	104.0
Outpatient services[1]	- - -	- - -	- - -	- - -	138.7	204.6	215.1	224.9	233.2
Hospital rooms	9.3	23.6	68.0	115.4	175.4	251.2	261.0	- - -	- - -
Other inpatient services[1]	- - -	- - -	- - -	- - -	142.7	206.8	216.9	- - -	- - -
Nursing home services[2]	- - -	- - -	- - -	- - -	- - -	- - -	- - -	102.3	107.1
Medical care commodities	46.9	46.5	75.4	115.2	163.4	204.5	210.4	215.3	221.8
Prescription drugs	54.0	47.4	72.5	120.1	181.7	235.0	242.9	249.3	258.6
Nonprescription drugs and medical supplies[1]	- - -	- - -	- - -	- - -	120.6	140.5	143.1	145.4	147.7
Internal and respiratory over-the-counter drugs	- - -	42.3	74.9	112.2	145.9	167.0	170.2	173.1	175.4
Nonprescription medical equipment and supplies	- - -	- - -	79.2	109.6	138.0	166.3	169.1	171.5	174.9
				Average annual percent change from previous year shown					
All items	...	4.3	8.9	5.5	4.0	3.1	3.0	2.3	1.6
All items excluding medical care	...	4.1	8.8	5.3	3.7	2.9	2.8	2.3	1.5
All services	...	5.6	10.2	7.1	4.8	3.9	3.2	3.0	2.7
Selected items									
Food	...	4.0	7.7	4.0	4.6	2.3	3.3	2.6	2.2
Apparel	...	4.4	4.6	2.9	3.4	1.2	−0.2	0.9	0.1
Housing	...	- - -	9.9	5.8	3.6	2.9	2.9	2.6	2.3
Energy	...	2.2	15.4	3.4	0.1	0.6	4.7	1.3	−7.7
Medical care	...	6.2	9.5	8.7	7.5	6.3	3.5	2.8	3.2
Components of medical care									
Medical care services	...	7.3	9.9	8.6	7.5	6.6	3.7	2.9	3.2
Professional medical services	...	- - -	8.9	7.8	6.6	5.2	3.6	3.4	3.2
Physicians' services	...	6.6	9.7	8.2	7.3	5.4	3.6	3.0	3.0
Dental services	...	5.3	8.2	7.7	6.4	5.8	4.7	4.7	4.2
Eye care[1]	...	- - -	- - -	- - -	- - -	3.2	1.7	1.6	1.8
Services by other medical professionals[1]	...	- - -	- - -	- - -	- - -	3.7	1.9	3.5	2.4
Hospital and related services	...	- - -	- - -	10.9	8.9	7.7	4.5	3.3	3.3
Hospital services[2]	...	- - -	- - -	- - -	- - -	- - -	- - -	- - -	3.2
Inpatient services[2]	...	- - -	- - -	- - -	- - -	- - -	- - -	- - -	2.7
Outpatient services[1]	...	- - -	- - -	- - -	- - -	8.1	5.1	4.6	3.7
Hospital rooms	...	13.9	12.2	11.2	8.7	7.4	3.9	- - -	- - -
Other inpatient services[1]	...	- - -	- - -	- - -	- - -	7.7	4.9	- - -	- - -
Nursing home services[2]	...	- - -	- - -	- - -	- - -	- - -	- - -	- - -	4.7
Medical care commodities	...	0.7	7.2	8.8	7.2	4.6	2.9	2.3	3.0
Prescription drugs	...	−0.2	7.2	10.6	8.6	5.3	3.4	2.6	3.7
Nonprescription drugs and medical supplies[1]	...	- - -	- - -	- - -	- - -	3.1	1.9	1.6	1.6
Internal and respiratory over-the-counter drugs	...	1.6	7.7	8.4	5.4	2.7	1.9	1.7	1.3
Nonprescription medical equipment and supplies	...	- - -	- - -	6.7	4.7	3.8	1.7	1.4	2.0

- - - Data not available.   . . . Category not applicable.
[1]Dec. 1986 = 100.   [2]Dec. 1996 = 100.

NOTES: 1982–84 = 100, except where noted. Data for additional years are available.

U.S. Department of Labor, Bureau of Labor Statistics. Consumer Price Index. Various releases.

Source: *Health, United States, 1999*, National Center for Health Statistics, Hyattsville, MD, 1999

TABLE 5.5

Personal Health Care Expenditures Aggregate and Per Capita Amounts and Percent Distribution, by Source of Funds: Selected Calendar Years 1980-97

Year	Total	Out-of-Pocket Payments	Third-Party Payments						Medicare[1]	Medicaid[2]
			Total	Private Health Insurance	Other Private Funds	Government				
						Total	Federal	State and Local		
					Amount in Billions					
1980	$217.0	$60.3	$156.8	$62.0	$7.8	$87.0	$63.4	$23.6	$36.4	$24.8
1985	376.4	100.7	275.8	114.1	14.0	147.7	111.1	36.6	70.0	39.1
1990	614.7	145.0	469.6	207.7	20.8	241.1	177.0	64.2	108.6	71.4
1991	679.6	153.3	526.2	229.8	23.1	273.4	203.2	70.2	117.8	89.6
1992	740.7	161.8	578.9	250.6	24.7	303.6	230.5	73.0	132.7	101.5
1993	790.5	167.1	623.5	265.2	26.8	331.4	252.3	79.1	144.7	115.8
1994	834.0	168.5	665.5	274.5	28.9	362.0	275.7	86.3	162.6	126.9
1995	879.3	171.0	708.3	286.6	31.6	390.1	299.0	91.2	180.7	137.2
1996	924.0	178.1	745.9	299.8	33.5	412.6	319.8	92.8	194.9	146.3
1997	969.0	187.6	781.5	313.5	35.6	432.4	337.3	95.1	208.9	152.3
					Per Capita Amount					
1980	$923	$256	$667	$264	$33	$370	$270	$100	(3)	(3)
1985	1,523	407	1,116	462	57	598	449	148	(3)	(3)
1990	2,364	558	1,806	799	80	927	681	247	(3)	(3)
1991	2,586	584	2,003	875	88	1,040	773	267	(3)	(3)
1992	2,790	609	2,181	944	93	1,143	868	275	(3)	(3)
1993	2,947	623	2,325	989	100	1,236	941	295	(3)	(3)
1994	3,080	622	2,458	1,014	107	1,337	1,018	319	(3)	(3)
1995	3,218	626	2,592	1,049	116	1,428	1,094	334	(3)	(3)
1996	3,351	646	2,705	1,087	121	1,496	1,160	337	(3)	(3)
1997	3,482	674	2,808	1,126	128	1,554	1,212	342	(3)	(3)
					Percent Distribution					
1980	100.0	27.8	72.2	28.6	3.6	40.1	29.2	10.9	16.8	11.4
1985	100.0	26.7	73.3	30.3	3.7	39.2	29.5	9.7	18.6	10.4
1990	100.0	23.6	76.4	33.8	3.4	39.2	28.8	10.4	17.7	11.6
1991	100.0	22.6	77.4	33.8	3.4	40.2	29.9	10.3	17.3	13.2
1992	100.0	21.8	78.2	33.8	3.3	41.0	31.1	9.9	17.9	13.7
1993	100.0	21.1	78.9	33.6	3.4	41.9	31.9	10.0	18.3	14.6
1994	100.0	20.2	79.8	32.9	3.5	43.4	33.1	10.3	19.5	15.2
1995	100.0	19.4	80.6	32.6	3.6	44.4	34.0	10.4	20.6	15.6
1996	100.0	19.3	80.7	32.4	3.6	44.7	34.6	10.0	21.1	15.8
1997	100.0	19.4	80.6	32.3	3.7	44.6	34.8	9.8	21.6	15.7

[1] Subset of Federal funds.

[2] Subset of Federal and State and local funds.

[3] Calculation of per capita estimates is inappropriate.

NOTES: Per capita amounts based on July 1 Social Security area population estimates for each year, 1980-97. Numbers and percents may not add to totals because of rounding.

Source: Bradley R. Braden et al., "National Health Expenditures, 1997," *Health Care Financing Review*, vol. 20, no. 1, Fall 1998

TABLE 5.6

Personal Health Care Expenditures, by Type of Expenditure and Source of Funds: Calendar Years 1990-97

Amount in Billions

Source of Funds	Total	Hospital Care	Physician Services	Dental Services	Other Professional Services	Home Health Care	Drugs and Other Medical Non-Durables	Vision Products and Other Medical Durables	Nursing Home Care	Other Personal Health Care
1996										
Personal Health Care Expenditures	$924.0	$360.8	$208.5	$47.5	$57.5	$31.2	$98.3	$13.4	$79.4	$27.4
Out-of-Pocket Payments	178.1	11.8	31.1	22.1	21.9	6.5	51.0	6.9	26.7	—
Third-Party Payments	745.9	348.9	177.4	25.5	35.5	24.7	47.3	6.5	52.7	27.4
Private Health Insurance	299.8	110.0	106.9	23.2	18.0	3.5	33.9	0.6	3.7	—
Other Private	33.5	16.1	4.3	0.2	4.3	3.7	—	—	1.5	3.4
Government	412.6	222.8	66.2	2.1	13.2	17.5	13.4	5.9	47.4	24.0
Federal	319.8	179.6	54.4	1.2	10.4	15.5	7.5	5.8	31.3	14.1
Medicare	194.9	116.3	42.8	0.1	8.4	13.2	0.7	5.4	8.0	—
Medicaid	88.0	37.4	9.1	1.0	0.9	2.3	6.5	—	21.6	9.2
Other	37.0	25.9	2.6	0.2	1.0	—	0.3	0.3	1.7	5.0
State and Local	92.8	43.2	11.8	0.9	2.8	2.0	5.9	0.1	16.2	9.9
Medicaid	58.4	21.6	6.1	0.8	0.7	1.9	4.6	—	16.0	6.7
Other	34.5	21.6	5.7	0.1	2.2	0.1	1.3	0.1	0.1	3.2
1997										
Personal Health Care Expenditures	969.0	371.1	217.6	50.6	61.9	32.3	108.9	13.9	82.8	29.9
Out-of-Pocket Payments	187.6	12.4	34.1	23.9	24.6	7.0	53.0	6.8	25.7	—
Third-Party Payments	781.5	358.6	183.6	26.8	37.3	25.3	55.9	7.1	57.0	29.9
Private Health Insurance	313.5	113.0	109.1	24.3	18.9	3.7	39.9	0.5	4.0	—
Other Private	35.6	17.2	4.3	0.2	4.8	3.9	—	—	1.6	3.6
Government	432.4	228.4	70.1	2.3	13.6	17.7	16.0	6.6	51.4	26.3
Federal	337.3	185.6	58.4	1.3	10.8	15.4	9.2	6.4	34.5	15.6
Medicare	208.9	123.7	46.4	0.1	8.8	12.8	1.0	6.0	10.1	—
Medicaid	91.1	36.2	9.3	1.1	1.0	2.6	7.8	—	22.6	10.4
Other	37.3	25.7	2.7	0.1	1.1	—	0.4	0.4	1.7	5.1
State and Local	95.1	42.8	11.7	1.0	2.8	2.3	6.8	0.1	16.9	10.7
Medicaid	61.2	21.4	6.4	0.9	0.7	2.1	5.5	—	16.8	7.5
Other	33.9	21.4	5.3	0.1	2.1	0.1	1.4	0.1	0.1	3.3

NOTES: The figure 0.0 denotes amounts less than $50 million. Medicaid expenditures exclude Part B premium payments to Medicare by States under buy-in agreements to cover premiums for eligible Medicaid recipients. Numbers may not add to totals because of rounding.

Source: Bradley R. Braden et al., "National Health Expenditures, 1997," *Health Care Financing Review*, vol. 20, no. 1, Fall 1998

tutional services. Hospital care and nursing home care accounted for nearly two-thirds (64 percent) of combined federal and state Medicaid spending.

From 1974 through 1989, the annual number of Medicaid recipients fluctuated between 22 million and 23 million people. From 1990 to 1995, the number of recipients increased 44 percent from 25.3 million to 36.3 million. In 1997, the number dropped to 33.6 million. Children under the age of 21 years made up 45.5 percent of Medicaid recipients but accounted for only 12.7 percent of expenditures. The aged, blind, and disabled accounted for 30 percent of recipients and 74 percent of expenditures.

In 1997, average Medicaid payments per recipient varied substantially by eligibility category, ranging from $1,027 for children under 21 years of age to $9,539 for the aged. In 1997, Medicaid payments per recipient averaged $3,679.

INSURANCE COVERAGE

Over the past 20 years, Americans have changed the way they insure themselves. In 1965, almost all insured people were covered either by insurance companies or the Federal Employee Program. While these two categories still remain the major private insurers, an increasing number of Americans are being covered by self-insured plans in which a large company, government authority, or perhaps a school district insures itself. The institution may administer the plan itself or hire a company to do it. In addition, a growing number of companies are turning to Health Maintenance Organizations (HMOs, see below) in an attempt to control increasing medical costs.

Between 1994 and 1998, the proportion of the population under 65 years of age with private health insurance remained stable at 70 to 71 percent, after declining from 77 percent to 70 percent between 1984 and 1994. Changes in Medicaid eligibility rules increased the proportion of the population covered by Medicaid from 7.3 percent in 1984 to 10 to 12 percent from 1994 through 1997. The pro-

portion of the population under 65 years of age without any health care coverage hovered around 17 percent from 1994 through 1997, up from 14.2 percent in 1984. (See Table 5.7.) In 1998, 44.3 million people in the United States were without health insurance coverage (16.3 percent). (See Figure 5.2. The percentages shown by type of health insurance coverage are not mutually exclusive; persons can be covered by more than one type of health insurance.)

In 1997, most people over 65 years of age were covered by Medicare. Of the 70 percent with private insurance, 92 percent also had Medicare. About 8 percent were covered by both Medicare and Medicaid, and 20.7 percent were covered by Medicare only. (See Table 5.8.)

People with low incomes, young people, Blacks, and persons of Hispanic origin were more likely not to have health insurance. In 1998, despite programs such as Medicaid and Medicare, 32.3 percent of the poor (11.2 million) had no health insurance of any kind, twice the percentage for the general population. (See Figure 5.2.) Although poor people accounted for only 12.7 percent of the total population, they made up 25.2 percent of all uninsured people.

In 1998, young adults aged 18 to 24 were more likely than other age groups to lack coverage (30 percent). Because of Medicare, the elderly were most likely to be covered — only 1.1 percent lacked coverage. (See Figure 5.3.) The number of uninsured children less than 18 years of age grew to 11.1 million (15.4 percent) in 1998, compared to 9.8 million (13.8 percent) in 1995. Even though the number of uninsured children went up in 1998, the long-term trend has been downward. Indeed, expansions in the Medicaid program in recent years led to a decline in the percentage of uninsured children from 18 percent in 1984 to 13 percent in 1995.

Among poor children, 3.4 million (25.2 percent) were uninsured in 1998. Poor children comprised nearly one-third of all uninsured children. Of those children who had health insurance (84.6

TABLE 5.7

Health care coverage for persons under 65 years of age, according to type of coverage and selected characteristics: United States, selected years 1984–97

[Data are based on household interviews of a sample of the civilian noninstitutionalized population]

Characteristic	Private insurance						Private insurance obtained through workplace[1]					
	1984	1989	1994[2]	1995	1996	1997[2,3]	1984	1989	1994[2]	1995	1996	1997[2,3]
	Number in millions											
Total[4]	157.5	162.7	160.7	165.0	165.9	165.8	141.8	146.3	146.7	151.4	151.4	152.5
	Percent of population											
Total, age adjusted[4]	76.6	75.7	69.9	71.2	71.1	70.4	68.9	68.1	63.8	65.4	64.8	64.7
Total, crude[4]	76.8	75.9	70.3	71.6	71.4	70.7	69.1	68.3	64.2	65.7	65.1	65.0
Age												
Under 18 years	72.6	71.8	63.8	65.7	66.4	66.1	66.5	65.8	59.0	60.9	61.1	61.3
Under 6 years	68.1	67.9	58.3	60.1	61.1	61.3	62.1	62.3	53.9	55.6	56.5	57.3
6–17 years	74.9	74.0	66.8	68.7	69.1	68.5	68.7	67.7	61.8	63.7	63.4	63.4
18–44 years	76.5	75.5	69.8	71.2	70.6	69.4	69.6	68.4	63.9	65.6	64.7	64.4
18–24 years	67.4	64.5	58.3	61.2	60.4	59.3	58.7	55.3	50.7	53.9	52.3	53.8
25–34 years	77.4	75.9	69.4	70.3	69.5	68.1	71.2	69.5	64.1	65.3	64.4	63.6
35–44 years	83.9	82.7	77.1	78.0	77.5	76.4	77.4	76.2	71.6	72.9	72.0	71.2
45–64 years	83.3	82.5	80.3	80.4	79.5	79.1	71.8	71.6	71.8	72.4	71.4	70.8
45–54 years	83.3	83.4	81.3	81.1	80.4	80.4	74.6	74.4	74.6	74.9	74.0	73.6
55–64 years	83.3	81.6	78.8	79.3	78.1	76.9	69.0	68.3	67.9	68.6	67.5	66.6
Sex[5]												
Male	77.1	76.0	70.4	71.6	71.4	70.7	69.7	68.6	64.3	65.9	65.2	65.0
Female	76.0	75.4	69.5	70.8	70.8	70.1	68.1	67.6	63.4	64.8	64.4	64.4
Race[5,6]												
White	79.7	79.0	73.5	74.4	74.2	74.1	71.9	71.1	67.0	68.4	67.6	67.9
Black	58.3	57.8	51.5	54.2	54.9	54.9	52.4	52.9	48.8	50.4	51.8	52.6
Asian or Pacific Islander	69.8	71.1	67.3	68.0	67.8	68.0	63.6	60.2	57.4	59.8	59.3	60.4
Hispanic origin and race[5,6]												
All Hispanic	56.3	52.6	48.6	47.3	47.5	47.3	52.3	48.0	44.5	44.0	43.8	44.0
Mexican	54.3	48.0	45.7	43.9	43.8	43.3	51.1	45.2	43.7	41.9	40.9	41.2
Puerto Rican	48.8	45.9	48.3	47.9	50.7	47.2	46.4	42.6	45.2	44.7	48.1	44.6
Cuban	71.7	69.0	63.9	62.4	65.4	70.5	57.7	55.8	46.5	53.1	54.4	56.0
Other Hispanic	61.6	61.9	52.3	52.2	52.6	50.7	57.4	55.4	46.2	47.1	47.6	47.1
White, non-Hispanic	82.3	82.4	77.3	78.6	78.5	77.9	74.0	74.1	70.4	72.1	71.5	71.4
Black, non-Hispanic	58.5	57.9	51.9	54.6	55.4	55.1	52.6	53.0	49.2	50.9	52.2	52.8
Age and percent of poverty level[6,7]												
All ages:[5]												
Below 100 percent	32.4	26.7	21.3	21.9	20.0	22.7	23.7	19.4	16.1	17.0	15.5	18.9
100–149 percent	62.4	54.9	46.8	47.8	47.1	42.1	51.9	45.8	40.9	41.9	40.8	37.0
150–199 percent	77.7	71.3	65.7	66.5	67.9	64.0	69.5	62.9	59.0	60.4	60.9	58.7
200 percent or more	91.7	91.2	88.9	89.3	89.5	87.7	85.2	84.2	83.0	83.7	83.2	82.0
Under 18 years:												
Below 100 percent	28.7	22.3	14.9	16.8	16.1	17.4	23.2	17.5	12.4	13.4	13.4	15.4
100–149 percent	66.2	59.6	47.8	48.5	49.5	42.5	58.3	52.5	43.2	43.6	43.7	38.5
150–199 percent	80.9	75.9	69.3	68.5	73.0	66.8	75.8	70.1	64.0	63.0	67.4	63.1
200 percent or more	92.3	92.7	89.7	90.4	90.7	88.9	86.9	86.7	84.5	85.5	84.6	83.7
Geographic region[5]												
Northeast	80.1	81.8	74.8	75.1	74.9	74.0	73.8	74.9	69.5	69.5	68.7	69.4
Midwest	80.4	81.4	77.2	77.2	78.4	76.9	71.9	73.3	71.0	71.1	72.3	71.1
South	74.0	71.1	65.0	66.7	65.9	66.8	65.9	63.3	59.1	61.7	60.4	61.0
West	71.8	71.3	65.2	67.9	67.1	65.3	64.5	63.9	58.1	60.7	59.6	58.9
Location of residence[5]												
Within MSA[8]	77.2	76.3	70.4	72.1	72.5	71.0	70.6	69.5	64.8	66.6	66.5	65.6
Outside MSA[8]	75.1	73.6	68.1	67.7	65.8	68.0	65.1	63.4	60.4	60.5	58.6	61.4

See footnotes at end of table.

(continued)

percent), private insurance covered 67.5 percent and Medicaid, 19.8 percent.

One-third of all Hispanics (35.3 percent), one-fifth each of Blacks (22.2 percent) and Asians and Pacific Islanders (21.1 percent), and 1 out of 8 non-Hispanic Whites (11.9 percent) were not covered. While the likelihood of being uninsured generally declined as the level of education rose, among those who were poor there were no significant differences across the education groups. (See Figure 5.3.)

110

TABLE 5.7 (Continued)

Health care coverage for persons under 65 years of age, according to type of coverage and selected characteristics: United States, selected years 1984–97

[Data are based on household interviews of a sample of the civilian noninstitutionalized population]

Characteristic	Medicaid[9]						Not covered[10]					
	1984	1989	1994[2]	1995	1996	1997[2,3]	1984	1989	1994[2]	1995	1996	1997[2,3]
	Number in millions											
Total[4]	14.0	15.4	24.1	25.3	25.0	22.9	29.8	33.4	40.4	37.4	38.9	41.0
	Percent of population											
Total, age adjusted[4]	7.3	7.8	11.5	12.0	11.7	10.7	14.2	15.2	17.1	15.6	16.1	16.8
Total, crude[4]	6.8	7.2	10.6	11.0	10.8	9.7	14.5	15.6	17.7	16.2	16.7	17.5
Age												
Under 18 years	11.9	12.6	20.0	20.6	20.1	18.4	13.9	14.7	15.3	13.6	13.4	14.0
Under 6 years	15.5	15.7	27.2	28.3	27.4	24.7	14.9	15.1	13.7	11.9	11.9	12.5
6–17 years	10.1	10.9	16.2	16.6	16.4	15.2	13.4	14.5	16.2	14.5	14.1	14.7
18–44 years	5.1	5.2	7.3	7.4	7.3	6.6	17.1	18.4	21.9	20.5	21.2	22.4
18–24 years	6.4	6.8	9.6	9.7	9.2	8.8	25.0	27.1	31.1	28.2	29.6	30.1
25–34 years	5.3	5.2	7.7	7.7	7.5	6.8	16.2	18.3	22.1	21.3	22.5	23.8
35–44 years	3.5	4.0	5.4	5.6	6.0	5.2	11.2	12.3	16.0	15.2	15.2	16.7
45–64 years	3.4	4.3	4.5	5.3	5.2	4.6	9.6	10.5	12.0	11.0	12.1	12.4
45–54 years	3.2	3.8	3.8	4.9	4.8	4.0	10.5	11.0	12.6	11.7	12.5	12.8
55–64 years	3.6	4.9	5.5	6.0	5.7	5.6	8.7	10.0	11.2	10.0	11.6	11.8
Sex[5]												
Male	6.1	6.5	9.8	10.3	10.1	9.4	14.8	16.1	18.1	16.7	17.2	17.8
Female	8.5	9.1	13.2	13.6	13.3	11.9	13.6	14.3	16.1	14.6	15.1	15.9
Race[5,6]												
White	5.0	5.6	8.7	9.4	9.3	8.2	13.3	14.1	16.4	15.0	15.4	15.8
Black	20.5	19.3	27.0	27.0	24.5	22.7	19.5	21.0	19.5	17.9	19.0	19.3
Asian or Pacific Islander	10.1	11.8	10.2	11.4	12.4	10.3	17.8	18.2	19.9	17.8	18.6	18.8
Hispanic origin and race[5,6]												
All Hispanic	13.1	13.5	19.6	21.2	20.1	17.8	29.0	32.4	31.4	30.8	31.6	33.2
Mexican	11.8	12.3	18.3	20.1	19.0	17.1	33.1	38.6	35.7	35.4	36.7	38.1
Puerto Rican	31.1	28.0	36.2	32.7	33.8	30.9	17.9	23.3	15.4	17.8	14.4	18.5
Cuban	5.0	8.0	9.8	15.3	13.9	9.2	21.6	21.8	26.1	21.6	17.6	19.8
Other Hispanic	8.0	11.2	16.2	18.4	16.3	15.6	27.1	24.8	30.2	29.0	29.8	31.8
White, non-Hispanic	4.0	4.6	7.1	7.5	7.5	6.8	11.6	11.7	14.2	12.7	12.9	13.3
Black, non-Hispanic	20.8	19.4	27.0	26.7	24.2	22.5	19.2	20.8	19.1	17.8	18.9	19.3
Age and percent of poverty level[6,7]												
All ages:[5]												
Below 100 percent	32.1	37.0	45.0	46.9	46.8	41.6	34.0	35.2	32.7	30.9	32.7	32.8
100–149 percent	7.7	11.2	16.0	18.4	17.2	19.1	26.4	30.6	34.0	31.2	32.8	34.8
150–199 percent	3.3	5.1	5.9	7.7	7.7	8.0	16.7	21.0	24.9	22.8	22.5	25.1
200 percent or more	0.6	1.1	1.4	1.6	1.6	1.9	5.6	6.5	8.4	7.8	7.4	8.5
Under 18 years:												
Below 100 percent	43.1	47.8	63.6	65.6	65.9	59.9	28.9	31.6	23.3	20.6	21.3	22.4
100–149 percent	9.0	12.3	22.9	26.3	24.8	30.2	22.8	26.1	27.7	25.5	25.2	26.1
150–199 percent	4.4	6.1	8.6	11.7	10.8	12.2	12.7	15.8	19.0	17.7	16.1	19.7
200 percent or more	0.8	1.6	2.2	2.7	2.6	2.9	4.2	4.4	6.8	6.0	5.3	6.1
Geographic region[5]												
Northeast	9.4	7.4	12.0	12.5	12.3	12.4	9.8	10.5	13.3	12.7	13.2	12.8
Midwest	7.9	8.2	10.4	11.0	9.4	9.2	10.9	10.2	11.9	11.8	11.9	12.6
South	5.5	7.0	11.3	11.6	12.0	9.8	17.4	19.4	20.9	19.1	19.7	20.3
West	7.5	9.1	12.6	13.2	13.4	12.5	17.6	18.1	20.2	17.3	18.1	19.8
Location of residence[5]												
Within MSA[8]	7.8	7.7	11.7	11.8	11.1	10.6	13.2	14.7	16.6	14.9	15.3	16.2
Outside MSA[8]	6.4	8.3	11.1	12.8	13.9	11.0	16.3	16.7	18.8	18.4	19.2	19.4

[1]Private insurance originally obtained through a present or former employer or union.
[2]The questionnaire changed compared with previous years.
[3]Preliminary data.   [4]Includes all other races not shown separately and unknown poverty level.
[5]Age adjusted.
[6]The race groups white, black, and Asian or Pacific Islander include persons of Hispanic and non-Hispanic origin; persons of Hispanic origin may be of any race.
[7]Poverty level is based on family income and family size using Bureau of the Census poverty thresholds.
[8]Metropolitan statistical area.
[9]Includes other public assistance through 1996. In 1997 includes state-sponsored health plans. In 1997 the age-adjusted percent of the population under 65 years of age covered by Medicaid was 9.5 percent, and 1.2 percent were covered by state-sponsored health plans.
[10]Includes persons not covered by private insurance, Medicaid, public assistance (through 1996), state-sponsored or other government-sponsored health plans (1997), Medicare, or military plans. Estimates of the percentage of persons lacking health care coverage based on the National Health Interview Survey (NHIS) are slightly higher than those based on the March Current Population Survey (CPS).

NOTE: Percents do not add to 100 because the percent with other types of health insurance (for example, Medicare, military) is not shown, and because persons with both private insurance and Medicaid appear in both columns.

Source: *Health, United States, 1999*, National Center for Health Statistics, Hyattsville, MD, 1999

Noncoverage rates fall as household income rises. In 1998, the percentage of persons without health insurance ranged from 8.3 percent among those in households with incomes of $75,000 or more to 25.2 percent among those in households with incomes less than $25,000. Nearly 12 percent of those earning $50,000 to $74,999 and 18.8 percent of those earning $25,000 to $29,999 were not covered.

HEALTH MAINTENANCE ORGANIZATIONS (HMOs)

Health Maintenance Organizations (HMOs) are group practices organized to provide complete coverage for subscribers' health needs at pre-established prices. The number of HMOs more than tripled from 174 in 1976 to 647 in 1987, dropped to 543 in 1994, and then rose to 651 in 1998. (See Table 5.9.)

As an alternative to traditional health insurance coverage, many major companies have turned to HMOs in an attempt to lower health-coverage costs. While this has increased the number of people using HMOs, it has also meant that HMOs can no longer be as selective in their membership. This has exposed HMOs to higher-risk individuals who would, in general, otherwise be served by traditional health insurance companies. This wider mix of clients has made it more difficult for many HMOs to be profitable.

The number of people enrolled in HMOs skyrocketed from 6 million in 1976 to 76.6 million in 1998. HMOs are most popular in the West (the home of Kaiser-Permanente, the largest not-for-profit HMO) where almost 2 of every 5 persons are enrolled in an HMO. They are least preferred in the South and Midwest, where 1 in 5 persons is a member. (See Table 5.9.)

HOSPITAL CARE

Responses to Rising Hospital Costs

In the mid-1970s, growth in health-care spending greatly exceeded growth in the overall economy. This led to the first cost-containment effort focused on health-care costs. In 1977, the government asked hospitals to voluntarily control rising costs. This voluntary effort met with initial success in controlling hospital costs, and growth rates from 1977 through 1979 were lower than in the mid-1970s. However, by 1980, hospital costs were again growing rapidly, and economists predicted the exhaustion of Medicare's Hospital Insurance fund by the early 1990s.

In response, Congress passed several provisions in the Tax Equity and Fiscal Responsibility Act of 1982 (PL 97-248) intended to reduce the rate of increase per case that Medicare paid to hospitals. Hospitals were to be paid on a per-case rather

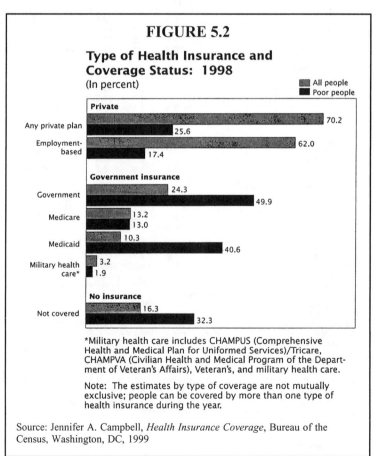

FIGURE 5.2

Type of Health Insurance and Coverage Status: 1998
(In percent)

Legend: All people / Poor people

Private
- Any private plan: 70.2 (All people), 25.6 (Poor people)
- Employment-based: 62.0 (All people), 17.4 (Poor people)

Government insurance
- Government: 24.3 (All people), 49.9 (Poor people)
- Medicare: 13.2 (All people), 13.0 (Poor people)
- Medicaid: 10.3 (All people), 40.6 (Poor people)
- Military health care*: 3.2 (All people), 1.9 (Poor people)

No insurance
- Not covered: 16.3 (All people), 32.3 (Poor people)

*Military health care includes CHAMPUS (Comprehensive Health and Medical Plan for Uniformed Services)/Tricare, CHAMPVA (Civilian Health and Medical Program of the Department of Veteran's Affairs), Veteran's, and military health care.

Note: The estimates by type of coverage are not mutually exclusive; people can be covered by more than one type of health insurance during the year.

Source: Jennifer A. Campbell, *Health Insurance Coverage*, Bureau of the Census, Washington, DC, 1999

TABLE 5.8

Health care coverage for persons 65 years of age and over, according to type of coverage and selected characteristics: United States, selected years 1984–97

[Data are based on household interviews of a sample of the civilian noninstitutionalized population]

Characteristic	Private insurance[1]						Private insurance obtained through workplace[1,2]					
	1984	1989	1994[3]	1995	1996	1997[3,4]	1984	1989	1994[3]	1995	1996	1997[3,4]
	Number in millions											
Total[5]	19.4	22.4	24.0	23.5	22.9	22.3	10.2	11.2	12.5	12.5	12.1	12.0
	Percent of population											
Total, age adjusted[5]	73.5	76.6	77.5	74.9	72.0	69.6	39.1	38.8	41.0	40.1	38.6	38.2
Total, crude[5]	73.3	76.5	77.3	74.8	72.0	69.5	38.8	38.4	40.4	39.6	38.1	37.5
Age												
65–74 years	76.5	78.2	78.4	75.3	72.4	69.9	45.1	43.7	45.6	43.3	41.5	42.0
75 years and over	68.1	73.9	75.8	74.2	71.3	69.1	28.6	30.2	33.0	34.3	33.3	31.6
75–84 years	70.8	75.9	77.9	76.0	73.3	70.2	30.8	32.0	35.0	36.1	35.5	33.2
85 years and over	56.8	65.5	67.9	67.8	63.9	64.7	18.9	22.8	25.1	27.5	25.3	25.6
Sex[6]												
Male	74.3	77.5	78.9	76.5	73.6	72.0	44.2	43.4	45.1	44.3	42.7	42.9
Female	72.9	76.2	76.5	73.9	71.0	67.8	35.7	35.6	38.1	37.0	35.5	34.9
Race[6,7]												
White	76.8	80.3	81.2	78.6	75.3	72.9	40.9	40.3	42.7	41.6	39.8	39.1
Black	42.3	43.0	44.7	41.9	44.0	43.5	24.0	24.9	26.5	26.4	30.1	32.1
Hispanic origin and race[6,7]												
All Hispanic	40.5	44.6	51.2	40.9	38.6	31.9	25.4	24.3	22.1	20.1	19.4	19.0
Mexican	41.4	36.6	44.6	33.0	35.6	32.4	25.5	22.4	23.1	17.4	18.7	19.0
White, non-Hispanic	77.9	81.5	82.6	80.7	77.2	75.0	41.4	40.9	43.8	42.9	40.8	40.2
Black, non-Hispanic	42.0	43.1	45.2	41.7	44.8	43.7	23.8	24.9	26.8	26.1	30.7	32.1
Percent of poverty level[6,8]												
Below 100 percent	43.0	45.3	40.1	36.8	32.7	31.0	13.4	11.5	10.6	11.3	10.2	7.3
100–149 percent	67.3	66.7	68.0	67.4	58.8	53.2	27.8	22.4	25.2	25.3	22.3	17.2
150–199 percent	78.6	81.1	81.3	77.4	75.0	69.0	41.4	39.8	37.3	39.9	37.3	32.9
200 percent or more	85.7	86.2	88.9	86.6	84.0	81.4	52.8	51.5	54.0	51.7	49.9	49.4
Geographic region[6]												
Northeast	76.8	76.7	78.3	76.0	72.9	73.0	43.9	44.2	45.2	45.3	42.5	43.8
Midwest	79.6	82.3	84.6	82.5	80.8	78.5	40.6	41.4	43.6	46.0	42.3	41.9
South	68.0	73.5	71.2	71.6	67.2	66.3	35.3	33.5	36.8	35.1	34.7	34.2
West	70.8	75.1	78.2	69.3	69.0	59.5	38.2	38.5	40.1	34.9	36.2	34.4
Location of residence[6]												
Within MSA[9]	74.5	77.2	78.0	75.1	72.2	68.4	42.3	41.6	42.6	42.0	40.5	39.8
Outside MSA[9]	71.8	75.1	76.0	74.4	71.3	73.6	33.7	31.3	36.5	33.5	32.2	33.0

See footnotes at end of table.

(continued)

than per-day basis. To implement this, Congress passed the PPS (preadmission payment system) in 1983, which established average costs per case for 467 medical procedures for which Medicare would pay. In addition to Medicare, other third-party payers have made changes to control costs, such as preadmission review and mandatory second opinions. Also, to keep down costs, insurance companies, through managed care, negotiate with hospitals and doctors on how much the insurance companies will pay for services.

Uncompensated Care

Rising costs have forced some people to forego insurance coverage. People who are uninsured frequently rely on hospitals for their primary care and often do not seek care until their illnesses require hospitalization. In many cases, these persons cannot afford to pay their hospital bills, resulting in hospitals delivering care for which they are not compensated (paid). Uncompensated care is a concern for hospitals because revenues must cover ex-

TABLE 5.8 (Continued)

Health care coverage for persons 65 years of age and over, according to type of coverage and selected characteristics: United States, selected years 1984–97

[Data are based on household interviews of a sample of the civilian noninstitutionalized population]

Characteristic	Medicaid[1,10]						Medicare only[11]					
	1984	1989	1994[3]	1995	1996	1997[3,4]	1984	1989	1994[3]	1995	1996	1997[3,4]
	Number in millions											
Total[5]	1.8	2.0	2.5	2.9	2.7	2.5	4.7	4.5	4.1	4.6	5.7	6.7
	Percent of population											
Total, age adjusted[5]	6.9	7.0	7.8	9.0	8.3	7.8	17.7	15.3	13.1	14.7	18.1	20.7
Total, crude[5]	7.0	7.0	7.9	9.2	8.5	7.9	17.9	15.4	13.2	14.8	18.1	20.8
Age												
65–74 years	6.0	6.3	6.8	8.3	7.5	7.5	15.2	13.8	12.3	14.4	18.0	20.3
75 years and over	8.5	8.2	9.6	10.4	9.9	8.4	22.3	17.8	14.5	15.2	18.2	21.5
75–84 years	7.7	7.9	8.4	9.5	9.0	7.9	20.6	16.2	13.3	14.1	16.8	20.5
85 years and over	11.7	9.7	14.2	13.7	13.0	10.2	29.8	24.9	19.1	19.3	23.4	25.2
Sex[6]												
Male	4.5	5.0	4.7	5.6	5.5	5.2	17.4	14.6	12.9	14.4	17.1	19.6
Female	8.6	8.4	10.0	11.5	10.4	9.7	18.1	15.6	13.3	14.9	18.7	21.5
Race[6,7]												
White	5.0	5.4	6.0	6.9	6.6	6.4	16.5	13.4	11.6	13.4	16.9	19.2
Black	24.9	20.4	21.7	26.8	21.8	19.3	30.7	34.5	28.7	28.6	30.1	33.9
Hispanic origin and race[6,7]												
All Hispanic	24.9	25.6	26.5	31.1	28.9	27.6	28.5	21.6	18.7	24.5	29.0	34.9
White, non-Hispanic	4.4	4.7	5.1	5.6	5.4	5.4	16.1	13.1	11.3	12.8	16.3	18.3
Black, non-Hispanic	25.2	20.4	21.2	27.0	21.7	19.0	30.8	34.5	28.8	28.7	29.3	34.0
Percent of poverty level[6,8]												
Below 100 percent	28.0	29.0	37.4	40.6	39.9	41.0	27.5	26.0	23.0	22.1	25.6	26.9
100–149 percent	6.9	9.2	10.8	13.3	12.5	14.6	22.5	21.1	19.0	18.3	26.6	28.6
150–199 percent	3.3	4.7	3.8	5.2	4.6	5.1	16.2	13.5	12.8	16.2	19.6	23.1
200 percent or more	1.8	2.3	1.8	1.8	1.9	2.5	11.0	10.4	7.8	9.9	12.4	15.0
Geographic region[6]												
Northeast	5.3	5.4	7.3	8.9	7.3	6.4	17.1	16.8	14.0	15.4	20.3	19.5
Midwest	4.2	3.6	3.7	5.6	5.1	5.0	15.2	13.4	10.7	10.9	12.8	15.2
South	9.5	9.1	10.3	10.8	9.9	9.7	19.8	16.3	16.0	15.8	19.7	21.3
West	7.9	9.3	9.4	10.8	10.8	9.9	18.4	13.8	10.3	17.3	18.6	28.5
Location of residence[6]												
Within MSA[9]	6.2	6.4	7.3	8.4	7.7	7.4	17.6	15.3	12.9	14.9	18.7	22.2
Outside MSA[9]	8.1	8.4	9.2	11.1	10.4	9.2	17.9	15.2	13.9	14.1	15.9	15.6

[1]Almost all persons 65 years of age and over are covered by Medicare also. In 1997, 92 percent of older persons with private insurance also had Medicare.
[2]Private insurance originally obtained through a present or former employer or union.
[3]The questionnaire changed compared with previous years.
[4]Preliminary data.
[5]Includes all other races not shown separately and unknown poverty level.
[6]Age adjusted.
[7]The race groups white and black include persons of Hispanic and non-Hispanic origin; persons of Hispanic origin may be of any race.
[8]Poverty level is based on family income and family size using Bureau of the Census poverty thresholds.
[9]Metropolitan statistical area.
[10]Includes public assistance through 1996. In 1997 includes state-sponsored health plans. In 1997 the age-adjusted percent of the population 65 years of age and over covered by Medicaid was 7.4 percent, and 0.4 percent were covered by state-sponsored health plans.
[11]Persons covered by Medicare but not covered by private health insurance, Medicaid, public assistance (through 1996), state-sponsored or other government-sponsored health plans (1997), or military plans.

NOTE: Percents do not add to 100 because persons with both private health insurance and Medicaid appear in more than one column, and because the percent of persons without health insurance (1.1 percent in 1997) is not shown.

Source: *Health, United States, 1999*, National Center for Health Statistics, Hyattsville, MD, 1999

penses so that facilities can maintain operations. Hospitals set charges, such as room rates and operating room fees, anticipating that a certain portion of billed amounts will not be paid.

Delivery of Care

The cost-containment efforts of the federal government and insurance companies have

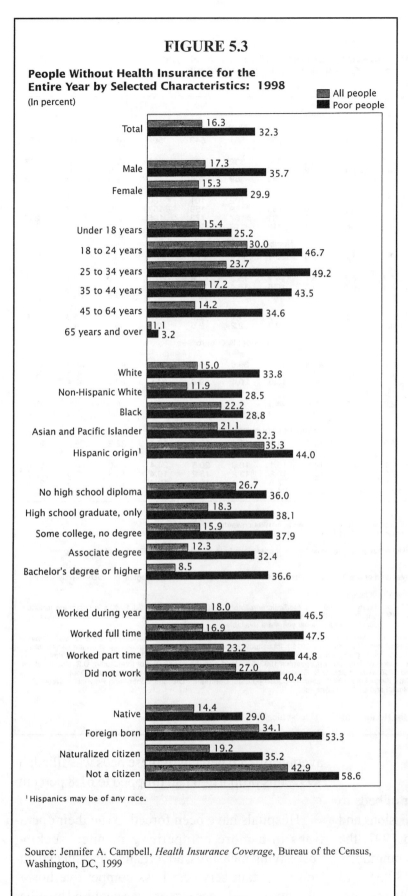

FIGURE 5.3

People Without Health Insurance for the Entire Year by Selected Characteristics: 1998

(In percent)

Legend: All people / Poor people

Characteristic	All people	Poor people
Total	16.3	32.3
Male	17.3	35.7
Female	15.3	29.9
Under 18 years	15.4	25.2
18 to 24 years	30.0	46.7
25 to 34 years	23.7	49.2
35 to 44 years	17.2	43.5
45 to 64 years	14.2	34.6
65 years and over	1.1	3.2
White	15.0	33.8
Non-Hispanic White	11.9	28.5
Black	22.2	28.8
Asian and Pacific Islander	21.1	32.3
Hispanic origin[1]	35.3	44.0
No high school diploma	26.7	36.0
High school graduate, only	18.3	38.1
Some college, no degree	15.9	37.9
Associate degree	12.3	32.4
Bachelor's degree or higher	8.5	36.6
Worked during year	18.0	46.5
Worked full time	16.9	47.5
Worked part time	23.2	44.8
Did not work	27.0	40.4
Native	14.4	29.0
Foreign born	34.1	53.3
Naturalized citizen	19.2	35.2
Not a citizen	42.9	58.6

[1] Hispanics may be of any race.

Source: Jennifer A. Campbell, *Health Insurance Coverage*, Bureau of the Census, Washington, DC, 1999

changed the methods of health care. Preadmission testing in outpatient departments and physicians' offices has replaced early admission to the hospital and reduced the length of hospital stays. The delivery of hospital care has shifted from more costly inpatient care to less costly outpatient care. Medical procedures that were once performed on an inpatient basis are now being done either in a doctor's office or outpatient departments located in hospitals, thus not requiring the individual to spend the night.

In 1980, 16.3 percent of surgeries in community hospitals were done on an outpatient basis; by 1997, this proportion had risen to 60.7 percent. Between 1985 and 1997, the number of inpatient admissions to short-stay community hospitals decreased by 6 percent to 31.6 million. During the same time period, outpatient visits in short-stay community hospitals more than doubled, to 450.1 million.

Technological Advances

Since 1980, technological advances have allowed more patients to be treated on an outpatient basis. Less invasive techniques (often nonsurgical treatments) have made less traumatic treatments possible so that patients are able to return home sooner. For example, extracorporeal shock wave lithotripsy pulverizes kidney stones, eliminating the need for surgery. Magnetic resonance imaging (MRI) machines allow diagnosis without surgery. New anesthetics wear off more quickly, allowing surgery patients to go home the same day. On the other hand, new technology has contributed to higher costs for outpatient care.

TABLE 5.9

Health maintenance organizations (HMO's) and enrollment, according to model type, geographic region, and Federal program: United States, selected years 1976–98

[Data are based on a census of health maintenance organizations]

Plans and enrollment	1976	1980	1985[1]	1990	1992	1993	1994[2]	1995[2]	1996[2]	1997[2]	1998[2]
Plans						Number					
All plans	174	235	478	572	555	551	543	562	630	652	651
Model type:[3]											
Individual practice association[4]	41	97	244	360	340	332	321	332	367	284	317
Group[5]	122	138	234	212	166	150	118	108	122	98	116
Mixed	- - -	- - -	- - -	- - -	49	69	104	122	141	258	212
Geographic region:											
Northeast	29	55	81	115	111	102	101	100	111	110	107
Midwest	52	72	157	160	165	169	159	157	182	184	185
South	23	45	141	176	161	167	173	196	218	236	237
West	70	63	99	121	118	113	110	109	119	121	122
Enrollment						Number of persons in millions					
Total	6.0	9.1	21.0	33.0	36.1	38.4	45.1	50.9	59.1	66.8	76.6
Model type:[3]											
Individual practice association[4]	0.4	1.7	6.4	13.7	14.7	15.3	17.8	20.1	26.0	26.7	32.6
Group[5]	5.6	7.4	14.6	19.3	16.5	15.4	13.9	13.3	14.1	11.0	13.8
Mixed	- - -	- - -	- - -	- - -	4.9	7.7	13.4	17.6	19.0	29.0	30.1
Federal program:[6]											
Medicaid[7]	- - -	0.3	0.6	1.2	1.7	1.7	2.6	3.5	4.7	5.6	7.8
Medicare	- - -	0.4	1.1	1.8	2.2	2.2	2.5	2.9	3.7	4.8	5.7
						Percent of HMO enrollees					
Model type:[3]											
Individual practice association[4]	6.6	18.7	30.4	41.6	40.7	39.8	39.4	39.4	44.1	39.9	42.6
Group[5]	93.4	81.3	69.6	58.4	45.9	40.1	30.7	26.0	23.7	16.5	18.0
Mixed	- - -	- - -	- - -	- - -	13.5	20.1	29.9	34.5	32.2	43.4	39.2
Federal program:[6]											
Medicaid[7]	- - -	2.9	2.7	3.5	4.8	4.4	5.8	6.9	8.0	8.2	10.2
Medicare	- - -	4.3	5.1	5.4	6.0	5.7	5.5	5.7	6.3	7.2	7.4
						Percent of population enrolled in HMO's					
Total	2.8	4.0	8.9	13.4	14.3	15.1	17.3	19.4	22.3	25.2	28.6
Geographic region:											
Northeast	2.0	3.1	7.9	14.6	16.1	18.0	20.8	24.4	25.9	32.4	37.8
Midwest	1.5	2.8	9.7	12.6	12.8	13.2	15.2	16.4	18.8	19.5	22.7
South	0.4	0.8	3.8	7.1	7.8	8.4	10.2	12.4	15.2	17.9	21.0
West	9.7	12.2	17.3	23.2	24.7	25.1	27.4	28.6	33.2	36.4	39.1

- - - Data not available.

[1]Increases partly due to changes in reporting methods.

[2]Open-ended enrollment in HMO plans, amounting to 11.6 million on Jan. 1, 1998, is included from 1994 onwards.

[3]In 1976, 11 HMO's with 35,000 enrollment did not report model type. In 1997, 11 HMO's with 153,000 enrollment did not report model type. In 1998, 6 HMO's with 109,000 enrollment did not report model type.

[4]An HMO operating under an individual practice association model contracts with an association of physicians from various settings (a mixture of solo and group practices) to provide health services.

[5]Group includes staff, group, and network model types.

[6]Federal program enrollment in HMO's refers to enrollment by Medicaid or Medicare beneficiaries, where the Medicaid or Medicare program contracts directly with the HMO to pay the appropriate annual premium.

[7]Data for 1990 and later include enrollment in managed care health insuring organizations.

NOTES: Data as of June 30 in 1976–80, December 31 in 1985, and January 1 in 1990–98. Medicaid enrollment in 1990 is as of June 30. HMO's in Guam are included starting in 1994; HMO's in Puerto Rico, starting in 1998. In 1998 HMO enrollment in Guam was 84,000 and in Puerto Rico, 390,000. Some numbers for 1997 have been revised and differ from the previous edition of *Health, United States*. Data for additional years are available.

Office of Health Maintenance Organizations: Summary of the National HMO census of prepaid plans—June 1976 and National HMO Census 1980. Public Health Service. Washington. U.S. Government Printing Office. DHHS Pub. No. (PHS) 80–50159; InterStudy: National HMO Census: Annual Report on the Growth of HMO's in the U.S., 1984–1985 Editions; The InterStudy Edge, 1990, vol. 2; Competitive Edge, vols. 1–8, 1991–1998; 1986 December Update of Medicare Enrollment in HMO's. 1988 January Update of Medicare Enrollment in HMO's. Excelsior, Minnesota (Copyrights 1983–98: Used with the permission of InterStudy); U.S. Bureau of the Census. Current Population Reports. Series P–25, Nos. 998 and 1058. Washington: U.S. Government Printing Office, Dec. 1986 and Mar. 1990. U.S. Dept. of Commerce. Press release CB 91–100. Mar. 11, 1991; Health Care Financing Administration: Unpublished data; Centers for Disease Control and Prevention, National Center for Health Statistics: Data computed by the Division of Health and Utilization Analysis.

Source: *Health, United States, 1999*, National Center for Health Statistics, Hyattsville, MD, 1999

Other Changes

Hospitals have reduced the number of beds to accommodate the lower number of admissions and shorter lengths of stay. From 1980 to 1997, the number of beds for use in short-stay community hospitals fell 13.7 percent, from 988,387 to 853,287. However, these reductions still have not kept up with reduced inpatient use. In 1980, an average of 75.6 percent of these beds was filled; in 1997, this proportion had dropped to 61.8 percent.

Hospitals have been forced to run their operations in a more competitive manner, seeking cost-saving measures, advertising, and specialization in certain services. Less competitive hospitals have closed, merged, or been acquired by other hospitals. Between 1980 and 1997, the number of

TABLE 5.10

Discharges, days of care, and average length of stay in short-stay hospitals, according to selected characteristics: United States, 1964, 1990, and 1996

[Data are based on household interviews of a sample of the civilian noninstitutionalized population]

Characteristic	Discharges			Days of care			Average length of stay		
	1964	1990	1996	1964	1990	1996	1964	1990	1996
	Number per 1,000 population						Number of days		
Total[1,2]	109.1	91.0	82.4	970.9	607.1	469.9	8.9	6.7	5.7
Age									
Under 15 years	67.6	46.7	37.3	405.7	271.3	212.3	6.0	5.8	5.7
Under 5 years	94.3	79.9	73.6	731.1	496.4	480.7	7.8	6.2	6.5
5–14 years	53.1	29.0	19.0	229.1	150.8	76.6	4.3	5.2	4.0
15–44 years	100.6	62.6	54.6	760.7	340.5	258.3	7.6	5.4	4.7
45–64 years	146.2	135.7	113.7	1,559.3	911.5	621.4	10.7	6.7	5.5
65 years and over	190.0	248.8	268.7	2,292.7	2,092.4	1,818.0	12.1	8.4	6.8
65–74 years.	181.2	215.4	228.8	2,150.4	1,719.3	1,491.6	11.9	8.0	6.5
75 years and over	206.7	300.6	323.7	2,560.4	2,669.9	2,267.6	12.4	8.9	7.0
Sex[1]									
Male.	103.8	91.0	82.5	1,010.2	622.7	487.6	9.7	6.8	5.9
Female.	113.7	91.7	83.1	933.4	592.9	458.0	8.2	6.5	5.5
Race[1]									
White.	112.4	89.5	79.9	961.4	580.9	423.0	8.6	6.5	5.3
Black[3]	84.0	112.0	104.6	1,062.9	875.9	800.3	12.7	7.8	7.7
Family income[1,4]									
Less than $16,000.	102.4	142.2	146.0	1,051.2	1,141.2	960.8	10.3	8.0	6.6
$16,000–$24,999.	116.4	98.4	97.7	1,213.9	594.5	572.2	10.4	6.0	5.9
$25,000–$34,999.	110.7	85.1	76.7	939.8	560.6	429.1	8.5	6.6	5.6
$35,000–$49,999.	109.2	73.2	62.3	882.6	380.3	272.0	8.1	5.2	4.4
$50,000 or more	110.7	72.5	54.2	918.9	446.2	257.7	8.3	6.2	4.8
Geographic region[1]									
Northeast	98.5	84.9	67.0	993.8	623.4	405.2	10.1	7.3	6.0
Midwest	109.2	91.5	91.3	944.9	570.8	524.8	8.7	6.2	5.7
South	117.8	106.4	95.3	968.0	713.6	549.5	8.2	6.7	5.8
West	110.5	70.5	66.2	985.9	444.6	339.5	8.9	6.3	5.1
Location of residence[1]									
Within MSA[5]	107.5	85.9	75.7	1,015.4	599.6	444.2	9.4	7.0	5.9
Outside MSA[5]	113.3	109.5	105.7	871.9	636.0	556.3	7.7	5.8	5.3

[1]Age adjusted.
[2]Includes all other races not shown separately and unknown family income.
[3]1964 data include all other races.
[4]Family income categories for 1996. In 1990 the two lowest income categories are less than $14,000 and $14,000–$24,999; the three higher income categories are as shown. Income categories in 1964 are less than $2,000; $2,000–$3,999; $4,000–$6,999; $7,000–$9,999; and $10,000 or more.
[5]Metropolitan statistical area.

NOTES: Estimates of hospital utilization from the National Health Interview Survey (NHIS) and the National Hospital Discharge Survey (NHDS) may differ because NHIS data are based on household interviews of the civilian noninstitutionalized population and exclude deliveries, whereas NHDS data are based on hospital discharge records of all persons. NHDS includes records for persons discharged alive or deceased and institutionalized persons, and excludes newborn infants. Differences in hospital utilization estimated by the two surveys are particularly evident for the elderly and for women.

Source: *Health, United States, 1999*, National Center for Health Statistics, Hyattsville, MD, 1999

short-stay community hospitals was 5,057, a decline of 15 percent.

Hospital Stays

Because of these changes, the number of admissions, the days of care, and the length of stay in the nation's hospitals have been dropping. The National Center for Health Statistics reported that the number of hospital discharges dropped from 109.1 per 1,000 population in 1964 to 82.4 per 1,000 in 1996, the number of days of care per 1,000 population declined from 970.9 to 469.9 days, and the average stay decreased from 8.9 days to 5.7 days. Blacks and the poor were more likely to be admitted to a hospital and more likely to stay longer. (See Table 5.10.)

VISITING THE DOCTOR

Americans generally visit the doctor quite regularly. The periodic *National Health Interview Sur-*

TABLE 5.11

Interval since last physician contact, according to selected patient characteristics: United States, 1964, 1990, and 1996

[Data are based on household interviews of a sample of the civilian noninstitutionalized population]

Characteristic	Total	Less than 1 year			1 year–less than 2 years			2 years or more[1]		
		1964	1990	1996	1964	1990	1996	1964	1990	1996
					Percent distribution[2]					
Total[3,4]	100.0	66.9	78.2	80.1	14.0	10.1	9.5	19.1	11.7	10.4
Age										
Under 15 years	100.0	68.4	82.9	85.6	14.8	10.7	9.4	16.7	6.4	5.0
Under 5 years	100.0	80.7	93.6	94.9	11.1	5.0	4.2	8.2	1.4	0.9
5–14 years	100.0	61.7	77.2	81.0	16.9	13.7	12.0	21.4	9.1	7.0
15–44 years	100.0	66.3	73.3	74.2	15.0	11.6	11.6	18.7	15.0	14.2
45–64 years	100.0	64.5	77.3	79.3	13.0	8.6	8.3	22.5	14.1	12.4
65 years and over	100.0	69.7	87.1	90.1	9.3	4.7	4.0	21.0	8.2	5.9
65–74 years.	100.0	68.8	85.7	88.3	9.4	5.1	4.5	21.8	9.1	7.1
75 years and over	100.0	71.3	89.3	92.4	9.3	4.1	3.3	19.5	6.6	4.3
Sex and age										
Male[3]	100.0	63.5	73.3	74.9	15.0	11.3	10.8	21.5	15.4	14.3
Under 15 years	100.0	- - -	82.8	85.7	- - -	10.7	9.4	- - -	6.5	4.9
15–44 years.	100.0	- - -	64.2	64.9	- - -	13.8	13.8	- - -	22.0	21.3
45–64 years.	100.0	- - -	72.4	72.7	- - -	9.8	10.1	- - -	17.8	17.2
65–74 years.	100.0	- - -	84.2	87.7	- - -	5.8	4.8	- - -	10.0	7.6
75 years and over	100.0	- - -	86.9	91.8	- - -	4.7	3.5	- - -	8.4	4.7
Female[3]	100.0	69.9	82.9	85.1	13.1	9.0	8.3	17.0	8.1	6.7
Under 15 years	100.0	- - -	83.0	85.5	- - -	10.7	9.4	- - -	6.4	5.1
15–44 years.	100.0	- - -	82.1	83.3	- - -	9.5	9.4	- - -	8.3	7.4
45–64 years.	100.0	- - -	81.9	85.5	- - -	7.6	6.6	- - -	10.6	7.9
65–74 years.	100.0	- - -	86.9	88.9	- - -	4.6	4.4	- - -	8.4	6.8
75 years and over	100.0	- - -	90.7	92.8	- - -	3.7	3.2	- - -	5.6	4.0
Race and age										
White[3]	100.0	68.1	78.7	80.3	13.8	9.9	9.3	18.1	11.5	10.4
Under 15 years	100.0	- - -	83.6	86.0	- - -	10.3	9.0	- - -	6.1	5.0
15–44 years.	100.0	- - -	73.9	74.5	- - -	11.4	11.3	- - -	14.8	14.1
45–64 years.	100.0	- - -	77.3	79.1	- - -	8.7	8.2	- - -	14.1	12.6
65–74 years.	100.0	- - -	86.0	88.1	- - -	5.0	4.6	- - -	9.0	7.3
75 years and over	100.0	- - -	89.3	92.7	- - -	4.2	3.1	- - -	6.5	4.1
Black[3,5]	100.0	58.3	77.5	81.3	15.1	11.0	9.8	26.6	11.6	8.8
Under 15 years	100.0	- - -	79.9	84.9	- - -	12.6	10.8	- - -	7.5	4.3
15–44 years.	100.0	- - -	72.3	75.9	- - -	12.7	11.6	- - -	15.0	12.5
45–64 years.	100.0	- - -	80.2	82.9	- - -	8.0	7.7	- - -	11.8	9.3
65–74 years.	100.0	- - -	84.4	90.2	- - -	5.9	*3.9	- - -	9.7	5.9
75 years and over	100.0	- - -	89.4	89.6	- - -	*3.4	*4.2	- - -	7.3	*6.2
Family income[3,6]										
Less than $16,000.	100.0	58.6	77.3	77.6	13.2	9.8	10.1	28.2	12.9	12.2
$16,000–$24,999.	100.0	62.5	76.7	75.4	14.2	10.2	10.9	23.3	13.2	13.7
$25,000–$34,999.	100.0	66.8	78.7	78.9	14.5	10.0	9.9	18.7	11.4	11.2
$35,000–$49,999.	100.0	70.2	80.1	81.0	14.0	9.4	9.3	15.7	10.4	9.7
$50,000 or more	100.0	73.6	81.7	84.3	12.9	8.9	8.2	13.5	9.4	7.5
Geographic region[3]										
Northeast	100.0	68.0	81.6	83.7	14.1	9.1	8.0	17.9	9.3	8.4
Midwest	100.0	66.6	79.5	80.1	14.2	9.6	9.9	19.2	10.9	10.0
South	100.0	65.2	76.0	79.2	13.9	11.3	10.1	20.9	12.7	10.7
West	100.0	69.0	77.5	78.2	13.7	9.4	9.5	17.3	13.1	12.3
Location of residence[3]										
Within MSA[7]	100.0	68.2	79.0	80.4	14.0	9.7	9.4	17.8	11.3	10.2
Outside MSA[7]	100.0	64.0	75.7	78.8	14.1	11.4	10.1	21.9	12.9	11.1

- - - Data not available.
* Relative standard error greater than 30 percent.
[1]Includes persons who never visited a physician.
[2]Denominator excludes persons with unknown interval.
[3]Age adjusted.
[4]Includes all other races not shown separately and unknown family income.
[5]1964 data include all other races.
[6]Family income categories for 1996. In 1990 the two lowest income categories are less than $14,000 and $14,000–$24,999; the three higher income categories are as shown. Income categories in 1964 are less than $2,000; $2,000–$3,999; $4,000–$6,999; $7,000–$9,999; and $10,000 or more.
[7]Metropolitan statistical area.

Source: *Health, United States, 1999*, National Center for Health Statistics, Hyattsville, MD, 1999

TABLE 5.12

Persons with a dental visit within the past year among persons 25 years of age and over, according to selected patient characteristics: United States, selected years 1983–93

[Data are based on household interviews of a sample of the civilian noninstitutionalized population]

Characteristic	1983[1]	1989[1]	1990	1991	1993
	\multicolumn{5}{Percent of persons with a visit within the past year}				
Total[2,3]	53.9	58.9	62.3	58.2	60.8
Age					
25–34 years	59.0	60.9	65.1	59.1	60.3
35–44 years	60.3	65.9	69.1	64.8	66.9
45–64 years	54.1	59.9	62.8	59.2	62.0
65 years and over	39.3	45.8	49.6	47.2	51.7
65–74 years	43.8	50.0	53.5	51.1	56.3
75 years and over	31.8	39.0	43.4	41.3	44.9
Sex[3]					
Male	51.7	56.2	58.8	55.5	58.2
Female	55.9	61.4	65.6	60.8	63.4
Poverty status[3,4]					
Below poverty	30.4	33.3	38.2	33.0	35.9
At or above poverty	55.8	62.1	65.4	61.9	64.3
Race and Hispanic origin[3]					
White, non-Hispanic	56.6	61.8	64.9	61.5	64.0
Black, non-Hispanic	39.1	43.3	49.1	44.3	47.3
Hispanic[5]	42.1	48.9	53.8	43.1	46.2
Education[3]					
Less than 12 years	35.1	36.9	41.2	35.2	38.0
12 years	54.8	58.2	61.3	56.7	58.7
13 years or more	70.9	73.9	75.7	72.2	73.8
Education, race, and Hispanic origin[3]					
Less than 12 years:					
White, non-Hispanic	36.1	39.1	41.8	38.1	41.2
Black, non-Hispanic	31.7	32.0	37.9	33.0	33.1
Hispanic[5]	33.8	36.5	42.7	28.9	33.0
12 years:					
White, non-Hispanic	56.6	59.8	62.8	58.8	60.4
Black, non-Hispanic	40.5	44.8	51.1	43.1	48.2
Hispanic[5]	48.7	56.5	59.9	49.5	54.6
13 years or more:					
White, non-Hispanic	72.6	75.8	77.3	74.2	75.8
Black, non-Hispanic	54.4	57.2	64.4	61.7	61.3
Hispanic[5]	58.4	66.2	67.9	61.2	61.8

[1]Data for 1983 and 1989 are not strictly comparable with data for later years. Data for 1983 and 1989 are based on responses to the question "About how long has it been since you last went to a dentist?" Starting in 1990 data are based on the question "During the past 12 months, how many visits did you make to a dentist?"
[2]Includes all other races not shown separately and unknown poverty status and education level.
[3]Age adjusted.
[4]Poverty status is based on family income and family size using Bureau of the Census poverty thresholds.
[5]Persons of Hispanic origin may be of any race.

NOTES: Denominators exclude persons with unknown dental data. Estimates for 1983 and 1989 are based on data for all members of the sample household. Beginning in 1990 estimates are based on one adult member per sample household. Estimates for 1993 are based on responses during the last half of the year only.

Source: *Health, United States, 1999*, National Center for Health Statistics, Hyattsville, MD, 1999

---

vey, prepared by the National Center for Health Statistics, reported that about 4 of every 5 Americans (80.1 percent) had seen their physicians within the last year. Children under five years old, people over 65 years old, and women tended to see their doctors somewhat more often than the general population. (See Table 5.11.) The average person contacted his or her doctor six times a year, usually by visiting the physician's office. Blacks and poorer citizens were more likely than the rest of the population to see a doctor in a hospital outpatient department.

VISITING THE DENTIST

In 1993, the last year the *National Health Interview Survey* asked a question about visits to the dentist, three-fifths (60.8 percent) of the population visited the dentist at least once. Females, those above the poverty level, non-Hispanic Whites, and

TABLE 5.13

Respondent-assessed health status, according to selected characteristics: United States, 1991–96

[Data are based on household interviews of a sample of the civilian noninstitutionalized population]

	Percent with fair or poor health								
	Both sexes			Male			Female		
Characteristic	1991	1995	1996	1991	1995	1996	1991	1995	1996
Total[1,2]	9.2	9.3	9.2	8.9	8.9	8.7	9.6	9.8	9.7
Age									
Under 18 years................	2.6	2.6	2.6	2.7	2.7	2.5	2.6	2.4	2.7
Under 6 years	2.7	2.7	2.6	2.9	3.1	2.6	2.4	2.2	2.5
6–17 years	2.6	2.5	2.6	2.5	2.4	2.4	2.6	2.6	2.8
18–44 years..................	6.1	6.6	6.7	5.2	5.5	5.6	6.9	7.7	7.7
45–54 years..................	13.4	13.4	13.1	12.5	12.5	12.3	14.2	14.3	13.9
55–64 years..................	20.7	21.4	21.2	20.7	20.6	21.4	20.8	22.2	21.1
65 years and over.............	29.0	28.3	27.0	29.2	28.8	26.6	28.9	28.0	27.4
65–74 years.................	26.0	25.6	23.8	26.7	26.3	23.2	25.5	25.0	24.4
75–84 years.................	32.6	31.4	30.2	33.2	31.7	31.3	32.3	31.2	29.4
85 years and over	37.3	35.3	36.2	36.5	38.5	34.9	37.6	33.8	36.8
Race[1,3]									
White.......................	8.5	8.6	8.4	8.3	8.3	8.0	8.7	8.8	8.7
Black.......................	15.0	15.3	15.0	14.0	13.7	13.7	15.9	16.6	16.0
American Indian or Alaska Native	16.8	15.9	18.9	16.1	16.1	19.2	17.0	16.0	17.8
Asian or Pacific Islander.................	6.7	8.2	8.3	5.9	7.0	6.5	7.3	9.2	10.0
Race and Hispanic origin[1]									
White, non-Hispanic.................	8.0	8.0	7.9	7.9	7.8	7.6	8.1	8.1	8.1
Black, non-Hispanic.................	15.0	15.4	14.9	14.1	13.8	13.7	15.9	16.6	15.9
Hispanic[3]	13.7	13.6	12.9	12.3	12.3	11.8	14.9	14.8	14.1
Mexican[3]	14.9	14.9	13.7	13.0	13.9	11.9	16.8	16.0	15.4
Poverty status[1,4]									
Poor........................	21.8	22.5	22.2	22.4	22.1	21.6	21.5	23.0	22.8
Near poor....................	13.5	14.2	14.1	13.5	14.9	14.4	13.5	13.8	14.0
Nonpoor.....................	5.5	5.6	5.5	5.4	5.3	5.3	5.7	5.8	5.6
Race and Hispanic origin and poverty status[1,4]									
White, non-Hispanic:									
Poor.....................	21.1	21.4	21.6	22.7	21.6	22.5	20.2	21.5	21.1
Near poor.................	12.9	13.6	13.8	13.5	15.0	14.7	12.5	12.5	13.2
Nonpoor..................	5.2	5.2	5.1	5.2	5.1	5.0	5.3	5.3	5.1
Black, non-Hispanic:									
Poor.....................	24.9	26.7	26.9	25.2	26.2	26.0	24.8	27.1	27.8
Near poor.................	15.5	17.2	16.6	14.6	15.9	15.2	16.3	18.1	17.6
Nonpoor..................	8.5	8.1	8.5	7.6	7.3	7.6	9.5	8.9	9.3
Hispanic:[3]									
Poor.....................	21.1	21.2	19.9	20.2	20.1	17.7	21.7	22.3	21.8
Near poor.................	15.8	15.5	14.7	14.3	14.1	14.3	17.4	16.9	15.5
Nonpoor..................	7.9	7.0	7.7	7.1	6.4	7.6	8.7	7.6	7.5
Geographic region[1]									
Northeast....................	7.4	8.0	8.2	7.2	7.7	7.7	7.6	8.3	8.7
Midwest.....................	8.0	8.5	8.1	7.7	8.3	7.7	8.3	8.7	8.6
South.......................	11.6	10.9	10.7	11.3	10.3	10.1	11.9	11.4	11.3
West	8.6	8.9	8.7	8.1	8.2	8.4	9.1	9.6	9.2
Location of residence[1]									
Within MSA[5]	8.8	8.9	8.4	8.3	8.4	7.8	9.3	9.4	9.0
Outside MSA[5]	10.6	11.1	11.8	10.9	10.8	11.5	10.4	11.4	12.1

[1]Age adjusted.
[2]Includes all other races not shown separately and unknown family income.
[3]The race groups, white, black, American Indian or Alaska Native, and Asian or Pacific Islander, include persons of Hispanic and non-Hispanic origin; persons of Hispanic origin may be of any race.
[4]Poverty status is based on family income and family size using Bureau of the Census poverty thresholds. Poor persons are defined as below the poverty threshold. Near poor persons have incomes of 100 percent to less than 200 percent of poverty threshold. Nonpoor persons have incomes of 200 percent or greater than the poverty threshold.
[5]Metropolitan statistical area.

Source: *Health, United States, 1999*, National Center for Health Statistics, Hyattsville, MD, 1999

the more educated were more likely to visit the dentist. (See Table 5.12.)

HOW DO AMERICANS FEEL?

Generally, according to the *National Health Interview Survey*, Americans feel pretty good. In

TABLE 5.14

Leading causes of death and numbers of deaths: United States, 1980 and 1997

[Data are based on the National Vital Statistics System]

Sex, race, Hispanic origin, and rank order	1980		1997	
	Cause of death	Deaths	Cause of death	Deaths
All persons				
...	All causes	1,989,841	All causes	2,314,245
1............	Diseases of heart	761,085	Diseases of heart	726,974
2............	Malignant neoplasms	416,509	Malignant neoplasms	539,577
3............	Cerebrovascular diseases	170,225	Cerebrovascular diseases	159,791
4............	Unintentional injuries	105,718	Chronic obstructive pulmonary diseases	109,029
5............	Chronic obstructive pulmonary diseases	56,050	Unintentional injuries	95,644
6............	Pneumonia and influenza	54,619	Pneumonia and influenza	86,449
7............	Diabetes mellitus	34,851	Diabetes mellitus	62,636
8............	Chronic liver disease and cirrhosis	30,583	Suicide	30,535
9............	Atherosclerosis	29,449	Nephritis, nephrotic syndrome, and nephrosis	25,331
10............	Suicide	26,869	Chronic liver disease and cirrhosis	25,175

Source: *Health, United States, 1999*, National Center for Health Statistics, Hyattsville, MD, 1999

1996, only about 9.2 percent responded that they felt in only fair or poor health. The older the person, the more likely he or she was to admit to not feeling very well. Blacks, American Indians or Alaska Natives, and poorer Americans were far more likely than the general population to feel their health was not up to par. (See Table 5.13.)

AIDS

Through December 31, 1998, the Centers for Disease Control and Prevention (Atlanta, Georgia) reported a cumulative total of 688,200 persons with AIDS. Of these, 83 percent were adult/adolescent men, 16 percent were adult/adolescent women, and 1 percent were children (under 13 years of age). Of the adults/adolescents reported during the 12 months (July 1998 to June 1999), 33 percent were White, 46 percent were Black, and 20 percent were Hispanic. Men who had sex with men accounted for the largest proportion of reported cases (34 percent) during the year. Injecting drugs accounted for another 23 percent of the cases.

Among the 322 children reported with AIDS in the 12-month period, 11 percent were White, 63 percent were Black, and 25 percent were Hispanic. Over 90 percent of these children were infected perinatally (in the womb or at the time of birth). In addition, 30 states that maintain records on cases of HIV infection (not AIDS) reported 104,784 persons who were diagnosed with HIV (excluding persons tested anonymously) but not yet diagnosed with AIDS.

In 1996, for the first time, the estimated deaths among persons with AIDS declined to 37,359 from 49,897 in 1995. In 1998, AIDS deaths further declined to 17,171. The cumulative number of persons estimated to have been diagnosed with AIDS and who are still living continued to increase from 217,504 estimated cases in 1995 to 297,135 cases in 1998. The introduction of new drugs is keeping many AIDS patients alive for longer periods. (For a complete discussion, see *AIDS*, Information Plus, Wylie, Texas, 1998.)

CAUSES OF DEATH

Heart disease continued to be the leading cause of death, followed by malignant neoplasms (cancer). (See Table 5.14.) In 1996, AIDS was the eighth leading cause of death, but AIDS deaths declined 48 percent from 1996 to 1997. By 1999, AIDS was no longer one of the top fifteen causes of death.

CHAPTER VI

EDUCATION*

Despite the continuing debate over the quality and direction of American education, the United States is one of the most highly educated nations in the world. In fall 1998, approximately 75.4 million Americans were involved, directly or indirectly, in providing or receiving formal education. About 67.3 million people were enrolled in American schools and colleges, and 3.8 million instructors were teaching at the elementary, secondary, and college levels. Other professional, administrative, and support staff at educational institutions numbered 4.2 million. In a nation with a population of about 270.3 million, 1 out of every 4 persons participated in the educational process. (See Table 6.1.)

AN INCREASINGLY EDUCATED POPULATION

Over the past two and one-half generations, the median number of school years completed has risen from 8.4 years in 1930 to 13.0 years. As late as 1930, fewer than 1 in 5 Americans had completed at least four years of high school. Since that time, the proportion has steadily increased, reaching 82.1 percent of those 25 and older in 1997. Among young people 25 to 29 years of age, 87.4 percent completed at least four years of high school. (See Table 6.2 and Figures 6.1 and 6.2.)

*For a complete discussion of education, See *Education — Reflecting Our Society?*, Information Plus, Wylie, Texas, 2000.

TABLE 6.1

Estimated number of participants in elementary and secondary education and in higher education: Fall 1998

[In millions]

Participants	All levels (elementary, secondary, and higher education)	Elementary and secondary schools			Institutions of higher education		
		Total	Public	Private	Total	Public	Private
1	2	3	4	5	6	7	8
Total	**75.4**	**58.6**	**52.0**	**6.6**	**16.8**	**12.9**	**3.9**
Enrollment [1]	67.3	52.7	46.8	5.9	14.6	11.4	3.2
Teachers and faculty	3.8	3.1	2.7	0.4	0.7	0.5	0.2
Other professional, administrative, and support staff	4.2	2.8	2.5	0.2	1.5	1.0	0.5

[1] Includes enrollments in local public school systems and in most private schools (religiously affiliated and nonsectarian). Excludes subcollegiate departments of institutions of higher education, residential schools for exceptional children, and federal schools. Elementary and secondary includes most kindergarten and some nursery school enrollment. Excludes preprimary enrollment in schools that do not offer first grade or above. Higher education comprises full-time and part-time students enrolled in degree-credit and non-degree-credit programs in universities, other 4-year colleges, and 2-year colleges.

NOTE.—The enrollment figures include all students in elementary and secondary schools and colleges and universities. However, the data for teachers and other staff in public and private elementary and secondary schools and colleges and universities are reported in terms of full-time equivalents. Because of rounding, details may not add to totals.

SOURCE: U.S. Department of Education, National Center for Education Statistics, unpublished projections and estimates. (This table was prepared July 1998.)

Source: *Digest of Education Statistics 1998*, National Center for Education Statistics, Washington, DC, 1999

TABLE 6.2

Years of school completed by persons age 25 and over and 25 to 29, by race/ethnicity and sex: 1910 to 1997

Age, year, and sex	Percent, by years of school completed											
	All races			White, non-Hispanic[1]			Black, non-Hispanic[1]			Hispanic		
	Less than 5 years of elementary school	High school completion or higher[2]	4 or more years of college[3]	Less than 5 years of elementary school	High school completion or higher[2]	4 or more years of college[3]	Less than 5 years of elementary school	High school completion or higher[2]	4 or more years of college[3]	Less than 5 years of elementary school	High school completion or higher[2]	4 or more years of college[3]
1	2	3	4	5	6	7	8	9	10	11	12	13

Males and females

25 and over

Age, year, and sex	2	3	4	5	6	7	8	9	10	11	12	13
1910[4]	23.8	13.5	2.7	—	—	—	—	—	—	—	—	—
1920[4]	22.0	16.4	3.3	—	—	—	—	—	—	—	—	—
1930[4]	17.5	19.1	3.9	—	—	—	—	—	—	—	—	—
April 1940	13.7	24.5	4.6	10.9	26.1	4.9	41.8	7.7	1.3	—	—	—
April 1950	11.1	34.3	6.2	8.9	36.4	6.6	32.6	13.7	2.2	—	—	—
April 1960	8.3	41.1	7.7	6.7	43.2	8.1	23.5	21.7	3.5	—	—	—
March 1970	5.3	55.2	11.0	4.2	57.4	11.6	14.7	36.1	6.1	—	—	—
March 1980	3.4	68.6	17.0	1.9	71.9	18.4	9.1	51.4	7.9	15.8	44.5	7.6
March 1985	2.7	73.9	19.4	1.4	77.5	20.8	6.1	59.9	11.1	13.5	47.9	8.5
March 1986	2.7	74.7	19.4	1.4	78.2	20.1	5.3	62.5	10.9	12.9	48.5	8.4
March 1987	2.4	75.6	19.9	1.3	79.0	20.5	4.9	63.6	10.8	11.9	50.9	8.6
March 1988	2.5	76.2	20.3	1.2	79.8	21.8	4.8	63.5	11.2	12.2	51.0	10.0
March 1989	2.5	76.9	21.1	1.2	80.7	22.8	5.2	64.7	11.7	12.2	50.9	9.9
March 1990	2.5	77.6	21.3	1.1	81.4	23.1	5.1	66.2	11.3	12.3	50.8	9.2
March 1991	2.4	78.4	21.4	1.1	82.4	23.3	4.7	66.8	11.5	12.5	51.3	9.7
March 1992	2.1	79.4	21.4	0.9	83.4	23.2	3.9	67.7	11.9	11.8	52.6	9.3
March 1993	2.1	80.2	21.9	0.8	84.1	23.8	3.7	70.5	12.2	11.8	53.1	9.0
March 1994	1.9	80.9	22.2	0.8	84.9	24.3	2.7	73.0	12.9	10.8	53.3	9.1
March 1995	1.9	81.7	23.0	0.7	85.9	23.4	2.5	73.8	13.3	10.6	53.4	9.3
March 1996	1.8	81.7	23.6	0.6	86.0	25.9	2.2	74.6	13.8	10.4	53.1	9.3
March 1997	1.7	82.1	23.9	0.6	86.3	26.2	2.0	75.3	13.3	9.4	54.7	10.3

25 to 29

Age, year, and sex	2	3	4	5	6	7	8	9	10	11	12	13
1920[4]	—	—	—	12.9	22.0	4.5	44.6	6.3	1.2	—	—	—
April 1940	5.9	38.1	5.9	3.4	41.2	6.4	27.0	12.3	1.6	—	—	—
April 1950	4.6	52.8	7.7	3.3	56.3	8.2	16.1	23.6	2.8	—	—	—
April 1960	2.8	60.7	11.0	2.2	63.7	11.8	7.2	38.6	5.4	—	—	—
March 1970	1.1	75.4	16.4	0.9	77.8	17.3	2.2	58.4	10.0	—	—	—
March 1980	0.8	85.4	22.5	0.3	89.2	25.0	0.7	76.7	11.6	6.7	58.0	7.7
March 1985	0.7	86.1	22.2	0.2	89.5	24.4	0.4	80.5	11.6	6.0	60.9	11.1
March 1986	0.9	86.1	22.4	0.4	89.6	25.2	0.5	83.5	11.8	5.6	59.1	9.0
March 1987	0.9	86.0	22.0	0.4	89.4	24.7	0.4	83.5	11.5	4.8	59.8	8.7
March 1988	1.0	85.9	22.7	0.3	89.7	25.1	0.3	80.9	12.0	6.0	62.3	11.3
March 1989	1.0	85.5	23.4	0.3	89.3	26.3	0.5	82.3	12.7	5.4	61.0	10.1
March 1990	1.2	85.7	23.2	0.3	90.1	26.4	1.0	81.7	13.4	7.3	58.2	8.2
March 1991	1.0	85.4	23.2	0.3	89.8	26.7	0.5	81.8	11.0	5.8	56.7	9.2
March 1992	0.9	86.3	23.6	0.3	90.7	27.2	0.8	80.9	11.1	5.2	60.9	9.5
March 1993	0.7	86.7	23.7	0.3	91.2	27.2	0.2	82.7	13.3	4.0	60.9	8.3
March 1994	0.8	86.1	23.3	0.3	91.1	27.1	0.6	84.1	13.6	3.6	60.3	8.0
March 1995	1.0	86.9	24.7	0.3	92.5	28.8	0.2	86.7	15.4	4.9	57.2	8.9
March 1996	0.8	87.3	27.1	0.2	92.6	31.6	0.4	86.0	14.6	4.3	61.1	10.0
March 1997	0.8	87.4	27.8	0.1	92.9	32.6	0.6	86.9	14.2	4.2	61.8	11.0

Males

25 and over

Age, year, and sex	2	3	4	5	6	7	8	9	10	11	12	13
April 1940	15.1	22.7	5.5	12.0	24.2	5.9	46.2	6.9	1.4	—	—	—
April 1950	12.2	32.6	7.3	9.8	34.6	7.9	36.9	12.6	2.1	—	—	—
April 1960	9.4	39.5	9.7	7.4	41.6	10.3	27.7	20.0	3.5	—	—	—
March 1970	5.9	55.0	14.1	4.5	57.2	15.0	17.9	35.4	6.8	—	—	—
March 1980	3.6	69.2	20.9	2.0	72.4	22.8	11.3	51.2	7.7	16.5	44.9	9.2
March 1990	2.7	77.7	24.4	1.3	81.6	26.7	6.4	65.8	11.9	12.9	50.3	9.8
March 1994	2.1	81.1	25.1	0.8	85.1	27.8	3.9	71.8	12.7	11.4	53.4	9.6
March 1995	2.0	81.7	26.0	0.8	86.0	28.9	3.4	73.5	13.7	10.8	52.9	10.1
March 1996	1.9	81.9	26.0	0.7	86.1	28.8	2.9	74.6	12.5	10.2	53.0	10.3
March 1997	1.8	82.0	26.2	0.6	86.3	29.0	2.9	73.8	12.5	9.2	54.9	10.6

Females

25 and over

Age, year, and sex	2	3	4	5	6	7	8	9	10	11	12	13
April 1940	12.4	26.3	3.8	9.8	28.1	4.0	37.5	8.4	1.2	—	—	—
April 1950	10.0	36.0	5.2	8.1	38.2	5.4	28.6	14.7	2.4	—	—	—
April 1960	7.4	42.5	5.8	6.0	44.7	6.0	19.7	23.1	3.6	—	—	—
March 1970	4.7	55.4	8.2	3.9	57.7	8.6	11.9	36.6	5.6	—	—	—
March 1980	3.2	68.1	13.6	1.8	71.5	14.4	7.4	51.5	8.1	15.3	44.2	6.2
March 1990	2.2	77.5	18.4	1.0	81.3	19.8	4.1	66.5	10.8	11.7	51.3	8.7
March 1994	1.7	80.8	19.6	0.7	84.7	21.1	1.8	73.9	13.1	10.3	53.2	8.6
March 1995	1.7	81.6	20.2	0.6	85.8	22.2	1.8	74.1	13.0	10.4	53.8	8.4
March 1996	1.7	81.6	21.4	0.5	85.9	23.2	1.6	74.6	14.8	10.6	53.3	8.3
March 1997	1.6	82.2	21.7	0.5	86.3	23.7	1.3	76.5	14.0	9.5	54.6	10.1

[1] Includes persons of Hispanic origin for years prior to 1980.
[2] Data for years prior to 1993 include all persons with at least 4 years of high school.
[3] Data for 1993 and later years are for persons with a bachelor's degree or higher.
[4] Estimates based on Bureau of the Census retrojection of 1940 Census data on education by age.
—Data not available.

NOTE.—Data for 1980 and subsequent years are for the noninstitutional population.

SOURCE: U.S. Department of Commerce, Bureau of the Census, *U.S. Census of Population, 1960*, Vol. 1, part 1; *Current Population Reports*, Series P-20 and unpublished data; and *1960 Census Monograph*, "Education of the American Population," by John K. Folger and Charles B. Nam. (This table was prepared July 1998.)

Source: *Digest of Education Statistics 1998*, National Center for Education Statistics, Washington, DC, 1999

In 1930, barely 4 percent of the population had completed four or more years of college. By 1997, nearly 24 percent had done so. Among those 25 to 29 years old, 27.8 percent had graduated college. (See Table 6.2 and Figures 6.1 and 6.2.) Whites were more likely to have completed high school and college than were Blacks and other minorities, but over the decades the percentage difference has narrowed dramatically. (See Table 6.2.) Figure 6.3 shows the highest levels of education earned. Less than half the students continued their education beyond high school, while 17.9 percent had never earned a high school diploma.

MOST CHILDREN STILL IN SCHOOL

In October 1997, more than half (55.6 percent) of all Americans between the ages of 3 and 34 years were enrolled in school. Because of compulsory attendance requirements, close to 100 percent of all young people ages 5 to 16 years were enrolled in school. This proportion dropped sharply to 61.5 percent among 18- and 19-year-olds, as many people graduated or left high school and did not go on to college. The proportion of children enrolled in school at ages 3 and 4 rose from 10.6 percent in 1965 to around 44.4 percent in 1990, dropping to 39.7 percent in 1992, and then rising to 52.6 percent in 1997 (see below). The percent-

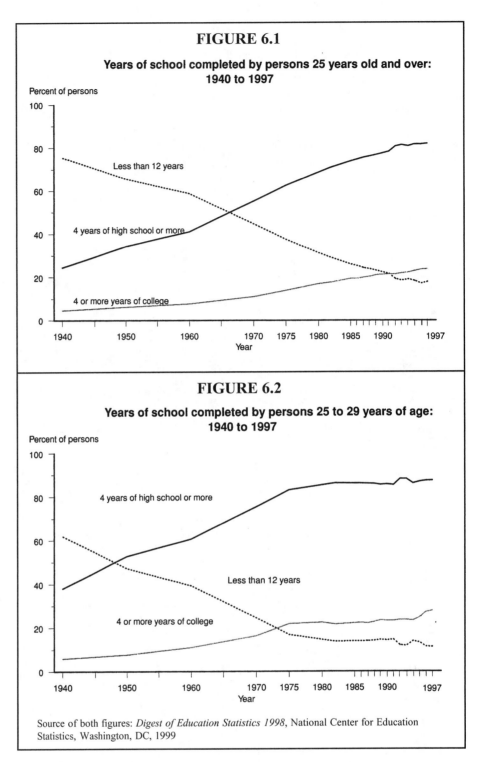

FIGURE 6.1

Years of school completed by persons 25 years old and over: 1940 to 1997

FIGURE 6.2

Years of school completed by persons 25 to 29 years of age: 1940 to 1997

Source of both figures: *Digest of Education Statistics 1998*, National Center for Education Statistics, Washington, DC, 1999

age of 5- and 6-year-olds attending school rose from 84.9 to 96.5 percent over the same period.

According to the 1997 *Current Population Survey*, conducted by the U.S. Census Bureau, about 4.3 percent of all students in the tenth, eleventh, and twelfth grades dropped out of high school during the 1996-97 school year. Students of Hispanic origin had the highest dropout rate (8.6 percent). Students from lower-income families were more likely to drop out of high school than those from families with higher incomes. The drop-out risk was higher for twelfth graders than the lower two grades. (See Table 6.3.)

SCHOOL ENROLLMENT

Elementary and secondary school enrollment grew rapidly during the 1950s and 1960s, peaking in 1975. This enrollment rise was caused by the baby boom, the dramatic increase in births following World War II. From 1971 to 1984, total elementary and secondary school enrollment decreased steadily, reflecting the drop in the school-age population over that period. In the fall of 1985, enrollment in elementary and secondary schools began to increase once again as the children of the baby boomers became school age. (See Figure 6.4.) Public school enrollment in kindergarten through grade eight rose from 28.5 million in fall 1988 to an estimated 33.5 million in fall 1998. Enrollment in the upper grades declined from 11.7 million in 1988 to 11.3 million in 1990, but has since increased to 13.3 million in 1998.

The increase from 1988 to 1998 was concentrated in the elementary grades, but this pattern is expected to change. The growing numbers of young students that have been filling the elementary schools mean significant increases at the secondary school level during the next decade. While public elementary school enrollment is expected to stay fairly stable, public secondary school en-

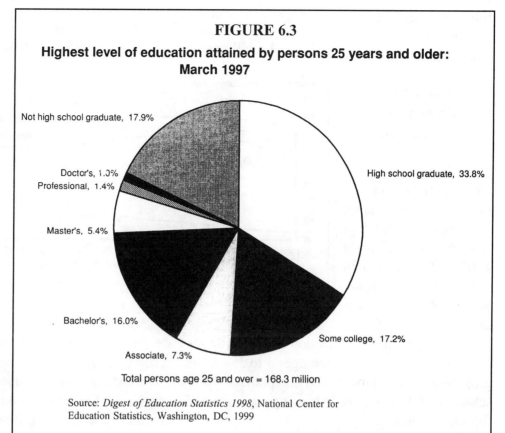

FIGURE 6.3

Highest level of education attained by persons 25 years and older: March 1997

Not high school graduate, 17.9%

Doctor's, 1.3%
Professional, 1.4%

Master's, 5.4%

High school graduate, 33.8%

Bachelor's, 16.0%

Some college, 17.2%

Associate, 7.3%

Total persons age 25 and over = 168.3 million

Source: *Digest of Education Statistics 1998*, National Center for Education Statistics, Washington, DC, 1999

TABLE 6.3
Annual High School Dropout Rates, by Gender, Race, Hispanic Origin, Family Income, and Grade Level: October 1997

	Dropout Rate
Total	**4.3**
Male	4.7
Female	3.8
White	4.2
Black	4.8
Asian and Pacific Islanders	2.6
Hispanic Origin	8.6
Family Income	
less than $20,000	8.2
$20,000-$39,999	3.8
$40,000 and over	1.6
Grade Level	
10th Grade	2.1
11th Grade	3.7
12th Grade	7.7

Note: Hispanics may be of any race. The number of students in the three race groups shown do not add to the total because data for American Indians, Eskimos, and Aleuts, are not shown.

Source: U.S. Census Bureau, Current Population Survey, October 1997.

Contact: U.S. Census Bureau, Education and Social Stratification Branch, 301-457-2464.

Source: *School Enrollment — Social and Economic Characteristics of Students, 1997*, U.S. Bureau of the Census, Washington, DC, 1999

rollment is expected to rise by 11 percent between 1998 and 2008.

Growth in Preprimary Enrollment

Between 1987 and 1997, preprimary enrollment grew substantially. Preprimary enrollment rose from 3.4 million in 1965 to 5.9 million in 1987 and to 7.9 million in 1997. The 33 percent increase from 1987 to 1997 is not so much a reflection of growth in the numbers of younger children ages 3 to 5, but the growth in the availability and acceptance of preschool education and the increasing proportion of full-day programs.

By the mid-1980s, approximately 55 percent of the nearly 11 million 3- to 5-year-olds were enrolled in preprimary programs. In 1990, the percentage rose to 59.4 percent, dropping to 55.7 percent in 1991 and 55.1 percent in 1993. The slight

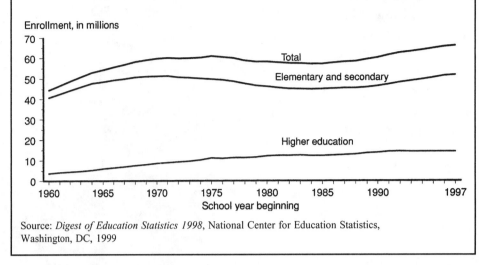

FIGURE 6.4

Enrollment by Level of Education: 1960-61 to 1997-98

Source: *Digest of Education Statistics 1998*, National Center for Education Statistics, Washington, DC, 1999

decrease in the early 1990s can be attributed to a recession, causing some parents not to send their children to preschool and some mothers to elect to stay home. The economy began to recover in 1993, and enrollment in preprimary programs again increased, reaching nearly 65 percent in 1997.

Just as significant as the increase in participation rates over the past decades is the increase in the number of full-day programs. In 1970, only 17 percent of young children in preprimary programs

TABLE 6.4

Enrollment of 3-, 4-, and 5-year-old children in preprimary programs, by level and control of program and by attendance status: October 1965 to October 1997

[In thousands]

Year and age	Total population, 3 to 5 years old	Enrollment by level and control						Enrollment by attendance		
		Total	Percent enrolled	Nursery school		Kindergarten		Full-day	Part-day	Percent full-day
				Public	Private	Public	Private			
1	2	3	4	5	6	7	8	9	10	11
Total, 3 to 5 years old										
1965	12,549	3,407	27.1	127	393	2,291	596	—	—	—
1970	10,949	4,104	37.5	332	762	2,498	511	698	3,405	17.0
1975	10,185	4,955	48.7	570	1,174	2,682	528	1,295	3,659	26.1
1980	9,284	4,878	52.5	628	1,353	2,438	459	1,551	3,327	31.8
1985	10,733	5,865	54.6	846	1,631	2,847	541	2,144	3,722	36.6
1986	10,866	5,971	55.0	829	1,715	2,859	567	2,241	3,730	37.5
1987	10,872	5,931	54.6	819	1,736	2,842	534	2,090	3,841	35.2
1988	10,993	5,978	54.4	851	1,770	2,875	481	2,044	3,935	34.2
1989	11,039	6,026	54.6	930	1,894	2,704	497	2,238	3,789	37.1
1990	11,207	6,659	59.4	1,199	2,180	2,772	509	2,577	4,082	38.7
1991	11,370	6,334	55.7	996	1,828	2,967	543	2,408	3,926	38.0
1992	11,545	6,402	55.5	1,073	1,783	2,995	550	2,410	3,992	37.6
1993	11,954	6,581	55.1	1,205	1,779	3,020	577	2,642	3,939	40.1
1994[1]	12,328	7,514	61.0	1,848	2,314	2,819	534	3,468	4,046	46.2
1995[1]	12,518	7,739	61.8	1,950	2,381	2,800	608	3,689	4,051	47.7
1996[1]	12,378	7,580	61.2	1,830	2,317	2,853	580	3,562	4,019	47.0
1997[1]	12,121	7,860	64.9	2,207	2,231	2,847	575	3,922	3,939	49.9

Source: *Digest of Education Statistics 1998*, National Center for Education Statistics, Washington, DC, 1999

126

attended all-day programs. By the mid-1980s, well over one-third did, and by 1997, about half were in full-day programs. (See Table 6.4 and Figure 6.5.) This growth reflects an increased emphasis on early schooling and the growth in the labor force participation among mothers of preschoolers.

PUBLIC ELEMENTARY AND SECONDARY SCHOOLS

Generally, over the past decades, the number of schools has decreased, usually as a result of school consolidation. In the 1930s, there were more than 247,000 schools, compared to around 86,000 in 1954. The total number of schools remained relatively stable through the 1980s but has slowly risen during the 1990s as consolidation has generally come to an end and the growing population has required more schools.

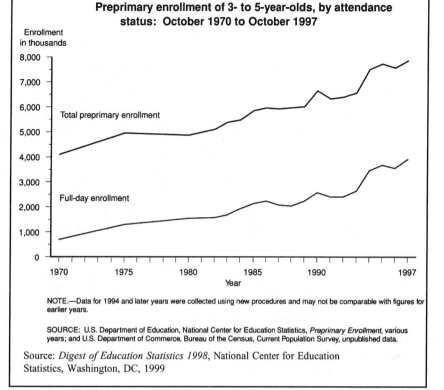

FIGURE 6.5

Preprimary enrollment of 3- to 5-year-olds, by attendance status: October 1970 to October 1997

NOTE.—Data for 1994 and later years were collected using new procedures and may not be comparable with figures for earlier years.

SOURCE: U.S. Department of Education, National Center for Education Statistics, *Preprimary Enrollment*, various years; and U.S. Department of Commerce, Bureau of the Census, Current Population Survey, unpublished data.

Source: *Digest of Education Statistics 1998*, National Center for Education Statistics, Washington, DC, 1999

For the 1996-97 school year, 45.4 million public school students attended the nation's 88,223 public schools. An estimated 29.6 million elementary students went to the 61,805 public elemen-

TABLE 6.5

Public elementary and secondary schools, by type and size of school: 1996–97

Enrollment size of school	Number of schools, by type						Enrollment, by type of school [1]					
	Total [2]	Elemen-tary [3]	Secondary [4]		Com-bined elemen-tary/sec-ondary [5]	Other [2]	Total [2]	Elemen-tary [3]	Secondary [4]		Com-bined elemen-tary/sec-ondary [5]	Other [2]
			All schools	Regular schools [6]					All schools	Regular schools [6]		
1	2	3	4	5	6	7	8	9	10	11	12	13
Total	88,223	61,805	21,307	18,207	2,980	2,131	45,364,791	29,572,370	14,564,205	14,138,959	1,151,966	76,250
Percent [7]	100.00	100.00	100.00	100.00	100.00	100.00	100.00	100.00	100.00	100.00	100.00	100.00
Under 100	9.22	5.98	14.26	8.03	31.54	60.04	0.82	0.60	0.96	0.59	3.59	19.40
100 to 199	9.43	8.70	10.54	9.66	15.23	18.65	2.68	2.75	2.20	1.84	5.68	19.33
200 to 299	11.27	12.21	8.61	8.66	10.27	10.83	5.39	6.47	3.04	2.78	6.44	19.31
300 to 399	13.20	15.38	7.66	8.07	7.79	6.04	8.75	11.24	3.80	3.63	7.02	15.12
400 to 499	13.24	15.79	6.90	7.52	6.51	1.95	11.27	14.81	4.40	4.34	7.53	6.34
500 to 599	11.77	13.83	6.66	7.29	6.51	0.53	12.23	15.83	5.20	5.16	9.20	2.07
600 to 699	8.78	9.87	6.24	6.88	5.57	0.00	10.78	13.33	5.76	5.74	9.33	0.00
700 to 799	6.15	6.64	5.21	5.79	3.46	0.36	8.71	10.36	5.55	5.59	6.72	1.98
800 to 999	7.41	7.13	8.76	9.85	5.23	0.53	12.47	13.16	11.15	11.35	12.14	3.38
1,000 to 1,499	6.22	3.96	13.30	14.92	4.87	0.71	14.08	9.60	23.13	23.50	15.15	6.49
1,500 to 1,999	2.00	0.41	6.82	7.66	1.88	0.18	6.51	1.42	16.71	16.99	8.35	2.05
2,000 to 2,999	1.11	0.08	4.26	4.81	0.84	0.00	4.96	0.39	14.27	14.57	5.11	0.00
3,000 or more	0.20	0.00	0.76	0.86	0.30	0.18	1.36	0.04	3.84	3.94	3.75	4.51
Average enrollment [7]	527	478	703	777	387	135	527	478	703	777	387	135

[1] These enrollment data should be regarded as approximations only. Totals differ from those reported in other tables because this table represents data reported by schools rather than by states or school districts. Percent distribution and average enrollment calculations exclude data for schools not reporting enrollment.
[2] Includes special education, alternative, and other schools not classified by grade span.
[3] Includes schools beginning with grade 6 or below and with no grade higher than 8.
[4] Includes schools with no grade lower than 7.

[5] Includes schools beginning with grade 6 or below and ending with grade 9 or above.
[6] Excludes special education schools, vocational schools, and alternative schools.
[7] Data are for schools reporting their enrollment size.

NOTE.—Because of rounding, details may not add to totals.

SOURCE: U.S. Department of Education, National Center for Education Statistics, Common Core of Data survey. (This table was prepared August 1998.)

Source: *Digest of Education Statistics 1998*, National Center for Education Statistics, Washington, DC, 1999

127

TABLE 6.6

Public elementary and secondary schools, by type of school: 1967–68 to 1996–97

Year	Total, all public schools	Schools with reported grade spans										Combined elementary/secondary schools [6]	Other schools [7]
		Total [1]	Elementary schools				Secondary schools						
			Total [2]	Middle schools [3]	One-teacher schools	Other elementary schools	Total [4]	Junior high [5]	3-year or 4-year high schools	5-year or 6-year high schools	Other secondary schools		
1	2	3	4	5	6	7	8	9	10	11	12	13	14
1967–68	—	94,197	67,186	—	4,146	63,040	23,318	7,437	10,751	4,650	480	3,693	—
1970–71	—	89,372	64,020	2,080	1,815	60,125	23,572	7,750	11,265	3,887	670	1,780	—
1972–73	—	88,864	62,942	2,308	1,475	59,159	23,919	7,878	11,550	3,962	529	2,003	—
1974–75	—	87,456	61,759	3,224	1,247	57,288	23,837	7,690	11,480	4,122	545	1,860	—
1975–76	88,597	87,034	61,704	3,916	1,166	56,622	23,792	7,521	11,572	4,113	586	1,538	1,563
1976–77	—	86,501	61,123	4,180	1,111	55,832	23,857	7,434	11,658	4,130	635	1,521	—
1978–79	—	84,816	60,312	5,879	1,056	53,377	22,834	6,282	11,410	4,429	713	1,670	—
1980–81	85,982	83,688	59,326	6,003	921	52,402	22,619	5,890	10,758	4,193	1,778	1,743	2,294
1982–83	84,740	82,039	58,051	6,875	798	50,378	22,383	5,948	11,678	4,067	690	1,605	2,701
1983–84	84,178	81,418	57,471	6,885	838	49,748	22,336	5,936	11,670	4,046	684	1,611	2,760
1984–85	84,007	81,147	57,231	6,893	825	49,513	22,320	5,916	11,671	4,021	712	1,596	2,860
1986–87	83,455	82,190	58,801	7,452	763	50,586	21,406	5,142	11,453	4,197	614	1,983	[8] 1,265
1987–88	83,248	81,416	57,575	7,641	729	49,205	21,662	4,900	11,279	4,048	1,435	2,179	[8] 1,832
1988–89	83,165	81,579	57,941	7,957	583	49,401	21,403	4,687	11,350	3,994	1,372	2,235	[8] 1,586
1989–90	83,425	81,880	58,419	8,272	630	49,517	21,181	4,512	11,492	3,812	1,365	2,280	[8] 1,545
1990–91	84,538	82,475	59,015	8,545	617	49,853	21,135	4,561	11,537	3,723	1,314	2,325	2,063
1991–92	84,578	82,506	59,258	8,829	569	49,860	20,767	4,298	11,528	3,699	1,242	2,481	2,072
1992–93	84,497	82,896	59,676	9,152	430	50,094	20,671	4,115	11,651	3,613	1,292	2,549	1,601
1993–94	85,393	83,431	60,052	9,573	442	50,037	20,705	3,970	11,858	3,595	1,282	2,674	1,962
1994–95	86,221	84,476	60,808	9,954	458	50,396	20,904	3,859	12,058	3,628	1,359	2,764	1,745
1995–96	87,125	84,958	61,165	10,205	474	50,486	20,997	3,743	12,168	3,621	1,465	2,796	2,167
1996–97	88,223	86,092	61,805	10,499	487	50,819	21,307	3,707	12,424	3,614	1,562	2,980	2,131

[1] Excludes special education, alternative, and other schools not classified by grade span.
[2] Includes schools beginning with grade 6 or below and with no grade higher than 8.
[3] Includes schools with grade spans beginning with 4, 5, or 6 and ending with grade 6, 7, or 8.
[4] Includes schools with no grade lower than 7.
[5] Includes schools with grades 7 and 8 or grades 7 through 9.
[6] Includes schools beginning with grade 6 or lower and ending with grade 9 or above.
[7] Includes special education, alternative, and other schools not classified by grade span.

[8] Because of revision in data collection procedures, figures not comparable to data for other years.
—Data not available.

NOTE.—Some data revised from previously published figures.

SOURCE: U.S. Department of Education, National Center for Education Statistics, *Statistics of State School Systems;* and Common Core of Data surveys. (This table was prepared August 1998.)

TABLE 6.7

Private elementary and secondary enrollment and schools, by amount of tuition, level, and orientation of school: 1993–94

Orientation and tuition	Kindergarten through 12th grade enrollment [1]				Schools				Average tuition paid by students [2]			
	Total	Elementary	Secondary	Combined	Total	Elementary	Secondary	Combined	Total	Elementary	Secondary	Combined
1	2	3	4	5	6	7	8	9	10	11	12	13
Total	4,970,646	2,803,359	811,087	1,356,199	26,093	15,538	2,551	8,004	$3,116	$2,138	$4,578	$4,266
Catholic	2,516,130	1,848,257	592,011	75,862	8,351	6,924	1,161	266	2,178	1,628	3,643	4,153
Less then $1,000	393,901	378,724	(3)	(3)	1,786	1,706	(3)	(3)	—	—	—	—
$1,000 to $2,499	1,368,046	1,274,601	81,955	(3)	4,834	4,542	235	(3)	—	—	—	—
$2,500 to $4,999	675,708	188,123	452,901	(3)	1,533	642	782	(3)	—	—	—	—
$5,000 or more	71,929	(3)	(3)	(3)	(3)	(3)	(3)	(3)	—	—	—	—
Other religious	1,686,064	718,170	124,447	843,448	12,180	6,328	612	5,240	2,915	2,606	5,261	2,831
Less then $1,000	113,382	66,259	(3)	45,878	2,435	1,386	(3)	1,044	—	—	—	—
$1,000 to $2,499	839,447	387,917	(3)	435,788	6,759	3,645	(3)	3,012	—	—	—	—
$2,500 to $4,999	513,773	187,164	62,993	263,615	2,198	970	316	913	—	—	—	—
$5,000 or more	203,014	68,255	38,655	96,104	738	303	172	263	—	—	—	—
Non-sectarian	768,451	236,932	94,629	436,890	5,563	2,287	778	2,498	6,631	4,693	9,525	7,056
Less then $1,000	49,128	(3)	(3)	(3)	912	(3)	(3)	(3)	—	—	—	—
$1,000 to $2,499	121,869	(3)	(3)	(3)	666	(3)	(3)	(3)	—	—	—	—
$2,500 to $4,999	200,857	119,326	(3)	74,395	1,810	1,301	(3)	465	—	—	—	—
$5,000 or more	396,244	82,596	74,283	239,364	2,166	456	408	1,302	—	—	—	—

[1] Only includes kindergarten students who attend schools that offer first grade or above.
[2] Tuition weighted by the number of students enrolled in schools.
[3] Too few sample cases (fewer than 30 schools) for reliable estimates.
—Data not applicable.

NOTE.—Data are based upon a sample survey and may not be strictly comparable with data reported elsewhere. Elementary schools have grade 6 or lower and no grade higher than 8. Secondary schools have no grade lower than 7. Combined schools have grades lower than 7 and higher than 8. Excludes prekindergarten students. Because of rounding and missing values in cells with too few sample cases, details may not add to totals.

SOURCE: U.S. Department of Education, National Center for Education Statistics, "Schools and Staffing Survey, 1993–94." (This table was prepared August 1995.)

Source of both tables: *Digest of Education Statistics 1998*, National Center for Education Statistics, Washington, DC, 1999

TABLE 6.8

Total fall enrollment in institutions of higher education, by attendance status, sex of student, and control of institution: 1947 to 1996

Year	Total enrollment	Attendance status		Sex of student		Control of institution			
		Full-time	Part-time	Men	Women	Public	Private		
							Total	Nonprofit	Proprietary
1	2	3	4	5	6	7	8	9	10

				Institutions of higher education					
1947 [1]	2,338,226	—	—	1,659,249	678,977	1,152,377	1,185,849	—	—
1948 [1]	2,403,396	—	—	1,709,367	694,029	1,185,588	1,217,808	—	—
1949 [1]	2,444,900	—	—	1,721,572	723,328	1,207,151	1,237,749	—	—
1950 [1]	2,281,298	—	—	1,560,392	720,906	1,139,699	1,141,599	—	—
1951 [1]	2,101,962	—	—	1,390,740	711,222	1,037,938	1,064,024	—	—
1952 [1]	2,134,242	—	—	1,380,357	753,885	1,101,240	1,033,002	—	—
1953 [1]	2,231,054	—	—	1,422,598	808,456	1,185,876	1,045,178	—	—
1954 [1]	2,446,693	—	—	1,563,382	883,311	1,353,531	1,093,162	—	—
1955 [1]	2,653,034	—	—	1,733,184	919,850	1,476,282	1,176,752	—	—
1956 [1]	2,918,212	—	—	1,911,458	1,006,754	1,656,402	1,261,810	—	—
1957	3,323,783	—	—	2,170,765	1,153,018	1,972,673	1,351,110	—	—
1959	3,639,847	2,421,016	[2] 1,218,831	2,332,617	1,307,230	2,180,982	1,458,865	—	—
1961	4,145,065	2,785,133	[2] 1,359,932	2,585,821	1,559,244	2,561,447	1,583,618	—	—
1963	4,779,609	3,183,833	[2] 1,595,776	2,961,540	1,818,069	3,081,279	1,698,330	—	—
1964	5,280,020	3,573,238	[2] 1,706,782	3,248,713	2,031,307	3,467,708	1,812,312	—	—
1965	5,920,864	4,095,728	[2] 1,825,136	3,630,020	2,290,844	3,969,596	1,951,268	—	—
1966	6,389,872	4,438,606	[2] 1,951,266	3,856,216	2,533,656	4,348,917	2,040,955	—	—
1967	6,911,748	4,793,128	[2] 2,118,620	4,132,800	2,778,948	4,816,028	2,095,720	—	—
1968	7,513,091	5,210,155	2,302,936	4,477,649	3,035,442	5,430,652	2,082,439	—	—
1969	8,004,660	5,498,883	2,505,777	4,746,201	3,258,459	5,896,868	2,107,792	—	—
1970	8,580,887	5,816,290	2,764,597	5,043,642	3,537,245	6,428,134	2,152,753	—	—
1971	8,948,644	6,077,232	2,871,412	5,207,004	3,741,640	6,804,309	2,144,335	—	—
1972	9,214,820	6,072,389	3,142,471	5,238,757	3,976,103	7,070,635	2,144,185	—	—
1973	9,602,123	6,189,493	3,412,630	5,371,052	4,231,071	7,419,516	2,182,607	—	—
1974	10,223,729	6,370,273	3,853,456	5,622,429	4,601,300	7,988,500	2,235,229	—	—
1975	11,184,859	6,841,334	4,343,525	6,148,997	5,035,862	8,834,508	2,350,351	—	—
1976	11,012,137	6,717,058	4,295,079	5,810,828	5,201,309	8,653,477	2,358,660	2,314,298	44,362
1977	11,285,787	6,792,925	4,492,862	5,789,016	5,496,771	8,846,993	2,438,794	2,386,652	52,142
1978	11,260,092	6,667,657	4,592,435	5,640,998	5,619,094	8,785,893	2,474,199	2,408,331	65,868
1979	11,569,899	6,794,039	4,775,860	5,682,877	5,887,022	9,036,822	2,533,077	2,461,773	71,304
1980	12,096,895	7,097,958	4,998,937	5,874,374	6,222,521	9,457,394	2,639,501	2,527,787	[3] 111,714
1981	12,371,672	7,181,250	5,190,422	5,975,056	6,396,616	9,647,032	2,724,640	2,572,405	[3] 152,235
1982	12,425,780	7,220,618	5,205,162	6,031,384	6,394,396	9,696,087	2,729,693	2,552,739	[3] 176,954
1983	12,464,661	7,261,050	5,203,611	6,023,725	6,440,936	9,682,734	2,781,927	2,589,187	192,740
1984	12,241,940	7,098,388	5,143,552	5,863,574	6,378,366	9,477,370	2,764,570	2,574,419	190,151
1985	12,247,055	7,075,221	5,171,834	5,818,450	6,428,605	9,479,273	2,767,782	2,571,791	195,991
1986	12,503,511	7,119,550	5,383,961	5,884,515	6,618,996	9,713,893	2,789,618	2,572,479	[4] 217,139
1987	12,766,642	7,231,085	5,535,557	5,932,056	6,834,586	9,973,254	2,793,388	2,602,350	[4] 191,038
1988	13,055,337	7,436,768	5,618,569	6,001,896	7,053,441	10,161,388	2,893,949	2,673,567	220,382
1989	13,538,560	7,660,950	5,877,610	6,190,015	7,348,545	10,577,963	2,960,597	2,731,174	229,423
1990	13,818,637	7,820,985	5,997,652	6,283,909	7,534,728	10,844,717	2,973,920	2,760,227	213,693
1991	14,358,953	8,115,329	6,243,624	6,501,844	7,857,109	11,309,563	3,049,390	2,819,041	230,349
1992	14,487,359	8,162,118	6,325,241	6,523,989	7,963,370	11,384,567	3,102,792	2,872,523	230,269
1993	14,304,803	8,127,618	6,177,185	6,427,450	7,877,353	11,189,088	3,115,715	2,888,897	226,818
1994	14,278,790	8,137,776	6,141,014	6,371,898	7,906,892	11,133,680	3,145,110	2,910,107	235,003
1995	14,261,781	8,128,802	6,132,979	6,342,539	7,919,242	11,092,374	3,169,407	2,929,044	240,363
1996 [5]	14,300,255	8,213,490	6,086,765	6,343,992	7,956,263	11,090,171	3,210,084	2,940,557	269,527

				Degree-granting institutions [6]					
1996 [5]	14,367,520	8,302,953	6,064,567	6,352,825	8,014,695	11,120,499	3,247,021	2,942,556	304,465

[1] Degree-credit enrollment only.

[2] Includes part-time resident students and all extension students.

[3] Large increases are due to the addition of schools accredited by the Accrediting Commission of Career Schools and Colleges of Technology.

[4] Because of imputation techniques, data are not consistent with figures for other years.

[5] Preliminary data.

[6] Data are for 4-year and 2-year degree-granting higher education institutions that were eligible to participate in Title IV federal financial aid programs.

—Data not available.

NOTE.—Trend tabulations of institutions of higher education data are based on institutions that were accredited by an agency or association that was recognized by the U.S. Department of Education. The Department of Education no longer distinguishes between those institutions and other institutions that are eligible to participate in Title IV programs. The new degree-granting classification is very similar to the earlier higher education classification, except that it includes some additional, primarily 2-year colleges, and excludes a few higher education institutions that did not award degrees.

SOURCE: U.S. Department of Education, National Center for Education Statistics, Higher Education General Information Survey (HEGIS), "Fall Enrollment in Colleges and Universities" surveys; and Integrated Postsecondary Education Data System (IPEDS), "Fall Enrollment" surveys. (This table was prepared April 1998.)

Source: *Digest of Education Statistics 1998*, National Center for Education Statistics, Washington, DC, 1999

TABLE 6.9

Total fall enrollment in institutions of higher education and degree-granting institutions, by level of enrollment, sex, attendance status, and type and control of institution: 1996 [1]

Attendance status, and type and control of institution	Total			Undergraduate			First-professional			Graduate		
	Total	Men	Women	Total	Men	Women	Total	Men	Women	Total	Men	Women
1	2	3	4	5	6	7	8	9	10	11	12	13
	Higher education institutions											
Total	14,300,255	6,343,992	7,956,263	12,259,417	5,411,058	6,848,359	297,739	172,462	125,277	1,743,099	760,472	982,627
Full-time	8,213,490	3,815,519	4,397,971	7,210,698	3,303,961	3,906,737	266,812	153,983	112,829	735,980	357,575	378,405
Part-time	6,086,765	2,528,473	3,558,292	5,048,719	2,107,097	2,941,622	30,927	18,479	12,448	1,007,119	402,897	604,222
Total 4-year	8,802,835	3,995,901	4,806,934	6,762,544	3,063,089	3,699,455	297,739	172,462	125,277	1,742,552	760,350	982,202
Full-time	6,226,868	2,933,912	3,292,956	5,224,166	2,422,374	2,801,792	266,812	153,983	112,829	735,890	357,555	378,335
Part-time	2,575,967	1,061,989	1,513,978	1,538,378	640,715	897,663	30,927	18,479	12,448	1,006,662	402,795	603,867
Total 2-year	5,497,420	2,348,091	3,149,329	5,496,873	2,347,969	3,148,904	—	—	—	547	122	425
Full-time	1,986,622	881,607	1,105,015	1,986,532	881,587	1,104,945	—	—	—	90	20	70
Part-time	3,510,798	1,466,484	2,044,314	3,510,341	1,466,382	2,043,959	—	—	—	457	102	355
Public, total	11,090,171	4,887,537	6,202,634	9,905,339	4,368,021	5,537,318	116,385	63,608	52,777	1,068,447	455,908	612,539
Full-time	5,964,174	2,767,918	3,196,256	5,410,564	2,490,931	2,919,633	111,395	60,951	50,444	442,215	216,036	226,179
Part-time	5,125,997	2,119,619	3,006,378	4,494,775	1,877,090	2,617,685	4,990	2,657	2,333	626,232	239,872	386,360
Public 4-year	5,806,904	2,646,777	3,160,127	4,622,497	2,127,360	2,495,137	116,385	63,608	52,777	1,068,022	455,809	612,213
Full-time	4,106,094	1,943,086	2,163,008	3,552,484	1,666,099	1,886,385	111,395	60,951	50,444	442,215	216,036	226,179
Part-time	1,700,810	703,691	997,119	1,070,013	461,261	608,752	4,990	2,657	2,333	625,807	239,773	386,034
Public 2-year	5,283,267	2,240,760	3,042,507	5,282,842	2,240,661	3,042,181	—	—	—	425	99	326
Full-time	1,858,080	824,832	1,033,248	1,858,080	824,832	1,033,248	—	—	—	—	—	—
Part-time	3,425,187	1,415,928	2,009,259	3,424,762	1,415,829	2,008,933	—	—	—	425	99	326
Private, total	3,210,084	1,456,455	1,753,629	2,354,078	1,043,037	1,311,041	181,354	108,854	72,500	674,652	304,564	370,088
Full-time	2,249,316	1,047,601	1,201,715	1,800,134	813,030	987,104	155,417	93,032	62,385	293,765	141,539	152,226
Part-time	960,768	408,854	551,914	553,944	230,007	323,937	25,937	15,822	10,115	380,887	163,025	217,862
Private 4-year	2,995,931	1,349,124	1,646,807	2,140,047	935,729	1,204,318	181,354	108,854	72,500	674,530	304,541	369,989
Full-time	2,120,774	990,826	1,129,948	1,671,682	756,275	915,407	155,417	93,032	62,385	293,675	141,519	152,156
Part-time	875,157	358,298	516,859	468,365	179,454	288,911	25,937	15,822	10,115	380,855	163,022	217,833
Private 2-year	214,153	107,331	106,822	214,031	107,308	106,723	—	—	—	122	23	99
Full-time	128,542	56,775	71,767	128,452	56,755	71,697	—	—	—	90	20	70
Part-time	85,611	50,556	35,055	85,579	50,553	35,026	—	—	—	32	3	29

[1] Preliminary data.

—Not applicable.

NOTE.—Institutions of higher education data are based on institutions that were accredited by an agency or association that was recognized by the U.S. Department of Education. The Department of Education no longer distinguishes between those institutions and other institutions that are eligible to participate in Title IV programs. The new degree-granting classification is very similar to the earlier higher education classification, except that it includes some additional institutions, primarily 2-year colleges, and excludes a few higher education institutions that did not award degrees.

SOURCE: U.S. Department of Education, National Center for Education Statistics, Integrated Postsecondary Education Data System (IPEDS), "Fall Enrollment" surveys. (This table was prepared May 1998.)

Source: *Digest of Education Statistics 1998*, National Center for Education Statistics, Washington, DC, 1999

tary schools, while approximately 14.6 million secondary students attended the 21,307 public secondary schools. Another 1.2 million went to the 2,980 combined elementary/secondary schools, while about 76,000 attended the 2,131 "other" schools, usually schools providing special or alternative education. (See Table 6.5.)

Middle schools (sixth through eighth grades), virtually unknown a generation ago, now play a major role in the nation's education system. The number of elementary schools rose by 8 percent between 1984-85 and 1996-97, but middle schools accounted for a disproportionate share of this increase, rising by 52 percent. On the other hand, a significant decrease has occurred in the number of

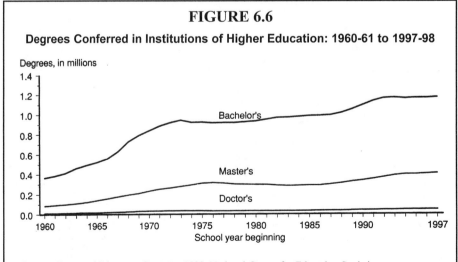

FIGURE 6.6

Degrees Conferred in Institutions of Higher Education: 1960-61 to 1997-98

Source: *Digest of Education Statistics 1998*, National Center for Education Statistics, Washington, DC, 1999

TABLE 6.10

Earned degrees conferred by institutions of higher education, by level of degree and sex of student: 1869–70 to 2007–08

Year	Associate degrees			Bachelor's degrees			Master's degrees			First-professional degrees			Doctor's degrees		
	Total	Men	Women	Total	Men	Women	Total	Men	Women	Total	Men	Women	Total	Men	Women
1	2	3	4	5	6	7	8	9	10	11	12	13	14	15	16
1869–70	—	—	—	¹9,371	¹7,993	¹1,378	0	0	0	(²)	(²)	(²)	1	1	0
1879–80	—	—	—	¹12,896	¹10,411	¹2,485	879	868	11	(²)	(²)	(²)	54	51	3
1889–90	—	—	—	¹15,539	¹12,857	¹2,682	1,015	821	194	(²)	(²)	(²)	149	147	2
1899–1900	—	—	—	¹27,410	¹22,173	¹5,237	1,583	1,280	303	(²)	(²)	(²)	382	359	23
1909–10	—	—	—	¹37,199	¹28,762	¹8,437	2,113	1,555	558	(²)	(²)	(²)	443	399	44
1919–20	—	—	—	¹48,622	¹31,980	¹16,642	4,279	2,985	1,294	(²)	(²)	(²)	615	522	93
1929–30	—	—	—	¹122,484	¹73,615	¹48,869	14,969	8,925	6,044	(²)	(²)	(²)	2,299	1,946	353
1939–40	—	—	—	¹186,500	¹109,546	¹76,954	26,731	16,508	10,223	(²)	(²)	(²)	3,290	2,861	429
1949–50	—	—	—	¹432,058	¹328,841	¹103,217	58,183	41,220	16,963	(²)	(²)	(²)	6,420	5,804	616
1959–60	—	—	—	¹392,440	¹254,063	¹138,377	74,435	50,898	23,537	(²)	(²)	(²)	9,829	8,801	1,028
1960–61	—	—	—	365,174	224,538	140,636	84,609	57,830	26,779	25,253	24,577	676	10,575	9,463	1,112
1961–62	—	—	—	383,961	230,456	153,505	91,418	62,603	28,815	25,607	24,836	771	11,622	10,377	1,245
1962–63	—	—	—	411,420	241,309	170,111	98,684	67,302	31,382	26,590	25,753	837	12,822	11,448	1,374
1963–64	—	—	—	461,266	265,349	195,917	109,183	73,850	35,333	27,209	26,357	852	14,490	12,955	1,535
1964–65	—	—	—	493,757	282,173	211,584	121,167	81,319	39,848	28,290	27,283	1,007	16,467	14,692	1,775
1965–66	111,607	63,779	47,828	520,115	299,287	220,828	140,602	93,081	47,521	30,124	28,982	1,142	18,237	16,121	2,116
1966–67	139,183	78,356	60,827	558,534	322,711	235,823	157,726	103,109	54,617	31,695	30,401	1,294	20,617	18,163	2,454
1967–68	159,441	90,317	69,124	632,289	357,682	274,607	176,749	113,552	63,197	33,939	32,402	1,537	23,089	20,183	2,906
1968–69	183,279	105,661	77,618	728,845	410,595	318,250	193,756	121,531	72,225	35,114	33,595	1,519	26,158	22,722	3,436
1969–70	206,023	117,432	88,591	792,316	451,097	341,219	208,291	125,624	82,667	34,918	33,077	1,841	29,866	25,890	3,976
1970–71	252,311	144,144	108,167	839,730	475,594	364,136	230,509	138,146	92,363	37,946	35,544	2,402	32,107	27,530	4,577
1971–72	292,014	166,227	125,787	887,273	500,590	386,683	251,633	149,550	102,083	43,411	40,723	2,688	33,363	28,090	5,273
1972–73	316,174	175,413	140,761	922,362	518,191	404,171	263,371	154,468	108,903	50,018	46,489	3,529	34,777	28,571	6,206
1973–74	343,924	188,591	155,333	945,776	527,313	418,463	277,033	157,842	119,191	53,816	48,530	5,286	33,816	27,365	6,451
1974–75	360,171	191,017	169,154	922,933	504,841	418,092	292,450	161,570	130,880	55,916	48,956	6,960	34,083	26,817	7,266
1975–76	391,454	209,996	181,458	925,746	504,925	420,821	311,771	167,248	144,523	62,649	52,892	9,757	34,064	26,267	7,797
1976–77	406,377	210,842	195,535	919,549	495,545	424,004	317,164	167,783	149,381	64,359	52,374	11,985	33,232	25,142	8,090
1977–78	412,246	204,718	207,528	921,204	487,347	433,857	311,620	161,212	150,408	66,581	52,270	14,311	32,131	23,658	8,473
1978–79	402,702	192,091	210,611	921,390	477,344	444,046	301,079	153,370	147,709	68,848	52,652	16,196	32,730	23,541	9,189
1979–80	400,910	183,737	217,173	929,417	473,611	455,806	298,081	150,749	147,332	70,131	52,716	17,415	32,615	22,943	9,672
1980–81	416,377	188,638	227,739	935,140	469,883	465,257	295,739	147,043	148,696	71,956	52,792	19,164	32,958	22,711	10,247
1981–82	434,526	196,944	237,582	952,998	473,364	479,634	295,546	145,532	150,014	72,032	52,223	19,809	32,707	22,224	10,483
1982–83	449,620	203,991	245,629	969,510	479,140	490,370	289,921	144,697	145,224	73,054	51,250	21,804	32,775	21,902	10,873
1983–84	452,240	202,704	249,536	974,309	482,319	491,990	284,263	143,595	140,668	74,468	51,378	23,090	33,209	22,064	11,145
1984–85	454,712	202,932	251,780	979,477	482,528	496,949	286,251	143,390	142,861	75,063	50,455	24,608	32,943	21,700	11,243
1985–86	446,047	196,166	249,881	987,823	485,923	501,900	288,567	143,508	145,059	73,910	49,261	24,649	33,653	21,819	11,834
1986–87	436,304	190,839	245,465	991,264	480,782	510,482	289,349	141,269	148,080	71,617	46,523	25,094	34,041	22,061	11,980
1987–88	435,085	190,047	245,038	994,829	477,203	517,626	299,317	145,163	154,154	70,735	45,484	25,251	34,870	22,615	12,255
1988–89	436,764	186,316	250,448	1,018,755	483,346	535,409	310,621	149,354	161,267	70,856	45,046	25,810	35,720	22,648	13,072
1989–90	455,102	191,195	263,907	1,051,344	491,696	559,648	324,301	153,653	170,648	70,988	43,961	27,027	38,371	24,401	13,970
1990–91	481,720	198,634	283,086	1,094,538	504,045	590,493	337,168	156,482	180,686	71,948	43,846	28,102	39,294	24,756	14,538
1991–92	504,231	207,481	296,750	1,136,553	520,811	615,742	352,838	161,842	190,996	74,146	45,071	29,075	40,659	25,557	15,102
1992–93	514,756	211,964	302,792	1,165,178	532,881	632,297	369,585	169,258	200,327	75,387	45,153	30,234	42,132	26,073	16,059
1993–94	530,632	215,261	315,371	1,169,275	532,422	636,853	387,070	176,085	210,985	75,418	44,707	30,711	43,185	26,552	16,633
1994–95	539,691	218,352	321,339	1,160,134	526,131	634,003	397,629	178,598	219,031	75,800	44,853	30,947	44,446	26,916	17,530
1995–96	555,216	219,514	335,702	1,164,792	522,454	642,338	406,301	179,081	227,220	76,734	44,748	31,986	44,652	26,841	17,811
1996–97³	528,000	211,000	317,000	1,166,000	523,000	643,000	402,000	181,000	221,000	79,700	46,000	33,700	44,700	27,100	17,600
1997–98³	520,000	209,000	311,000	1,172,000	523,000	649,000	406,000	183,000	223,000	78,400	46,100	32,300	45,200	27,200	18,000
1998–99³	528,000	209,000	319,000	1,166,000	510,000	655,000	410,000	185,000	225,000	75,800	43,700	32,000	45,800	27,300	18,500
1999–2000³	532,000	208,000	323,000	1,161,000	502,000	659,000	414,000	187,000	227,000	74,000	42,000	32,000	46,400	27,400	19,000
2000–01³	543,000	210,000	333,000	1,173,000	506,000	667,000	418,000	189,000	229,000	73,100	41,100	32,000	46,800	27,300	19,500
2001–02³	550,000	211,000	339,000	1,195,000	510,000	685,000	422,000	191,000	231,000	72,400	40,500	31,800	47,200	27,200	20,000
2002–03³	555,000	212,000	343,000	1,214,000	515,000	699,000	426,000	193,000	233,000	71,900	40,100	31,800	47,600	27,100	20,500
2003–04³	559,000	213,000	346,000	1,227,000	519,000	708,000	430,000	195,000	235,000	71,800	39,800	32,000	47,900	27,000	20,900
2004–05³	560,000	213,000	347,000	1,235,000	520,000	716,000	434,000	197,000	237,000	72,300	39,900	32,400	48,300	26,900	21,400
2005–06³	565,000	214,000	351,000	1,243,000	524,000	719,000	438,000	199,000	239,000	73,100	40,100	33,000	48,700	26,800	21,900
2006–07³	572,000	215,000	357,000	1,256,000	527,000	729,000	442,000	201,000	241,000	74,100	40,500	33,600	49,100	26,700	22,400
2007–08³	579,000	216,000	363,000	1,270,000	530,000	739,000	446,000	203,000	243,000	75,000	40,800	34,200	49,500	26,600	22,900

¹ Includes first-professional degrees.
² First-professional degrees are included with bachelor's degrees.
³ Projected.
—Data not available.

NOTE.—Some data have been revised from previously published figures. Because of rounding, details may not add to totals.

SOURCE: U.S. Department of Education, National Center for Education Statistics, Earned Degrees Conferred; Projections of Education Statistics to 2008; Higher Education General Information Survey (HEGIS), "Degrees and Other Formal Awards Conferred" surveys; and Integrated Postsecondary Education Data System (IPEDS), "Completions" surveys. (This table was prepared May 1998.)

Source: *Digest of Education Statistics 1998*, National Center for Education Statistics, Washington, DC, 1999

one-teacher schools. In 1967-68, there were 4,146 one-teacher schools; by 1992-93, there were only 430 such schools. The number of one-teacher schools has risen slightly to 487 in 1996-1997. (See Table 6.6.)

PRIVATE SCHOOLS

In 1993-94, almost 5 million students, a decrease of about 9 percent from 1987-88, attended the nation's private schools. About 2.8 million went to the 15,538 elementary schools; 811,087 attended 2,551 secondary schools; and 1.4 million went to the 8,004 combined elementary and secondary schools. Catholic institutions accounted for 45 percent of the elementary and secondary schools. About two-thirds of the combined schools were "other religiously affiliated" schools. About one-fifth of private schools were not religiously affiliated. (See Table 6.7.)

The Census Bureau reported that about 1 in 10 students attended private schools in 1997. Private school enrollment is more likely for children from families with higher family incomes. Fewer than 3 percent of children from families with incomes under $20,000 attended private elementary or high schools, compared to 13.4 percent of those from families with incomes of $40,000 or more.

COLLEGE AND UNIVERSITY EDUCATION

College enrollment increased more than 40 percent between 1970 and 1980. Since 1980, enrollments have risen more slowly. Between 1980 and 1992, enrollment increased about 20 percent from 12.1 million to a record 14.5 million. Most of this growth was in part-time enrollment. (See Table 6.8.)

Between 1992 and 1996, college enrollment fell slightly from 14.5 million to 14.3 million. Between 1980 and 1996, the number of men enrolled increased by 8 percent, while the number of women rose by 28 percent. (See Table 6.8.) Total college enrollment is expected to rise as increasing numbers of high school graduates pursue higher education.

In 1996, nearly 12.3 million students were attending undergraduate school, 297,739 were going to a first-professional degree program (medical, dental, law, or theological school), and 1.7 million were in graduate school. (See Table 6.9.) Barely 1 in 6 students attended two-year schools in 1963. By the 1970s, two-year schools were playing a major role in American higher education, with almost 2 out of 5 students attending during the 1980s and in 1996.

TABLE 6.11

Mean Earnings of Workers 18 Years or Older by Highest Level of Educational Attainment

Year	Not a High School Graduate	High School Graduate (or equiv.)	Some College or Assoc. Degree	Bachelor's Degree Only	Not a High School Graduate	High School Graduate (or equiv.)	Some College or Assoc. Degree	Bachelor's Degree Only
	MALE				FEMALE			
1997	19,574	28,307	32,641	50,056	10,725	16,906	19,856	30,119
1996	17,826	27,642	31,426	46,702	10,421	16,161	18,933	28,701
1995	16,747	26,333	29,851	46,111	9,790	15,970	17,962	26,841
1994	16,633	25,038	27,636	46,278	9,189	14,955	16,928	26,483
1993	14,946	23,973	26,614	43,499	9,462	14,446	16,555	25,232
1992	14,934	22,978	25,660	40,039	9,311	14,128	16,023	23,991
1991	15,056	22,663	25,345	38,484	8,818	13,523	15,643	22,802
1990	14,991	22,378	26,120	38,901	8,808	12,986	15,002	21,933
1989	14,727	22,508	25,555	38,692	8,268	12,468	14,688	21,089
1988	14,551	21,481	23,827	35,906	7,711	11,857	14,009	19,216
1987	14,544	20,364	22,781	33,677	7,504	11,309	13,158	18,217
1986	13,703	19,453	21,784	33,376	7,109	10,606	12,029	17,623
1985	13,124	18,575	20,698	31,433	6,874	10,115	11,504	16,114
1984	12,775	18,016	18,863	29,203	6,644	9,561	10,614	14,865
1983	12,052	16,728	18,052	27,239	6,292	9,147	9,981	13,808
1982	11,513	16,160	17,108	25,758	5,932	8,715	9,348	12,511
1981	11,668	15,900	16,870	24,353	5,673	8,063	8,811	11,384
1980	11,042	15,002	15,871	23,340	5,263	7,423	8,256	10,628
1979	10,628	14,317	14,716	21,482	4,840	6,741	7,190	9,474
1978	9,894	13,188	13,382	19,861	4,397	6,192	6,441	8,408
1977	8,939	12,092	12,393	18,187	4,032	5,624	5,856	7,923
1976	8,522	11,189	11,376	16,714	3,723	5,240	5,301	7,383
1975	7,843	10,475	10,805	15,758	3,438	4,802	5,109	6,963

Source: Created by the U.S. Congressional Research Service from U.S. Bureau of the Census data.

Note: Prior to 1991, workers with less than 1 year of college were included in the high school graduate category. Since then, they have been included in the some college or associate degree category.

Source: Linda Levine, *Education Matters: Earnings by Highest Year of Schooling Completed*, Congressional Research Service, Washington, DC, 1998

DEGREES CONFERRED

At the end of the 1995-96 school year, 555,216 associate degrees, 1.2 million bachelor's degrees, 406,301 master's degrees, 76,734 first-professional degrees, and 44,652 doctor's degrees were awarded. (See Figure 6.6 and Table 6.10.) While more women than men earned associate, bachelor's, and master's degrees, more men than women earned first-professional and doctor's degrees.

Of the 1.2 million bachelor's degrees conferred in 1995-1996, 19 percent were for business, far ahead of the 11 percent for social sciences and 9 percent for education. Interest in the fields of parks, recreation, leisure, and fitness; agriculture and natural resources; biological sciences; and multi/interdisciplinary studies has been growing in recent years, with at least a 50 percent increase in the number of degrees conferred in those subjects since 1990-1991. Computer and information sciences, virtually unknown a generation ago, now account

TABLE 6.12

Total expenditures of educational institutions related to the gross domestic product, by level of institution: 1959–60 to 1997–98

Year	Gross domestic product (in billions)	School year	Total expenditures for education (amounts in millions of current dollars)					
			All educational institutions		All elementary and secondary schools		All colleges and universities	
			Amount	As a percent of gross domestic product	Amount	As a percent of gross domestic product	Amount	As a percent of gross domestic product
1	2	3	4	5	6	7	8	9
1959	$507.2	1959–60	$23,860	4.7	$16,713	3.3	$7,147	1.4
1961	544.8	1961–62	28,503	5.2	19,673	3.6	8,830	1.6
1963	617.4	1963–64	34,440	5.6	22,825	3.7	11,615	1.9
1965	719.1	1965–66	43,682	6.1	28,048	3.9	15,634	2.2
1967	833.6	1967–68	55,652	6.7	35,077	4.2	20,575	2.5
1969	982.2	1969–70	68,459	7.0	43,183	4.4	25,276	2.6
1970	1,035.6	1970–71	75,741	7.3	48,200	4.7	27,541	2.7
1971	1,125.4	1971–72	80,672	7.2	50,950	4.5	29,722	2.6
1972	1,237.3	1972–73	86,875	7.0	54,952	4.4	31,923	2.6
1973	1,382.6	1973–74	95,396	6.9	60,370	4.4	35,026	2.5
1974	1,496.9	1974–75	108,664	7.3	68,846	4.6	39,818	2.7
1975	1,630.6	1975–76	118,706	7.3	75,101	4.6	43,605	2.7
1976	1,819.0	1976–77	126,417	6.9	79,194	4.4	47,223	2.6
1977	2,026.9	1977–78	137,042	6.8	86,544	4.3	50,498	2.5
1978	2,291.4	1978–79	148,308	6.5	93,012	4.1	55,296	2.4
1979	2,557.5	1979–80	165,627	6.5	103,162	4.0	62,465	2.4
1980	2,784.2	1980–81	182,849	6.6	112,325	4.0	70,524	2.5
1981	3,115.9	1981–82	197,801	6.3	120,486	3.9	77,315	2.5
1982	3,242.1	1982–83	212,081	6.5	128,725	4.0	83,356	2.6
1983	3,514.5	1983–84	228,597	6.5	139,000	4.0	P3,597	2.5
1984	3,902.4	1984–85	247,657	6.3	149,400	3.8	98,257	2.5
1985	4,180.7	1985–86	269,485	6.4	161,800	3.9	107,685	2.6
1986	4,422.2	1986–87	291,974	6.6	175,200	4.0	116,774	2.6
1987	4,692.3	1987–88	313,375	6.7	187,999	4.0	125,376	2.7
1988	5,049.6	1988–89	346,883	6.9	209,377	4.1	137,506	2.7
1989	5,438.7	1989–90	381,525	7.0	230,970	4.2	150,555	2.8
1990	5,743.8	1990–91	412,652	7.2	248,930	4.3	163,722	2.9
1991	5,916.7	1991–92	432,987	7.3	261,255	4.4	171,732	2.9
1992	6,244.4	1992–93	456,070	7.3	274,335	4.4	181,735	2.9
1993	6,558.1	1993–94	477,237	7.3	287,507	4.4	189,730	2.9
1994	6,947.0	1994–95	503,925	7.3	302,400	4.4	201,525	2.9
1995	7,269.6	[1] 1995–96	529,561	7.3	318,211	4.4	211,350	2.9
1996	7,661.6	[2] 1996–97	559,500	7.3	336,000	4.4	223,500	2.9
1997	8,110.9	[2] 1997–98	583,800	7.2	351,300	4.3	232,500	2.9

[1] Preliminary.
[2] Estimated.

NOTE.—Total expenditures for public elementary and secondary schools include current expenditures, interest on school debt, and capital outlay. Data for private elementary and secondary schools are estimated. Total expenditures for colleges and universities include current-fund expenditures and additions to plant value. Excludes expenditures of noncollegiate postsecondary institutions. Data for 1995–96 through 1997–98 are for 4-year and 2-year degree-granting institutions that were eligible to participate in Title IV federal financial aid programs. Some data revised from previously published figures. Because of rounding, details may not add to totals.

SOURCE: U.S. Department of Education, National Center for Education Statistics, *Statistics of State School Systems; Revenues and Expenditures for Public Elementary and Secondary Education; Financial Statistics of Institutions of Higher Education*; Common Core of Data survey; Higher Education General Information Survey (HEGIS), "Financial Statistics of Institutions of Higher Education" survey, Integrated Postsecondary Education Data System (IPEDS) "Finance" survey, and unpublished data; Council of Economic Advisers, *Economic Indicators*; and National Education Association, *Estimates of School Statistics*, various years. (This table was prepared November 1998.)

Source: *Digest of Education Statistics 1998*, National Center for Education Statistics, Washington, DC, 1999

for 2 percent of bachelor's degrees.

THE INFLUENCE OF EDUCATION ON EARNINGS

Higher levels of education generally lead to higher incomes. In fact, the wage gap between more- and less-educated workers has widened over the past two decades. In 1977, the average male college graduate earned about 50 percent more than the average male high school graduate; in 1997, the male college graduate earned 77 percent more. The growth in the wage gap between women with bachelor's degrees and women with high school degrees was even wider. In 1977, the average female college graduate earned 41 percent more than female high school graduates. By 1997, the female college graduate earned 78 percent more. (See Table 6.11.)

Similarly, workers without a high school degree, or its equivalent, earn less than those with high school degrees, although the gap is not as wide. In 1997, male workers with a high school degree earned about 45 percent more than male workers without, while female workers with a high school degree earned 58 percent more than females who did not graduate from high school. (See Table 6.11.)

Over the past two decades, the average earnings of males with high school degrees or less increased at a slower rate than those of comparably educated female workers. This may be at least partly explained by cutbacks in high-wage, generally blue-collar factory jobs that historically have

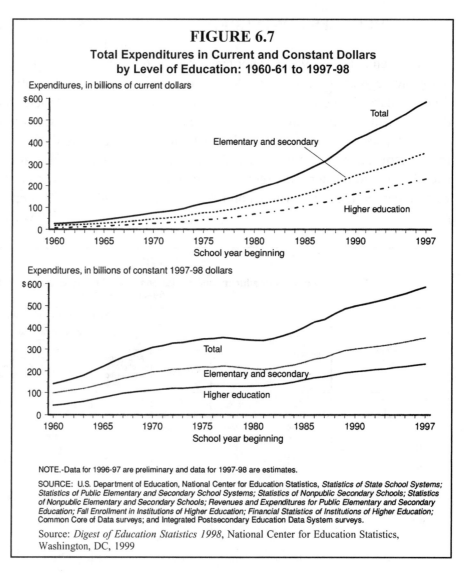

FIGURE 6.7
Total Expenditures in Current and Constant Dollars by Level of Education: 1960-61 to 1997-98

NOTE.-Data for 1996-97 are preliminary and data for 1997-98 are estimates.

SOURCE: U.S. Department of Education, National Center for Education Statistics, *Statistics of State School Systems; Statistics of Public Elementary and Secondary School Systems; Statistics of Nonpublic Secondary Schools; Statistics of Nonpublic Elementary and Secondary Schools; Revenues and Expenditures for Public Elementary and Secondary Education; Fall Enrollment in Institutions of Higher Education; Financial Statistics of Institutions of Higher Education; Common Core of Data surveys; and Integrated Postsecondary Education Data System surveys.*

Source: *Digest of Education Statistics 1998*, National Center for Education Statistics, Washington, DC, 1999

not required more than a high school education and that were predominately held by men.

HOW MUCH DO WE SPEND ON EDUCATION?

Expenditures for public and private education from preprimary through graduate school were estimated at $583.8 billion (current dollars*) for the 1997-98 school year. Expenditures for elementary and secondary schools were estimated at $351.3 billion, while institutions of higher learning spent around $232.5 billion. The United States spent about 7.2 percent of its gross domestic product on education. (See Table 6.12 and Figure 6.7.)

In 1995-1996, as a group, the nation's public schools received most of their funding from state (43.9 percent) and local sources (31 percent), with

134

TABLE 6.13

Estimated total expenditures of educational institutions, by level, control of institution, and source of funds: 1979–80 to 1995–96

[In billions of current dollars]

Level and control of institution and source of funds	1979–80 Amount	1979–80 Percent	1984–85 Amount	1984–85 Percent	1989–90 Amount	1989–90 Percent	1990–91 Amount	1990–91 Percent	1994–95[1] Amount	1994–95[1] Percent	1995–96[2] Amount	1995–96[2] Percent
1	2	3	4	5	6	7	8	9	10	11	12	13
All levels												
Total public and private	$165.6	100.0	$247.7	100.0	$381.5	100.0	$412.7	100.0	$503.9	100.0	$529.6	100.0
Federal	18.9	11.4	21.3	8.6	31.6	8.3	34.1	8.3	43.7	8.7	45.0	8.5
State	64.3	38.8	96.1	38.8	142.2	37.3	151.6	36.7	177.9	35.3	188.6	35.6
Local	43.3	26.1	63.3	25.6	97.9	25.7	105.5	25.6	127.6	25.3	132.9	25.1
All other	39.1	23.6	66.9	27.0	109.8	28.8	121.5	29.4	154.7	30.7	163.1	30.8
Total public	137.4	100.0	200.7	100.0	309.2	100.0	333.9	100.0	406.6	100.0	426.4	100.0
Federal	14.8	10.8	15.8	7.9	23.0	7.4	24.9	7.5	33.1	8.1	34.2	8.0
State	63.9	46.5	95.5	47.6	140.8	45.5	150.3	45.0	176.3	43.4	187.0	43.9
Local	43.1	31.4	63.1	31.4	97.5	31.6	105.0	31.5	127.2	31.3	132.3	31.0
All other	15.6	11.3	26.3	13.1	47.9	15.5	53.7	16.1	70.0	17.2	72.8	17.1
Total private	28.2	100.0	47.0	100.0	72.4	100.0	78.8	100.0	97.3	100.0	103.2	100.0
Federal	4.1	14.5	5.5	11.7	8.6	11.9	9.2	11.6	10.6	10.9	10.8	10.5
State	0.4	1.6	0.7	1.4	1.4	1.9	1.3	1.7	1.6	1.6	1.5	1.5
Local	0.2	0.6	0.2	0.5	0.4	0.6	0.4	0.5	0.4	0.4	0.6	0.5
All other	23.5	83.4	40.6	86.4	62.0	85.6	67.9	86.1	84.7	87.0	90.3	87.5
Elementary and secondary schools												
Total public and private	103.2	100.0	149.4	100.0	231.0	100.0	248.9	100.0	302.4	100.0	318.2	100.0
Federal	9.4	9.1	9.1	6.1	13.0	5.6	14.2	5.7	19.0	6.3	19.5	6.1
State	44.7	43.3	66.8	44.7	100.6	43.6	108.2	43.5	130.5	43.1	139.5	43.8
Local	41.6	40.3	60.8	40.7	94.0	40.7	101.2	40.6	122.1	40.4	126.9	39.9
All other	7.5	7.3	12.8	8.6	23.3	10.1	25.4	10.2	30.9	10.2	32.4	10.2
Total public	96.0	100.0	137.0	100.0	212.8	100.0	229.4	100.0	279.0	100.0	293.6	100.0
Federal	9.4	9.8	9.1	6.6	13.0	6.1	14.2	6.2	19.0	6.8	19.5	6.6
State	44.7	46.6	66.8	48.7	100.6	47.3	108.2	47.2	130.5	46.8	139.5	47.5
Local	41.6	43.3	60.8	44.3	94.0	44.2	101.2	44.1	122.1	43.8	126.9	43.2
All other	0.3	0.3	0.4	0.3	[3] 5.1	[3] 2.4	[3] 5.9	[3] 2.6	[3] 7.5	[3] 2.7	[3] 7.8	[3] 2.6
Total private [4]	7.2	100.0	12.4	100.0	18.2	100.0	19.5	100.0	23.4	100.0	24.6	100.0
All other	7.2	100.0	12.4	100.0	18.2	100.0	19.5	100.0	23.4	100.0	24.6	100.0
Institutions of higher education												
Total public and private	62.5	100.0	98.3	100.0	150.6	100.0	163.7	100.0	201.5	100.0	211.3	100.0
Federal	9.5	15.2	12.2	12.4	18.6	12.3	19.9	12.2	24.8	12.3	25.5	12.1
State	19.6	31.4	29.4	29.9	41.6	27.6	43.4	26.5	47.4	23.5	49.1	23.2
Local	1.7	2.7	2.5	2.6	3.9	2.6	4.3	2.6	5.5	2.7	6.0	2.8
All other	31.6	50.6	54.1	55.1	86.5	57.4	96.1	58.7	123.8	61.5	130.7	61.8
Total public	41.4	100.0	63.7	100.0	96.4	100.0	104.4	100.0	127.6	100.0	132.8	100.0
Federal	5.4	13.1	6.7	10.6	9.9	10.3	10.7	10.3	14.1	11.1	14.7	11.1
State	19.2	46.3	28.7	45.1	40.2	41.7	42.1	40.3	45.8	35.9	47.6	35.8
Local	1.5	3.7	2.3	3.6	3.5	3.7	3.9	3.7	5.1	4.0	5.5	4.1
All other	15.3	36.9	25.9	40.7	42.7	44.3	47.7	45.7	62.6	49.0	65.0	49.0
Total private	21.0	100.0	34.6	100.0	54.2	100.0	59.3	100.0	73.9	100.0	78.6	100.0
Federal	4.1	19.4	5.5	15.9	8.6	15.9	9.2	15.4	10.6	14.4	10.8	13.8
State	0.4	2.1	0.7	1.9	1.4	2.6	1.3	2.3	1.6	2.1	1.5	1.9
Local	0.2	0.8	0.2	0.6	0.4	0.7	0.4	0.7	0.4	0.6	0.6	0.7
All other	16.3	77.7	28.2	81.6	43.8	80.8	48.4	81.6	61.3	82.9	65.7	83.6

[1] Revised from previously published data.

[2] Preliminary data.

[3] Revenues from individuals including fees for transportation and books and food service receipts. This expenditure includes only the individual contributions for these categories and excludes contributions from public sources.

[4] Some private elementary and secondary school revenues come from federal, state, and local sources. However, comprehensive data are not available to delineate the sources of revenues for private schools.

NOTE.—Estimated distribution of expenditures by source of funds are obtained from distribution of revenue sources for current funds. Federally-supported student aid that goes to higher education institutions through students' tuition payments is shown under "All other" rather than "federal." Such payments would add substantial amounts and several percentage points to the federal share. Other federal programs, not included in this table because they do not support regular educational institutions, would increase the federal share even further. Typical examples of these payments would be federal support for libraries and museums. Additionally, the federal contribution to education through tax expenditures is not reflected in this table. Because of rounding, details may not add to totals.

SOURCE: U.S. Department of Education, National Center for Education Statistics, Common Core of Data; Higher Education General Information Survey (HEGIS), "Financial Statistics of Institutions of Higher Education" survey; Integrated Postsecondary Education Data System (IPEDS) "Finance" survey, unpublished data. (This table was prepared November 1998.)

Source: *Digest of Education Statistics 1998*, National Center for Education Statistics, Washington, DC, 1999

the federal government contributing 8 percent. At the public elementary and secondary level, almost all funding came from state (47.5 percent) and local (43.2 percent) governments, with about 6.6 percent coming from the federal government. The percentage of total federal funding for all schools has dropped by 25 percent since the 1979-80 school year. Federal funding dropped a similar amount for the public schools. (See Table 6.13.)

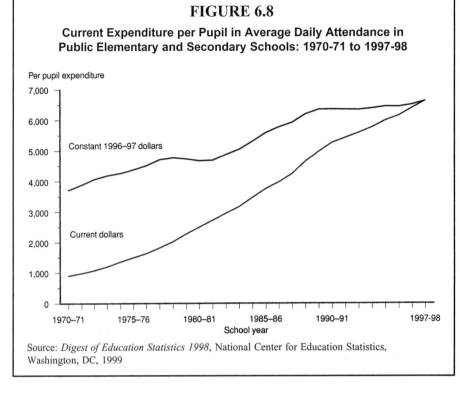

FIGURE 6.8

Current Expenditure per Pupil in Average Daily Attendance in Public Elementary and Secondary Schools: 1970-71 to 1997-98

Per pupil expenditure

Constant 1996–97 dollars

Current dollars

School year

Source: *Digest of Education Statistics 1998*, National Center for Education Statistics, Washington, DC, 1999

Private institutions received almost all of their funding from private sources (87.5 percent), with most of the remainder coming from the federal government (10.5 percent). (See Table 6.13.) Most of the federal funds went to colleges and universities.

Expenditures Per Student

In 1997, the average per student spending for elementary and secondary schools in the United States was $6,146. Huge differences exist in per capita spending by state. New Jersey ($9,955), New York ($9,549), Alaska ($9,012), and Connecticut ($8,817) spent well above the average, while Utah ($3,867), Mississippi ($4,250), and Idaho ($4,465) spent well below the average. While money spent is not the only indicator of a state's commitment to education or financial ability to offer an education (it is often a reflection of the cost of living), it is one indicator of the quality of education students are receiving in that state. (See Figure 6.8 for trends in per pupil spending in public schools.)

---

* *Current* dollars equal the actual dollars of the current year, with no adjustment for inflation. *Constant* dollars are inflation-adjusted, so that the purchasing power of various years' currency can be compared.

CHAPTER VII

VOTER PARTICIPATION

VOTER TURNOUT BEFORE 1920

Although voting is generally considered one of the most important rights of citizenship in a democratic country, a substantial number of Americans choose not to exercise their right to vote. In the nation's first elections (from 1798 to 1824), the popular vote played a secondary role. The state legislatures frequently selected the electors who then elected the president. It was not until Andrew Jackson's victory in 1828 that the popular vote became the determining factor in electing the nation's leader. Just over 1 in 5 Americans of voting age* actually voted in that election, and only 1 out of 8 wanted Jackson. Voter participation remained light throughout the nineteenth century, with a low of less than 21 percent voting in Jackson's 1832 run for reelection and a high of 37 percent voting in the 1876 Hayes-Tilden contest.

BLACK AND WOMEN'S SUFFRAGE

The U.S. Constitution allows the states to set qualifications for the conduct of elections, as long as they do not violate guarantees provided by the Constitution through its amendments. In 1868, Congress ratified the Fourteenth Amendment, granting citizenship to Black Americans. Two years later the adoption of the Fifteenth Amendment gave all citizens the right to vote, regardless of race, color, or previous condition of servitude. However, several states continued to deprive Blacks of their voting rights. Ploys such as grandfather clauses (the grandfather had to have been a U.S. citizen), poll taxes, and literacy tests effectively limited Black voting participation for another 100 years.

The Fifteenth Amendment did not grant voting rights to women. Individual states first gave women the right to vote, beginning with Wyoming in 1869. Before the adoption of the national amendment, 15 states permitted women full voting privileges, 12 states allowed them to vote only in presidential elections, 2 states permitted them to vote in primary elections, and 19 states did not grant any voting rights to women. On August 26, 1920, the Nineteenth Amendment, granting women the right to vote, was ratified.

FELONY DISENFRANCHISEMENT LAWS

All mentally competent adults now have the right to vote with one exception: felony offenders. Forty-six states (all but Maine, Massachusetts, Utah, and Vermont) and the District of Columbia have laws denying the right to vote to convicted criminal offenders in prison. Thirty-two states prohibit felons on parole from voting, and 29 also ban those on probation. In 10 states, laws prohibit ex-

---

* Because of the difficulty in determining the historical population who were legally eligible to register and vote, the population of voting age who voted is often used as the standard of national voting. Consequently, it is important to understand that women, slaves (and later Black Americans), Native Americans, illiterates, convicted felons, those who could not afford a poll tax, and many others at one time or another were denied the vote.

offenders, those who have fully served their sentences, from ever voting. Four additional states ban some ex-offenders, and Texas bars ex-offenders from voting for two years after the completion of their sentences. (See Table 7.1.)

According to The Sentencing Project and Human Rights Watch, two non-profit research and advocacy groups, in *Losing the Vote: The Impact of Felony Disenfranchisement Laws in the United States* (1998), about 3.9 million Americans, or 1 in 50 adults, cannot vote because of a felony conviction. Over one-third are ex-offenders who have completed their sentences, one-third are on probation or parole, and the rest are currently in prison.

Thirteen percent of Black men have lost their voting rights as a result of a felony conviction. At the current rate of incarceration, an estimated 3 in 10 Black men in the next generation will be prohibited from voting at some time in their lives. In those states that deny the vote to ex-offenders, 40 percent may permanently lose their voting rights. According to the report,

No other democratic country in the world denies as many people ... the right to vote because of felony convictions.... Restrictions on the fran-

TABLE 7.1

Categories of Felons Disenfranchised under State Law

State	Prison	Probation	Parole	Ex-felons
Alabama	X	X	X	X
Alaska	X	X	X	
Arizona	X	X	X	X (2nd felony)
Arkansas	X	X	X	
California	X		X	
Colorado	X		X	
Connecticut	X	X	X	
Delaware	X	X	X	X
District of Columbia	X			
Florida	X	X	X	X
Georgia	X	X	X	
Hawaii	X			
Idaho	X			
Illinois	X			
Indiana	X			
Iowa	X	X	X	X
Kansas	X			
Kentucky	X	X	X	X
Louisiana	X			
Maine				
Maryland	X	X	X	X (2nd felony)
Massachusetts				
Michigan	X			
Minnesota	X	X	X	
Mississippi	X	X	X	X
Missouri	X	X	X	
Montana	X			
Nebraska	X	X	X	
Nevada	X	X	X	X
New Hampshire	X			
New Jersey	X	X	X	
New Mexico	X	X	X	X
New York	X		X	
North Carolina	X	X	X	
North Dakota	X			
Ohio	X			
Oklahoma	X	X	X	
Oregon	X			
Pennsylvania	X			
Rhode Island	X	X	X	
South Carolina	X	X	X	
South Dakota	X			
Tennessee	X	X	X	X (pre-1986)
Texas	X	X	X	X (2years)
Utah				
Vermont				
Virginia	X	X	X	X
Washington	X	X	X	X (pre- 1984)
West Virginia	X	X	X	
Wisconsin	X	X	X	
Wyoming	X	X	X	X
U.S. Total	**47**	**29**	**32**	**15**

Source: Jamie Fellner and Mark Maur, *Losing the Vote: The Impact of Felony Disenfranchisement Laws in the United States*, Human Rights Watch and The Sentencing Project, New York, NY, and Washington, DC, 1998

chise in the United States seem to be singularly unreasonable as well as racially discriminatory, in violation of democratic principles and international human rights law.

At the time of this writing, legislation has been introduced in the House of Representatives (H.R. 906) to allow non-incarcerated felons and ex-felons to vote in federal elections, regardless of whether state laws prohibit their voting in state elections.

LOW VOTER TURNOUT

The 1928 Hoover-Smith contest saw over one-half of the electorate turn out for the first time. Voter participation in presidential elections has remained over 50 percent ever since, ranging from a low of 51 percent in Truman's upset victory in 1948 to a high of 69 percent in Johnson's landslide victory over Goldwater in 1964. The voter turnout (54.2 percent) for the 1996 Clinton-Dole race was the lowest since 1948. In every election in American history, the number of voting-age Americans who did not vote outnumbered those who voted for the winning candidates.

Some observers believe low voter turnout indicates tacit approval of the way things are going (the people are generally happy and, therefore, see no reason to go out and vote). Others claim low voter turnout reflects a general dissatisfaction with the system (the people are unhappy, but do not think it will change anything if they go out and vote). Some say the cause is uninformed and apathetic people.

Other observers believe that if it were easier to register and elections were not held on a Tuesday, a workday for most people, more people would turn out to vote. European elections, where voter turnout often exceeds 90 percent, are generally held on Sundays. In January 1996, Oregon had its first special election in which voters could mail in their ballots, although this method is currently being challenged in court. Other jurisdictions, such as Texas, have set up places for early voting. However, overall, these efforts appear to have had little significant effect in increasing voter participation. (See below for reasons people cited for not voting in the 1996 presidential election.)

Over the past decade, many states have tried to make registration easier. Some states have mailed out registration forms, while others have permitted registration in public buildings and at public agencies. The Supreme Court has declared the residency requirement unconstitutional, so it is no longer necessary to have lived in an area for six months to a year to be able to vote (*Dunn v. Blumstein*, 405 U.S. 330, 1971).

In 1993, Congress passed the National Voter Registration Act ("Motor Voter Law" — PL 103-30). This legislation permits people to register

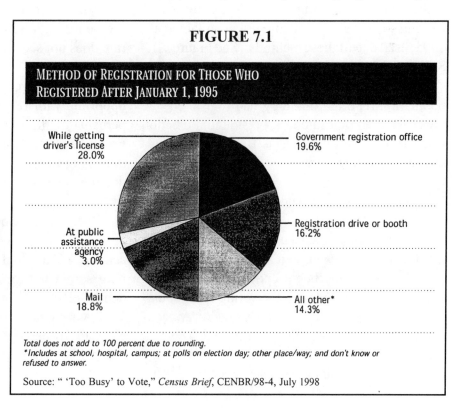

FIGURE 7.1

METHOD OF REGISTRATION FOR THOSE WHO
REGISTERED AFTER JANUARY 1, 1995

While getting driver's license 28.0%

Government registration office 19.6%

At public assistance agency 3.0%

Registration drive or booth 16.2%

Mail 18.8%

All other* 14.3%

Total does not add to 100 percent due to rounding.
*Includes at school, hospital, campus; at polls on election day; other place/way; and don't know or refused to answer.

Source: " 'Too Busy' to Vote," *Census Brief*, CENBR/98-4, July 1998

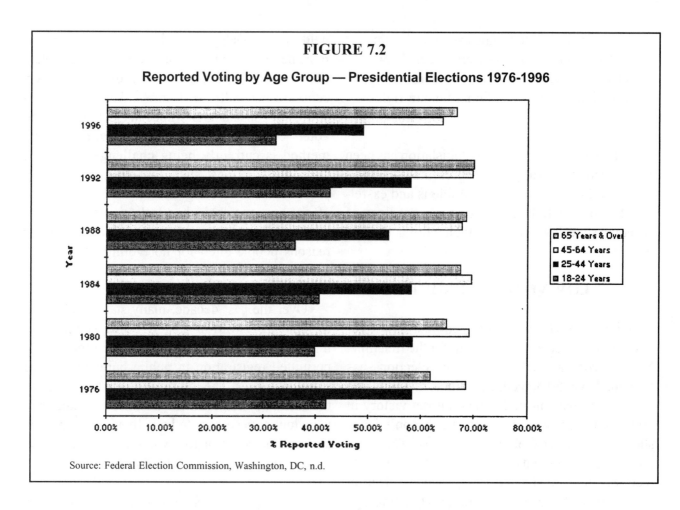

FIGURE 7.2

Reported Voting by Age Group — Presidential Elections 1976-1996

Legend:
- 65 Years & Over
- 45-64 Years
- 25-44 Years
- 18-24 Years

Y-axis (Year): 1996, 1992, 1988, 1984, 1980, 1976

X-axis (% Reported Voting): 0.00%, 10.00%, 20.00%, 30.00%, 40.00%, 50.00%, 60.00%, 70.00%, 80.00%

Source: Federal Election Commission, Washington, DC, n.d.

while obtaining a driving permit or visiting a public assistance office. It also allows people to mail in their registration forms. About half of those registering since the act went into effect on January 1, 1995, used one of these methods. (See Figure 7.1.) Still, the downward trend in voter registration has continued. In 1996, 65.9 percent of the voting-age population reported that they had registered, the lowest registration rate in a presidential election since 1968, when the Census Bureau began collecting this information.

Age

The Bureau of the Census attributes much of the decline in voter turnout since 1964 to the entrance of the "baby boom" population (born between 1946 and 1964) into the voting-age population and to the passage of the Twenty-sixth Amendment (1971), lowering the voting age to 18 years old. The earliest of the "baby boom" cohorts (age groups) reached the age of 18 around 1964. This substantially raised the number of younger voters, an age group known for low voter participation. Nonetheless, many of these "baby boomers" are now entering middle age, but the overall voting rate does not seem to be increasing.

The 1972 presidential election was the first opportunity for 18-year-olds to vote, and half (49.6 percent) of the population ages 18 to 24 voted. From 1972 to 1996, however, the percentage of the youngest group voting in presidential elections declined to 32.4 percent. (See Figure 7.2.)

Over the same period, the percentage of those 65 and older who voted increased from 63.5 percent in 1972 to a high of 70.1 percent in 1992, dropping somewhat to 67 percent in the 1996 presidential election. In the twenty years from 1972 to 1992, voting rates of those ages 45 to 64 remained close to 70 percent, dropping to 64.4 percent in the 1996 election. (See Figure 7.2.)

Gender

For about 60 years following the ratification of the Nineteenth Amendment, voter turnout rates for women were considerably lower than men's rates. However, in every presidential election since 1980, women have voted at a slightly higher rate than men have (Table 7.2). Because they make up an increasing share of voters, women have the potential to determine the results of elections at all levels.

Race and Ethnicity

In 1976, the voting gap between Whites and Blacks was 12 percentage points (60.9 percent versus 48.7 percent). By 1992, it had dropped to 10 points (63.6 percent and 54 percent, respectively). In the 1996 presidential election, 56 percent of White and 50.6 percent of Black voting-age populations turned out to vote, a difference of slightly more than 5 points. (See Figure 7.3.)

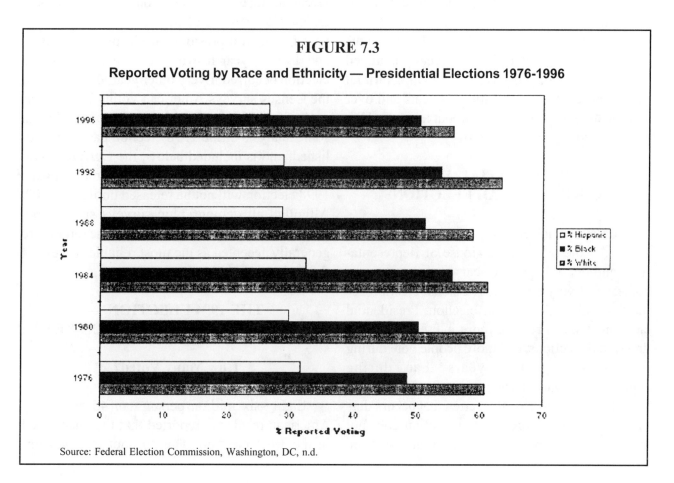

FIGURE 7.3

Reported Voting by Race and Ethnicity — Presidential Elections 1976-1996

Source: Federal Election Commission, Washington, DC, n.d.

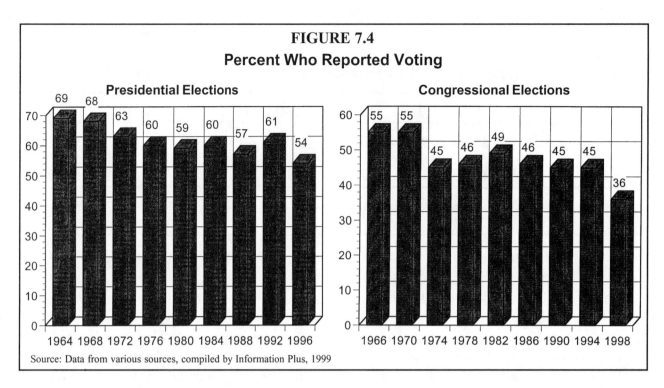

FIGURE 7.4
Percent Who Reported Voting

Presidential Elections

69 68 63 60 59 60 57 61 54

1964 1968 1972 1976 1980 1984 1988 1992 1996

Congressional Elections

55 55 45 46 49 46 45 45 36

1966 1970 1974 1978 1982 1986 1990 1994 1998

Source: Data from various sources, compiled by Information Plus, 1999

The voting rate for persons of Hispanic origin has been about half the rate for Whites, declining from 37.5 percent in 1972 to 26.7 percent in 1996 (Figure 7.3). The low turnout rate among Hispanics reflects, in part, the large proportion of noncitizens among the Hispanic population. The *Current Population Survey*, conducted by the Bureau of the Census, counts persons; it only recently included some questions on citizenship. Estimating turnout rates for the citizen population 18 years and over significantly increased voter turnout levels for Hispanics to 44.3 percent in 1996.

PRESIDENTIAL AND CONGRESSIONAL ELECTIONS

Congressional elections are held every two years. All the seats in the House of Representatives and one-third of the seats in the Senate are contested. Every other congressional election coincides with a presidential election. Presidential elections tend to receive more interest than congressional elections, and more people vote during presidential election years than during congressional-only election years. (See Figure 7.4.) In fact, the congressional election that occurs during the year that a presidential election does not take place is often called an "off-year" election,

implying that this election is less important than the presidential election.

Since the voting and registration rates are different during these two election periods, this chapter includes studies of both the 1996 election, a year in which a presidential election took place, and 1994, a year in which only a congressional election occurred. Every other year, the Bureau of the Census surveys American voting behavior as part of its *Current Population Reports*. Though some analysis of the 1998 election has been published, and is included below, the *Current Population Reports* on voting and registration in the 1998 election will not be released until mid-2000. Although all demographic surveys suffer from undercoverage of the population, these reports are generally accepted as the most reliable surveys of the voting population.

THE 1994 ELECTION — A CONGRESSIONAL ELECTION YEAR

How Many Voted?

Eighty-six million persons, or 45 percent of American residents, reported that they had voted in the 1994 election. This turnout rate was un-

TABLE 7.3

Characteristics of the Voting-Age Population Reported Having Registered or Voted: November 1994

(Numbers in thousands)

Characteristic	Number of persons	1994 Percent registered	Percent voted
TOTAL:			
18 yrs & over	190,267	62.5	45.0
RACE:			
White	160,317	64.6	47.3
Black	21,799	58.5	37.1
Hispanic 1/	17,476	31.3	20.2
GENDER:			
Male	91,006	61.2	44.7
Female	99,260	63.7	45.3
AGE:			
18 - 24 yrs	25,182	42.3	20.1
25 - 44 yrs	83,006	57.9	39.4
45 - 64 yrs	50,934	71.7	56.7
65 yrs & over	31,144	76.3	61.3
REGION:			
Northeast	38,387	61.5	45.6
Midwest	44,507	68.9	48.9
South	66,365	61.1	40.9
West	41,009	58.9	47.1
EDUCATION:			
Elem: 0 - 8 yrs	14,734	40.7	23.6
High: 1 - 3 yrs	20,717	45.0	27.3
4 years	64,929	59.2	40.7
Coll: 1 - 3 yrs	50,441	68.9	49.5
4 or more yrs	39,446	77.2	63.8
LABOR FORCE:			
In civ lab force	129,076	62.6	44.7
Employed	122,584	63.4	45.6
Agri	3,388	62.0	45.0
Nonagri	119,196	63.5	45.6
Private	91,772	59.9	41.2
Gov't	18,367	78.9	63.7
Self 2/	9,057	68.4	53.2
Unemployed	6,492	46.9	28.6
Not in lab force	61,191	62.4	45.8
FAMILY INCOME 3/:			
Under $5,000	4,510	40.6	20.0
$5,000-$9,999	8,086	43.2	23.5
$10,000-$14,999	11,477	51.0	33.0
$15,000-$24,999	20,267	58.0	40.4
$25,000-$34,999	21,837	63.1	44.9
$35,000-$49,999	25,902	68.1	50.1
$50,000 & over	44,530	76.8	60.6
Not reported	10,788	54.6	41.3
TENURE 4/:			
Owner occupied	130,636	70.9	53.4
Renter occupied	56,237	43.7	26.3

1/ Persons of Hispanic origin may be of any race.
2/ Includes unpaid family workers.
3/ Restricted to members of families. Income in current dollars.
4/ Excludes persons with no cash rent and not reported on home ownership.

Source: Bureau of the Census, Washington, DC, 1996

changed from the previous mid-term election in 1990. Historically, the Census Bureau has calculated voter rates on the basis of the total resident population because estimates regarding citizenship status were not directly asked or consistently edited in prior surveys. Beginning with the *1994 Current Population Survey*, detailed questions on place of birth and citizenship status were asked as basic items on the *Survey*. Computing voter turnout rates for citizens only, instead of all residents, increased the level of voter turnout for the nation as a whole from 45 to 48 percent.

Characteristics of Voters

Older Citizens Vote More

As shown in Table 7.3, the older the voter, the more likely he or she is to vote. Sixty-one percent of persons age 65 and over and 56.7 percent of those ages 45 to 64 reported voting in 1994. On the other hand, only 39.4 percent of those 25 to 44 years old and just 20.1 percent of 18- to 24-year-olds reported voting.

TABLE 7.4 (Continued)
Reported Voting and Registration by Selected Characteristics: November 1996

(Numbers in thousands)

Characteristics	All persons	Total Population				Citizen Population		
		Reported registered		Reported voted		Total Citizens	Percent registered	Percent voted
		Number	Percent	Number	Percent			
Employment Status								
In the civilian labor force	132,043	87,532	66.3	71,682	54.3	122,791	71.3	58.4
Employed	125,634	84,166	67.0	69,300	55.2	117,048	71.9	59.2
Unemployed	6,409	3,365	52.5	2,383	37.2	5,743	58.6	41.5
Not in the labor force	61,608	40,129	65.1	33,335	54.1	57,146	70.2	58.3
Occupation[2]								
Total employed	125,634	84,166	67.0	69,300	55.2	117,048	71.9	59.2
Managerial and professional	37,462	29,889	79.8	26,309	70.2	35,975	83.1	73.1
Technical, sales, and admin.	36,973	26,068	70.5	21,530	58.2	35,366	73.7	60.9
Service occupations	16,238	9,083	55.9	6,992	43.1	14,336	63.4	48.8
Farming, forestry, and fishing	3,171	1,893	59.7	1,557	49.1	2,713	69.8	57.4
Precision product, craft, and repair	13,647	7,811	57.2	5,988	43.9	12,598	62.0	47.5
Operators, fabricators, and laborers	18,143	9,423	51.9	6,923	38.2	16,060	58.7	43.1
Annual Family Income[3]								
Total persons in families	149,487	100,599	67.3	83,734	56.0	138,582	72.6	60.4
Less than $5,000	3,590	1,719	47.9	1,179	32.8	3,109	55.3	37.9
$5,000 to $9,999	6,302	3,025	48.0	2,064	32.8	5,384	56.2	38.3
$10,000 to $14,999	10,281	5,494	53.4	4,057	39.5	8,692	63.2	46.7
$15,000 to $24,999	19,135	11,169	58.4	8,778	45.9	16,886	66.2	52.0
$25,000 to $34,999	20,187	13,059	64.7	10,499	52.0	18,541	70.4	56.6
$35,000 to $49,999	25,319	18,008	71.1	15,037	59.4	24,019	75.0	62.6
$50,000 to $74,999	27,451	21,169	77.1	18,347	66.8	26,440	80.1	69.4
$75,000 and over	23,348	19,243	82.4	17,177	73.6	22,531	85.4	76.2
Income not reported	13,875	7,712	55.6	6,598	47.6	12,981	59.4	50.8
Tenure								
Owner-occupied units	135,104	98,562	73.0	83,579	61.9	129,906	75.9	64.3
Renter-occupied units	55,762	27,450	49.2	20,107	36.1	47,458	57.8	42.4
Occupied without payment of cash rent	2,785	1,649	59.2	1,332	47.8	2,572	64.1	51.8
Duration of Residence								
Less than 1 month	3,126	1,410	45.1	849	27.2	2,766	51.0	30.7
1 to 6 months	19,249	9,910	51.5	7,149	37.1	16,871	58.7	42.4
7 to 11 months	8,255	4,426	53.6	3,220	39.0	7,184	61.6	44.8
1 to 2 years	28,986	17,319	59.7	13,671	47.2	25,523	67.9	53.6
3 to 4 years	25,263	16,855	66.7	13,965	55.3	22,921	73.5	60.9
5 years or longer	97,804	77,216	78.9	65,759	67.2	94,456	81.8	69.6
Not reported	10,969	525	4.8	404	3.7	10,215	5.1	4.0
Metropolitan Residence								
Metropolitan	155,735	101,042	64.9	83,984	53.9	142,641	70.8	58.9
In central cities	57,934	35,414	61.1	29,181	50.4	51,003	69.4	57.2
Outside central cities	97,801	65,627	67.1	54,802	56.0	91,638	71.6	59.8
Nonmetropolitan	37,916	26,619	70.2	21,033	55.5	37,294	71.4	56.4
Region								
Northeast	38,263	24,772	64.7	20,852	54.5	35,147	70.5	59.3
Midwest	45,177	32,364	71.6	26,798	59.3	43,861	73.8	61.1
South	68,080	44,891	65.9	35,550	52.2	64,726	69.4	54.9
West	42,131	25,634	60.8	21,816	51.8	36,202	70.8	60.3

[1] For selected race categories.
[2] Limited to employed people.
[3] Limited to people in families.

Source: Lynne M. Casper and Loretta E. Bass, *Voting and Registration in the Election of November 1996*, P20-504, Bureau of the Census, Washington, DC, 1998

Gender

A generation ago, men were more likely to vote in congressional elections than women were. In the 1994 elections, however, there was little overall difference in voter turnout rates between men and women. (See Table 7.3.) Women 18 to 44 years old reported slightly higher turnout rates than did men (36 percent versus 34 percent). In the 1994 election, as in previous congressional elections, men 65 years old and over continued to report higher rates of voter turnout than women (67 and 58 percent, respectively). This difference, however, was less than it was almost 30 years ago in the 1966 election when the gap was 14 percentage points in favor of men.

Race and Ethnicity

Voter turnout for Whites was 47.3 percent, 10 percentage points higher than for Blacks (37.1 percent). Only 20.2 percent of Hispanics voted (Table

145

7.3); however, estimating turnout rates for the citizen population only, this rate increased significantly to 34 percent. Asians/Pacific Islanders voted at levels similar to Hispanics, recording a turnout rate of only 22 percent. However, estimating turnout rates for the citizen population almost doubled the rate for the Asian or Pacific Islander population to 39 percent.

Education and Income

Persons with more education were far more likely to vote than those with less education. In 1994, a far lower percentage of Americans with only an elementary education (23.6 percent) voted than those with a high school diploma (40.7 percent) or a college degree (63.8 percent) (Table 7.3).

Generally, those in the upper-income brackets were more likely to vote than those in the lower-income brackets. Only about 1 of 5 eligible voters in families earning less than $10,000 went to the polls, compared to 3 out of 5 of those earning $50,000 or more. Renters (26.3 percent) were far less likely to vote than homeowners (53.4 percent). (See Table 7.3.)

Employment

Of those participating in the labor force, about 44.7 percent voted. The unemployed (28.6 percent) were much less likely to vote than the employed (45.6 percent). (The unemployed are considered part of the labor force because they are still looking for work.) Those not in the labor force (including retired people) were as likely to vote (45.8 percent) as those in the labor force. (See Table 7.3.)

THE 1996 ELECTION — A PRESIDENTIAL ELECTION YEAR

According to the *1996 Current Population Survey* (CPS), 54.2 percent of the voting-age population reported that they voted in the 1996 presidential election, compared to 61.3 percent in 1992 and 57.4 percent in 1988. (See Figure 7.4.)

Voter Registration Versus Voter Participation

Sixty-six percent of the population were registered to vote in 1996, 67.3 percent of women and 64.4 percent of men (Table 7.4). However, 21.3 million registered voters did not vote. More than one in five (21.5 percent) claimed they did not vote because they could not take time off from work or school or because they were too busy, three times the proportion who gave this reason in 1980 (Figure 7.5). Nearly 17 percent did not vote because they had no interest in the elections, while 13 percent disliked the candidates. About 15 percent reported that they were ill, disabled, or had a family emergency. Other reasons included "out of town," "forgot," or "no transportation to the polls."

Characteristics of Voters

Gender, Race and Ethnicity, and Age

In the 1996 presidential election, a somewhat higher percentage of women (55.5 percent) turned out to vote than men (52.8 percent) (Table 7.4). Only half of the non-Hispanic Blacks (50.9 percent) of voting-age population participated in the 1996 election, compared to 59.6 percent of non-Hispanic Whites. About 26.9 percent of Hispanics voted in 1996. Hispanic turnout appears much lower because a large proportion of Hispanics of voting age were not U.S. citizens. Considering only the citizen population, the rate increases to 44.3. (See Table 7.4.)

The older the person, the more likely he or she is to vote. Approximately 7 in 10 of those 65 to 74 years old participated in the 1996 election, compared to less than one-third of those 18 to 24 years old. Not surprisingly, while three-fourths or more of older voters are registered, just one-half of the younger voters are registered.

Education and Employment

In 1996, as in past elections, the more education a person had, the more likely he or she was to vote. Almost 3 out of 4 college-educated persons

146

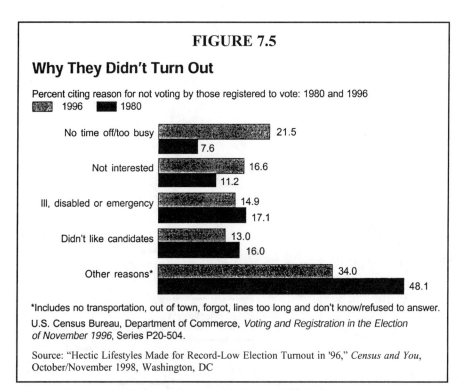

FIGURE 7.5

Why They Didn't Turn Out

Percent citing reason for not voting by those registered to vote: 1980 and 1996

1996 ▪ 1980

No time off/too busy — 21.5 / 7.6

Not interested — 16.6 / 11.2

Ill, disabled or emergency — 14.9 / 17.1

Didn't like candidates — 13.0 / 16.0

Other reasons* — 34.0 / 48.1

*Includes no transportation, out of town, forgot, lines too long and don't know/refused to answer.

U.S. Census Bureau, Department of Commerce, *Voting and Registration in the Election of November 1996*, Series P20-504.

Source: "Hectic Lifestyles Made for Record-Low Election Turnout in '96," *Census and You*, October/November 1998, Washington, DC

voted, while only 32.3 percent of those with less than a high-school education voted. More employed people (55.2 percent) than unemployed (37.2 percent) voted. More than half (54.1 percent) of those not in the labor force, which included retirees, went to the polls. (See Table 7.4.)

Voter Profile Remains Similar

Despite the increases in the level of turnout, the typical voter profile remained similar to past years. People in the Midwest, those with four years or more of college, those who owned their homes, older people, and the employed were most likely to vote. (See Table 7.4.)

THE 1998 ELECTION — A CONGRESSIONAL ELECTION YEAR

The Committee for the Study of the American Electorate (CSAE), a Washington-based, non-par-

tisan, non-profit research institution, reported on voter turnout in the 1998 mid-term general election. For the CSAE, turnout in "off-year," or "mid-term," elections is based upon the total vote cast for the highest office contested on the ballot in each of the 50 states and the District of Columbia. In most cases, this figure represents total votes cast for either U.S. senator or for state governor. In a few instances, U.S. representative was the highest office on the ballot.

According to the CSAE, fewer Americans cast their ballots in the 1998 congressional election than in 1994 even though nearly 8 million more Americans were eligible to vote and 4 million more had registered to vote. About 73 million Americans voted in 1998, dropping the turnout rate (36.4 percent) to its lowest level since 1942, when millions of Americans were fighting in World War II.

Minnesota had the highest turnout, where about 60 percent of the voting-age population voted in the governor's race. The second highest level of voting was in Montana, where 50.2 percent voted for that state's only congressional seat. Wyoming and South Dakota had about half of their eligible voters turn out for their governor's races; nearly half (48.5 percent) turned out for the Vermont senate race. Tennessee (23.6 percent), Arizona (25.8 percent), Texas (26.2 percent), and Louisiana (30.8 percent) had the lowest turnouts in states with 1998 statewide races.

CHAPTER VIII

CRIME*

Virtually every U.S. president since John F. Kennedy has committed his administration to a "war on crime," often without much success. The Bush Administration tied its "war on crime" to a "war on drugs" as street violence, often capped by random shooting and death and frequently associated with illegal drug activities, became a major concern in virtually every major American city.

Under President Clinton, Congress passed the Violent Crime Control and Law Enforcement Act of 1994 (PL 103-322), which provided funds for 100,000 new police officers. The law also required mandatory life sentences for violent, three-time federal offenders. In addition, it expanded the federal death penalty to cover more than 60 offenses and permitted the prosecution as adults of juvenile offenders, ages 13 or older, who commit federal crimes of violence or federal crimes involving a firearm. The law increased the penalties for repeat federal sex offenders and created a program for the registration of sexual predators.

The annual *Crime in the United States*, prepared by the Federal Bureau of Investigation (FBI), is generally used as an indicator of the level of crime in the United States. Its findings are based on reports by city, county, and state police agencies. The Crime Index is composed of selected offenses, including the violent crimes of murder and nonnegligent manslaughter, forcible rape, robbery, and aggravated assault and the property crimes of burglary, larceny-theft, motor vehicle theft, and arson. In 1998, a Crime Index offense occurred ev-

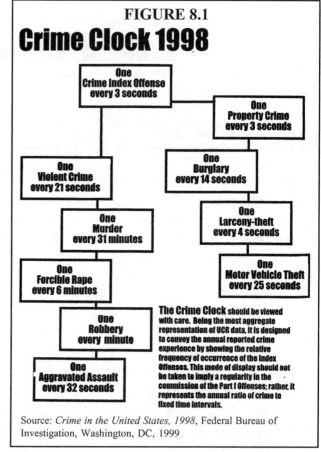

Source: *Crime in the United States, 1998*, Federal Bureau of Investigation, Washington, DC, 1999

ery 3 seconds, a violent crime every 21 seconds, and a property crime every 3 seconds. (See Figure 8.1.)

NUMBER AND RATE OF CRIMES

The FBI reported that the number of Crime Index offenses more than doubled between 1967 (5.9 million) and 1980 (13.4 million). From 1982 to 1984, the number of these crimes decreased;

---

* For a complete discussion of crime, see *Crime — A Serious American Problem*, Information Plus, Wylie, Texas, 1998.

however, from 1984 through 1991, the number of crimes grew 25 percent. In 1992, the number of crimes again began to decline.

By 1998, the total of crimes committed dropped to just under 12.5 million offenses. This is the lowest annual serious crime count since 1985 and the seventh consecutive annual decline. From 1980 through 1984, the Crime Index rate (offenses per 100,000 inhabitants) began to drop, reaching a low of 5,031 per 100,000 people in 1984. After that, the rate increased, reaching 5,898 crimes per 100,000 people in 1991, an increase of 16 percent. Since then, however, the rate has been dropping. By 1998, the crime rate had fallen to 4,615.5 per 100,000, the lowest rate since 1973. (See Table 8.1.)

TABLE 8.1

Index of Crime, United States, 1979-1998

Population[1]	Crime Index total[2]	Modified Crime Index total[3]	Violent crime[4]	Property crime[4]	Murder and non-negligent man-slaughter	Forcible rape	Robbery	Aggravated assault	Burglary	Larceny-theft	Motor vehicle theft	Arson[3]
					Number of Offenses							
Population by year:												
1979-220,099,000	12,249,500		1,208,030	11,041,500	21,460	76,390	480,700	629,480	3,327,700	6,601,000	1,112,800	
1980-225,349,264	13,408,300		1,344,520	12,063,700	23,040	82,990	565,840	672,650	3,795,200	7,136,900	1,131,700	
1981-229,146,000	13,423,800		1,361,820	12,061,900	22,520	82,500	592,910	663,900	3,779,700	7,194,400	1,087,800	
1982-231,534,000	12,974,400		1,322,390	11,652,000	21,010	78,770	553,130	669,480	3,447,100	7,142,500	1,062,400	
1983-233,981,000	12,108,600		1,258,090	10,850,500	19,310	78,920	506,570	653,290	3,129,900	6,712,800	1,007,900	
1984-236,158,000	11,881,800		1,273,280	10,608,500	18,690	84,230	485,010	685,350	2,984,400	6,591,900	1,032,200	
1985-238,740,000	12,431,400		1,328,770	11,102,600	18,980	88,670	497,870	723,250	3,073,300	6,926,400	1,102,900	
1986-241,077,000	13,211,900		1,489,170	11,722,700	20,610	91,460	542,780	834,320	3,241,400	7,257,200	1,224,100	
1987-243,400,000	13,508,700		1,484,000	12,024,700	20,100	91,100	517,700	855,090	3,236,200	7,499,900	1,288,700	
1988-245,807,000	13,923,100		1,566,220	12,356,900	20,680	92,490	542,970	910,090	3,218,100	7,705,900	1,432,900	
1989-248,239,000	14,251,400		1,646,040	12,605,400	21,500	94,500	578,330	951,710	3,168,200	7,872,400	1,564,800	
1990-248,709,873	14,475,600		1,820,130	12,655,500	23,440	102,560	639,270	1,054,860	3,073,900	7,945,700	1,635,900	
1991-252,177,000	14,872,900		1,911,770	12,961,100	24,700	106,590	687,730	1,092,740	3,157,200	8,142,200	1,661,700	
1992-255,082,000	14,438,200		1,932,270	12,505,900	23,760	109,060	672,480	1,126,970	2,979,900	7,915,200	1,610,800	
1993-257,908,000	14,144,800		1,926,020	12,218,800	24,530	106,010	659,870	1,135,610	2,834,800	7,820,900	1,563,100	
1994-260,341,000	13,989,500		1,857,670	12,131,900	23,330	102,220	618,950	1,113,180	2,712,800	7,879,800	1,539,300	
1995-262,755,000	13,862,700		1,798,790	12,063,900	21,610	97,470	580,510	1,099,210	2,593,800	7,997,700	1,472,400	
1996-265,284,000	13,493,900		1,688,540	11,805,300	19,650	96,250	535,590	1,037,050	2,506,400	7,904,700	1,394,200	
1997-267,637,000[5]	13,194,600		1,636,100	11,558,500	18,210	96,150	498,530	1,023,200	2,460,500	7,743,800	1,354,200	
1998-270,296,000	12,475,600		1,531,040	10,944,600	16,910	93,100	446,630	974,400	2,330,000	7,373,900	1,240,800	
Percent change, number of offenses:												
1998/1997	-5.4		-6.4	-5.3	-7.1	-3.2	-10.4	-4.8	-5.3	-4.8	-8.4	
1998/1994	-10.8		-17.6	-9.8	-27.5	-8.9	-27.8	-12.5	-14.1	-6.4	-19.4	
1998/1989	-12.5		-7.0	-13.2	-21.3	-1.5	-22.8	+2.4	-26.5	-6.3	-20.7	
					Rate per 100,000 Inhabitants							
Year:												
1979	5,565.5		548.9	5,016.6	9.7	34.7	218.4	286.0	1,511.9	2,999.1	505.6	
1980	5,950.0		596.6	5,353.3	10.2	36.8	251.1	298.5	1,684.1	3,167.0	502.2	
1981	5,858.2		594.3	5,263.9	9.8	36.0	258.7	289.7	1,649.5	3,139.7	474.7	
1982	5,603.6		571.1	5,032.5	9.1	34.0	238.9	289.2	1,488.8	3,084.8	458.8	
1983	5,175.0		537.7	4,637.4	8.3	33.7	216.5	279.2	1,337.7	2,868.9	430.8	
1984	5,031.3		539.2	4,492.1	7.9	35.7	205.4	290.2	1,263.7	2,791.3	437.1	
1985	5,207.1		556.6	4,650.5	8.0	37.1	208.5	302.9	1,287.3	2,901.2	462.0	
1986	5,480.4		617.7	4,862.6	8.6	37.9	225.1	346.1	1,344.6	3,010.3	507.8	
1987	5,550.0		609.7	4,940.3	8.3	37.4	212.7	351.3	1,329.6	3,081.3	529.4	
1988	5,664.2		637.2	5,027.1	8.4	37.6	220.9	370.2	1,309.2	3,134.9	582.9	
1989	5,741.0		663.1	5,077.9	8.7	38.1	233.0	383.4	1,276.3	3,171.3	630.4	
1990	5,820.3		731.8	5,088.5	9.4	41.2	257.0	424.1	1,235.9	3,194.8	657.8	
1991	5,897.8		758.1	5,139.7	9.8	42.3	272.7	433.3	1,252.0	3,228.8	659.0	
1992	5,660.2		757.5	4,902.7	9.3	42.8	263.6	441.8	1,168.2	3,103.0	631.5	
1993	5,484.4		746.8	4,737.6	9.5	41.1	255.9	440.3	1,099.2	3,032.4	606.1	
1994	5,373.5		713.6	4,660.0	9.0	39.3	237.7	427.6	1,042.0	3,026.7	591.3	
1995	5,275.9		684.6	4,591.3	8.2	37.1	220.9	418.3	987.1	3,043.8	560.4	
1996	5,086.6		636.5	4,450.1	7.4	36.3	201.9	390.9	944.8	2,979.7	525.6	
1997[5]	4,930.0		611.3	4,318.7	6.8	35.9	186.3	382.3	919.4	2,893.4	506.0	
1998	4,615.5		566.4	4,049.1	6.3	34.4	165.2	360.5	862.0	2,728.1	459.0	
Percent change, rate per 100,000 inhabitants:												
1998/1997	-6.4		-7.3	-6.2	-7.4	-4.2	-11.3	-5.7	-6.2	-5.7	-9.3	
1998/1994	-14.1		-20.6	-13.1	-30.0	-12.5	-30.5	-15.7	-17.3	-9.9	-22.4	
1998/1989	-19.6		-14.6	-20.3	-27.6	-9.7	-29.1	-6.0	-32.5	-14.0	-27.2	

[1] Populations are Bureau of the Census provisional estimates as of July 1, except 1980 and 1990 which are the decennial census counts.

[2] Because of rounding, the offenses may not add to total.

[3] Although arson data are included in the trend and clearance tables, sufficient data are not available to estimate totals for this offense.

[4] Violent crimes are offenses of murder, forcible rape, robbery, and aggravated assault. Property crimes are offenses of burglary, larceny-theft, and motor vehicle theft. Data are not included for the property crime of arson.

[5] The 1997 figures have been adjusted.

Complete data for 1998 were not available for the states of Illinois, Kansas, Kentucky, Montana, New Hampshire, and Wisconsin.

All rates were calculated on the offenses before rounding.

Source: *Crime in the United States, 1998*, Federal Bureau of Investigation, Washington, DC, 1999

Crime Index offenses include both violent crimes (murder, forcible rape, robbery, and aggravated assault) and property crimes (burglary, larceny-theft, and motor vehicle theft). In 1998, 12 percent of the crimes reported to law enforcement were violent crimes, while 88 percent were property crimes. Nearly 3 of 5 offenses (59.1 percent) were larceny-theft offenses.

In the first half of 1999, the number of serious crimes reported to police dropped 10 percent from 1998 to the lowest level in 25 years. This decline even surprised crime experts, who cited such explanations as anti-crime measures, a growing economy, the aging of baby boomers, efforts to control availability of guns, and the decline of crack-cocaine markets. Overall, violent crimes dropped 8 percent, with murder leading the decrease at 13 percent. Property crime fell 10 percent, with burglary dropping 14 percent and motor vehicle theft, 12 percent.

The nation's murder rate — 6.3 per 100,000 — was at the lowest point since 1968. In general, the preliminary 1999 FBI figures showed that the smaller the city, the larger the decline in murders. In cities of more than 1 million residents, murders increased by 1 percent, an insignificant increase according to experts. Earlier in the 1990s, big-city murders saw steep declines. According to James Alan Fox, a professor of criminal justice at Northeastern University, "There is a point where crime gets as low as it can go."

Crime Rate by Region and Area

In 1998, for the first time, the crime rate in cities outside of metropolitan areas (4,987 per 100,000 residents) was slightly higher than in metropolitan areas (4,975 per 100,000). Both rates were considerably higher than in rural areas (1,998 per 100,000). (See Table 8.2.) Overall, southern and western states accounted for a somewhat higher

---

TABLE 8.2

Index of Crime, United States, 1998

Area	Population[1]	Crime Index total	Modified Crime Index total[2]	Violent crime[3]	Property crime[3]	Murder and non-negligent man-slaughter	Forcible rape	Robbery	Aggravated assault	Burglary	Larceny-theft	Motor vehicle theft	Arson[2]
United States Total	270,296,000	12,475,634		1,531,044	10,944,590	16,914	93,103	446,625	974,402	2,329,950	7,373,886	1,240,754	
Rate per 100,000 inhabitants		4,615.5		566.4	4,049.1	6.3	34.4	165.2	360.5	862.0	2,728.1	459.0	
Metropolitan Statistical Area	215,575,223												
Area actually reporting[4]	92.7%	10,119,626		1,306,087	8,813,539	14,036	71,744	416,390	803,917	1,834,598	5,868,594	1,110,347	
Estimated totals	100.0%	10,724,952		1,359,174	9,365,778	14,538	77,788	426,706	840,142	1,940,002	6,276,315	1,149,461	
Rate per 100,000 inhabitants		4,975.0		630.5	4,344.6	6.7	36.1	197.9	389.7	899.9	2,911.4	533.2	
Cities outside metropolitan area	21,991,208												
Area actually reporting[4]	77.1%	870,077		81,827	788,250	732	6,172	12,236	62,687	157,975	589,853	40,422	
Estimated totals	100.0%	1,096,760		97,708	999,052	884	7,825	14,517	74,482	194,599	755,413	49,040	
Rate per 100,000 inhabitants		4,987.3		444.3	4,543.0	4.0	35.6	66.0	338.7	884.9	3,435.1	223.0	
Rural Counties	32,729,569												
Area actually reporting[4]	76.0%	534,982		62,497	472,485	1,344	5,861	4,639	50,653	159,113	278,450	34,922	
Estimated totals	100.0%	653,922		74,162	579,760	1,492	7,490	5,402	59,778	195,349	342,158	42,253	
Rate per 100,000 inhabitants		1,998.0		226.6	1,771.4	4.6	22.9	16.5	182.6	596.9	1,045.4	129.1	

[1] Populations are Bureau of the Census provisional estimates as of July 1, 1996-1998, and are subject to change.

[2] Although arson data are included in the trend and clearance tables, sufficient data are not available to estimate totals for this offense.

[3] Violent crimes are offenses of murder, forcible rape, robbery, and aggravated assault. Property crimes are offenses of burglary, larceny-theft, and motor vehicle theft. Data are not included for the property crime of arson.

[4] The percentage representing area actually reporting will not coincide with the ratio between reported and estimated crime totals, since these data represent the sum of the calculations for individual states which have varying populations, portions reporting, and crime rates.

Complete data for 1998 were not available for the states of Illinois, Kansas, Kentucky, Montana, New Hampshire, and Wisconsin.

Source: *Crime in the United States, 1998*, Federal Bureau of Investigation, Washington, DC, 1999

TABLE 8.3

Index of Crime
Regional Offense and Population Distribution, 1998

Region	Population	Crime Index total	Modified Crime Index total[1]	Violent crime[2]	Property crime[2]	Murder and non-negligent manslaughter	Forcible rape	Robbery	Aggravated assault	Burglary	Larceny-theft	Motor vehicle theft	Arson[1]
United States Total[3]	100.0	100.0		100.0	100.0	100.0	100.0	100.0	100.0	100.0	100.0	100.0	
Northeastern States	19.1	14.4		16.9	14.0	13.1	13.1	21.4	15.3	13.1	14.1	15.5	
Midwestern States	23.3	22.1		20.3	22.3	21.4	24.8	19.9	20.0	20.9	23.1	20.1	
Southern States	35.3	40.0		39.5	40.0	43.9	39.1	36.1	40.9	42.8	39.8	36.2	
Western States	22.3	23.6		23.3	23.6	21.7	22.9	22.6	23.8	23.2	23.0	28.2	

[1] Although arson data are included in the trend and clearance tables, sufficient data are not available to estimate totals for this offense.

[2] Violent crimes are offenses of murder, forcible rape, robbery, and aggravated assault. Property crimes are offenses of burglary, larceny-theft, and motor vehicle theft. Data are not included for the property crime of arson.

[3] Because of rounding, the percentages may not add to totals.

Complete data for 1998 were not available for the states of Illinois, Kansas, Kentucky, Montana, New Hampshire, and Wisconsin.

Source: *Crime in the United States, 1998*, Federal Bureau of Investigation, Washington, DC, 1999

proportion of crimes relative to their percentage of the total population (Table 8.3). The South had the highest homicide rate, 8 per 100,000 residents, compared to 6 per 100,000 residents of the Midwest and West and only 4 per 100,000 residents of the Northeast.

VICTIMS OF CRIME

Many observers believe the *National Crime Victimization Survey* (NCVS), prepared annually by the Bureau of Justice Statistics (BJS) since 1972, is a more accurate indicator of crime than the FBI's *Crime in the United States*. The crime increase reported in the Bureau of Justice Statistics' victimization rate between 1973 and 1979 was not nearly as dramatic as the rise reported in the FBI reports. While the data in *Crime in the United States* indicated an increase in crime during the last half of the 1980s, the BJS *National Crime Victimization Survey* showed a general decline over the same period. However, the 1998 BJS statistics are in general agreement with those in *Crime in the United States* for 1998.

The BJS victimization survey asks a representative sample* of American households if they have been the victims of a crime and whether they reported it. Those who believe this method to be more accurate than the reporting used by the FBI note that large numbers of crimes are unreported. Many victims believe that reporting the crime to the police will bring no results. Others are too embarrassed (as in the case of fraud), or they fear they will become subjects of an investigation (as in the case of rape). Still others believe the crime is too insignificant to report (as in the case of petty larceny).

Reported Victimizations

Based on the findings of past *National Crime Victimization Surveys*, researchers estimate that almost half of all violent victimizations and about one-third of all property crimes are reported to the police. Murder, the major crime most likely to be reported to the police, is not included in the victimization studies because the survey is based on victim interviews. (The FBI's 1998 Crime Index reported 17,000 murders. Murders were the least frequent violent victimization. In 1998, about 6.3 murders occurred per 100,000 persons — see Table 8.1.)

In 1998, victims reported 35 percent of all property crimes; not surprisingly, motor vehicle thefts were more likely than any other crime to be reported (80 percent). Victims reported 46 percent of violent crimes to the police — 62 percent of robberies, 58 percent of aggravated assaults, and

---

*In 1998, approximately 43,000 households and 80,000 people age 12 or older were interviewed.

TABLE 8.4

Criminal victimization, 1997-98

Type of crime	Number of victimizations (1,000's)		Victimization rates (per 1,000 persons age 12 or older or per 1,000 households)		
	1997	1998	1997	1998	Percent change, 1997-98
All crimes	34,788	31,307	...	...	
Personal crimes[a]	8,971	8,412	40.8	37.9	-7.1%*
Crimes of violence	8,614	8,116	39.2	36.6	-6.6‡
Completed violence	2,679	2,564	12.2	11.6	-4.9
Attempted/threatened violence	5,935	5,553	27.0	25.0	-7.4‡
Rape/Sexual assault	311	333	1.4	1.5	7.1
Rape/attempted rape	194	200	0.9	0.9	0.0
Rape	115	110	0.5	0.5	0.0
Attempted rape	79	89	0.4	0.4	0.0
Sexual assault	117	133	0.5	0.6	20.0
Robbery	944	886	4.3	4.0	-7.0
Completed/property taken	607	610	2.8	2.7	-3.6
With injury	243	170	1.1	0.8	-27.3‡
Without injury	363	439	1.7	2.0	17.6
Attempted to take property	337	277	1.5	1.2	-20.0
With injury	73	70	0.3	0.3	0.0
Without injury	265	207	1.2	0.9	-25.0
Assault	7,359	6,897	33.5	31.1	-7.2‡
Aggravated	1,883	1,674	8.6	7.5	-12.8‡
With injury	595	547	2.7	2.5	-7.4
Threatened with weapon	1,288	1,126	5.9	5.1	-13.6‡
Simple	5,476	5,224	24.9	23.5	-5.6
With minor injury	1,258	1,175	5.7	5.3	-7.0
Without injury	4,218	4,048	19.2	18.2	-5.2
Personal theft[b]	357	296	1.6	1.3	-18.8
Property crimes	25,817	22,895	248.3	217.4	-12.4%*
Household burglary	4,635	4,054	44.6	38.5	-13.7*
Completed	3,893	3,380	37.4	32.1	-14.2*
Forcible entry	1,497	1,310	14.4	12.4	-13.9*
Unlawful entry without force	2,396	2,070	23.0	19.7	-14.3*
Attempted forcible entry	742	674	7.1	6.4	-9.9
Motor vehicle theft	1,433	1,138	13.8	10.8	-21.7*
Completed	1,007	822	9.7	7.8	-19.6*
Attempted	426	316	4.1	3.0	-26.8*
Theft	19,749	17,703	189.9	168.1	-11.5*
Completed[c]	18,960	17,074	182.3	162.1	-11.1*
Less than $50	7,218	6,169	69.4	58.6	-15.6*
$50-$249	6,680	6,083	64.2	57.8	-10.0*
$250 or more	3,955	3,693	38.0	35.1	-7.6‡
Attempted	789	629	7.6	6.0	-21.1*

Note: Completed violent crimes include rape, sexual assault, robbery with or without injury, aggravated assault with injury, and simple assault with minor injury. The total population age 12 or older was 221,880,960 in 1998 and 219,839,810 in 1997. The total number of households was 105,322,920 in 1998 and 103,988,670 in 1997.
. . .Not applicable.
*The difference from 1997 to 1998 is significant at the 95% confidence level.
‡The difference from 1997 to 1998 is significant at the 90% confidence level.
[a]The NCVS is based on interviews with victims and therefore cannot measure murder.
[b]Includes pocket picking, purse snatching, and attempted purse snatching not shown separately.
[c]Includes thefts with unknown losses.

Source: Callie Marie Rennison, *Criminal Victimization 1998 — Changes 1997-98 with Trends 1993-98*, Bureau of Justice Statistics, Washington, DC, 1999

40 percent of simple assaults. Females were more likely than males and Blacks more likely than Whites to report a victimization to the police.

Numbers and Rates of Crimes

In 1998, U.S. residents age 12 and older experienced a total of 31.3 million crimes, of which one-quarter (8.1 million) were violent crimes and the other three-quarters (22.9 million) were property crimes. The victimization rate was 36.6 violent victimizations per 1,000 persons and 217.4 property crimes per 1,000 households. From 1997 to 1998, the violent crime rate decreased 6.6 percent, and the rate of property crime went down 12.4 percent, a significant decrease in one year. (See Table 8.4.) These declines followed a general downward trend of criminal victimization rates over the past five years. Indeed, the victimization rates are the lowest recorded by the NCVS since its inception in 1973.

Violent Victimizations

From 1993 to 1998, rates of violent victimizations fell 27 percent, from 50 per 1,000 Americans age 12 or older to about 37 per 1,000. The 8.1 million violent crimes occurring in 1998 included almost 333,000 rapes and sexual assaults, 886,000 robberies, 1.7 million aggravated assaults, and 5.2 million simple assaults. During 1998, there were fewer than 1 rape, 4 completed or attempted robberies, 7.5 aggravated assaults, and 23.5 simple assaults per 1,000 persons age 12 and older. (See Table 8.4.)

Property Crimes

In 1998, most crimes (73 percent) committed were property crimes (burglaries, motor vehicle thefts, or thefts). About 4 million household burglaries occurred in 1998. Almost one-third (32 percent) of the total (1.3 million victimizations) were forcible entries, and just over 2 million were unlawful entries without force. About 674,000 were unsuccessful attempts to enter using force. About 1.1 million car thefts were reported. For every 1,000 households, there were 38.5 burglaries, nearly 11 motor vehicle thefts, and 168 property thefts in 1998. (See Table 8.4.)

Characteristics of Victims

Personal Crimes

Males, young persons, Blacks, residents of central cities, and the poor tend to have higher rates of victimization than other persons. For every violent crime category except rape and sexual assault, victimization rates were significantly higher for males than females. Males were twice as likely to experience aggravated assault.

Blacks were somewhat more likely than Whites and significantly more likely than persons of other races, such as Asians or Native Americans, to be victims of violent crime. Blacks were more than one and one-half times as likely as Whites to be robbed or to experience aggravated assault. In 1998, 11.9 aggravated assaults per 1,000 Black persons age 12 or older occurred, compared to 7 per 1,000 Whites and 6.6 per 1,000 persons in other racial

TABLE 8.5

Rates of violent crime and personal theft, by gender, age, race, and Hispanic origin, 1998

Characteristic of victim	Population	Victimizations per 1,000 persons age 12 or older						Personal theft
		Violent crimes						
		All crimes of violence*	Rape/ Sexual assault	Robbery	Assault			
					Total	Aggra- vated	Simple	
Gender								
Male	107,595,530	43.1	0.2	4.6	38.3	10.5	27.8	1.2
Female	114,285,430	30.4	2.7	3.5	24.3	4.7	19.5	1.5
Age								
12-15	15,781,590	82.4	3.5	7.7	71.2	12.2	58.9	2.0
16-19	15,620,290	91.1	5.0	11.4	74.7	19.0	55.7	2.3
20-24	17,663,220	67.3	4.6	7.9	54.8	16.0	38.8	1.8
25-34	39,263,480	41.5	1.7	4.2	35.6	8.4	27.3	1.0
35-49	63,428,180	29.9	0.7	3.2	26.1	6.8	19.3	1.2
50-64	37,939,800	15.4	0.2	1.7	13.5	3.3	10.2	1.6
65 or older	32,184,400	2.8	0.0	0.5	2.3	0.5	1.8	0.8
Race								
White	185,831,440	36.3	1.5	3.7	31.1	7.0	24.2	1.2
Black	27,020,600	41.7	2.0	5.9	33.7	11.9	21.8	2.1
Other	9,028,930	27.6	0.7	4.4	22.5	6.6	15.9	1.4
Hispanic origin								
Hispanic	21,699,490	32.8	0.8	6.3	25.6	6.1	19.5	1.7
Non-Hispanic	197,506,660	36.8	1.6	3.7	31.5	7.6	23.9	1.3

*The National Crime Victimization Survey includes as violent crime rape/sexual assault, robbery, and assault, but not murder and manslaughter.

TABLE 8.6

Rates of violent crime and personal theft, by household income, marital status, region, and location of residence of victims, 1998

Characteristic of victim	Population	Victimizations per 1,000 persons age 12 or older						Personal theft
		Violent crimes						
		All*	Rape/ Sexual assault	Robbery	Assault			
					Total	Aggra- vated	Simple	
Household income								
Less than $7,500	11,724,160	63.8	3.2	6.5	54.2	19.6	34.5	1.7
$7,500 - $14,999	21,132,940	49.3	2.4	5.8	41.0	11.8	29.3	1.8
$15,000 - $24,999	29,783,090	39.4	2.3	3.6	33.5	7.9	25.7	1.3
$25,000 - $34,999	28,314,520	42.0	2.4	6.9	32.8	6.3	26.5	1.1
$35,000 - $49,999	34,039,640	31.7	0.5	3.1	28.1	6.2	21.9	1.6
$50,000 - $74,999	33,179,460	32.0	0.7	2.8	28.5	6.2	22.3	1.1
$75,000 or more	29,414,500	33.1	1.2	2.9	29.0	6.2	22.8	1.0
Marital status								
Never married	68.860.090	66.6	3.1	8.0	55.5	12.9	42.5	2.0
Married	114.134.930	17.7	0.5	1.3	15.9	3.9	11.9	0.9
Divorced/separated	23.948.180	57.4	2.6	6.8	48.0	12.8	35.2	2.0
Widowed	13.632.600	6.7	0.3	1.2	5.2	1.5	3.7	0.8
Region								
Northeast	42,008,340	31.3	1.7	3.2	26.2	5.9	20.3	2.0
Midwest	53,236,240	40.2	1.8	3.8	34.5	8.5	26.0	1.0
South	79,513,720	31.0	1.1	3.8	26.2	7.2	19.0	1.2
West	47,122,670	46.7	1.6	5.2	39.9	8.4	31.5	1.3
Residence								
Urban	62,685,860	46.3	1.7	6.5	38.1	10.9	27.2	2.4
Suburban	102,775,530	35.5	1.4	3.2	30.9	6.9	24.0	1.1
Rural	56,419,570	27.6	1.5	2.6	23.6	4.9	18.7	0.5

*The National Crime Victimization Survey includes as violent crime rape/sexual assault, robbery, and assault, but not murder and manslaughter.

Source of both tables: Callie Marie Rennison, *Criminal Victimization 1998 — Changes 1997-98 with Trends 1993-98*, Bureau of Justice Statistics, Washington, DC, 1999

categories. Non-Hispanics had slightly higher violent victimization rates than Hispanics and were twice as likely as Hispanics to fall victim to rape and sexual assault. (See Table 8.5.) For Hispanics, the violent victimization rate in 1998 decreased significantly from the previous year, falling from 43 to about 33 victimizations per 1,000 Hispanics.

Victimization rates generally decline with age. Persons under age 25 had higher victimization rates than older persons. Persons ages 16 to 19 were more than twice as likely as those ages 25 to 34 and about three times as likely as those ages 35 to 49 to be victims of violent crimes. People ages 16 to 19 had a violent crime victimization rate 30 times higher than those age 65 or older. (See Table 8.5.)

Victimization rates usually decrease with increases in family income. Persons with household incomes of less than $7,500 were twice as likely to experience violent crime than persons in households with incomes of $35,000 or more. Persons in households in the middle ranges of income ($15,000 to $24,999 and $25,000 to $34,999) had similar rates of victimization, about 40 per 1,000 persons. (See Table 8.6.)

Residents of urban areas had higher victimization rates for all personal crimes than did residents of the suburbs or rural areas. They were more than twice as likely as rural residents to experience aggravated assault. Urban residents were robbed at

a rate two and one-half times the rate of residents of rural areas and twice that of suburban residents. (See Table 8.6.)

Property Crimes

Certain groups had higher property victimization rates than others. Black households experienced a higher rate of property crime (248 per 1,000 Black households) than did White households (212.6 per 1,000 White households). Hispanics had a higher rate (267.6 per 1,000 Hispanic households) than did non-Hispanics (212.5 per 1,000 non-Hispanic households). Black and Hispanic households were more than twice as likely as White non-Hispanic households to be victimized by motor vehicle theft. (See Table 8.7.)

TABLE 8.7

Household property crime victimization, by race, Hispanic origin, household income, region, and home ownership of households victimized, 1998

Characteristic of household or head of household	Number of households, 1998	Victimizations per 1,000 households			
		Total	Burglary	Motor vehicle theft	Theft
Race					
White	88.616.850	212.6	36.3	9.4	166.9
Black	12,992,210	248.0	54.8	20.1	173.1
Other	3,713,860	224.5	33.2	12.5	178.9
Hispanic origin					
Hispanic	8,497,710	267.6	44.9	22.0	200.7
Non-Hispanic	96,037,610	212.5	37.7	9.7	165.0
Household income					
Less than $7,500	7,427,400	209.0	55.4	11.1	142.5
$7,500 - $14,999	11,641,910	229.8	57.8	9.0	162.9
$15,000 - $24,999	14,878,040	211.0	42.6	12.0	156.5
$25,000 - $34,999	13,249,500	233.8	38.2	12.3	183.2
$35,000 - $49,999	14,903,750	221.7	32.7	10.8	178.3
$50,000 - $74,999	13,490,230	248.6	30.1	10.6	208.0
$75,000 or more	11,843,870	248.6	28.0	11.2	209.4
Region					
Northeast	20,186,010	159.3	26.0	8.4	124.8
Midwest	25,481,910	214.0	39.3	9.9	164.7
South	37,990,330	213.5	41.1	9.9	162.5
West	21,664,680	282.3	44.6	15.6	222.1
Residence					
Urban	31,153,220	274.2	49.3	17.8	207.0
Suburban	47,853,910	204.5	32.5	10.2	161.8
Rural	26,315,800	173.5	36.6	3.5	133.4
Home ownership					
Owned	69,145,000	189.6	31.7	8.5	149.3
Rented	36,177,920	270.6	51.5	15.1	204.0

Source: Callie Marie Rennison, *Criminal Victimization 1998 — Changes 1997-98 with Trends 1993-98*, Bureau of Justice Statistics, Washington, DC, 1999

In general, households with higher annual family incomes were victimized by household property crimes at greater rates than the lowest income households. Households with annual incomes of $50,000 or more experienced nearly 30 percent more thefts than those with incomes less than $15,000. However, households earning under $15,000 annually sustained burglaries at twice the rate of households with the highest annual earnings of $75,000 or more — 55 to 58 per 1,000 households compared to 28 per 1,000. In 1998, income was unrelated to motor vehicle theft rates. (See Table 8.7.)

For each type of property crime, urban residents had consistently higher rates than suburban or rural residents. For example, households in urban areas experienced burglaries at one and one-half times the rate of suburban households (49.3 versus 32.5). Households that rented their residences had significantly higher victimization rates than households that owned their homes. Households that rented sustained motor vehicle thefts at rates almost twice that of households that owned their residences, with 15.1 thefts per 1,000 households compared to 8.5 thefts per 1,000 households. Urban households experienced motor vehicle thefts at five times the rate of rural households. (See Table 8.7.)

Use of Weapons

In 1998, offenders used a weapon in about one-fourth (24 percent) of violent victimizations. Thirty-nine percent of robberies and 22 percent of assaults were committed by an offender with a weapon. Guns were used in 21 percent of robbery victimizations and 8 percent of all violent victimizations, while knives were used in 10 percent of robbery victimizations and 6 percent of violent victimizations. Other weapons used were either not specifically identified as to type or the weapon used was unknown.

CHAPTER IX

SPENDING OUR MONEY

The Bureau of the Census, under contract to the Bureau of Labor Statistics (BLS), conducts an ongoing two-part *Consumer Expenditure Survey* of the spending habits of the American people. The first part is the *Interview Survey,* which obtains data on the types of expenditures respondents can be expected to recall for a period of three months or longer. Respondents are interviewed every three

TABLE 9.1

Average annual expenditures of all consumer units and percent changes, Consumer Expenditure Survey, 1995-97

Item	1995	1996	1997	Percent change	
				1995-96	1996-97
Number of consumer units (in thousands)	103,123	104,212	105,576		
Income before taxes [1]	$36,918	$38,014	$39,926		
Averages:					
Age of reference person	48.0	47.7	47.7		
Number of persons in consumer unit	2.5	2.5	2.5		
Number of earners	1.3	1.3	1.3		
Number of vehicles	1.9	1.9	2.0		
Percent homeowner	64	64	64		
Average annual expenditures	$32,264	$33,797	$34,819	4.8	3.0
Food	4,505	4,698	4,801	4.3	2.2
Food at home	2,803	2,876	2,880	2.6	.1
Cereals and bakery products	441	447	453	1.4	1.3
Meats, poultry, fish, and eggs	752	737	743	-2.0	.8
Dairy products	297	312	314	5.1	.6
Fruits and vegetables	457	490	476	7.2	-2.9
Other food at home	856	889	895	3.9	.7
Food away from home	1,702	1,823	1,921	7.1	5.4
Alcoholic beverages	277	309	309	11.6	-
Housing	10,458	10,747	11,272	2.8	4.9
Shelter	5,928	6,064	6,344	2.3	4.6
Utilities, fuels, and public services	2,191	2,347	2,412	7.1	2.8
Household operations	509	522	548	2.6	5.0
Housekeeping supplies	430	464	455	7.9	-1.9
Housefurnishings and equipment	1,401	1,350	1,512	-3.6	12.0
Apparel and services	1,704	1,752	1,729	2.8	-1.3
Transportation	6,014	6,382	6,457	6.1	1.2
Vehicle purchases (net outlay)	2,638	2,815	2,736	6.7	-2.8
Gasoline and motor oil	1,006	1,082	1,098	7.6	1.5
Other vehicle expenses	2,015	2,058	2,230	2.1	8.4
Public transportation	355	427	393	20.3	-8.0
Health care	1,732	1,770	1,841	2.2	4.0
Entertainment	1,612	1,834	1,813	13.8	-1.1
Personal care products and services	403	513	528	27.3	2.9
Reading	162	159	164	-1.9	3.1
Education	471	524	571	11.3	9.0
Tobacco products and supplies	269	255	264	-5.2	3.5
Miscellaneous	766	855	847	11.6	-.9
Cash contributions	925	940	1,001	1.6	6.5
Personal insurance and pensions	2,964	3,060	3,223	3.2	5.3
Life and other personal insurance	373	353	379	-5.4	7.4
Pensions and Social Security	2,591	2,707	2,844	4.5	5.1

[1] Income values are derived from "complete income reporters" only.

Source: *Consumer Expenditures in 1997*, Report 927, Bureau of Labor Statistics, Washington, DC, 1999

TABLE 9.2

Distribution of total annual expenditures by major category, Consumer Expenditure Survey, 1994-97

Item	1994	1995	1996	1997
Average annual expenditures	100.0	100.0	100.0	100.0
Food	13.9	14.0	13.9	13.8
Food at home	8.5	8.7	8.5	8.3
Food away from home	5.4	5.3	5.4	5.5
Housing	31.8	32.4	31.8	32.4
Apparel and services	5.2	5.3	5.2	5.0
Transportation	19.0	18.6	18.9	18.5
Vehicles	8.6	8.2	8.3	7.9
Gasoline and motor oil	3.1	3.1	3.2	3.2
Other transportation	7.4	7.3	7.4	7.5
Health care	5.5	5.4	5.2	5.3
Entertainment	4.9	5.0	5.4	5.2
Personal insurance and pensions	9.3	9.2	9.1	9.3
Life and other personal insurance	1.3	1.2	1.0	1.1
Pensions and Social Security	8.0	8.0	8.0	8.2
Other expenditures[1]	10.3	10.1	10.5	10.6

[1] Includes alcoholic beverages, personal care products and services, reading, education, tobacco products and supplies, cash contributions, and miscellaneous.

Source: *Consumer Expenditures in 1997*, Report 927, Bureau of Labor Statistics, Washington, DC, 1999

months over a period of five calendar quarters. In general, these recollections include relatively large expenditures, such as real property, automobiles, and major appliances, or expenditures that occur on a fairly regular basis, such as rent, utilities, or insurance premiums. Overnight trips are also included in this category, but business-related expenditures are not. Approximately 95 percent of all expenditures are covered in this survey.

Part two, the *Diary Survey*, is designed to obtain expenditures on small, frequently purchased items, which are normally difficult for people to remember. In the *Diary Survey*, 5,000 households are asked to keep a diary of all expenses for two one-week periods, resulting in a total of 10,000 diaries. These diaries cover spending for groceries, eating out, tobacco, housekeeping supplies, nonprescription drugs, and personal care products and services.

The *Consumer Expenditure Survey* is the only national survey that thoroughly examines consumer spending in all types of households. Survey results are used by government and private agencies and companies to determine the spending patterns of Americans.

GENERAL SPENDING

In 1997, the average family earned about $39,926 before taxes, had 2.5 people in the household, was headed by a 48-year-old person, and had 2 vehicles. About 1.3 members of the household worked outside the home. (See Table 9.1.) The typical family spent almost two-thirds of its total expenditures on housing (32.4 percent), transportation (18.5 percent), and food (13.8 percent). (See Table 9.2.) The distribution of expenditures among the major spending components changed very little from 1994 to 1997.

Average annual expenditures per consumer unit rose about 3 percent from 1996 to 1997. (See Table 9.1.) This increase continued the trend of modest increases over the past several years. The change in expenditures in 1997 was slightly more than the 2.3 percent increase in general price levels. Spending on education increased 9 percent; on cash contributions, 6.5 percent; eating out, 5.4 percent; personal insurance and pensions, 5.3 percent; housing, 4.9 percent (including a 12 percent increase in furnishings and equipment); and health care, 4 percent.

TABLE 9.3

Income before taxes: Average annual expenditures and characteristics, Consumer Expenditure Survey, 1997

Item	Complete reporting of income									
	Total complete reporting	Less than $5,000	$5,000 to $9,999	$10,000 to $14,999	$15,000 to $19,999	$20,000 to $29,999	$30,000 to $39,999	$40,000 to $49,999	$50,000 to $69,999	$70,000 and over
Number of consumer units (in thousands) ..	84,991	4,178	8,904	9,096	7,424	12,415	10,392	7,949	11,930	12,705
Consumer unit characteristics:										
Income before taxes [1]	$39,926	$2,050	$7,708	$12,411	$17,393	$24,599	$34,583	$44,396	$58,249	$107,170
Age of reference person	47.8	39.9	54.6	54.6	51.1	48.6	45.1	44.4	44.3	45.5
Average number in consumer unit:										
Persons	2.5	1.8	1.7	2.1	2.3	2.4	2.6	2.8	3.0	3.1
Children under 18	.7	.5	.4	.6	.6	.6	.7	.8	.9	.9
Persons 65 and over	.3	.2	.5	.6	.5	.4	.2	.2	.2	.1
Earners	1.3	.8	.5	.7	1.0	1.2	1.5	1.7	1.9	2.1
Vehicles	2.0	1.0	.9	1.3	1.7	1.8	2.2	2.4	2.7	3.0
Percent homeowner	64	31	40	53	57	58	62	72	81	88
Average annual expenditures	$36,146	$16,545	$15,154	$18,737	$23,940	$27,836	$34,376	$40,779	$48,417	$71,656
Food	4,902	2,711	2,601	3,006	3,764	4,109	4,888	5,429	6,220	8,279
Food at home	2,970	1,714	1,853	2,155	2,634	2,701	3,062	3,221	3,556	4,315
Cereals and bakery products	465	277	275	322	412	421	489	506	549	691
Meats, poultry, fish, and eggs	756	452	498	604	726	728	774	774	880	1,024
Dairy products	329	190	195	242	281	295	332	374	395	487
Fruits and vegetables	485	289	317	361	433	444	479	496	565	735
Other food at home	935	506	569	626	782	813	987	1,072	1,167	1,378
Food away from home	1,932	997	748	851	1,129	1,408	1,826	2,208	2,664	3,964
Alcoholic beverages	330	180	145	128	190	256	319	363	417	699
Housing	11,348	5,993	5,587	6,878	8,047	8,782	10,653	12,359	14,380	21,816
Shelter	6,339	3,446	2,980	3,765	4,376	4,832	6,004	6,969	7,827	12,590
Owned dwellings	3,933	1,255	976	1,591	1,878	2,253	3,243	4,454	5,793	9,898
Rented dwellings	1,980	2,003	1,910	2,048	2,292	2,371	2,536	2,137	1,540	1,266
Other lodging	426	189	94	126	206	208	225	378	494	1,425
Utilities, fuels, and public services	2,408	1,386	1,568	1,835	2,136	2,218	2,403	2,599	2,933	3,478
Household operations	562	206	187	315	304	354	359	500	754	1,496
Housekeeping supplies	485	240	250	301	347	394	482	524	651	833
Household furnishings and equipment	1,554	713	602	662	885	985	1,405	1,767	2,214	3,420
Apparel and services	1,786	948	769	771	1,184	1,363	1,772	1,778	2,614	3,442
Transportation	6,669	2,540	2,218	3,146	4,234	5,249	7,139	8,444	9,436	12,387
Vehicle purchases (net outlay)	2,856	944	872	1,260	1,728	2,276	3,382	4,074	4,085	4,900
Gasoline and motor oil	1,110	546	490	646	841	963	1,181	1,331	1,547	1,758
Other vehicle expenses	2,312	857	711	1,090	1,448	1,753	2,288	2,681	3,319	4,683
Public transportation	390	193	145	150	217	257	288	358	485	1,046
Health care	1,898	842	1,219	1,563	1,830	1,918	1,820	2,052	2,214	2,642
Entertainment	1,868	752	648	832	1,062	1,274	1,514	2,054	2,654	4,300
Personal care products and services	551	216	255	329	402	497	594	571	708	957
Reading	171	74	70	93	113	141	159	170	233	346
Education	548	676	385	293	287	354	398	499	722	1,131
Tobacco products and smoking supplies	271	210	215	248	272	263	321	286	316	262
Miscellaneous	888	532	479	441	662	705	881	1,207	1,170	1,456
Cash contributions	1,085	568	232	381	828	999	841	1,176	1,188	2,635
Personal insurance and pensions	3,830	303	331	629	1,066	1,926	3,077	4,390	6,145	11,304
Life and other personal insurance	387	96	123	169	214	295	306	360	571	921
Pensions and Social Security	3,444	207	208	460	852	1,630	2,770	4,030	5,574	10,382

[1] Components of income and taxes are derived from "complete income reporters" only.

Source: *Consumer Expenditures in 1997*, Report 927, Bureau of Labor Statistics, Washington, DC, 1999

CHARACTERISTICS OF CONSUMERS

The greater the number of working household members, the more the family earned, with those in the highest one-fifth (quintile) averaging 2.1 earners per family. Not surprisingly, the more a family earned, the more vehicles they owned. Those in the highest 20 percent averaged 2.9 vehicles. Families in the first and second quintiles had 1.0 and 1.6 vehicles, respectively. Furthermore,

TABLE 9.4

Housing tenure, type of area, race of reference person, and Hispanic origin of reference person:
Average annual expenditures and characteristics, Consumer Expenditure Survey, 1997

Item	All consumer units	Housing tenure		Type of area		Race of reference person		Hispanic origin of reference person	
		Homeowner	Renter	Urban	Rural	White and other	Black	Hispanic	Non-Hispanic
Number of consumer units (in thousands) ..	105,576	67,249	38,327	92,216	13,360	93,004	12,572	8,905	96,670
Consumer unit characteristics:									
Income before taxes [1]	$39,926	$47,898	$26,031	$41,072	$32,299	$41,382	$28,678	$29,976	$40,907
Age of reference person	47.7	52.2	39.9	47.4	50.2	48.1	45.0	42.0	48.3
Average number in consumer unit:									
Persons	2.5	2.7	2.2	2.5	2.5	2.5	2.8	3.4	2.4
Children under 18	.7	.7	.7	.7	.6	.7	1.0	1.3	.6
Persons 65 and over	.3	.4	.1	.3	.3	.3	.2	.2	.3
Earners	1.3	1.4	1.2	1.3	1.4	1.4	1.2	1.6	1.3
Vehicles	2.0	2.4	1.2	1.9	2.5	2.1	1.2	1.7	2.0
Percent homeowner	64	100	n.a.	61	79	66	44	47	65
Average annual expenditures	$34,819	$40,480	$24,866	$35,614	$29,353	$36,076	$25,509	$29,333	$35,325
Food	4,801	5,432	3,684	4,897	4,150	4,967	3,571	4,869	4,796
Food at home	2,880	3,219	2,280	2,905	2,707	2,929	2,515	3,363	2,839
Cereals and bakery products	453	510	352	459	413	463	376	468	452
Meats, poultry, fish, and eggs	743	818	611	752	684	727	861	1,057	716
Dairy products	314	352	246	316	301	328	210	346	311
Fruits and vegetables	476	526	386	486	407	485	402	607	464
Other food at home	895	1,013	685	893	902	925	666	884	896
Food away from home	1,921	2,214	1,404	1,992	1,442	2,038	1,056	1,506	1,958
Alcoholic beverages	309	324	283	329	174	332	137	206	318
Housing	11,272	12,712	8,742	11,712	8,238	11,573	9,044	9,907	11,397
Shelter	6,344	6,726	5,673	6,716	3,778	6,512	5,098	5,797	6,394
Owned dwellings	3,935	6,143	61	4,115	2,691	4,165	2,235	2,672	4,051
Rented dwellings	1,983	33	5,405	2,151	827	1,883	2,721	2,972	1,892
Other lodging	426	550	207	450	260	464	143	153	451
Utilities, fuels, and public services	2,412	2,864	1,619	2,404	2,472	2,406	2,461	2,169	2,435
Household operations	548	686	308	586	287	571	379	322	569
Housekeeping supplies	455	557	275	454	459	477	289	398	460
Household furnishings and equipment ...	1,512	1,879	867	1,552	1,243	1,606	818	1,220	1,539
Apparel and services	1,729	1,991	1,266	1,772	1,435	1,742	1,631	1,958	1,709
Transportation	6,457	7,622	4,412	6,455	6,472	6,687	4,754	5,585	6,537
Vehicle purchases (net outlay)	2,736	3,253	1,829	2,691	3,042	2,830	2,036	2,367	2,770
Gasoline and motor oil	1,098	1,276	784	1,065	1,322	1,138	798	1,095	1,098
Other vehicle expenses	2,230	2,649	1,497	2,273	1,939	2,310	1,640	1,785	2,271
Public transportation	393	444	303	426	168	408	280	339	398
Health care	1,841	2,289	1,054	1,819	1,988	1,950	1,035	1,167	1,903
Entertainment	1,813	2,202	1,130	1,851	1,551	1,940	872	1,137	1,875
Personal care products and services	528	602	397	542	425	514	631	479	532
Reading	164	199	102	169	125	175	77	66	173
Education	571	582	550	616	257	612	269	456	581
Tobacco products and smoking supplies	264	265	261	251	349	276	170	111	278
Miscellaneous	847	976	621	865	727	886	563	694	862
Cash contributions	1,001	1,284	504	1,032	789	1,046	669	398	1,056
Personal insurance and pensions	3,223	4,000	1,861	3,303	2,673	3,377	2,086	2,299	3,308
Life and other personal insurance	379	510	148	378	381	386	321	205	395
Pensions and Social Security	2,844	3,490	1,712	2,925	2,291	2,990	1,765	2,095	2,913

[1] Components of income and taxes are derived from "complete income reporters" only.
n.a. Not applicable

Source: *Consumer Expenditures in 1997*, Report 927, Bureau of Labor Statistics, Washington, DC, 1999

the more the family earned, the more likely they were to be homeowners. (See Table 9.3.)

Black families generally earned less than White and other families, Hispanics less than non-Hispanics, renters less than homeowners, and rural residents less than those in urban settings. Indeed, although the number of wage earners was not very different for Black families (1.2 wage earners) than for White and other families (1.4 wage earners),

159

Blacks earned much less. Hispanic families had somewhat more wage earners (1.6) per family than non-Hispanics (1.3) but earned significantly less income. (See Table 9.4.)

Black families owned 1.2 cars, compared to 2.1 cars for Whites and others. Ownership of vehicles differed somewhat between Hispanics (1.7 per family) and non-Hispanics (2.0 per family). Black and Hispanic families were somewhat less likely to own their homes (44 and 47 percent, respectively) than Whites and others and non-Hispanic families (66 and 65 percent, respectively). (See Table 9.4.)

SPENDING PATTERNS

Just as the U.S. economy is affected by wars, economic declines, technological advances, and changes in population demographics and the labor force, spending patterns also change. In the mid-1930s, the average family spent over one-third of its total expenditures on food. By 1960-1961, housing had replaced food as the largest portion of total spending. The share spent on apparel, like the share spent on food, decreased by 50 percent from 1935-1936 to 1996-1997.

Not surprisingly, spending varies dramatically depending on the earnings of the household. In 1997, on average, the lowest, second, and third quintiles spent more than they earned, reflecting at least some dependence on government assistance, support from friends and/or family, and debt. Generally, for virtually every quintile, the more the family earned, the more they spent on most categories. However, the proportion of the income spent varied significantly. While the richest 20 percent spent more than three times as much as the poorest 20 percent, the richest spent only 21 percent of their pretax income on housing, while the poorest spent 84 percent. Similarly, while the richest 20 percent spent three times as much on food as the poorest 20 percent, the poorest fifth spent about 38 percent of their income on food, compared to just over 8 percent for the wealthiest quintile. (See Table 9.3.)

Little Left for "a Rainy Day"

With at least three-fifths of American households spending more than they earn, most Americans have little left to put aside for "a rainy day" — their children's college education, the down payment on a home, retirement (above and beyond what they contribute to a pension fund or to Social Security), or an investment that might earn them money. Even the fourth quintile had just $5,632 left over for taxes and other payments after their other expenditures were considered. Consequently, the amount of money saved for retirement among 80 percent of the population was little more than the Social Security contributions automatically taken from their salaries.

CHAPTER X

HOUSING

OVERVIEW

Every two years, the Bureau of the Census surveys housing in the United States. The latest is the *American Housing Survey for the United States in 1997* (1999). In addition, the Census Bureau releases periodic updates on various housing indicators.

In 1997, there were an estimated 112.4 million housing units in the United States, up 37 million homes from 75.5 million in 1973. About 46 percent of these homes were in the suburbs, 30 percent were in central cities of Metropolitan Statistical Areas (MSAs — defined as an urban area of at least 50,000 population with a total metropolitan population of at least 100,000; 75,000 in New England), and one-quarter (24 percent) were in areas outside of MSAs. (See Table 10.1.) By third quarter 1999, there were an estimated 119.6 housing units in the United States.

Recently, most housing growth has been in the South, accounting for 45 percent of the homes constructed from 1994 to 1998. In 1997, the largest proportion (36 percent) of the nation's housing was also in the South. Approximately one-quarter (24 percent) of all U.S. housing was located in the Midwest, followed by the West (21 percent) and the Northeast (19 percent). (See Table 10.1.)

HOME OWNERSHIP

Home ownership is at the highest rate it has ever been.* In the third quarter 1999, home-ownership had risen to 67 percent. (See Table 10.2.) Historically, the home-ownership rate plunged to about 44 percent in 1940 from 77 percent in 1930 as a result of the Great Depression. Since then, home ownership increased virtually every year through 1980, after which it leveled off. The rate started to rise again in 1995. Mortgage rates soared during the late 1970s and early 1980s, and while they have dropped sharply since, the cost of buying a home is still beyond the reach of many prospective house buyers. In 1997, according to the National Association of Home Builders, in *Housing Facts, Figures and Trends* (Washington, DC, 1998), only a little more than one-third of all American households could afford to buy a median-priced house.

Home ownership was most frequent among those living outside the central cities (suburbs) and outside the metropolitan areas (MSAs). Only half of those living in the central cities owned their

---

* Owning one's own home has traditionally meant that the householder arranges a mortgage with a bank. The bank loans money to the buyer, who uses it to purchase the home; the homeowner then repays the bank. This payment to the bank includes interest on the borrowed money that, along with the actual cost of the house, is the major factor that determines the amount of the monthly payment. It is unusual for a person to be able to pay for a home outright without help from a bank. In 1998, for example, only 5 percent of homes were bought with cash.

TABLE 10.1

Introductory Characteristics—All Housing Units

[Numbers in thousands. Consistent with the 1990 Census. ... means not applicable or sample too small. – means zero or rounds to zero]

| Characteristics | Total housing units | Seasonal | Year-round | | | | | | | | | | | New construction 4 years | Mobile homes |
| | | | Occupied | | | | Vacant | | | | | | | | |
			Total	Total	Owner	Renter	Total	For rent	Rental vacancy rate	For sale only	Rented or sold	Occasional use/URE	Other vacant		
Total	112 357	3 166	109 191	99 487	65 487	34 000	9 704	2 884	7.8	1 043	753	2 796	2 228	6 503	8 301
Units in Structure															
1, detached	68 109	1 831	66 278	62 111	53 756	8 355	4 167	574	6.4	682	377	1 277	1 257	3 912	...
1, attached	6 778	157	6 622	5 840	3 030	2 810	781	280	9.0	98	68	181	154	453	...
2 to 4	10 363	129	10 234	8 973	1 756	7 216	1 261	646	8.1	69	75	197	274	239	...
5 to 9	5 657	78	5 579	4 852	491	4 361	727	412	8.5	24	64	153	74	231	...
10 to 19	5 025	59	4 966	4 264	319	3 945	702	398	9.1	18	45	182	59	233	...
20 to 49	3 877	75	3 801	3 292	355	2 936	509	239	7.5	17	27	192	34	201	...
50 or more	4 247	108	4 139	3 611	524	3 087	528	203	6.1	17	45	192	72	72	...
Mobile home or trailer	8 301	729	7 572	6 544	5 255	1 289	1 028	132	9.2	119	51	423	303	1 163	8 301
Cooperatives and Condominiums															
Cooperatives	775	47	727	618	382	236	109	23	8.9	16	16	47	8	7	52
Condominiums	6 922	499	6 423	5 308	3 167	2 141	1 115	220	9.2	124	82	510	180	498	115
Metropolitan/Nonmetropolitan Areas															
Inside metropolitan statistical areas	85 466	1 283	84 183	77 417	48 998	28 418	6 767	2 245	7.3	745	611	1 659	1 507	4 741	4 093
In central cities	34 062	199	33 864	30 533	14 938	15 595	3 331	1 310	7.7	280	266	695	781	918	422
Suburbs	51 404	1 084	50 320	46 884	34 061	12 823	3 436	935	6.8	466	345	964	726	3 823	3 671
Outside metropolitan statistical areas	26 891	1 884	25 007	22 070	16 489	5 582	2 937	639	10.2	297	142	1 138	721	1 762	4 207
Regions															
Northeast	21 776	747	21 029	19 484	12 241	7 242	1 546	478	6.1	158	129	451	330	562	705
Midwest	26 580	718	25 862	23 951	16 902	7 050	1 911	620	8.0	214	187	463	427	1 391	1 479
South	40 403	1 119	39 283	34 808	23 650	11 157	4 476	1 215	9.7	469	279	1 404	1 109	3 101	4 489
West	23 599	583	23 016	21 245	12 694	8 551	1 772	571	6.2	202	159	478	362	1 449	1 627

Source: *American Housing Survey for the United States: 1997*, Bureau of the Census, Washington, DC, 1999

---

homes. By the third quarter 1999, people living in the Midwest (72.1 percent) and South (69.3 percent) were more likely to own their own homes than those in the Northeast (63.6 percent) and West (60.8 percent). (See Table 10.3.) While only 20.4 percent of householders under 25 owned homes, by the time householders were 45 years old or older, more than three-fourths owned their own homes. (See Table 10.4.)

PAYING FOR HOMES

Although the rise in the cost of housing has slowed recently, past increases have been significant. The average price of a new, single-family home rose from $30,500 in 1972 to $154,500 in 1994. By 1998, the price had reached $181,900. In September 1999, the price for a home averaged $196,900, the highest average price ever. The median price (half the homes cost more and half cost less) for a home in 1998 was $152,500 and $160,000 in September 1999. (See Table 10.5.)

General inflation played a major role in the price rise over the last 25 years. Another contrib-

uting factor is that, in the 1980s, builders began constructing larger houses with more conveniences, making them more expensive.

Regional Price Differences

Regionally, new housing prices can vary substantially. Housing costs in the Northeast were considerably higher than in the other regions. The average new house in the Northeast rose 31 percent from $183,600 in 1993 to $240,100 in 1998. Meanwhile the huge increases that had once characterized housing prices in the West have slowed. Between 1993 and 1998, new housing prices increased 25 percent in the Midwest, 24 percent in the West, and 19.5 percent in the South. (See Table 10.6.)

The Price Range of New Homes Sold

In 1974, more than 8 of 10 houses sold for less than $50,000. By the 1980s, the *Current Housing Surveys* raised the lowest category to "under $60,000," and in the 1990s, the bottom category became "under $80,000." In 1986, about 2 out of

TABLE 10.2

Homeownership Rates for the United States

Year	First Quarter	Second Quarter	Third Quarter	Fourth Quarter
1999.....	66.7	66.6	67.0	
1998.....	65.9	66.0	66.8	66.4
1997.....	65.4	65.7	66.0	65.7
1996.....	65.1	65.4	65.6	65.4
1995.....	64.2	64.7	65.0	65.1
1994.....	63.8	63.8	64.1	64.2
1993\r...	63.7	63.9	64.2	64.2
1993.....	64.2	64.4	64.7	64.6
1992.....	64.0	63.9	64.3	64.4
1991.....	63.9	63.9	64.2	64.2
1990.....	64.0	63.7	64.0	64.1
1989\r...	63.9	63.8	64.1	63.8
1989.....	63.9	63.9	64.0	63.8
1988.....	63.7	63.7	64.0	63.8
1987.....	63.8	63.8	64.2	64.1
1986.....	63.6	63.8	63.8	63.9
1985.....	64.1	64.1	63.9	63.5
1984.....	64.6	64.6	64.6	64.1
1983.....	64.7	64.7	64.8	64.4
1982.....	64.8	64.9	64.9	64.5
1981.....	65.6	65.3	65.6	65.2
1980.....	65.5	65.5	65.8	65.5
1979\r...	64.8	64.9	65.8	65.4
1979.....	65.3	65.1	66.0	65.8
1978.....	64.8	64.4	65.2	65.4
1977.....	64.8	64.5	65.0	64.9
1976.....	64.6	64.6	64.9	64.8
1975.....	64.4	64.9	64.6	64.5
1974.....	64.8	64.8	64.6	64.4
1973.....	64.9	64.4	64.4	64.4
1972.....	64.3	64.5	64.3	64.4
1971.....	64.0	64.1	64.4	64.5
1970.....	64.3	64.0	64.4	64.0
1969.....	64.1	64.4	64.4	64.4
1968.....	63.6	64.1	64.1	63.6
1967.....	63.3	63.9	63.8	63.5
1966.....	63.5	63.2	63.3	63.8
1965.....	62.9	62.9	62.9	63.4

\r Revised.

Source: *Housing Vacancy Survey: Third Quarter 1999*, Bureau of the Census, Washington, DC, 1999

5 houses (38 percent) sold for less than $80,000. By 1990, about 21 percent did; by 1998, fewer than 5 percent of houses sold for less than $80,000.

While only the rich even thought of a house costing more than $100,000 in 1976, more than 4 of 5 homes (85 percent) sold for more than $100,000 in 1998. A $200,000 home, bought by barely 1 in 12 in 1986, was purchased by 28 percent of those buying homes in 1998. (See Table 10.5 for 1994 through September 1999 statistics.)

Value of All Homes

In 1997, the median value (half cost more, half cost less) of all homes was $98,815. Homes built in the previous four years had a median value of $130,701. The median value of homes owned by Black householders was $72,750 and by Hispanic householders, $86,770. The median value of homes owned by the elderly was $89,294. Suburban homes in metropolitan areas ($118,548) were more expensive than homes in the central cities ($92,623) and in rural areas ($90,489). The median value of homes outside metropolitan areas was $73,478. Regionally, the median value of homes in the West ($141,236) ran much higher than homes in other regions. (See Table 10.7.)

Housing Costs

The *Consumer Expenditure Survey* (Bureau of Labor Statistics) estimated that Americans spent about one-third (32 percent) of their annual expenditures on housing in 1997 (Table 9.2 in Chapter IX). For the past five years, the cost of housing has been increasing slightly less than the consumer price index (CPI). The CPI measures the rate of inflation based on the years 1982-1984 (100). The CPI for all items in 1998 was 163.0; for housing, 160.4; for food, 160.7; and for health care, 242.1. (See Table 10.8.)

In 1997, the median monthly cost for housing was $542. Renters ($549) paid somewhat more a month than homeowners ($534), in contrast to

TABLE 10.3

Homeownership Rates by Area: Third Quarter 1999 and 1998

Area	Third quarter 1999	Third quarter 1998
United States.....................	67.0	66.8
Inside MAs......................	64.9	64.8
In central cities.............	50.5	50.5
Not in central cities (suburbs)	73.7	73.8
Outside MAs.....................	75.8	75.0
Northeast........................	63.6	63.4
Midwest..........................	72.1	71.7
South............................	69.3	68.8
West.............................	60.8	61.1

Source: *Housing Vacancy Survey: Third Quarter 1999*, Bureau of the Census, Washington, DC, 1999

163

TABLE 10.4

Homeownership Rates by Age of Householder:
Third Quarter 1999 and 1998

Age of householder	Third Quarter 1999	Third Quarter 1998
United States..............	67.0	66.8
Less than 25 years.....	20.4	18.1
25 to 29 years.........	36.9	35.8
30 to 34 years.........	54.2	54.6
35 to 39 years.........	65.1	64.6
40 to 44 years.........	69.6	71.0
45 to 49 years.........	75.1	74.7
50 to 54 years.........	77.8	78.3
55 to 59 years.........	80.1	79.9
60 to 64 years.........	81.3	82.4
65 to 69 years.........	82.9	82.1
70 to 74 years.........	83.2	82.1
75 years and over......	78.2	77.1
Less than 35 years...	40.1	39.5
35 to 44 years.......	67.4	67.8
45 to 54 years.......	76.3	76.3
55 to 64 years.......	80.7	81.1
65 years and over....	80.8	79.7

Source: *Housing Vacancy Survey: Third Quarter 1999*, Bureau of the Census, Washington, DC, 1999

1995, when renters paid less. Those who moved in the past year ($593) paid more than the median monthly costs, as did those who lived in the suburbs of metropolitan areas ($639). (See Table 10.9.)

WHO CAN AFFORD TO BUY A HOME?

In *Who Can Afford to Buy a House in 1995?* (Washington, DC, 1999), the Bureau of the Census concluded that 55.6 percent of families could afford a modestly priced house in the area where they lived, a percentage that has been declining. (This proportion was based on 30-year conventional fixed-rate financing with a 5 percent down payment.) (See Table 10.10.) (A modestly priced house is one priced so that 25 percent of all owner-occupied houses in the area are below this value and 75 percent are above.)

Regional Comparisons

Almost half of all families and unrelated individuals in the South and the Northeast could af-

ford a modestly priced house in 1995. A home was more affordable in the Midwest (55 percent), but less so in the West (39 percent). In central cities of metropolitan areas, 38 percent could afford a modestly priced house, compared to 55 percent in suburban areas and 51 percent outside metropolitan areas.

Owners or Renters

The ability to purchase a modestly priced house differed significantly by whether people currently owned or rented their present residence. For renters, only 10 percent could afford a modestly priced home in 1995. In contrast, 71 percent of owners could afford to relocate to a modestly priced home in the same area in 1995.

Marital Status, Race, and Ethnicity

While half of all families could afford a modestly priced house in 1995, affordability varied greatly by type of family and marital status. Two-thirds (66 percent) of married couples, one-third (36 percent) of male-householder families, 1 of 5 (22 percent) female-householder families, and one-third (34 percent) of all unrelated individuals could afford a modestly priced house. For married couples with children under 18, 56 percent could afford a house, while for those with no children under 18, about three-quarters (74 percent) could afford a house.

More Whites could afford modestly priced homes than Blacks and more non-Hispanics than Hispanics. More than three-quarters (78 percent) of White (non-Hispanic) families and those of non-Hispanic origin (76 percent) who owned homes could afford a modestly priced home, compared to 53 percent of Black families and 52 percent of Hispanic-origin families. (See Figure 10.1.)

About 1 of 5 (19 percent) White married-couple renters could qualify to buy a modestly priced house, compared to only 8 percent of Black mar-

TABLE 10.5

Houses Sold by Sales Price

[Thousands of houses. Components may not add to total because of rounding. Percents computed from unrounded figures]

Period	Total	Number of houses[1]						Percent distribution[2]						Median sales price (dollars)	Average sales price (dollars)
		Under $80,000	$80,000 to $99,999	$100,000 to $119,999	$120,000 to $149,999	$150,000 to $199,999	$200,000 and over	Under $80,000	$80,000 to $99,999	$100,000 to $119,999	$120,000 to $149,999	$150,000 to $199,999	$200,000 and over		
ANNUAL DATA															
1994	670	72	108	93	140	129	127	11	16	14	21	19	19	130,000	154,500
1995	667	58	101	99	144	127	138	9	15	15	22	19	21	133,900	158,700
1996	757	59	104	101	159	160	175	8	14	13	21	21	23	140,000	166,400
1997	804	51	93	103	173	177	207	6	12	13	21	22	26	146,000	176,200
1998	886	41	91	112	183	208	251	5	10	13	21	23	28	152,500	181,900
MONTHLY DATA															
1997: January	61	3	8	8	13	13	15	6	13	13	22	21	25	145,000	171,900
February	69	5	9	9	15	14	18	7	13	13	21	20	26	143,000	171,100
March	81	7	9	12	15	19	20	8	11	14	18	23	25	148,000	172,700
April	70	5	7	9	14	16	19	7	10	13	20	23	28	150,000	179,500
May	71	4	9	9	15	15	17	6	13	13	22	22	24	141,000	170,700
June	71	4	9	9	17	14	19	5	12	12	24	20	27	145,000	179,400
July	69	4	8	9	15	15	18	6	12	13	21	22	26	145,900	175,500
August	72	5	9	10	15	17	17	6	13	14	21	24	23	144,000	170,700
September	67	4	8	8	14	15	17	6	12	12	21	23	25	146,300	177,500
October	62	3	7	9	14	13	15	5	11	15	23	21	24	141,500	172,900
November	61	4	8	7	13	13	16	6	13	12	22	22	25	145,000	175,400
December	51	4	5	6	12	11	13	7	10	11	23	23	25	145,900	175,800
1998: January	64	3	8	9	13	14	17	4	12	14	21	22	27	148,000	178,600
February	75	3	8	11	13	18	23	4	10	15	17	23	31	156,000	181,600
March	81	3	8	10	17	20	22	4	10	12	21	25	27	152,700	178,500
April	82	4	9	11	19	18	22	5	11	13	23	22	26	148,000	176,700
May	82	4	9	11	15	20	23	5	11	13	19	24	28	153,200	183,500
June	83	5	10	10	18	19	21	6	12	12	22	22	26	148,000	175,900
July	75	5	8	10	15	16	21	6	10	14	20	21	28	149,900	179,800
August	75	4	7	9	16	17	23	5	10	12	21	22	30	154,900	186,500
September	68	2	7	8	14	18	18	3	10	12	21	27	26	155,000	182,700
October	69	3	7	9	13	16	21	5	11	13	18	23	30	154,500	182,800
November	70	3	6	9	16	17	19	4	9	12	23	24	27	151,000	178,600
December	61	3	5	7	14	15	17	6	8	11	23	24	28	152,500	183,300
1999: January	67	3	7	7	15	17	18	4	11	11	23	25	27	152,500	182,800
February	78	3	6	10	17	17	26	4	7	13	21	21	33	159,900	191,400
March	86	3	8	11	18	21	26	3	9	13	21	24	30	155,000	189,400
April	88	2	10	9	18	21	28	3	11	11	20	23	32	160,000	191,400
May	83	3	7	10	19	18	26	4	8	13	23	21	31	154,800	188,200
June	86	3	6	10	18	20	28	4	7	12	21	23	33	158,300	193,400
July[r]	81	4	7	11	15	19	26	5	9	13	18	23	32	157,900	188,600
August[r]	83	3	7	9	21	19	25	4	8	11	26	22	29	153,900	192,400
September[p]	62	3	6	6	13	14	21	4	9	10	20	23	33	160,000	196,900
AVERAGE RELATIVE STANDARD ERRORS															
Annual (percent)	2	7	5	6	5	5	5	7	5	6	5	5	5	2	2
Monthly (percent)	4	24	16	13	8	8	7	24	15	12	7	7	6	4	2

pPreliminary.　rRevised.

[1]Houses for which sales price was not reported have been distributed proportionally to those for which sales price was reported.
[2]Total equals 100 percent.

Note: The sales price includes the land.

Source: *New One-Family Houses Sold: September 1999*, Bureau of the Census, Washington, DC, 1999

TABLE 10.6

Median and Average Sales Price of Houses Sold, by Region: September 1999

[Dollars]

Period	Median sales price					Average sales price				
	United States	Northeast	Midwest	South	West	United States	Northeast	Midwest	South	West
ANNUAL DATA										
1993........................	126,500	162,600	125,000	115,000	135,000	147,700	183,600	143,100	133,600	161,900
1994........................	130,000	169,000	132,900	116,900	140,400	154,500	200,500	152,700	136,800	168,900
1995........................	133,900	180,000	134,000	124,500	141,000	158,700	216,600	157,200	142,000	169,800
1996........................	140,000	186,000	138,000	126,200	153,900	166,400	226,100	158,900	144,200	186,200
1997........................	146,000	190,000	149,900	129,600	160,000	176,200	234,100	173,000	151,400	198,200
1998........................	152,500	200,000	157,500	135,800	163,500	181,900	240,100	179,200	159,700	200,500
QUARTERLY DATA										
1999										
1st quarter...................	156,900	195,000	165,000	142,800	168,600	189,100	227,900	183,600	166,900	217,500
2nd quarter^r.................	158,500	210,100	155,000	144,000	170,000	191,700	248,000	177,600	174,100	215,600
3rd quarter^p.................	157,100	202,900	161,500	137,000	174,900	191,900	239,000	188,100	163,200	222,900

^p Preliminary   ^r Revised

Source: *New One-Family Houses Sold: September 1999*, Bureau of the Census, Washington, DC, 1999

---

ried couples. Five percent of Hispanic married couples who rented could afford a modestly priced house, compared to 17 percent of non-Hispanic married couples.

About 82 percent of White married-couple homeowners could afford to buy another modestly priced house in the area where they lived, compared to about 7 out of 10 Black married-couple owners. About 59 percent of married-couple homeowners of Hispanic origin could afford to buy another modestly priced house, compared to 81 percent for non-Hispanic married-couple householders.

Age

Age is also a factor related to affordability. Householders in renter families who could not afford to buy a modestly priced house were slightly younger (median age 36) than householders in homeowner families who could not afford to buy another modestly priced house (median age 39).

Affording Higher-Priced Homes

The median maximum-priced house (highest-priced house a family or unrelated individual can afford, given limitations of income, debts, and financial assets) owner families could purchase using conventional financing was $136,100. The median maximum-priced house for unrelated individual owners was $84,600. The median maximum-priced house renter families and unrelated individuals could afford was less than $20,000.

HOUSING SATISFACTION

On a scale of 1 to 10, with 10 being the best, the 1997 *American Housing Survey* respondents were asked to rank their homes as structures to live in. About 75 percent in owner-occupied units rated their homes highly, providing scores of 8, 9, or 10, compared to 53 percent of renters. One-third (32 percent) of homeowners categorized their homes with the highest mark of a perfect "10."

Homeowners were somewhat less satisfied with their surroundings than they were their homes; 70 percent of homeowners provided high ratings for their neighborhood. About 28 percent were completely satisfied, giving the highest possible ranking of 10.

Of the 63 million homeowners who lived in neighborhoods, 39 percent thought that problems

TABLE 10.7

Value — Owner Occupied Units

[Numbers in thousands. Consistent with the 1990 Census.... means not applicable or sample too small. — means zero or rounds to zero]

	Characteristics	Total occupied units	Housing unit characteristics New construction 4 years	Mobile homes	Physical problems Severe	Physical problems Moderate	Black	Hispanic	Household characteristics Elderly (65 years and over)	Moved in past year	Below poverty level
1	Total	65 487	4 894	5 255	725	2 170	5 457	3 646	16 493	5 093	6 619
	Value										
2	Less than $10,000	2 081	96	1 575	78	156	204	159	501	211	583
3	$10,000 to $19,999	1 713	124	1 004	28	189	237	115	471	136	397
4	$20,000 to $29,999	2 047	238	838	41	207	298	202	658	183	388
5	$30,000 to $39,999	2 559	212	580	55	221	471	196	825	239	456
6	$40,000 to $49,999	3 044	140	353	46	173	442	195	938	250	432
7	$50,000 to $59,999	3 597	148	198	72	172	450	237	1 165	247	458
8	$60,000 to $69,999	4 328	143	238	40	155	493	247	1 183	303	450
9	$70,000 to $79,999	4 782	168	47	67	111	482	327	1 363	332	492
10	$80,000 to $99,999	9 133	449	185	101	224	763	428	2 458	644	777
11	$100,000 to $119,999	6 600	480	52	59	112	444	307	1 598	461	572
12	$120,000 to $149,999	8 114	702	75	66	124	434	448	1 747	707	559
13	$150,000 to $199,999	8 047	879	84	37	154	457	442	1 735	605	496
14	$200,000 to $249,999	3 771	486	15	18	49	124	157	749	323	215
15	$250,000 to $299,999	2 030	255	3	10	34	65	93	419	165	123
16	$300,000 or more	3 641	375	6	7	90	93	92	683	288	220
17	Median	98 815	130 701	20 570	70 300	58 146	72 750	86 770	89 294	100 101	72 953

	Total occupied units	In (P)MSAs Central cities	Suburbs	Outside MSAs	Urban Total	Urban Outside MSAs	Rural Total	Rural Suburbs	Rural Outside MSAs	Regions Northeast	Midwest	South	West
1	65 487	14 938	34 061	16 489	42 282	4 888	23 205	11 486	11 601	12 241	16 902	23 650	12 694
2	2 081	212	875	994	737	157	1 345	508	837	243	474	1 082	284
3	1 713	298	640	776	749	178	964	365	598	197	456	850	210
4	2 047	368	753	927	964	234	1 083	389	693	277	496	1 013	261
5	2 559	684	742	1 133	1 409	348	1 150	365	785	411	610	1 239	298
6	3 044	878	968	1 198	1 833	390	1 212	400	809	431	960	1 440	213
7	3 597	1 022	1 258	1 317	2 299	479	1 298	454	838	480	1 154	1 667	296
8	4 328	1 206	1 667	1 455	2 823	520	1 504	565	935	679	1 302	1 855	493
9	4 782	1 405	2 098	1 279	3 315	488	1 467	666	790	899	1 381	1 956	546
10	9 133	2 211	4 684	2 238	6 121	758	3 013	1 519	1 480	1 686	2 795	3 365	1 287
11	6 600	1 556	3 609	1 435	4 307	397	2 293	1 227	1 038	1 271	1 885	2 383	1 060
12	8 114	1 656	5 005	1 453	5 558	439	2 556	1 525	1 013	1 640	2 099	2 398	1 976
13	8 047	1 557	5 363	1 127	5 585	294	2 462	1 616	832	1 853	1 662	2 257	2 276
14	3 771	768	2 501	502	2 620	101	1 150	734	401	913	732	881	1 244
15	2 030	368	1 353	310	1 317	42	713	443	267	468	358	491	713
16	3 641	749	2 545	346	2 645	63	996	709	284	793	538	773	1 537
17	98 815	92 623	118 548	73 478	104 141	72 847	90 489	108 345	73 867	112 863	91 585	84 302	141 236

Source: *American Housing Survey for the United States: 1997*, Bureau of the Census, Washington, DC, 1999

TABLE 10.8

Consumer Price Index and average annual percent change for all items and selected items: United States, selected years 1960–98

[Data are based on reporting by samples of providers and other retail outlets]

Items and medical care components	1960	1970	1980	1985	1990	1995	1996	1997	1998
	Consumer Price Index (CPI)								
All items	29.6	38.8	82.4	107.6	130.7	152.4	156.9	160.5	163.0
All items excluding medical care	30.2	39.2	82.8	107.2	128.8	148.6	152.8	156.3	158.6
All services	24.1	35.0	77.9	109.9	139.2	168.7	174.1	179.4	184.2
Selected items									
Food	30.0	39.2	86.8	105.6	132.4	148.4	153.3	157.3	160.7
Apparel	45.7	59.2	90.9	105.0	124.1	132.0	131.7	132.9	133.0
Housing	- - -	36.4	81.1	107.7	128.5	148.5	152.8	156.8	160.4
Energy	22.4	25.5	86.0	101.6	102.1	105.2	110.1	111.5	102.9
Medical care	22.3	34.0	74.9	113.5	162.8	220.5	228.2	234.6	242.1
	Average annual percent change from previous year shown								
All items	...	4.3	8.9	5.5	4.0	3.1	3.0	2.3	1.6
All items excluding medical care	...	4.1	8.8	5.3	3.7	2.9	2.8	2.3	1.5
All services	...	5.6	10.2	7.1	4.8	3.9	3.2	3.0	2.7
Selected items									
Food	...	4.0	7.7	4.0	4.6	2.3	3.3	2.6	2.2
Apparel	...	4.4	4.6	2.9	3.4	1.2	-0.2	0.9	0.1
Housing	...	- - -	9.9	5.8	3.6	2.9	2.9	2.6	2.3
Energy	...	2.2	15.4	3.4	0.1	0.6	4.7	1.3	-7.7
Medical care	...	6.2	9.5	8.7	7.5	6.3	3.5	2.8	3.2

- - - Data not available.   ... Category not applicable.

NOTES: 1982–84 = 100, except where noted. Data for additional years are available.

U.S. Department of Labor, Bureau of Labor Statistics. Consumer Price Index. Various releases.

Source: *Health, United States, 1999*, National Center for Health Statistics, Hyattsville, MD, 1999

existed in their neighborhoods. A variety of problems were identified, and some respondents listed more than one problem. Of the 16.8 million homeowners who reported street noise or traffic present in their neighborhoods, 40 percent felt the condition was bothersome. Nearly 9 million reported the presence of crime in their neighborhoods; slightly more than 3 of 5 (62 percent) said it was a problem.

Renters generally expressed lower opinions concerning their homes than homeowners did. Just over half (53 percent) of renters rated their homes highly. The same percentage gave their neighborhoods high marks. About 18 percent ranked their neighborhoods with the best possible rating.

Of the 32.8 million renters who lived in neighborhoods, 52 percent said they were bothered by at least one problem. The problem most often cited was street noise or traffic (15 percent). About 14 percent of renters thought crime was a problem. Approximately 6 percent said people caused a

problem, 5 percent mentioned odors, 4 percent chose noise, 2 percent reported litter or housing deterioration, and less than 1 percent cited poor city or county services and undesirable commercial, institutional, or industrial areas. About 7 percent said they were bothered by other unlisted factors.

HOUSING CHARACTERISTICS

In 1997, about 58 percent of total U.S. housing units were owner-occupied, and about 30 percent were renter-occupied. The remaining houses were either empty (9 percent) or used by seasonal or migratory workers (3 percent). (See Table 10.11.)

Most housing units (67 percent) were single dwellings (61 percent detached; 6 percent, attached). Nine percent of the housing were made up of 2 to 4 units, and 5 percent were made up of 5 to 9 units, while nearly 4 percent were units of 50 or more. Seven percent were mobile homes or trailers. (See Table 10.1.)

TABLE 10.9

Selected Housing Costs—Occupied Units

[Numbers in thousands. Consistent with the 1990 Census. ... means not applicable or sample too small. – means zero or rounds to zero]

| Characteristics | Total occupied units | Tenure | | Housing unit characteristics | | | | Household characteristics | | | | |
		Owner	Renter	New construction 4 years	Mobile homes	Physical problems Severe	Physical problems Moderate	Black	Hispanic	Elderly (65 years and over)	Moved in past year	Below poverty level
Total	99 487	65 487	34 000	5 848	6 544	1 796	5 191	12 085	8 513	20 906	17 469	15 728
Monthly Housing Costs												
Less than $100	1 772	1 182	589	52	330	102	185	354	198	700	289	769
$100 to $199	9 651	7 844	1 808	377	1 301	231	693	1 437	692	4 378	772	2 944
$200 to $249	6 050	5 067	984	203	549	130	339	767	619	2 619	465	1 228
$250 to $299	5 966	4 796	1 169	231	467	91	308	686	381	1 296	540	1 090
$300 to $349	5 337	3 669	1 668	182	483	93	352	687	367	1 768	726	988
$350 to $399	5 407	3 267	2 140	231	456	79	360	750	428	1 380	1 002	1 066
$400 to $449	5 289	2 896	2 394	219	526	109	311	762	515	1 160	1 150	989
$450 to $499	5 023	2 472	2 551	202	398	108	285	749	483	910	1 169	885
$500 to $599	9 939	4 612	5 327	506	603	230	569	1 513	1 111	1 427	2 510	1 508
$600 to $699	8 615	4 251	4 365	445	474	159	422	1 098	982	1 114	2 097	1 101
$700 to $799	6 955	3 792	3 162	404	273	96	318	794	711	671	1 596	688
$800 to $999	9 535	6 402	3 133	735	241	148	314	938	852	699	1 918	696
$1,000 to $1,249	6 644	6 249	1 395	661	94	47	154	459	489	463	1 106	416
$1,250 to $1,499	4 158	3 602	556	472	38	42	83	295	289	251	646	182
$1,500 or more	6 975	6 386	589	910	52	36	225	371	225	616	929	323
No cash rent	2 171	–	2 171	46	257	95	272	425	225	454	553	855
Median (excludes no cash rent)	542	534	549	769	351	458	436	476	565	307	593	370

| | Total occupied units | In MSAs | | | Urban | | Rural | | | Regions | | | | |
		Central cities	Suburbs	Outside MSAs	Total	Outside MSAs	Total	Suburbs	Outside MSAs	Northeast	Midwest	South	West	
Total	99 487	30 533	46 884	22 070	71 317	7 858	28 170	13 793	14 212	19 484	23 951	34 808	21 245	1
Less than $100	1 772	485	563	724	1 002	174	770	218	550	225	310	929	306	2
$100 to $199	9 651	2 429	3 172	4 051	5 382	1 261	4 270	1 460	2 791	915	2 260	4 986	1 490	3
$200 to $249	6 050	1 554	2 391	2 104	3 785	769	2 265	918	1 335	760	1 822	2 425	1 043	4
$250 to $299	5 966	1 688	2 447	1 830	3 958	701	2 007	871	1 129	1 022	1 719	2 167	1 058	5
$300 to $349	5 337	1 625	2 203	1 509	3 677	600	1 660	751	909	1 096	1 716	1 832	840	6
$350 to $399	5 407	1 824	2 204	1 379	3 915	581	1 492	691	799	1 138	1 598	1 791	881	7
$400 to $449	5 289	1 834	2 219	1 236	3 904	530	1 385	664	719	1 004	1 453	1 763	908	8
$450 to $499	5 023	1 815	2 026	1 183	3 820	518	1 203	542	653	971	1 328	1 795	929	9
$500 to $599	9 939	3 840	4 076	1 852	7 758	758	2 181	1 076	1 095	2 054	2 495	3 399	991	10
$600 to $699	8 615	3 026	3 555	1 513	6 656	536	1 960	989	977	1 971	1 976	2 787	881	11
$700 to $799	6 955	2 328	5 249	1 072	5 381	382	1 593	887	690	1 491	1 571	2 295	597	12
$800 to $999	9 535	2 990	4 167	1 296	7 256	413	2 279	1 373	883	2 045	2 107	3 005	2 378	13
$1,000 to $1,249	6 644	1 837	2 772	640	5 012	203	1 632	1 177	437	1 494	1 388	1 876	1 886	14
$1,250 to $1,499	4 158	1 059	1 810	327	3 185	95	973	729	232	1 087	789	997	1 285	15
$1,500 or more	6 975	1 651	4 810	514	5 374	111	1 601	1 184	403	1 799	987	1 828	2 360	16
No cash rent	2 171	549	783	838	1 271	226	900	282	612	380	432	947	412	17
Median (excludes no cash rent)	542	545	639	364	572	377	442	560	355	617	483	479	652	18

Source: *American Housing Survey for the United States: 1997*, Bureau of the Census, Washington, DC, 1999

Age of Housing

The median age of owner-occupied housing was 29 years, meaning that one-half of the units were built during or before 1968 and the other half after that year. About 6 percent of all housing units were the most newly constructed units, built between 1993 and 1997.

Living Conditions

Owner-occupied homes had a median of 6.1 rooms, with 3 bedrooms. Seven out of 10 (69 percent) of these homes had more than one bathroom, while the remainder had a single bath or, in a few instances, none. Owner-occupied single detached and mobile homes had a median of 1,825 square feet of living space, amounting to some 760 square feet for every person in the household. (See Table 10.11.) Just 1 percent of owners maintained households that were crowded, that is, had more than one person per room. Owner-occupied units had a median of 2.4 people living in the housing.

There was a median of 4.1 rooms and 1.9 bedrooms in all renter-occupied housing. Renters lived in a median unit of 1,276 square feet. Nearly 6 percent of renters lived in homes considered crowded, with more than one person per room. Renter-occupied units had a median of two people living in the housing. About 27 percent had more than one bathroom, while about 1 percent was without any bathroom physically located in the unit. (See Table 10.11.)

Equipment

Virtually all units had sinks, refrigerators, and stoves. About 63 percent of owned homes, 35 percent of rental units, and 31 percent of mobile homes had a dishwasher; 93 percent of homeowners, 45 percent of the renters, and 74 percent of those living in mobile homes had a washing machine. Nine

TABLE 10.10

Affordability of a Modestly Priced House for Families and Unrelated Individuals, by Tenure: Selected Years, 1984-1995

Percentage who could afford to buy

	Families			Unrelated individuals		
	Total	Owner	Renter	Total	Owner	Renter
1984	60.4	79.6	12.6	33.5	60.2	13.4
1988	59.7	78.1	14.0	33.9	60.8	12.8
1991	57.6	75.2	13.1	33.4	59.0	12.2
1993	57.7	76.5	11.7	33.5	60.8	11.2
1995	55.6	74.6	9.9	34.3	62.3	10.6

Note: Assumes conventional, fixed-rate, 30-year financing, with a 5-percent down payment.

Source: *Who Could Afford to Buy a House in 1995?*, Bureau of the Census, Washington, DC, 1999

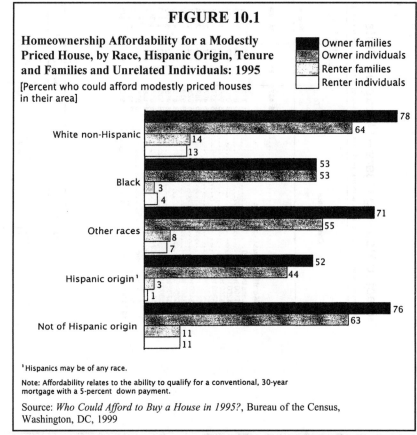

FIGURE 10.1

Homeownership Affordability for a Modestly Priced House, by Race, Hispanic Origin, Tenure and Families and Unrelated Individuals: 1995

[Percent who could afford modestly priced houses in their area]

- Owner families
- Owner individuals
- Renter families
- Renter individuals

[1] Hispanics may be of any race.

Note: Affordability relates to the ability to qualify for a conventional, 30-year mortgage with a 5-percent down payment.

Source: *Who Could Afford to Buy a House in 1995?*, Bureau of the Census, Washington, DC, 1999

170

out of 10 (89 percent) owners, 4 of 10 (39.5 percent) renters, and 70 percent of those living in mobile homes had clothes dryers. (See Table 10.11.)

Forty-two percent of owned homes, 12 percent of the rental units, and 9 percent of the mobile homes had a usable fireplace. Nearly 73 percent of the homes, 31 percent of the rental units, and 25 percent of those in mobile homes had a garage or carport with their unit. (See Table 10.11.)

More than half of owner-occupied housing (56 percent) had central air conditioning as did 38 percent of rentals and 47 percent of mobile homes. (See Table 10.11.) Most housing units were heated by a warm air furnace (59 percent), a steam or hot water system (12.5 percent), or electric heat pumps (11 percent). Piped gas provided the fuel in half (56 percent) the units, followed by electricity (30 percent), fuel oil (10 percent), and wood (2 percent).

Seventy percent of owned homes used a public sewer, while the remaining 30 percent used a septic tank or cesspool. Eighty-five percent of owned units and 95 percent of rented ones used a public system or private company for their water supply. About 15 percent of owned homes had

wells, while only 4 percent of rented units used wells. Nearly 9 percent of owners and 16 percent of renters reported that the water was not safe to drink.

Physical Problems

Renters (12 percent) experienced more physical problems with their housing than owners did (4 percent). While 9 percent of all renters had moderate physical problems, over 3 percent lived with severe problems. (Severe problems include specific critical problems in one or more of the following areas: plumbing, heating, electricity, or upkeep.) Only 1 percent of owners reported severe physical problems, and 3 percent had moderate problems.

NEW HOUSING CHARACTERISTICS

Privately Owned Homes

In 1998, 1.16 million one-unit privately owned homes were built, 82 percent of them in metropolitan statistical areas (MSAs) and 45 percent of them in the South. Of these, 815,000 houses were built to be sold; the rest were built for owner's occupancy on the owner's land.

TABLE 10.11

Housing Quality—All Housing Units

[Numbers in thousands. **Consistent with the 1990 Census.** ... means not applicable or sample too small. – means zero or rounds to zero]

Characteristics	Total housing units	Sea-sonal	Year-round											New con-struc-tion 4 years	Mobile homes
			Total	Occupied			Vacant								
				Total	Owner	Renter	Total	For rent	Rental vacan-cy rate	For sale only	Rent-ed or sold	Occa-sional use/ URE	Other vacant		
Total............................	112 357	3 166	109 191	99 487	65 487	34 000	9 704	2 884	7.8	1 043	753	2 796	2 228	6 503	8 301
Selected Amenities[1]															
Porch, deck, balcony, or patio	84 570	2 298	82 272	75 986	55 374	20 612	6 286	1 627	7.3	784	545	1 989	1 342	5 462	5 803
Usable fireplace	34 092	670	33 422	31 825	27 702	4 123	1 597	248	5.7	321	179	581	268	3 130	756
Separate dining room	41 858	422	41 435	39 077	31 411	7 666	2 359	564	6.8	405	243	582	564	2 767	1 362
With 2 or more living rooms or recreation rooms, etc.	18 033	233	17 800	17 059	15 371	1 688	741	96	5.4	154	90	257	143	1 169	522
Garage or carport included with home	62 427	914	61 513	58 027	47 488	10 539	3 486	666	5.9	607	379	1 096	737	4 248	2 110
Not included	49 670	2 252	47 418	41 431	33 601	17 982	23 448	5 987	2 190	8.5	429	373	1 600	1 394	2 251	6 176
Offstreet parking included	40 285	1 970	38 315	33 601	15 449	18 152	4 715	1 722	8.6	343	280	1 353	1 017	2 150	5 503
Offstreet parking not reported	23	–	23	21	2	18	2	–	–	–	–	–	2	–	–
Garage or carport not reported	260	–	260	29	16	13	231	27	67.8	6	1	100	96	4	15
Owner or Manager on Property															
Rental, multiunit[2]	...	...	...	...	...	21 548	...	1 899	8.0	...	207	364	...	741	4
Owner or manager lives on property..............	...	...	...	...	...	5 935	...	410	6.4	...	52	77	...	205	1
Neither owner nor manager lives on property	...	...	...	...	...	15 614	...	1 490	8.6	...	155	287	...	536	3

(continued)

TABLE 10.11 (Continued)

Size of Unit—All Housing Units

[Numbers in thousands. Consistent with the 1990 Census. ... means not applicable or sample too small. – means zero or rounds to zero]

Characteristics	Total housing units	Seasonal	Year-round Total	Occupied Total	Owner	Renter	Vacant Total	For rent	Rental vacancy rate	For sale only	Rented or sold	Occasional use/URE	Other vacant	New construction 4 years	Mobile homes
Total..........	112 357	3 166	109 191	99 487	65 487	34 000	9 704	2 884	7.8	1 043	753	2 796	2 228	6 503	8 301

Rooms

1 room	471	18	453	328	5	323	125	47	12.4	–	7	38	34	8	19
2 rooms	1 470	112	1 357	951	100	851	406	120	12.3	8	8	161	108	25	114
3 rooms	11 715	627	11 088	9 399	1 037	8 361	1 690	744	8.1	67	117	441	321	293	621
4 rooms	23 468	1 286	22 183	19 038	6 996	12 042	3 145	1 184	8.9	209	216	829	707	865	3 284
5 rooms	24 476	552	23 925	21 760	14 828	6 932	2 165	477	6.4	284	167	703	533	1 779	2 839
6 rooms	21 327	295	21 032	19 885	16 415	3 470	1 147	219	5.9	220	104	325	280	1 363	913
7 rooms	13 782	154	13 629	13 113	11 900	1 213	516	47	3.7	122	64	147	136	830	347
8 rooms	8 439	75	8 363	8 093	7 615	478	270	19	3.8	74	31	86	60	653	132
9 rooms	4 174	12	4 162	4 044	3 856	188	118	18	8.7	31	13	30	26	408	28
10 rooms or more	3 034	35	2 999	2 877	2 736	141	122	9	5.8	29	27	35	24	280	4
Median....................	5.3	4.1	5.3	5.4	6.1	4.1	4.3	3.9	...	5.3	4.7	4.4	4.4	5.7	4.5

Bedrooms

None.....................	619	30	589	439	41	398	150	53	11.5	–	10	44	43	8	22
1	15 117	651	14 466	12 399	1 846	10 554	2 066	946	8.2	64	130	550	376	391	780
2	34 609	1 575	33 034	28 899	14 340	14 559	4 135	1 357	8.5	363	288	1 194	934	1 345	4 034
3	43 782	647	43 135	40 597	33 800	6 797	2 539	439	6.0	443	239	744	673	3 356	3 205
4 or more	18 230	263	17 967	17 153	15 461	1 692	814	89	5.0	173	87	264	201	1 403	260
Median....................	2.6	2.1	2.7	2.7	3.0	1.9	2.1	1.8	...	2.7	2.3	2.2	2.2	2.9	2.3

Complete Bathrooms

None.....................	1 673	412	1 260	750	319	432	510	101	18.8	34	10	170	194	18	153
1	51 729	1 668	50 061	44 223	19 801	24 421	5 838	2 122	7.9	416	401	1 411	1 488	800	3 702
1 and one-half	16 162	232	15 930	14 987	11 628	3 360	943	222	6.2	126	109	294	192	370	949
2 or more	42 794	854	41 939	39 527	33 739	5 787	2 413	439	7.0	467	233	921	353	5 315	3 497

Square Footage of Unit

Single detached and mobile homes	76 410	2 560	73 850	68 655	59 011	9 644	5 195	706	6.8	800	429	1 700	1 559	5 075	8 301
Less than 500	1 402	369	1 032	778	491	287	254	37	11.3	16	11	112	79	79	616
500 to 749	3 188	381	2 808	2 286	1 369	917	521	65	6.5	42	31	188	196	97	1 261
750 to 999	6 576	364	6 212	5 586	4 121	1 465	627	109	6.9	64	22	191	240	236	2 194
1,000 to 1,499	17 030	468	16 562	15 432	12 886	2 546	1 130	181	6.6	188	87	348	325	1 047	2 114
1,500 to 1,999	15 007	196	14 811	14 071	12 598	1 473	741	102	6.4	151	79	220	188	1 087	714
2,000 to 2,499	10 680	113	10 567	10 194	9 526	668	373	36	5.1	72	43	109	112	774	165
2,500 to 2,999	5 944	45	5 898	5 660	5 315	345	238	17	4.7	53	32	82	53	428	39
3,000 to 3,999	5 469	45	5 424	5 212	4 966	245	212	18	6.9	62	36	52	44	514	20
4,000 or more	3 229	49	3 180	3 023	2 825	198	157	13	6.4	43	23	36	43	303	48
Not reported (includes don't know)	7 885	529	7 355	6 414	4 915	1 499	941	127	7.7	110	64	362	278	511	1 129
Median....................	1 702	932	1 724	1 750	1 825	1 276	1 321	1 218	...	1 619	1 696	1 255	1 193	1 879	945

Equipment

Lacking complete kitchen facilities	5 629	416	5 213	2 289	515	1 774	2 924	688	27.3	396	241	398	1 201	231	382
With complete kitchen (sink, refrigerator, and oven or burners).................................	106 728	2 750	103 978	97 198	64 972	32 226	6 780	2 195	6.3	646	513	2 398	1 027	6 272	7 919
Kitchen sink...............................	111 191	3 044	108 147	98 878	65 316	33 563	9 269	2 812	7.7	1 012	726	2 725	1 995	6 453	8 231
Refrigerator	109 357	2 922	106 434	99 017	65 310	33 707	7 417	2 348	6.5	688	542	2 568	1 271	6 361	8 050
Cooking stove or range	108 779	2 860	105 919	98 318	65 023	33 295	7 601	2 465	6.8	850	614	2 465	1 207	6 396	8 006
Burners, no stove or range	267	5	262	247	165	82	14	5	5.5	–	2	4	3	19	9
Microwave oven only	514	16	499	454	177	277	45	1	.5	5	–	22	16	25	26
Dishwasher	57 642	990	56 652	53 116	41 162	11 954	3 535	1 004	7.7	510	345	1 284	391	5 416	2 552
Washing machine..........................	80 133	1 258	78 875	75 901	60 708	15 193	2 974	405	2.6	359	226	1 398	586	5 771	6 151
Clothes dryer	76 470	1 334	75 136	71 669	58 231	13 438	3 467	513	3.7	392	260	1 504	798	5 693	5 808
Disposal in kitchen sink	45 843	740	45 103	41 984	28 888	13 096	3 118	985	6.9	393	317	1 063	361	4 051	1 053
Trash compactor	4 001	109	3 891	3 615	2 908	708	276	47	6.3	49	20	116	43	316	52

Air conditioning:

Central..................................	54 567	946	53 620	49 896	36 833	13 063	3 725	1 071	7.5	529	382	1 265	478	5 223	3 906
Additional Central	2 601	28	2 573	2 407	1 956	451	166	35	7.2	25	28	57	20	316	99
1 room unit	18 453	448	18 005	16 350	8 545	7 805	1 655	449	5.4	107	91	539	468	348	1 648
2 room units	7 422	96	7 326	7 055	4 888	2 168	270	83	3.7	26	20	83	59	57	638
3 room units or more	2 840	18	2 823	2 728	2 128	600	94	16	2.6	11	9	28	31	9	52

Source: *American Housing Survey for the United States: 1997*, Bureau of the Census, Washington, DC, 1999

Sales Prices

In 1998, just 2 percent of new one-family houses were sold for under $70,000, compared to 6 percent in 1994, and about 17 percent were sold for over $250,000, compared to 11 percent in 1994. The average price was $181,900, and the median price was $152,500. (See Table 10.12.) Seventy-nine percent were purchased with conventional mortgages; 5 percent were bought with cash.

TABLE 10.12

Sales Price of Houses by Location and Type of Financing: 1994 to 1998

[Components may not add to totals because of rounding. Percents computed from unrounded figures]

Sales price, location, and type of financing	Number of houses (thousands)					Percent distribution				
	1998	1997	1996	1995	1994	1998	1997	1996	1995	1994
United States	**886**	**804**	**757**	**667**	**670**	**100**	**100**	**100**	**100**	**100**
Under $70,000	19	22	26	26	37	2	3	3	4	6
$70,000 to $79,999	22	28	33	32	35	2	4	4	5	5
$80,000 to $99,999	91	93	104	101	108	10	12	14	15	16
$100,000 to $119,999	112	103	101	99	93	13	13	13	15	14
$120,000 to $149,999	183	173	159	144	140	21	21	21	22	21
$150,000 to $199,999	208	177	160	127	129	23	22	21	19	19
$200,000 to $249,999	104	83	79	63	55	12	10	10	9	8
$250,000 to $299,999	59	46	40	29	28	7	6	5	4	4
$300,000 and over	88	78	56	46	44	10	10	7	7	7
Average sales price	181 900	176 200	166 400	158 700	154 500	(X)	(X)	(X)	(X)	(X)
Median sales price	152 500	146 000	140 000	133 900	130 000	(X)	(X)	(X)	(X)	(X)

Source: *Characteristics of New Housing: 1998*, Bureau of the Census, Washington, DC, 1999

Physical Characteristics

The current American homeowner's dream contains just about every convenience needed for easy living. Among the houses sold in 1998, the vast majority (95 percent) included two or more bathrooms. Most (90 percent) had three or more bedrooms, and more than one-third (37 percent) contained four or more bedrooms. The homes sold were built with a brick exterior (21 percent), wood (15 percent), stucco (22 percent), or vinyl siding (34 percent). The remaining 9 percent were built with aluminum siding, cinder block, cement block, and stone. (See Table 10.13.)

Two-thirds of new homes (66 percent) had at least one fireplace. The homes were heated either by gas (76 percent), electricity (23 percent), or oil (2 percent). Eighty-five percent had central air-conditioning. While most (85 percent) had a two-or-more-car garage, about 1 in 14 (7 percent) had no garage or carport. About half (53 percent) were two stories or more. Close to half of new homes (45 percent) were from 1,200 to 1,999 square feet, with about 1 in 7 (14 percent) larger than 3,000 square feet. (See Table 10.13.)

Multi-Family Dwellings

Thirty-two thousand new multi-family buildings were built in 1998, of which all but 1,000 had one to three floors. Eight thousand were built in the Midwest and in the West. Thirteen thousand were constructed in the South, while only 3,000

new buildings were erected in the Northeast. Two-thirds (66 percent) of the buildings contained two to nine units, 20 percent had 10 to 19 units, and 13 percent had more than 20. Fewer than 500 buildings had 50 units or more.

Eighty-seven percent of the buildings had air conditioning, with the South having the most (100 percent) and the West having the least (65 percent). Sixty-nine percent of the buildings in the Northeast, and 92 percent of those in the Midwest had air conditioning.

Apartments

In 1998, a total of 274,000 apartments were completed in buildings with five or more units — a 76 percent increase from the 155,900 apartments completed in 1994, but a 7 percent drop from 1990 (294,400 apartments) and a 42 percent plunge from 1987 (474,200 apartments). Of the 274,000 apartments, 210,000 (77 percent) were privately subsidized unfurnished rental apartments in buildings of five units or less, and just 3,000 (1 percent) were furnished. Approximately 34,000 (12 percent) were condominiums, 20,000 (7 percent) were federally subsidized, and 2 percent were other (such as time-sharing and continuing-care retirement).

The large number of apartments built during the mid-1980s led to an excess of apartments, severe competition among apartment developers in many areas, and the bankruptcy of many developers and the savings and loan companies that fi-

173

TABLE 10.13

Selected Characteristics by Sales Price: 1998

[Value of improved lot included in sales price of house. Price per square foot of floor area excludes value of improved lot. Components may not add to totals because of rounding. Averages, medians, and percents computed from unrounded figures]

Characteristic	Total	Under $100,000	$100,000 to $149,999	$150,000 to $199,999	$200,000 to $249,999	$250,000 to $299,999	$300,000 and over	Average sales price (dollars)	Median sales price (dollars)
PHYSICAL CHARACTERISTICS									
Central Air-Conditioning									
Number of Houses (in thousands)									
Installed	756	122	257	168	85	49	73	179 800	149 000
Not installed	130	9	39	40	18	11	15	198 000	169 000
Percent Distribution									
Installed	85	93	87	81	82	82	83	(X)	(X)
Not installed	15	7	13	19	18	18	17	(X)	(X)
Number of Bathrooms									
Number of Houses (in thousands)									
1 1/2 bathrooms or less	42	17	17	5	(B)	(B)	(B)	115 400	110 700
2 bathrooms	363	102	178	63	13	5	3	128 000	120 000
2 1/2 bathrooms	332	11	83	106	62	36	35	200 000	182 500
3 bathrooms or more	149	(B)	17	34	28	18	50	296 200	236 000
Percent Distribution									
1 1/2 bathrooms or less	5	13	6	2	(B)	(B)	(B)	(X)	(X)
2 bathrooms	41	78	60	30	12	9	4	(X)	(X)
2 1/2 bathrooms	37	9	28	51	59	60	39	(X)	(X)
3 bathrooms or more	17	(B)	6	16	27	30	57	(X)	(X)
Number of Bedrooms									
Number of Houses (in thousands)									
2 bedrooms or less	85	22	36	15	6	3	(B)	141 900	126 900
3 bedrooms	474	102	200	101	34	16	19	149 100	132 000
4 bedrooms or more	327	7	60	91	64	40	67	241 400	202 200
Percent Distribution									
2 bedrooms or less	10	17	12	7	6	6	(B)	(X)	(X)
3 bedrooms	54	78	68	49	32	27	22	(X)	(X)
4 bedrooms or more	37	5	20	44	62	67	76	(X)	(X)
Principal Type of Exterior Wall Material									
Number of Houses (in thousands)									
Brick	187	40	57	39	20	12	18	173 400	145 500
Wood	133	18	37	35	16	9	17	197 900	162 000
Stucco	193	16	61	47	24	15	31	214 300	166 400
Vinyl siding	300	48	116	69	33	17	15	160 700	141 800
Aluminum siding	14	(B)	(B)	3	4	3	(B)	212 900	201 000
Other[2]	59	9	21	13	8	3	5	175 200	149 600
Percent Distribution									
Brick	21	30	19	19	19	20	20	(X)	(X)
Wood	15	14	12	17	15	16	20	(X)	(X)
Stucco	22	12	21	23	23	25	36	(X)	(X)
Vinyl siding	34	37	39	33	32	30	17	(X)	(X)
Aluminum siding	2	(B)	(B)	1	4	5	(B)	(X)	(X)
Other[2]	7	7	7	6	7	6	6	(X)	(X)
Number of Fireplaces									
Number of Houses (in thousands)									
No fireplace	300	83	126	53	20	8	8	137 600	124 800
1 fireplace	550	46	166	151	80	48	61	192 700	168 700
2 fireplaces or more	36	(B)	3	4	4	3	20	405 100	322 800
Percent Distribution									
No fireplace	34	64	42	25	19	13	9	(X)	(X)
1 fireplace	62	35	57	73	77	81	70	(X)	(X)
2 fireplaces or more	4	(B)	1	2	4	6	22	(X)	(X)
Floor Area									
Number of Houses (in thousands)									
Under 1,200 square feet	46	30	14	(B)	(B)	(B)	(B)	92 800	89 900
1,200 to 1,599 square feet	182	66	91	21	(B)	(B)	(B)	116 000	112 100
1,600 to 1,999 square feet	212	27	110	57	11	5	(B)	143 400	135 900
2,000 to 2,399 square feet	170	6	55	63	30	9	7	177 200	164 800
2,400 to 2,999 square feet	151	(B)	21	47	38	23	21	221 300	205 000
3,000 square feet or more	124	(B)	4	18	22	21	58	342 800	290 000
Percent Distribution									
Under 1,200 square feet	5	23	5	(B)	(B)	(B)	(B)	(X)	(X)
1,200 to 1,599 square feet	21	50	31	10	(B)	(B)	(B)	(X)	(X)
1,600 to 1,999 square feet	24	21	37	28	11	9	(B)	(X)	(X)
2,000 to 2,399 square feet	19	4	19	30	29	16	8	(X)	(X)
2,400 to 2,999 square feet	17	(B)	7	23	37	38	24	(X)	(X)
3,000 square feet or more	14	(B)	1	9	22	35	66	(X)	(X)
Type of Foundation									
Number of Houses (in thousands)									
Full or partial basement	306	17	77	83	50	31	46	213 400	184 500
Slab[3]	459	88	180	94	42	22	35	165 700	138 000
Crawl space	121	26	38	31	12	6	7	164 900	145 000
Percent Distribution									
Full or partial basement	35	13	26	40	48	53	52	(X)	(X)
Slab[3]	52	67	61	46	41	37	40	(X)	(X)
Crawl space	14	20	13	15	11	9	8	(X)	(X)

See footnotes at end of table.

(continued)

TABLE 10.13 (Continued)

Selected Characteristics by Sales Price: 1998—Con.

[Value of improved lot included in sales price of house. Price per square foot of floor area excludes value of improved lot. Components may not add to totals because of rounding. Averages, medians, and percents computed from unrounded figures]

Characteristic	Total	Under $100,000	$100,000 to $149,999	$150,000 to $199,999	$200,000 to $249,999	$250,000 to $299,999	$300,000 and over	Average sales price (dollars)	Median sales price (dollars)
PHYSICAL CHARACTERISTICS—Con.									
Type of Heating System									
Number of Houses (in thousands)									
Warm-air furnace	689	80	222	172	87	52	77	191 000	160 000
Heat pump	167	47	64	31	13	5	7	146 800	125 000
Hot water or steam	21	3	5	5	3	(B)	3	205 800	179 000
Other[4]	9	(B)	4	(B)	(B)	(B)	(B)	166 200	130 300
Percent Distribution									
Warm-air furnace	78	61	75	83	84	88	88	(X)	(X)
Heat pump	19	36	22	15	12	9	8	(X)	(X)
Hot water or steam	2	2	2	2	3	(B)	4	(X)	(X)
Other[4]	1	(B)	1	(B)	(B)	(B)	(B)	(X)	(X)
Type of Heating Fuel									
Number of Houses (in thousands)									
Gas	670	68	219	170	87	51	76	192 000	161 300
Electricity	200	62	74	35	14	6	8	143 200	120 000
Oil	15	(B)	(B)	3	3	(B)	4	301 700	220 000
Other types or none	(B)	(B)	(B)	(B)	(B)	(B)	(B)	250 600	250 000
Percent Distribution									
Gas	76	52	74	82	83	86	87	(X)	(X)
Electricity	23	48	25	17	14	10	9	(X)	(X)
Oil	2	(B)	(B)	1	3	(B)	4	(X)	(X)
Other types or none	(B)	(B)	(B)	(B)	(B)	(B)	(B)	(X)	(X)
Size of Lot									
Number of Houses (in thousands)									
Total reporting size of lot	760	113	254	179	88	51	75	182 000	152 000
Under 7,000 square feet	255	49	101	57	20	12	17	161 500	139 000
7,000 to 8,999 square feet	135	21	48	35	14	6	10	168 800	148 000
9,000 to 10,999 square feet	125	18	43	30	16	10	8	173 600	152 000
11,000 to 21,999 square feet	167	16	47	43	27	14	21	200 000	170 000
22,000 square feet or more	78	10	16	15	11	8	19	246 400	195 000
Average lot size	12 870	11 275	10 585	12 080	14 540	15 815	19 350	(X)	(X)
Median lot size	8 800	7 500	7 995	8 750	10 400	10 800	11 625	(X)	(X)
Percent Distribution									
Under 7,000 square feet	33	43	40	32	23	23	23	(X)	(X)
7,000 to 8,999 square feet	18	19	19	20	16	13	14	(X)	(X)
9,000 to 10,999 square feet	16	15	17	17	18	21	11	(X)	(X)
11,000 to 21,999 square feet	22	14	18	24	30	28	27	(X)	(X)
22,000 square feet or more	11	9	6	8	13	16	25	(X)	(X)
Type of Parking Facility									
Number of Houses (in thousands)									
Garage: 1 car	65	23	25	10	3	(B)	(B)	130 700	116 900
2 cars	620	74	233	160	74	37	42	172 100	150 000
3 cars or more	135	(B)	15	32	26	19	44	288 100	240 000
Carport	8	4	3	(B)	(B)	(B)	(B)	128 800	100 000
No garage or carport	58	29	19	6	(B)	(B)	(B)	109 700	98 900
Percent Distribution									
Garage: 1 car	7	18	9	5	3	(B)	(B)	(X)	(X)
2 cars	70	57	79	77	71	62	47	(X)	(X)
3 cars or more	15	(B)	5	15	25	33	51	(X)	(X)
Carport	1	3	1	(B)	(B)	(B)	(B)	(X)	(X)
No garage or carport	7	22	6	3	(B)	(B)	(B)	(X)	(X)
Number of Stories									
Number of Houses (in thousands)									
1 story	399	106	174	74	23	11	13	140 300	125 000
2 stories or more[5]	472	23	113	130	81	48	75	220 400	187 000
Split level	15	(B)	9	4	(B)	(B)	(B)	139 900	133 900
Percent Distribution									
1 story	45	81	59	36	22	19	15	(X)	(X)
2 stories or more[5]	53	18	38	63	78	80	85	(X)	(X)
Split level	2	(B)	3	2	(B)	(B)	(B)	(X)	(X)

B Withheld because estimate did not meet publication standards on the basis of sample size.   S Withheld because estimate did not meet publication standards on the basis of response rate, associated standard error, or a consistency review.   X Not applicable.   Z Fewer than 500 units or less than 0.5 percent.

[1]Includes other types of financing (not shown separately).
[2]Includes cinder block, stone, and other types.
[3]Includes a small number of other foundation types.
[4]Includes electric baseboard, panel, radiant heat, space heater, floor or wall furnace, solar, other types, or none.
[5]Includes houses with 1 1/2, 2 1/2, and 3 stories.

Source: *Characteristics of New Housing: 1998*, Bureau of the Census, Washington, DC, 1999

TABLE 10.14

Selected Characteristics of New Rental Apartments Completed by Asking Rent: 1998

[Preliminary data. Newly-constructed, privately financed, nonsubsidized, unfurnished apartments in buildings with 5 units or more. Components may not add to totals because of rounding. Medians computed from unrounded figures]

Characteristic	Total	Asking rent						Median asking rent (dollars)
		Less than $450	$450 to $549	$550 to $649	$650 to $749	$750 to $849	$850 or more	
New rental apartments completed (in thousands) ...	**210**	**13**	**26**	**30**	**41**	**32**	**68**	**735**
LOCATION								
Number of Apartments (in thousands)								
Inside MSAs	197	11	25	27	38	30	66	743
Outside MSAs	13	2	2	3	3	2	1	633
Northeast	11	(Z)	1	1	3	1	6	850+
Midwest	35	3	11	8	6	3	5	604
South	115	9	10	18	23	19	36	738
West	49	1	5	3	10	8	21	805
Percent Distribution								
Inside MSAs	94	84	94	89	92	95	98	(X)
Outside MSAs	6	16	6	11	8	5	2	(X)
Northeast	5	(S)	2	2	6	3	8	(X)
Midwest	17	20	40	28	13	10	8	(X)
South	55	69	39	60	55	61	53	(X)
West	23	9	19	11	25	25	31	(X)
BEDROOMS PER UNIT								
Number of Apartments (in thousands)								
Efficiencies	6	1	1	1	(Z)	(Z)	2	611
1 bedroom	71	6	12	13	17	8	14	670
2 bedrooms	104	5	11	14	20	18	36	760
3 bedrooms or more	29	(Z)	2	2	3	5	16	884
Percent Distribution								
Efficiencies	3	10	4	2	(S)	(S)	3	(X)
1 bedroom	34	47	47	44	42	25	20	(X)
2 bedrooms	50	40	41	46	49	57	53	(X)
3 bedrooms or more	14	(S)	8	8	8	17	23	(X)
FEATURES INCLUDED IN ASKING RENT								
Number of Apartments (in thousands)								
Swimming pool:								
Included in rent	157	5	12	21	33	28	57	775
Not included in rent	3	(Z)	(Z)	(Z)	(Z)	(Z)	1	(S)
Not available	50	8	14	9	8	3	9	582
Off-street parking:								
Included in rent	201	12	26	29	40	31	64	734
Not included in rent	6	(Z)	(Z)	1	1	1	3	850+
Not available	3	1	(Z)	1	(Z)	(Z)	1	(S)
Air-conditioning:								
Included in rent	69	5	10	11	13	8	20	704
Not included in rent	129	7	14	16	25	22	44	757
Not available	13	1	2	3	3	1	4	669
Dishwasher:								
Included in rent	195	10	20	27	41	31	65	747
Not included in rent	4	(Z)	3	1	(Z)	(Z)	(Z)	(S)
Not available	11	3	3	2			2	523
Percent Distribution								
Swimming pool:								
Included in rent	75	37	46	70	81	90	85	(X)
Not included in rent	1	(S)	(S)	(S)	(S)	(S)	2	(X)
Not available	24	62	53	29	18	9	13	(X)
Off-street parking:								
Included in rent	96	92	98	95	98	97	94	(X)
Not included in rent	3	(S)	(S)	2	2	3	5	(X)
Not available	1	5	(S)	3	(S)	(S)	1	(X)
Air-conditioning:								
Included in rent	33	40	39	38	32	27	30	(X)
Not included in rent	61	56	51	53	62	70	65	(X)
Not available	6	4	9	10	6	3	5	(X)
Dishwasher:								
Included in rent	93	77	77	90	99	100	97	(X)
Not included in rent	2	(S)	10	3	(S)	(S)	(S)	(X)
Not available	5	23	12	8	(S)	(S)	3	(X)

See footnotes at end of table.

(continued)

TABLE 10.14 (Continued)

Selected Characteristics of New Rental Apartments Completed by Asking Rent: 1998—Con.

[Preliminary data. Newly-constructed, privately financed, nonsubsidized, unfurnished apartments in buildings with 5 units or more. Components may not add to totals because of rounding. Medians computed from unrounded figures]

Characteristic	Total	Asking rent						Median asking rent (dollars)
		Less than $450	$450 to $549	$550 to $649	$650 to $749	$750 to $849	$850 or more	
UTILITIES INCLUDED IN ASKING RENT								
Number of Apartments (in thousands)								
Electricity:								
Included in rent	8	1	1	1	(Z)	(Z)	4	850+
Not included in rent	203	12	26	29	41	31	63	734
Gas:								
Included in rent	22	2	6	5	2	1	6	623
Not included in rent	83	3	6	10	18	14	31	779
Not available	105	9	14	15	21	16	30	716
Percent Distribution								
Electricity:								
Included in rent	4	5	3	4	(S)	(S)	6	(X)
Not included in rent	96	95	97	96	99	99	94	(X)
Gas:								
Included in rent	10	12	21	16	5	4	9	(X)
Not included in rent	40	21	24	33	44	46	46	(X)
Not available	50	68	54	51	51	50	44	(X)

S Withheld because estimate did not meet publication standards on the basis of response rate, associated standard error, or a consistency review. X Not applicable. Z Fewer than 500 units or less than 0.5 percent.

Source: *Characteristics of New Housing: 1998*, Bureau of the Census, Washington, DC, 1999

nanced them. These factors resulted, until recently, in a huge decline in apartment construction. A drop in the proportion of federally subsidized housing also contributed to the decline in apartment construction. By the late 1990s, the oversupply had been used, and apartment houses were being built again.

Fewer Federally Subsidized Apartments

From 1979 to 1981, federally subsidized housing accounted for about 20 percent of all apartment construction. Since then, however, the federal government has helped build only about 5 percent of the housing, rising to 8 percent in 1994, but back down to 6 percent in 1996 and 7 percent in 1998. These units were built under Department of Housing and Urban Development (HUD) programs, including Low Cost Housing Assistance (Section 8) and Senior Citizens Housing Direct Loans (Section 202).

The number of federally subsidized units plummeted from 87,500 in 1979 to 13,900 in 1990, dropping to 7,000 in 1992. Federal subsidies then increased to 12,000 in 1994, 14,000 in 1996, and 20,000 in 1998. Most (85 percent) of this housing was built inside MSAs (metropolitan statistical areas).

Rent and Conveniences

In 1998, the median rent of unfurnished privately subsidized apartments in buildings with five units or more was about $735 per month, with the least expensive units in the Midwest ($604) and the most expensive in the Northeast ($850 or more). Most apartment complexes offered swimming pools (76 percent), parking (99 percent), air conditioning (94 percent), and a dishwasher (95 percent). Only a small percentage included electricity (4 percent) or gas (10 percent) in the rent. (See Table 10.14.)

Condominium Apartments

A condominium is an apartment that is purchased as if it were a house. It is an investment, and the interest that is included in the monthly mortgage payment is tax-deductible. Condominiums have become very popular across the United States, particularly in Florida. About 31,000 condominium apartments were completed in 1998.

TABLE 10.15

New Condominiums Completed by Location and Number of Bedrooms by Asking Price: 1998

[Preliminary data. Newly-constructed, privately financed, nonsubsidized, unfurnished condominiums in buildings with 5 units or more. Components may not add to totals because of rounding. Medians computed from unrounded figures]

Characteristic	Total	Asking price						Median asking price (dollars)
		Less than $75,000	$75,000 to $99,999	$100,000 to $124,999	$125,000 to $149,999	$150,000 to $199,999	$200,000 or more	
New condominiums completed (in thousands)[1]	31	3	9	5	4	4	6	117 800
LOCATION								
Number of Condominiums (in thousands)								
Inside MSAs	24	2	5	5	4	4	5	128 800
Outside MSAs	7	1	4	1	(Z)	(Z)	1	90 000
Northeast	1	(Z)	(Z)	(Z)	(Z)	(Z)	1	(S)
Midwest	5	1	1	1	1	1	1	130 900
South	16	2	6	2	2	2	3	103 000
West	9	(Z)	2	2	1	1	2	120 400
Percent Distribution								
Inside MSAs	77	56	58	89	89	88	89	(X)
Outside MSAs	23	44	42	11	(S)	(S)	11	(X)
Northeast	4	(S)	(S)	(S)	(S)	(S)	13	(X)
Midwest	16	34	7	11	28	21	13	(X)
South	50	54	67	42	43	38	44	(X)
West	29	(S)	26	46	28	31	30	(X)
BEDROOMS PER UNIT								
Number of Condominiums (in thousands)								
Efficiencies	1	(Z)	(Z)	(Z)	(Z)	(Z)	(Z)	(S)
1 bedroom	3	1	(Z)	(Z)	(Z)	(Z)	1	129 800
2 bedrooms	21	2	7	4	3	2	3	107 900
3 bedrooms or more	7	(Z)	1	1	1	1	2	147 700
Percent Distribution								
Efficiencies	2	(S)	(S)	(S)	(S)	(S)	(S)	(X)
1 bedroom	9	24	(S)	(S)	(S)	(S)	10	(X)
2 bedrooms	66	66	81	69	65	60	46	(X)
3 bedrooms or more	22	(S)	11	27	24	25	41	(X)

S Withheld because estimate did not meet publication standards on the basis of response rate, associated standard error, or a consistency review.   X Not applicable.   Z Fewer than 500 units or less than 0.5 percent.

[1] Does not include cooperatively owned apartment units.

Source: *Characteristics of New Housing: 1998*, Bureau of the Census, Washington, DC, 1999

In 1998, half (50 percent) of all condominiums were built in the South, 29 percent in the West, 16 percent in the Midwest, and 4 percent in the Northeast. About 88 percent of all new condominiums contained two or more bedrooms. The median asking price for a condominium was $117,800, with condominiums generally costing more inside metropolitan statistical areas. (See Table 10.15.)

Mobile Homes or Manufactured Housing

Between 1984 and 1991, the mobile home market (the industry prefers the term manufactured housing) had declined as the number of units fell 40 percent from 288,000 units to 174,000 units. However, business has regained momentum, with 291,000 units built in 1994, almost the same number as 1984. This has continued to increase, with 338,000 sold in 1996 and 369,000 in 1998 (Table 10.16).

Modern mobile homes are often far from being mobile. Even the single-wide units (40 percent of all units sold) require a large truck to move them about, and double-wide homes may be indistinguishable from a builder-constructed home. About 35 percent of new mobile homes were located inside manufactured home communities (Table 10.16). Single-wide homes were more likely (45 percent) to be located within manufactured home communities than were double-wide homes (29 percent). About 88 percent of all new mobile homes had three or more bedrooms, with single-wide homes (76 percent) less likely to have three bed-

TABLE 10.16

Selected Characteristics by Type of Manufactured Home: 1994 to 1998

[Components may not add to totals because of rounding. Percents computed from unrounded figures]

Type of manufactured home, region, and characteristic	Number of new manufactured homes (thousands)					Percent distribution				
	1998	1997^r	1996^r	1995^r	1994^r	1998	1997^r	1996^r	1995^r	1994
ALL MANUFACTURED HOMES										
United States	369	338	338	319	291	100	100	100	100	100
Location:										
Inside manufactured home parks	130	113	113	109	99	35	33	33	34	34
Outside manufactured home parks	239	225	225	211	192	65	67	67	66	66
Number of bedrooms:										
2 or less	44	46	52	53	60	12	14	15	17	21
3 or more	325	292	287	266	231	88	86	85	83	79
Central air-conditioning:										
Installed	287	263	259	237	201	78	78	77	74	69
Not installed	83	75	79	83	90	22	22	23	26	31
Foundation:										
Concrete pads	50	37	30	25	21	13	11	9	8	7
Blocks	243	236	256	248	229	66	70	76	78	79
Masonry	60	47	34	33	30	16	14	10	10	10
Other²	16	18	18	13	11	4	5	5	4	4

Source: *Characteristics of New Housing: 1998*, Bureau of the Census, Washington, DC, 1999

rooms than double-wide homes (96 percent). About 78 percent of new mobile homes had central air conditioning (Table 10.16).

Manufacturers are producing larger mobile homes. The typical size of a mobile home built in 1988 was 1,175 square feet: 970 square feet for single-wide homes and 1,435 square feet for double-wide homes. By 1998, the typical mobile home was 1,450 square feet — 1,130 square feet for a single-wide home and 1,640 square feet for a double-wide home, almost the size of a typical builder-constructed home. The average mobile home cost $43,800 in 1998, with a single-wide home running $30,300 and a double-wide home costing $52,300.

KEEPING UP THE HOUSE

Houses are not built to last forever, and maintenance is a continuous process. In 1998, the nation's homeowners spent an estimated $120.7 billion improving, maintaining, and repairing their homes. Of that, $39 billion was spent on maintenance and repairs, and $81 billion went into construction improvements ($10 billion for additions, $33 billion for alterations, and over $27 billion on major replacements). (See Table 10.17.)

TABLE 10.17

Expenditures for Residential Properties: Quarterly 1995 to 1998

Not Seasonally Adjusted

[Millions of dollars. Components may not add to totals because of rounding]

Property type, year, and quarter	Total expenditures	Mainte-nance and repairs	Improvements					
			Total	Additions and alterations				Major replacements
				Total	To structures		To property outside of structures	
					Additions	Alterations		
ALL PROPERTIES								
Annual								
1995	111,683	42,047	69,636	44,726	7,936	26,893	9,897	24,910
1996	114,919	36,997	77,922	53,456	12,035	30,064	11,357	24,465
1997	118,569	38,576	79,993	55,530	11,042	33,046	11,442	24,463
1998^r	120,661	39,326	81,335	53,868	10,092	32,784	10,992	27,467
Relative standard error of annual estimates ....(percent)..	3	4	5	5	11	8	10	8

Source: *Expenditures for Residential Improvements and Repairs: 4th Quarter, 1998*, Bureau of the Census, Washington, DC, 1999

During the 1980s and into the 1990s, Americans spent increasingly more on home repairs and alterations because home owners were holding on to their property longer than in the past and, hence, had to repair it. Also, the huge volume of homes built during the middle to late 1970s now need painting, roofing, and other repairs.

HOMELESSNESS

Homelessness is a continuing problem in the United States. Estimates of the actual number of homeless people vary considerably. The 1990 census counted 240,140 homeless persons. Census officials made a special effort to count the homeless by sending out 15,000 census takers to visit 11,000 shelters and 11,000 open-air sites. The census takers did not count any homeless persons they saw other than those at the designated sites. In only a few instances were counts taken in cities of less than 50,000 population, so that number is generally considered to be well below the actual number.

The Urban Institute, in *America's Homeless* (Martha Burt and Barbara Cohen, Washington, DC, 1989), estimated that between 500,000 and 600,000 people were homeless during a seven-day period in March 1988. This implies that, since people go in and out of homelessness, more than one million persons in the United States were homeless at some time during 1988. In 1999, the National Law Center on Homelessness and Poverty updated this 500,000 to 600,000 estimate by projecting an increase to over 700,000 people homeless on any given night and up to 2 million people who experience homelessness during one year.

A 1998 survey by the U.S. Conference of Mayors did not offer an estimate of the total numbers of homeless but did report on the requests for emergency shelter in 30 representative cities. The conference found that requests for emergency shelter had increased an average of 11 percent from 1997 to 1998, with 72 percent of the survey cities reporting an increase. The city officials indicated that a growing number of families among the homeless were responsible for some of the increase. Requests by homeless families with children increased by 15 percent. The cities failed to meet an average of 26 percent of the requests for emergency shelter by homeless people overall and 30 percent of the requests by homeless families alone. The conference reported that one-quarter of the homeless population were children. (For a complete discussion of homelessness, see *Homeless in America — How Could It Happen Here?*, Information Plus, Wylie, Texas, 1999.)

IMPORTANT NAMES AND ADDRESSES

Bureau of the Census
Washington, DC 20233-6900
(301) 457-2135
(301) 763-2800 (Public Information)
FAX (301) 457-3761
www.census.gov

Bureau of the Census
Housing and Household Economic
Statistics
4700 Silver Hill Rd.
Suitland, MD 20746-8500
(301) 457-3234
FAX (301) 457-3248
http://blue.census.gov

Bureau of Economic Analysis
Commerce Department
1441 L St. NW, #6006
Washington, DC 20230
(202) 606-9600
FAX (202) 606-5311
www.bea.doc.gov
john.landefeld@bea.doc.gov

Bureau of Justice Statistics
810 7th St. NW, #2400
Washington, DC 20001
(202) 307-0765
FAX (202) 307-5846
www.ojp.usdoj.gov/bjs
askbjs@0jp.usdoj.gov

Bureau of Labor Statistics
2 Massachusetts Ave. NE, #2860
Washington, DC 20212
(202) 606-5886
FAX (202) 606-7890
www.bls.gov
labstathelpdesk@bls.gov

Centers for Disease Control and
Prevention
1600 Clifton Rd. NE
Atlanta, GA 30333
(404) 639-3534
www.cdc.gov

Federal Bureau of Investigation
935 Pennsylvania Ave. NW
Washington, DC 20535
(202) 324-3444
FAX (202) 324-4705
www.fbi.gov

Health Care Financing Administration
200 Independence Ave. SW, #314G
Washington, DC 20201
(202) 690-6726
FAX (202) 690-6262
www.hcfa.gov

Immigration and Naturalization Service
425 Eye St. NW, #7100
Washington, DC 20536
(202) 514-1900
FAX (202) 514-3296
www.ins.usdoj.gov

Justice Research and Statistics
Association
777 N. Capitol St. NE, #801
Washington, DC 20002
(202) 842-9330
FAX (202) 842-9329
www.jrsainfo.org
cjinfo@jrsa.org

National Agricultural Statistics Service
1400 Independence Ave. SW, #41175
Washington, DC 20250
(202) 720-2707
FAX (202) 720-9013
www.usda.gov/nass/
nass@nass.usda.gov

National Center for Education Statistics
555 New Jersey Ave. NW, #400
Washington, DC 20208-5574
(202) 219-1828
FAX (202) 219-1736
Toll-Free (800) 424-1616
http://nces.ed.gov
ncesinfo@inet.ed.gov

National Center for Health Statistics
6525 Belcrest Rd., #1140
Hyattsville, MD 20782
(301) 436-7016
FAX (301) 436-5202
www.cdc.gov/nchs

National Institute of Justice
810 7th St. NW
Washington, DC 20531
(202) 307-2942
FAX (202) 307-6394
www.ojp.usdoj.gov/nij

Population Reference Bureau
1875 Connecticut Ave. NW, #520
Washington, DC 20009-5728
(202) 483-1100
FAX (202) 328-3937
www.prb.org

U.S. Department of Agriculture
1400 Independence Ave. SW
Washington, DC 20250
(202) 720-3631
FAX (202) 720-2166
www.usda.gov

U.S. Department of Agriculture
Economic Research Service
1800 M St. NW
Washington, DC 20036
(202) 694-5000
FAX (202) 694-5757
www.econ.ag.gov

U.S. Department of Commerce
Main Commerce Building
14th St. and Constitution Ave., NW
#5854
Washington, DC 20230
(202) 482-2112
FAX (202) 482-4576
www.doc.gov

U.S. Department of Education
600 Independence Ave. SW
Washington, DC 20202
(202) 401-3000
FAX (202) 401-0596
www.ed.gov

U.S. Department of Health and Human
Services
200 Independence Ave. SW, #615F
Washington, DC 20201
(202) 690-7000
FAX (202) 690-7203
www.dhhs.gov

U.S. Department of Housing and Urban
Development
HUD Building
451 7th St. SW, #10000
Washington, DC 20410
(202) 708-0417
FAX (202) 619-8365
www.hud.gov

U.S. Department of Interior
1849 C St. NW, #6156
Washington, DC 20240
(202) 208-7351
FAX (202) 208-5048
www.doi.gov

U.S. Department of Justice
950 Pennsylvania Ave. NW
Washington, DC 20530
(202) 514-2001
FAX (202) 514-4371
www.usdoj.gov

U.S. Department of Labor
200 Constitution Ave. NW, #S2018
Washington, DC 20210
(202) 219-8271
FAX (202) 219-8822
www.dol.gov

RESOURCES

The Bureau of the Census of the U.S. Department of Commerce provides the most complete statistics on the life of the American people. The most valuable information comes from the national census, taken every 10 years. In addition to the national census, the Bureau surveys the nation in its annual *Current Population Surveys*. Among the dozens of valuable *Current Population Reports* based on these surveys are *1997 Population Profile of the United States* (1998), a statistical overview of the nation; *Population Projections of the United States by Age, Sex, Race, and Hispanic Origin: 1995 to 2050* (1996), *Population Projections: States, 1995-2025* (1997); *Household and Family Characteristics: March 1998* (1999*)*; and *Marital Status and Living Arrangements — March 1998 (Update)* (1998).

Other publications include *Geographic Mobility*: *March 1996-March 1997* (1998); *Asset Ownership of Households: 1993 (1995); Money Income in the United States: 1998* (1999); *Poverty in the United States: 1998* (1999*); Voting and Registration in the Election of November 1994* (1995); and *Voting and Registration in the Election of November 1996* (1998). Other reports based on the *Current Population Survey* are *A Brief Look at Postwar U.S. Income Inequality* (1996), *Measuring 50 Years of Economic Changes* (1998); *Profile of the Foreign-Born Population: 1997* (1999); and *Health Insurance Coverage: 1998* (1999).

The Bureau of the Census, in its series *Dynamics of Economic Well-Being*, publishes longitudinal studies of the nation. Longitudinal studies follow individuals over a period of time. Studies in this series include *Moving Up and Down the Income Ladder* (1998*); Poverty 1993-1994: Trap Door? Revolving Door? Or Both?* (1998); *Program Participation, 1993-1994 — Who Gets Assistance?* (1999); and *Extending Measures of Well-Being: Meeting Basic Needs, 1995* (1999). The Bureau of the Census provides the *World Population Profile: 1998* (1999), comparing population statistics, such as life expectancy, in various countries.

The Bureau of the Census publishes summaries of its various reports in its monthly *Census and You* and *Census Brief* and its *Commerce News*. Other publications include press releases, such as "Fastest-Growing Counties Are Southern, Western and Predominantly Metropolitan" (1999) and "Nearly 1 in 10 U.S. Residents Are Foreign-Born" (1999).

The National Agricultural Statistics Service of the U.S. Department of Agriculture prepared the *1997 Census of Agriculture* (1999). The Immigration and Naturalization Service of the U.S. Department of Justice published the annual report *Legal Immigration, Fiscal Year 1998* (1999). The Bureau of the Census and the U.S.

Department of Housing and Urban Development jointly monitored the housing market and produced *American Housing Survey for the United States in 1997* (1999) and numerous studies, including *Characteristics of New Housing: 1998* (1999) and *Who Can Afford to Buy a House in 1995?* (1999), as well as the quarterly *Expenditures for Residential Improvement and Repairs* and the monthly *New One-Family Houses Sold* and numerous invaluable one-time studies.

The Bureau of Labor Statistics (BLS) of the U.S. Department of Labor maintains the nation's employment and occupation statistics. Its monthly and annual compilation, *Employment and Earnings,* statistically covers the subject. Its *Monthly Labor Review* magazine provides monthly statistical updates and articles on the American labor force. The annual BLS study, *Consumer Expenditure Survey,* based on Bureau of the Census surveys, traces how Americans spend their money. The Federal Reserve surveys family finances in *Family Finances in the U.S.: Recent Evidence from the Survey of Consumer Finances* (1997).

The National Center for Health Statistics is the primary source for statistical information on health. Its annual *Health, United States* offers a statistical overview, while its *National Vital Statistics Reports* provides the most recent health information. The Health Care Financing Administration, in its quarterly *Health Care Financing Review*, maintains statistics and prepares valuable studies on health care spending.

America's Children: Key National Indicators of Well-Being (1999) is the third report in an annual series prepared by the Interagency Forum on Child and Family Statistics. The annual *Digest of Education Statistics*, prepared by the National Center for Education Statistics of the U.S. Department of Education, provides a complete overview of education. The Federal Bureau of Investigation (FBI), in the annual *Crime in the United States*, and the Bureau of Justice Statistics of the U.S. Department of Justice, in the yearly *National Crime Victimization Survey*, keep track of crime and justice statistics.

Human Rights Watch and The Sentencing Project jointly published *Losing the Vote: The Impact of Felony Disenfranchisement Laws in the United States* (1998). The Congressional Research Service prepares reports on various issues for members and committees of Congress, including *Women's Electoral Participation and Representation in Elective Office* (1999).

Information Plus wishes to thank The Gallup Organization (Princeton, New Jersey) for the use of its surveys.

INDEX

INDEX (Continued)